JOURNALS

VOLUME 1: 1889–1913

ANDRÉ GIDE

Photograph by
Laure Albin Guillot

ANDRÉ GIDE

Journals

VOLUME 1: 1889–1913

TRANSLATED FROM THE FRENCH,

WITH INTRODUCTION AND NOTES, BY

Justin O'Brien

FOREWORD BY RICHARD HOWARD

UNIVERSITY OF ILLINOIS PRESS

Urbana and Chicago

First paperback edition, 2000
Foreword © 2000 by the Board of Trustees
of the University of Illinois
Journals 1889–1939 © 1939 by Editions Gallimard
English translation of volume 1 © 1947 by Alfred A. Knopf, Inc.
Reprinted by arrangement with Editions Gallimard and Alfred A. Knopf, Inc.

Library of Congress Cataloging-in-Publication Data
Gide, André, 1869–1951.
[Journal. English]
Journals / André Gide ; translated from the French,
with introduction and notes, by Justin O'Brien.
p. cm.
Includes bibliographical references and index.
Contents: v. 1. 1889–1913 — v. 2. 1914–1927 — v. 3. 1928–1939
— vol. 4. 1939–1949.
ISBN 0-252-06929-3 (vol. 1 : pbk. : alk. paper) —
ISBN 0-252-06930-7 (vol. 2 : pbk. : alk. paper) —
ISBN 0-252-06931-5 (vol. 3 : pbk. : alk. paper) —
ISBN 0-252-06932-3 (vol. 4 : pbk. : alk. paper)
1. Gide, André, 1869–1951—Diaries. 2. Authors, French—20th century—Diaries.
I. O'Brien, Justin, 1906–1968. II. Title.
PQ2613.I2Z465413   2000
848'.91203—dc21
[B]   00-037715

P 5 4 3 2 1

CONTENTS

CONTENTS

FOREWORD
A Welcome Return

RICHARD HOWARD

In no way superficial, a great Frenchman nonetheless
always preserves his surface, a natural envelope
which surrounds his depths.
—Nietzsche, *The Dawn*

It is a great assuagement—indeed, for a whole new generation of readers, it will prove a great resource—to have all of Gide's journals in print
once again, for they constitute the cartilaginous tissue that secures and
sustains the otherwise discrepant and (particularly for Americans who
must rely on the vagaries of translation) diffuse oeuvre of the most
enantiotropic writer of Western culture. André Gide was a creature of
conflicts, reversals, contradictions, and antitheses so marked that without
the "natural envelope" of the *Journals,* we run the risk of missing, in the
flagrant multiformity of his production, those inveterately sounded notes
that constitute, as Auden once observed, *the restored relation.*

The journal was the first form of writing to occur to him. From his
own intermittent but inexhaustible text, which began with a single entry
for the year 1889 when he was twenty, to *Les cahiers d'André Walter,*
published anonymously in 1891, when he was twenty-two, to *Strait Is the
Gate,* a 1909 *récit* concluded by Alissa's lyric diary (later set to music as
a solo cantata by Darius Milhaud), to *La symphonie pastorale* (1919),
another *récit* entirely narrated in the pastor's two diaries, all the way to
Ainsi soit-il, a dateless deathbed meditation published posthumously in
1951, André Gide continually experimented with the genre. He kept a
journal of his progress—and his setbacks—in writing his only novel (a
large portion of which consists of the journal of a novelist writing a novel
to be called *The Counterfeiters*) and eventually published this journal as
a sort of appendix to the (real?) *Counterfeiters* (1926); he kept a journal
of his travels in the Congo to study—and to criticize severely—French
colonization in Africa; and he even aspired to keep a journal of his translation of *Hamlet.* Indeed, any enterprise Gide could conceive of as constituting an independent effort, a moral and esthetic project, he subjected
to the record (and the erosion) of his progress in consciousness, thereby
articulating the first of many besetting contradictions, for it is the nature
of a journal to be successive, and Gide was the most simultaneous of
beings in modern literature. After the first twenty years of journal keep-

ing, he was painfully conscious of the dilemma: "It is hard for [my crit-
ics] to admit that these different books cohabited, still cohabit, in my
mind. They follow one another only on paper and through the great impossibility of letting them be written together. Whatever the book I am
writing, I never give myself to it utterly, and the subject that claims me
most insistently immediately afterward, develops meanwhile at the other
extremity of me" (*Journals*, 1909). Not only is all of Gide somehow
present in any one work, but all of Gide is present in that initial diary
kept by that suicidal alter ego André Walter, and furthermore André
Walter is still present in Gide in 1947. That is why I doubt his journal
has much interest if reading Gide's work has not awakened some initial
curiosity as to the man who kept it.

Certainly Gide's journal is the one work that affords the mucilage or
masking tape to hold the diverging works together, affording us this man's
central determination to see himself as a being forever dual "and therefore not to be confined within any one thing." It is by means of the *Journals* that we can accompany Gide, or at least pursue him, through that
remarkable pattern of "returns" that characterize his labyrinthine life and
can be identified by his remarkably conflictory works: the return from
puritanism (*Fruits of the Earth* [1897] and *The Pastoral Symphony*
[1919]), from marriage (*The Immoralist* [1902] and *The School for Wives*
[1929]), and from narcissism (*Les cahiers d'André Walter* [1891] and *Le
retour de l'enfant prodigue* [1907]); the return from Symbolism (*Le voyage d'Urien* [1893] and *Paludes* [1896]) and from Christianity (*Strait Is
the Gate* [1909] and *Numquid et tu . . . ?* [1926]); from absurdist comedy (*Prometheus Ill-bound* [1899] and *Lafcadio's Adventures* [1914]) and
from the "grand machines" of classicism (*Philoctetes* [1899], *Oedipus*
[1931], and *Theseus* [1946]); from exotic dramatic gestures (*Saül* [1895]
and *King Candaules* [1901]) and from drama itself (stage versions of
Kafka's *Trial* and of his own *Lafcadio*); from literary responsibility (founding and directing the *Nouvelle revue française* [1908]) and from homosexuality as well as from "family values" (*Corydon* [1924] and fathering
a daughter); from the critique of capitalism (*Travels in the Congo* [1927–
28]) and of communism (*Return from the U.S.S.R.* [1936]); and from
controversiality, or at least from controversy (translations of Shakespeare,
Whitman, Conrad, Blake, Goethe, Pushkin, and Tagore). Even Gide's sole
novel, *The Counterfeiters*, might well be counted a return from Dostoyev-
ski, whose cult Gide had so eagerly furthered in lectures and articles in
1923.

I would emphasize by the word *return* that Gide does not *retreat from*
passions and positions espoused, however experimentally, in the
fluctuations of a notoriously self-conscious life and literary career; rather
he *returns to* a core of ironic fervors (it is not irrelevant to invoke a

Nietzschean intensity here) that afford him the possibility, ever and again, of escape from ideology, from fanaticism, from whatever Gide perceives as falsehood and fixity. The unremitting journal inveterately serves as an argumentative, sometimes lyrical, and often drastic corrective to any residual—and fallacious—commitment.

Along the way, almost as an incident in the journal enterprise, occurs Gide's life—"life too," as Alan Sheridan, Gide's latest and best biographer, reminds us, "has its autonomy: it does not require justification by works." Here the journal, with what can only be qualified as a thick-skinned intimacy (by 1916 Gide knew that every word he wrote in the journal would eventually and often immediately be published; a set of "pages de Journal" often jump-started *La nouvelle revue française* between the wars), articulates the life's notorious intimacies and alienations (Valéry, Claudel); hopeless forbearance and happy infatuation (Madeleine Gide, Marc Allégret); the exemplary instances of conscience and corruption (ascendancy of Mallarmé and of Oscar Wilde); the collaborative amities and collegial betrayals (Martin du Gard, Cocteau); the excursions into a permissive exoticism (*Amyntas* [1906]) and the withdrawals to an equally permissive family seat in Normandy (*Souvenirs de la Cour d'Assises* [1912]); and year by year, month by month, the inveterate vacillation— the constant autocritique, really—between modish classicism and modernist contraption, the reading lists and grammatical disputes, the education not only carried out but also ceremonially paraded in public.

An inveterate lineament of Gide's insisted-upon "life in the present," we have discovered since his death in 1951, was the letters. To the solicitations of the world's friendship and the world's hostility, Gide *corresponded*. In a hastier age, one wonders how he managed it. Between his works and his journal, between a simmering professional life in Paris and a lacerating private one in Cuverville, between his elaborately staged travels and a vast program of reading and rereading fanatically pursued over seven decades and faithfully glossed in the *Journals*, how did he ever find or make time for thousands and thousands of letters, letters written and, perhaps just as besetting, letters *read and answered*—over thirty complete correspondences published so far, some in two volumes, constituting another range altogether, often a corrective one, of the biographical dimension that so many of us had assumed was to be simply—simply!— accounted for in the *Journals, 1889–1949*. To think that these diaries are only a partial reticulation of the social and literary and political web in which this inky spider loomed over some sixty years of his generation!

Besides the correspondence, there is another body of writing that has released Gide's journal to be read not as a source, a disclosure, but as a work of concentrated and harmonious—no, *harmonized*—experience. This is *someone else's* journal, *Les cahiers de la petite dame* (the "little lady" being Maria van Rysselberghe, intrepid widow of a Belgian painter, whose daughter, Élisabeth, was to become the mother of Gide's only child, Catherine), four volumes covering the period from 1918 to Gide's death in 1951. *Covering* is the apposite word, for the incessant, accurate, and mercilessly affectionate reportage by this clear-eyed friend, amassed without the knowledge of her unwitting "subject" and published only after his death, has probably done more to eclipse and to disenchant Gide's demonic self-image than all the attacks from Rome and Moscow or all the horrified attentions of an offended literary orthodoxy; henceforth no biographer can resist these quotidian intimate revelations, but no heroic figure—especially the figure of an author committed to the unique presentation of an authentic, a "sincere" self—can withstand them. And of course such testimony from the rim discloses the *Journals'* core workings to be faulty—not precisely fraudulent, but not precise either: fallacious, if we are reading for the facts, ma'am. This will come as a veritable liberation to new readers of Gide's *Journals,* now to be attended as a truly Goethean muster of "poetry and truth," as opposed to scandal and parade. For the first time, we may come unburdened to the intersection at which Gide has remained, the most important and populous carrefour, where the two greatest roads of the Western world cross—the Greek and the Christian; here is the total situation Gide preferred, enclosed by nothing and protected by nothing, subject to every attack, accessible to every affection. To survive, to perdure in so perilous a situation—it is only "natural" that the very word *experience* should have the notion of *peril* at its root—required a certain hardness, out of which masterpieces are made.

"It is from the point of view of art that it is most fitting to judge what I write—a point of view the critic never, or almost never, takes. . . . It is, moreover, the only point of view that does not exclude any of the others" (*Journals,* 1918). Gide's works are the depths to which Nietzsche refers in the epigraph I have given to these remarks, depths surrounded by the "natural envelope" of his journal, which as Roland Barthes pointed out long ago, we must not suppose is in opposition to the work and not itself a work of art. The journal is not an explanatory, an external writing; it is not a chronicle like Saint-Simon's history but the masterpiece of a mind and body not free yet seeking to be free by means of those passionate inquiries, arguments, and contradictions that make him, rather, another Montaigne. Let us put an equal accent on both nouns to obtain his true portrait: Gide, or Civilization and its Discontents.

INTRODUCTION

BY

JUSTIN O'BRIEN

Wʜᴇɴ, at the age of eighteen or nineteen, André Gide began keeping his first journal, he already intended to be a writer. Indeed, he was even then elaborating his first literary work, a symbolic prose poem interspersed with poetry, which in recounting the conflicts of his awakening to life was to draw heavily upon that journal. His often interrupted formal education was drawing to a close, for he had left the strict and pious Protestant school that had once mortified his family by expelling him, and had even signed up at the university with a vague intention of working for an M.A. He was living in his native Paris with his widowed mother and Aunt Claire, who still treated him as an irresponsible child. Once a week he lunched with Miss Anna Shackleton, the Scottish spinster who, after tutoring his mother as a girl in Rouen, had become her lifelong companion, and with her he practiced his faltering German. Every day he played his beloved piano for hours. The summers he spent at the family estate not far from the sea in Normandy walking with his cousins, perfecting his technique at the piano, patiently herborizing with Anna Shackleton, and voraciously reading. Already versed in the French classics, he was during the next few years to discover Baudelaire and Verlaine, Dante and Goethe and Shakespeare, and the German philosophers.

But his inseparable companion — even more frequently opened than his piano, even more essential to his spiritual life than his cousin Emmanuèle, whom he was already planning to marry — was the Bible. All his thoughts were interpreted in the light of the Scriptures. If he "anointed his literary style with music," if he even dreamed of "writing in music," that style had already received its basic form from the Bible.

A tall, well-built youth, André Gide was inordinately austere and painfully shy. His upbringing had developed in him an excessive sensitivity and feminine grace. His hair fell below his ears, almost touching his stiff collar; his cheeks were covered with a soft down that was soon to become a full beard. Hypnotized by his keen dark eyes, everyone but Oscar Wilde failed to notice his full sensual lips and fine aquiline nose. He dressed with a somewhat antiquated elegance, preferring soft, flowing bow ties, a loose cape, and a broad-brimmed soft hat.

Such was the young man whose uncompromising intellectualism and devout faith rather embarrassed the other disciples at Mallarmé's charmed gatherings each Tuesday evening in the early nineties or in the more social *salon* of the poet Heredia, where, amidst literary discussion, his friends Pierre Louÿs and Henri de Régnier courted their future wives among the poet's daughters. The symbolist movement was at its height: the poetry of Baudelaire, Rimbaud, Verlaine, Laforgue, and the teachings of Mallarmé were forming the taste of a generation; little reviews and new theories of versification were rapidly multiplying; Schopenhauer was the rage and Nietzsche was beginning to be discovered; Wagner's music (against which Gide was perhaps the only one to revolt) made the young swoon at concerts and led to endless discussions of new art forms; painters like Gustave Moreau, Puvis de Chavannes, and Odilon Redon were producing literary allegories and painting symbolic visions; the art theaters were stirring audiences to ecstasy and indignation with novel and ambitious works that were most often singularly undramatic. From Paris the electric current flashed to *avant-garde* groups everywhere: in Italy Gabriele d'Annunzio recognized the call and subscribed at once to the new *Mercure de France;* Oscar Wilde, Whistler, George Moore, Aubrey Beardsley, and others came over frequently from London and took back ideas for their own *Yellow Book;* the young Maeterlinck came down from Brussels and was hailed in Paris as a second Shakespeare; in provincial Montpellier Louÿs met the young Paul-Ambroise Valéry and sent him to Gide in Paris.

In this world André Gide moved stiffly and cautiously. With his friends he started several little reviews and contributed to others, sometimes as far away as Liége. He shared Mallarmé's conception of the nobility of the artist and the sacrifice of everything to the work of art. His first works were poems in prose and in verse, symbols in limited editions and without name of author, legible only to the initiate.

Most appropriately his journals for these first years are concerned principally with himself. Notes on his reading, travel diaries, records of conversations with friends (which play such a large part in the later journals) occupy but few of these pages devoted almost exclusively to self-scrutiny and dreams, to philosophic hesitations and emotional unrest, to gropings after a rule of conduct and amorphous plans for future creation. The will figures importantly in those early years and he seems never to have faltered in his intention; in January 1890 he notes:

"My pride is constantly being irritated by a thousand minute slights. I suffer absurdly from the fact that everybody does not already know what I hope some day to be, what I shall be; that people cannot foretell the work to come just from the look in my eyes."

Fifty years later, when for the first time André Gide made his complete *Journals* widely accessible, the text (despite the passages removed for incorporation into other works and the suppressions) ran to over thirteen hundred pages. The author had become a great figure of European letters, and his reputation as novelist, dramatist, literary critic, and essayist was equaled only by the immense legend built about his name by unscrupulous critics and uncritical admirers. The *Nouvelle Revue Française* he had founded in 1909 had for thirty years occupied the forefront of modern literature, serving as a model for literary reviews in England, Germany, and America and molding literary taste more effectively than had publicity, prizes, and academies. The fifteen volumes of André Gide's *Œuvres complètes*, though they did not include anything published since 1930, still bore impressive testimony of a full literary life. His influence, perhaps the most widespread in France since that of Baudelaire, had been deeply felt by such Academicians as Jacques de Lacretelle, François Mauriac, and André Maurois and eagerly accepted by the Nobel prize-winner Roger Martin du Gard besides contributing significantly to the formation of such younger writers as Julien Green, Malraux, Saint Exupéry, and Giono. Outside the frontiers, it had touched Aldous Huxley and T. S. Eliot, Rilke, Thomas Mann, and a host of younger writers.

And yet he was not a member of the French Academy; nor did he wear in his buttonhole any of the little ribbons symbolic of national distinction that are so much appreciated in Europe. Honors had begun by fleeing him early in life, he said once, and later he had learned to flee them.

In appearance, too, André Gide had changed considerably from the æsthete of the early nineties, and this transformation corresponded to his growth in intellectual stature. In 1939 he was a vigorous, large-boned man who seemed much younger than his age. Long ago, like the hero of *L'Immoraliste*, he had sacrificed first beard and then mustache because they masked his emotion. The long hair had likewise yielded to a more modern style and had receded to reveal a noble brow. The firm, attentive eyes were still the striking feature of his face. His long stride and lithe step were those of a young man who would rather walk than ride. His deep, modulated voice, conforming to his precise diction, made one think of an actor or singer. The *lavallière* necktie had given way to the familiar four-in-hand, and the formal black suit to tweeds of excellent British quality. In fact, his appearance no longer had anything about it specifically marking him as an artist — save perhaps the long rough cape loosely thrown on his shoulders.

The man himself was as devoid of affectation as was his external appearance. André Gide had traveled widely both throughout the world and within himself, and he had come, oh, what a long way from the fervent, sentimental André Walter he had created to serve as the author of his first two books! In the interval he had identified himself with a great many characters, as any creative artist must, but the critics (and his legend) had narrowed that crowd down to but a few: the cynical hedonist Ménalque of the *Nourritures terrestres,* the cruel and bewildered superman Michel of *L'Immoraliste;* the seductive Lafcadio of *Les Caves du Vatican,* curious of the world and of himself, whose self-expression extends to committing a gratuitous murder; the Corydon of the four Socratic dialogues named after him; and the amoral novelist Édouard of *Les Faux-Monnayeurs.* For these writings, with a few others, were the ones that had created scandals periodically throughout the first fifty years of André Gide's career.

Like any original thinker and artist, he early began to scandalize. His contemporaries were shocked when he returned from his first trip to Africa in 1895 and mocked them in the first of his ironic works, *Paludes,* that brilliant satire on banality and moral stagnation written with special reference to the literary circles he knew so well. But already before he started out in the autumn of 1893, André Gide sensed — as is evident from his leaving behind his familiar Bible — that this trip was to effect more than his conscious break with symbolism; indeed, that it was to mark the great turning-point in his life. Doubtless this would have been so even if he had not fallen ill at Biskra and approached death so closely that his long convalescence seemed a resuscitation. For without the resultant discovery of the value of life and of that ardor which gives life its zest, he would nevertheless have learned the secret of his tormented nature. But the escape from death, the self-identification with Lazarus, helped form the resolve not to stifle his unorthodox inclinations.

"In the name of what God, of what ideal, do you forbid me to live according to my nature?" he cries in his memoirs. "And where would that nature lead me if I simply followed it? Until now I had followed the rule of Christ or at least a certain puritanism that had been taught me as the rule of Christ. My only reward for having striven to submit to it had been a complete physical and spiritual upset. I could not agree to live without a code, and the demands of my flesh required the consent of my mind. But then I began to wonder whether God himself called for such coercion; whether it was not blasphemous to resist constantly, and whether it was not against him; whether, in that struggle which was dividing me, it was logical to decide against the other. Eventually I sensed that this discordant dualism could perhaps be resolved into a harmony. And immediately it occurred to me that that harmony was to be my sovereign aim and seeking to achieve it the evident justification of my life."

Uprooting himself then from his entire past, he attempted to resolve his vital conflict by suppressing all that education, in the broadest sense, had added to nature. But how difficult this was for such a man one can realize from the capital entry in his journals for 10 October 1893 with its revealing remark: "Yet the habit of asceticism was such that in the beginning I had to force myself toward joy. . . ."

After such an experience it is but natural that the work that followed

Paludes, entitled *Les Nourritures terrestres*, is a handbook of revolt and a hymn to freedom. Breaking forth from the cloistered walls within which French literature was becoming ever more hermetic, André Gide instinctively voiced the message of Nietzsche and Walt Whitman and expressed more emphatically than had Pater or Wilde the doctrine of supreme individualism. While the very popular Maurice Barrès was teaching the need of rooting oneself firmly in one's native soil and keeping close contact with one's traditions, André Gide exhorted his reader: ". . . and when you have read me, throw this book away — and go out. I should like it to have made you want to get away — away from anywhere, from your town, from your family, from your room, from your thought."

As the *Journals* clearly indicate, the *fin-de-siècle* combination of persuasive prose and ejaculatory verse that made up *Les Nourritures terrestres* failed to reach a large public in 1897, when the work first appeared. But the fact remains that, in addition to marking the turning-point in its author's career, it struck the note of the future since, twenty years later, this little book preaching the cult of unrest and ardor with the attendant glorification of desire and spontaneity came to be the chief agent of that Gidian influence which to conservative critics has seemed nothing less than diabolical. It is dangerous indeed to describe "the savage and sudden savor of life" and to urge people to "act without *judging* whether the deed is good or evil." Many youths found in this volume a justification for indulging their worst instincts, but this is perhaps the inevitable result of freeing people. Had they shared the author's background, they would have been aware also of a more sober current in the book and noted the exhortation: "Let everyone follow his inclination . . . provided he go upward." In recent years André Gide himself has judged the work harshly on the basis of style and because of the misunderstandings to which it has given rise. But as the journal entry for 18 April 1928 states: "My writings can be compared to Achilles' spear, with which a second contact cured those it had first wounded. If one of my books disconcerts you, reread it; under the obvious poison I took care to hide the antidote; each one of them aims less to disturb than to warn."

Paludes in 1895 had showed Gide's associates to what an extent they were prisoners of their habits, their ideas, and even their emotions; two years later *Les Nourritures terrestres* was an urgent call to freedom. But as if the author felt that on this occasion the antidote deserved more attention and better labeling, he was for some time to devote himself to clarifying his message — as much in his own mind as in that of the reader.

"To free oneself is nothing; it's being free that is hard," says Michel of *L'Immoraliste*. This is the problem that André Gide examines from all sides during the next thirty years. The overgenerous Candaules and the too receptive Saul (heroes of the beautiful dramas *Le Roi Candaule* and *Saül*), together with the protagonist of *L'Immoraliste,* end tragically because of breaking with conventional morality in their search for self-realization and thus offer a commentary on the doctrine of *Les Nourritures terrestres.* In the philosophic dialogue couched in dramatic form *Philoctète,* the debate between two opposing systems of ethics ends with the victory of self-fulfillment. The heroine of the tale *La Porte étroite* (counterpart of *L'Immoraliste,* published seven years later, in 1909) illustrates the dangers of the other extreme, renunciation, and her very different form of selfishness leads to just as tragic a conclusion. In *Le Retour de l'enfant prodigue* the prodigal, while admitting his own errors, yet helps his younger brother to escape as he had done. And the attractive young hero of *Les Caves du Vatican,* born and educated without any reference to tradition, yet finds himself the prisoner of a free, unmotivated act he has committed simply to prove his own liberty.

During his period of full maturity between the two wars, André Gide constantly returns to the problem of personal freedom: in his memoirs entitled *Si le grain ne meurt;* in his dialogues ·on the subject of homosexuality (*Corydon*); in his studies of criminology (*L'Affaire Redureau* and *La Séquestrée de Poitiers*); in his drama of *Œdipe,* which enacts the struggle of the individualist against religious authority; and finally — because of all Gide's works it is the best-known abroad — in *Les Faux-Monnayeurs.*

The Counterfeiters (as this novel is known in English) is another break with the past. The earlier works of fiction, which most critics would be willing to classify as novels were it not for their author's insistence that they are tales, are all marked by a concentrated action performed by but three or four characters, a personal form of narration by one of the interested individuals, and a distinct simplicity of style. But now, obsessed with the example of Dostoyevsky, whom he had been rereading and analyzing in a series of lectures, André Gide set out to write a *summa* of modern life encompassing many plots and simulating the confusion of life itself. "What should I like this novel to be?" he asks in the *Journals* in 1923 and immediately replies: "A crossroads — a meeting of problems." This is why, within his own work, he has reserved the designation of novel for this single book. The four principal themes of the novel — the adolescent revolt against the older generation, the decay of the family, the creation of the work of art, and the counterfeit of life to which we all contribute — are interlocked in a contrapuntal composition inspired by Bach's *Art of the Fugue.*

All the problems raised and stylistic innovations attempted in *Les Faux-Monnayeurs* had occupied André Gide's mind for some time. Often the *Journals* are a revelation in this regard. For instance, before 1902 Gide notes his inability to find a single sentence spoken by Christ that authorizes the family, and again in 1921 he records his observation that of some forty families he knows particularly well there are hardly four in which the parents' actions do not make it desirable for the child to escape their influence. Likewise in the case of the novel within the novel (a complication that Gide had already broached in seven earlier works), the *Journals* contain a revealing passage dated 1893 about the transposition of the subject of a work into the work itself (as in the play scene in *Hamlet* or in certain Dutch paintings).

However fascinating the composition of the novel may be and however complicated the interweaving of themes, *Les Faux-Monnayeurs* strikes the reader most forcibly as a study of the free individual in opposition to the institution of the family. Once again André Gide's long preoccupation with self-realization fuses with his equally permanent concern with the nature of virtue. As we watch the evolution of the numerous characters, particularly the young Bernard and Olivier, we are reminded of the author's own early search for a rule of conduct that should combine expression and restraint. His particularly admirable form of equilibrium has nothing static about it.

The definition of virtue and the problem of self-realization are so fundamental in Gide's work as to make of him a *moraliste* or moral philosopher in the best French tradition. "The only drama that really interests me," he wrote in his *Journals* in 1930, "and that I should always be willing to depict anew, is the debate of the individual with whatever keeps him from being authentic, with whatever is opposed to his integrity, to his integration. Most often the obstacle is within him. And all the rest is merely accidental." This is a capital text for the understanding of *Les Faux-Monnayeurs* as of all his literary work. Bernard Profitendieu is not the only protagonist to wrestle with the angel, nor Prométhée the only one upon whom an eagle feeds.

But this text is also — since the obstacle is not always within the individual — a key to André Gide's social preoccupations. Having from his earliest years enjoyed an enviable economic independence permitting a life devoted wholly to disinterested art, he could have ignored such concerns. Had he remained faithful to the doctrines of pure art current during the nineties, he would have done so. But with his discovery of life beyond the confines of the *cénacles* came also a sense of responsibility and solidarity. His keenly sympathetic nature and anxiety for freedom caused him to become increasingly a champion of the oppressed. As mayor of a Commune in Normandy (1896), later as a juror in Rouen (1912), and finally as a special envoy of the Colonial Ministry (1925-6), he had ample opportunity to observe social injustice. His *Voyage au Congo* and *Retour du Tchad*, in fact, led to legal reform and eventually to curbing of the industrial concessions in the colonies.

He had done for the exploited Negroes of central Africa what he had earlier done for the homosexual instinct in his *Corydon*. Indeed, in a public debate that took place in 1935 André Gide emphasized the essential relationship of such literary "campaigns" when he said: "Enthusiastically and almost systematically I become the advocate of whatever voice society ordinarily seeks to stifle (oppressed peoples or races, human instincts), of whatever has hitherto been prevented from or incapable of speech, of anything to which the world has been, either intentionally or unintentionally, deaf."

The periodic scandals that punctuated André Gide's career have been alluded to in passing. Restricted in the earlier years by the voluntarily limited editions he issued and the correspondingly small public he reached, their repercussions were greater in the twenties and thirties. Naturally the chief scandals centered on *Corydon* and on what Gide now calls, with a slightly apologetic smile, his "honeymoon with Communism." In the early thirties when he announced his admiration for Soviet Russia and his sympathy toward Communism, he shocked even his most faithful admirers and raised another barrier between himself and official honors. At about this time, on the other hand, the *Soviet Encyclopedia* hailed Gide's abandonment of "the world outlook of the middle-class *rentier*" in favor of a realization "together with the best representatives of Western intelligentsia" of the collapse of the capitalist system.

But those who were more sophisticated than André Gide could appreciate the extent of his misunderstanding when they read the text of his enthusiastic message to the first Congress of Soviet Writers in August 1934 with its statement that

"The Communist ideal is not, as its enemies declare, the 'ideal of an anthill.' Its task today is to establish, in literature and art, a Communist individualism. . . .

"Communism cannot assert itself without taking into account the peculiarities of each individual. A society in which each man resembles all others is not desirable; I shall even say it is impossible; and this is even more true of a literature. Each artist is necessarily an individualist, however strong his Communist convictions may be and his attachment to the party. Only in this way can he create a useful work and serve society."

And when, in 1936, he undertook a trip through Russia to observe the realization of Utopia at close hand, he was quite naturally shocked by the lack of personal liberty, the intellectual regimentation, the "depersonalization," the continued existence of poverty he found there, and the reconstitution of social classes that he had hoped were forever abolished. In his *Retour de l'U.R.S.S.* and *Retouches à mon Retour de l'U.R.S.S.* he did not hesitate to say these things at the risk of another scandal, this time in other quarters. In addition to embarrassing those whom his influence had led into the ranks of Communism, he lost the handsome royalties that he had begun to receive from Russia.

Thus in his devotion to truth André Gide first refused to rely on second-hand evidence; and when he had seen for himself, he hastened to revoke his adherence to a cause he could no longer approve completely. He even warned the French Communist Party against dangerous errors and thus brought upon himself the attacks that have not ceased even now. In this whole episode, however, André Gide remained true to his own evolution. After its close he could truthfully repeat the statement he had made before his trip to Moscow:

"I believe that the value of a writer is linked to the revolutionary force that drives him, or more precisely (for I am not so foolish as to recognize artistic value only in leftist writers) in his force of opposition. That force can be found in Bossuet, Chateaubriand, or, even today, in Claudel as well as in Molière, Voltaire, Hugo, and so many others. In our form of society a great writer or great artist is essentially nonconformist. He swims against the current."

Once again Gide was ahead of his time. In Soviet Russia, as in the new Germany or Fascist Italy, he now discerned a current that he instinctively resisted. At considerable personal sacrifice and at the risk of losing his vast prestige with the young of the world, he once more resolutely took an independent attitude.

That the *Journals* throw new light upon his creative work is indubitable. In 1931 he himself expressed the hope in these pages that the *Journals* might help to prevent the misinterpretation of his works, which are so often misunderstood. Though Gide has frequently warned his reader that he writes to be reread, that he writes for posterity, that one work must be read in the light of another, it is still helpful to discover here his secret intentions and intimate hesitations. One is more inclined to give his creative writings the deep attention they deserve when one learns how carefully, almost painfully, many of them were elaborated. Often the reader is amazed to find out how long a certain subject has haunted the author — sometimes for ten or fifteen years before publication or even before composition. In fact, the *Journals* constantly bear out the rather presumptuous-seeming letter, written at the age of twenty-four, in which André Gide claimed that he could already see his unwritten works, so real they appeared to him, taking their preordained places *among* (rather than after) the already written works in such a way as to form a complete whole only when everything should finally be written.

Yet if the *Journals* merely provided marginal notes for Gide's works, they would interest only specialists. They represent considerably more than a notebook filled with confessions, acts of literary repentance, and raw material for future works. In an atmosphere which had so little use for real life that Mallarmé was shocked when he mistook Gide's imaginary description of a trip to Spitzbergen for the account of an actual voyage, the *Journals* were begun as a literary exercise. But little by little — the evolution can be traced in their pages — they assumed more importance until, as André Malraux says, they became almost an obsession with their author, gradually drawing him from art to life, away from Racine toward Stendhal. In their present form the *Journals* record a half-century of full and varied life — and not only that of André Gide. The period covered by these fifty years includes the Dreyfus case, the first World War, and the spread of Fascism and Communism. André Gide, though in each case a noncombatant, has significant things to say about these and other historical moments. In literature and art, however, he has occupied a position on the front line during the whole of this period and, in fact, still does so today.

But the interest of any journal remains essentially autobiographic; ultimately the journal is worth no more than the personality of its author. If this work is to have permanent value for us we must feel as François Mauriac felt when, interrupting his reading of the *Voyage au Congo*, he exclaimed: "And suddenly I am seized, not by Africa, but by this Gide so different from what the journalists have written about him. . . ." Until we have finished the whole of the *Journals* we should remember the words Gide so often quotes: "Judge not." Even then, his "*esprit ondoyant et divers*" will make it difficult to seize the real personality of André Gide, for never has a writer seemed to hesitate, to contradict himself, and to complicate his thought as he has done — not even the great Montaigne, who first used these words about himself. But whatever we decide about the many temperamental conflicts that produce those antinomies on which his dynamic equilibrium rests — the soul and the flesh, life and art, expression and restraint, the individual and society, ethics and æsthetics, classicism and romanticism, Christ and Christianity, God and the devil — we cannot fail to admire his genuine modesty, all-embracing sympathy, and proud independence. Nor can we fail to note, through all his transformation and growth, an unusual fidelity to his youth.

There is not one of André Gide's works that does not raise, over and above the particular destinies it unfolds, considerations of the most general and most basic kind. From his earliest writing to his latest André Gide has been consistently concerned with man's relation to man and especially with man's relation to himself. Despite his own periodic spiritual debates (of which the most sustained gave the deeply moving *Numquid et tu . . . ?* written between 1916 and 1919), his most constant attitude is that of the broadest humanism. It is perhaps as much for this reason as for any other that he deserves his position as one of the leading spokesmen of our age.

His Œdipus tells us that he knew his answer to the Sphinx long before the question was put to him, for every youth encounters an enigma to which the only solution is Man. Furthermore, for each one of us, says the King of Thebes, that man is necessarily himself. Again in the recent *Thésée* (1946) Gide has brought together toward the end of their lives blind Œdipus, the victim of the gods, and Theseus, the conqueror of the Minotaur and builder of Athens. In this supreme confrontation Œdipus vaunts the inner world he has discovered by blacking out the visible universe and releasing the divinity within, whereas the materialistic Theseus feels confirmed in his philosophic naturalism. This capital dialogue (has not the author told us he was a creature of dialogue?) receives light from a supplement to the *Journals* written in June 1942: "As soon as I understood that, instead of existing already, God was *becoming* and that it depended on each one of us that he should become, my ethical sense was restored." Gide refuses to see any impiety in this statement since it is also true that man culminates in God, and creation, which culminates in man, starts from God. Hence there is no question of blindly obeying God. Rather, one must infuse life into God, "demanding him of oneself through love and obtaining him through virtue." These words were written in Tunisia during some of the darkest days of the recent war. It is fair to consider them as representative of Gide's mature philosophy. It is characteristic of the author, as of the times, that he should add less than a week later: "But how slow God is in becoming!"

As a stylist André Gide has always been admired even by those of his countrymen who are least sympathetic to his "message." The apparent paradox of his basing his æsthetics on the very classical austerity that he had fled on the ethical plane has been pointed out by commentators. One even suggests that his original puritanism simply deviated into literary purism, since if the puritan is a purist in morals, the purist is also a puritan in taste.

In the *Journals* can be seen Gide's deliberate forging of a style at once classical and personal until the slightest thing he writes bears a peculiar mark. He tells why he purified his language of metaphors in his first book and then longed for an even poorer, nuder style, for which he sought inspiration in Stendhal. Later he confesses his desire to achieve inimitability by dint of the secret perfection of his sentences. On the other hand, he often sees the *Journals* themselves as an exercise in spontaneous rapid composition, since, disliking to write rapidly, he must force himself to do so here. Nothing could be more characteristically Gidian, as his adolescence and African experience abundantly illustrate, than this need of constraining himself to cast off constraint.

However difficult it may be to define his personality and credo, it is certain that the *Journals* of André Gide, like Goethe's *Conversations with Eckermann* and Montaigne's *Essays*, reveal a moral philosopher struggling with the fundamental problems of humanity. The comparison with those two giants of modern letters is not fortuitous, since they have been Gide's constant companions from his earliest years. Complaining at the age of fifty-nine that he had waited too long to write certain things, he comments that Montaigne's strength comes from distrusting his memory and writing on the spur of the moment rather than waiting until he had better organized his thought; "I have always counted too much on the future and had recourse to too much rhetoric," he adds. This reproach, just or unjust in the case of the other writing, cannot be addressed to the *Journals*. It may be simply because of their spontaneity that they will endure, for, more than any other work, they show us André Gide himself and prove that, like Montaigne and Goethe, he is first a man and secondly a writer.

NOTE

Fragments of the Journals of André Gide originally appeared from time to time in book form or in periodicals. Not until the edition of the complete works appeared in the thirties did the entire Journal kept between 1889 and 1932 become available. Even then it was divided arbitrarily according to the notebooks in which it had been kept rather than by years, and many names of persons were masked by initials. In 1939, on the eve of the war, the one-volume Pléiade edition of *Le Journal d'André Gide, 1889–1939* reinstated for the first time various "Detached Pages," "The Death of C.-L. Philippe," "The Turkish Journey," "Numquid et tu . . . ?" and so on, which had been the first fragments to reach the public and had since enjoyed independent existence. In this publication most of the names were written out clearly. A few explanatory notes had been supplied by the author and a still smaller number by the editor, Jacques Schiffrin. Since then a second Pléiade edition with slight corrections and a third edition, erroneously reproducing the first, have appeared, as well as the continuation of the Journals down to 1942; and fragments dated since 1942 have appeared in Paris literary reviews. The English translation has been made from the second Pléiade edition.

An editorial note to that edition warns the attentive reader that, the wartime Journal of 1914–18 having been kept often on loose sheets, some disorder may have crept into their classification. None of these slight errors, impossible to rectify now, is likely to confuse the reader.

In addition to the footnotes and Index, I have prepared a Glossary of Persons for the present edition.

J. O'B.

JOURNALS

VOLUME 1: 1889–1913

1889

With Pierre.[1] We climb to the sixth floor of a house in rue Monsieur-le-Prince, looking for a place where our group can meet. Up there we find a huge room seeming even larger because of the lack of furniture. To the left of the door the ceiling slopes downward as in a mansard. Near the floor a small door opens into an attic extending the whole length of the house under the roof. In the opposite wall a window, just waist-high, provides a view over the roofs of the Medical School, over the Latin Quarter, of an expanse of gray houses as far as the eye can see, the Seine and Notre-Dame in the setting sun, and, in the far distance, Montmartre barely visible in the evening mist.

And together we dream of the impecunious student's life in such a room, with an unfettered pen as the only means of earning a living. And at your feet, on the other side of your writing-table, all Paris. And take refuge there with the dream of your masterpiece, and not come out until it is finished.

Rastignac's famous cry as he looks down on the City from the heights of Père Lachaise: "And now . . . you and I come to grips!" [2]

[1] Pierre Louis (who later signed his name: Pierre Louÿs). [Note supplied by the author in the French edition. Such notes will hereafter be indicated by an A. in brackets.]

[2] At the end of Balzac's *Père Goriot.*

1890

V isit to Verlaine.[1]

Saturday

My Aunt Briançon in bed, very ill, her mind wandering so much as to prevent her from recognizing anyone. Her head on the pillow is transfigured, discolored, but not pale; rather a dull waxen yellow. The astonishing thing is that now she looks like my grandmother: her childhood features have reappeared under the deformation imposed by life but now obliterated by the suffering of death. She looks at me with dim eyes and I stand by her bed not knowing what to say. Finally the nurse leans toward her and shouts in her ear:

"But this is your nephew, madame. Don't you recognize him? It is Monsieur Gide."

And, without understanding, my aunt repeats: "Monsieur Gide . . . Monsieur Gide . . ." Then, all of a sudden, she cries out: "Oh! André! André, it's you!" And I see her hand feebly trying to reach mine. I take her feverish hand and squeeze it hard as if I could express my affection in that way. And perhaps she tried to reply to my gesture, for I hear her murmuring: "Oh! André! my child, my poor André! . . ."

A great effort to speak, but too weak to find her words. And I weep to see that affection trying so hard, but unable, to pour forth.

Then I am seized by a great desire to shout out: I love you, aunt! . . . But already she is relapsing into her semi-coma and her eyes become fixed and sightless. And I am afraid of speaking for fear of distracting that soul perhaps intent on higher things. I close the curtains on her sleep so that nothing may disturb it.

Friday

Aunt Briançon's funeral.

I shall not recount these things, for the emotion would lose its bloom of sincere spontaneity if I analyzed it for the purpose of my writing.

Moreover, it did not make a very strong impression. It was all still very objective. My mind told me what impressions to have: they did not grip me.

However, a very painful emotion on seeing Aunt Charles weep. Her tears hurt me more than if I had wept them. I should have preferred sorrow to respect her and leave that pretty, thoughtful smile on her lips. It seems to me now that what prevents me from feeling lively

---

[1] At the Broussais Hospital. That visit has been very accurately related by Pierre Louÿs (see *Vers et Prose*, September 1910). [A.]

impressions is the sense of not being alone. I pay too much attention to those around me. For instance, I should have liked to be alone and see my aunt's handsome corpse (this is a hideous word). The first dead body I have seen. Then I could have forgotten my tears, and my mind would have wandered.

Pierre Louis was there. He has the kind thought, which I appreciate, of wishing our friendship to be serene and strong in sorrows. I felt him to be better than I; more naturally and without trying to prove it to himself. Indeed, after having seen André,[2] I wonder what affection is and doubt whether I really love anyone. . . . And yet my heart vibrates with pity, oh! with an infinite pity, at every sorrow I meet.

If I had been alone, I would have kissed that little servant girl who was sobbing near me, shaken by grief. It was heartbreaking to hear her.

January

I had always felt vaguely that I communicated my zeal to others, but that they lacked the divine spark. I make an exception of Pierre, of course. When I excited them, I used to feel that they were almost on my level of enthusiasm and boldness.

Then it was that J. wanted to come in and that I saw the mediocrity of their writings.

André Walckenaër, if he wrote, would write too well; but he does not feel the need of writing; the work of others is enough for him. Léon Blum does not know; he is still seeking; he is groping; has too much intelligence and not enough personality. Fazy imitates Mendès too subtly; one can't make out what belongs to the pupil and what to the master. Drouin deserts charmingly, with a modesty that sounds so frank I like him for it. And I am left alone with my bankrupt hopes.

Nevertheless, so powerful is my enthusiasm, so naïve my faith, that all this amuses me and I cannot believe in my defeat. If I had more wit, more talent, and above all a more supple personality, less interested in asserting itself — I could have launched the review[3] alone with Louis, or almost alone, playing the parts of several people without anyone's suspecting it. . . . But such a feat is repellent to me; I could not keep it up.

My pride is constantly being irritated by a thousand minute slights. I suffer absurdly from the fact that everybody does not already know

---

[2] André Walckenaër. [A.]

[3] Louÿs and Gide dreamed of founding a literary review to add to those which were burgeoning under the influence of the symbolist movement. *La Conque,* edited by Louÿs, finally appeared in March 1891 and ran for eleven numbers, limited to 100 copies each. Several fragments by Gide and many of Valéry's early poems appeared in it.

what I hope some day to be, what I shall be; that people cannot foretell the work to come just from the look in my eyes.

· ·

18 March

I live in expectation. I no longer dare begin anything. My courage is all on edge from repeating over and over again: how I shall be working in two weeks, when I give all my time to *Allain!* [4] Oh, those long days of struggling with the work! The thought of them clings to me and keeps me from concentrating on other things now.

My head is cluttered with my work; it tosses about in my head; I can no more read than write; it always gets between the book and my eyes. This is an intolerable mental restlessness. At times I am seized by a mad desire to drop everything, at once, to cancel my lessons, to send everyone packing and ignore the necessity of paying visits, to take refuge in myself "as in a tower," and to develop my vision. . . . But I can do this only in a new, unknown environment. Unless my senses are disoriented I shall fall back into the familiar ruts, into day-dreams built on recollections. Life must be utterly new, and nothing in the surroundings must remind me that, outside, there are other things. The illusion of working in the absolute.

But where? The dream-cell; in the Causses, in the Dauphiné? I thought once of the room I had discovered in Paris; but active life is too close; besides, a real incognito would be impossible; my mind would be too restless. . . . Meanwhile, perhaps a week at Mortefontaine.

One thing is certain, and that is that I drop all lessons, all shackles, in twelve days, or fourteen.

My mind is so taut now that I am afraid it may relapse, may relax at the moment when . . .

8 May

I must do *Allain. Examen d'André Walter.* (Begin at once to gather notes.) *Traité du Narcisse.* [5]

Point out, for *André Walter*, the lack of conclusion, which baffles the reader. First of all I must prepare the *"ut Varietur* edition" to rest me from the *Cahiers*.

It is essential to work relentlessly, all at once, and without letting anything distract you; this is the real means of achieving the unity of a work of art. Then, once it is finished, while the written pages are resting, you must read relentlessly, voraciously, as is fitting after such a fast, and to the very end, for it is essential to know everything. Ideas will

---

[4] A part of Gide's first published work, the anonymous *Cahiers d'André Walter* (*André Walter's Notebooks*) (1891).

[5] *Treatise of the Narcissus* (1892), the first book Gide signed.

again begin to stir; you must let them have their way; one of them will soon dominate; then you can return to writing. At the moment of production, deliberately cease all reading. For me reading is the cause of excessive agitation and stirs up at once all the ideas in my head. No single one is dominant, or at least not for long. Besides, this movement of ideas makes me too well aware of how relative they all are. When one is working, the idea one stumbles upon must stand alone. You must believe that you are working in the absolute.

10 November

I am still clumsy; I should aim to be clumsy only when I wish to be. *I must learn to keep silent.* Merely from having talked to Albert yesterday about this projected book, my will to see it through was weakened. I must learn to take myself seriously; and not to hold any smug opinion of myself. To have more mobile eyes and a less mobile face. To keep a straight face when I make a joke. Not to applaud every joke made by others. Not to show the same colorless geniality toward everyone. To disconcert at the right moment by keeping a poker face. Especially never to praise two people in the same way, but rather to keep toward each individual a distinct manner from which I would never deviate without intending to.

At the baccalaureate examinations for the two Widmer brothers Georges passes; and I don't give a hang. I write this without shame and fail to understand how it could be otherwise.

What interested me was a youth, almost a child, small, pale, an obstinate chin, and white teeth; his hair in bangs down to his eyebrows. He seemed so little concerned that he had not even handed in his list of authors. He was sent back to write it and I did it with him on a sheet of paper I had given him. He gave the feeblest answers to all the questions. He was the last to come up. I pretended to go out with Georges, but I hid in an angle of the stairs and they went out without seeing me. When I went back upstairs, the room was almost empty.

They passed him though. He threw himself into his mother's arms, then into his sister's. The two women in full mourning had stood there trembling all over. I wanted to speak to him. I liked him enormously. I said a few words to him; he thanked me with a smile. His joy almost made him handsome. The three of them went up the boulevard and, to see him a bit longer, I followed them for a long time. I returned home very sad.

End of November

Whenever I get ready again to write really sincere notes in this notebook, I shall have to undertake such a disentangling in my cluttered brain that, to stir up all that dust, I am waiting for a series of vast empty hours, a long cold, a convalescence, during which my constantly re-awakened curiosities will lie at rest; during which my sole care will be to rediscover myself.

For the last two months I have not enjoyed a single moment of monologue. I am not even egotistical any longer. I am not even any longer. Lost, on the day when I began my book. . . .

RULE OF CONDUCT

First point: Necessity for a rule.

2. Morals consist in establishing a hierarchy among things and in using the lesser to obtain the greater. This is an ideal strategy.

3. Never lose sight of the end. Never prefer the means.

4. Look upon oneself as a means; hence never prefer oneself to the chosen end, to the work.

(At this point a blank space in which the question arises as to the choice of the work, and the free choice of that work. To manifest. And yet . . . Can one choose?)

Thinking of one's salvation: egotism.

The hero must not even think of his salvation. He has *voluntarily* and *fatally* consecrated himself, unto damnation, for the sake of others; in order to manifest.

RULE OF CONDUCT

Pay no attention to *appearing*. *Being* is alone important.

And do not long, through vanity, for a too hasty manifestation of one's essence.

Whence: do not seek to *be* through the vain desire to *appear;* but rather because it is *fitting* to be so.

1891

Right now I am again in the same intellectual state as before writing *André Walter:* the same emotional complexity, the same systems of vibrations that I noted in January '90. I am led to the conclusion that this is perhaps the state of mind which will always precede a new period of production and follow a long rest.

10 June

Yesterday a moment of sagging. I had forgotten that; for a long time now my mind has remained alert and triumphant. But yesterday, for a few hours during the afternoon, my head felt soft and I didn't dare speak, so deeply was I annoyed in advance by the inanities I knew I would say.

Today intelligence has returned, but it is calm, without that amusing fermentation which, a few days ago, prevented me from reading. Today I reached the doldrums; or rather a forewarning, a fear at the approach of the doldrums. The doldrums are made up especially of pride; I don't mind that; but one suffers dreadfully. One even goes so far as to long for physical suffering or for some mental degradation to push adrift that aimless anguish of the soul and wear it out.

The great figure of Byron appears to me again, as it did last summer when I had the blues for the first time. . . .

I am reading Carlyle, who annoys me and awakens my enthusiasm at one and the same time. I made the mistake of reading the second lecture (of *Heroes and Hero-Worship*) out of a sense of duty. I never penetrated it. This is absurd. I should never read anything in that way. The first lecture, on the other hand, made such an impression on me that I thought I should never finish reading it. Every line called for a quarter of an hour of reflexions and musings. It has given me the desire and already almost the habit of a certain moral defiance, slightly cantankerous but none the less admirable, and surely the only attitude capable of great things.

An impression worth noting (but I shall remember it anyway) is the sound of a piano in a closed-up house (the de Flaux house in Uzès). You open the shutters; the sounds reverberate. Above all the smell; of cretonne and mouse dung. And also the flat notes of the piano; a puny, almost tremulous sound; for playing Bach it is perfect.

One thing that is indisputable is that Pierre Louis is thoroughly practical while I am hardly at all. But I don't want to be. I take pride in not being. Then it is pointless to long for the advantages of something I abhor. *There are certain things that I shall never have.* Oh, if only I could really convince myself of that! But it is very hard. At least I shall not compromise myself by showing that I do desire them. Essential to remain tightly buttoned up in one's attitude like Barbey d'Aurevilly in his frock-coat.

But, in practical matters, I always flounder absurdly. I am bold in taking the first steps, but I stop after the first effort; and you never get returns before the second effort. I make many acquaintances and then neglect to go back and see them because they bore me.

I can never succeed in entirely convincing myself that certain things really exist. It has always seemed to me that they ceased to exist when I stopped thinking about them; or at least that they are no longer interested in me when I cease to be interested in them. To me the world is a mirror, and I am amazed when it gives a bad reflection of me.

One should want *only one thing* and want it constantly. Then one is sure of getting it. But I desire everything and consequently get nothing. Each time I discover, and too late, that one thing had come to me while I was running after another.

One of Louis's dodges, which has always worked, is imagining that he instinctively and passionately desires everything that serves his purpose.

I must stop puffing up my pride (in this notebook) just for the sake of doing as Stendhal did. The spirit of imitation; watch out for it. It is useless to do something simply because another has done it. One must remember the rule of conduct of the great after having isolated it from the contingent facts of their lives, rather than imitating the little facts.

Dare to be yourself. I must underline that in my head too.

Don't ever do anything through affectation or to make people like you or through imitation or for the pleasure of contradicting.

No compromise (either ethical or artistic). Perhaps it is very dangerous for me to see other people; I always have too great a desire to please; perhaps I need solitude. I might as well admit it frankly: my solitary and sullen childhood made me what I am. Perhaps it would be better to exaggerate that aspect. Perhaps I would find great strength in doing so. (But there should not be any "perhaps" in matters of conduct. There's no use creating question marks. Answer everything in advance. What a ridiculous undertaking! How rash!)

Brunetière talks of the men of the seventeenth century (at least most of them; not Pascal) who never indulged in profound thoughts on life (like Shakespeare's, for instance) or who never dared to express them because society had accustomed those writers to make their thought accessible to women.

I read in Taine (*English Literature*) his description of the celebrations and customs of the Renaissance. Perhaps that was real beauty; utterly physical. Some time ago all that luxurious display would have left me cold. I am reading it at the right moment, when it can most effectively intoxicate me. My mind is becoming voluptuously impious and pagan. I must stress that tendency. I can see the readings I should indulge in: Stendhal, the eighteenth-century *Encyclopedia*, Swift, Condillac . . . to dry up my heart (sear is a better word; everything is mildewed in my heart). Then the vigorous writers and especially the most virile: Aristophanes, Shakespeare, Rabelais . . . these are the ones I must read. . . . And don't worry about the rest. There is enough possibility of tears in my soul to irrigate thirty books.

17 June

Yesterday I spent the afternoon with Henri de Régnier; I like him enormously. Then with Manuel; we paid each other insipid compliments. This morning I missed Huysmans. Wrote a very long letter to Paul Valéry. Ended the day with the man of integrity.[1] He is the one whose company I enjoy most; we fan each other's enthusiasm to the utmost.

18 June

I am reading Stendhal, seated in front of a café (Place Médicis) where I note that I am delightfully uncomfortable for working.

Essential to make oneself irreproachable.

23 June

I spent the day Sunday with Marcel Drouin in the woods of Chaville. Marcel Drouin is the person whom I admire and maybe even like the most in the world. As soon as we are together we fan each other's enthusiasm magnificently; we are good for each other. He was tired from his examinations. We both slept on the grass. I read him my notes on Brittany.

I am becoming Walter again; and so much the better. Certainly nothing is so beautiful as nobility of soul; no, not beautiful, but rather, sublime.

25 June

I have seen Louis again. Good Lord! Are we going to make up?

He tore up my letter in my presence! Why? It was altogether sincere. Three times already we have had long explanations; we have already gone through that painful experience; we are incapable of "hitting it

---

[1] Marcel Drouin. [A.]

off"; therefore intimacy is impossible. Why begin again, then? I could remain his friend; why does he want to be my friend when I don't even admire him any longer and when these animated and paradoxical discussions only tire me and bore me. . . . Oh, how they bore me!

10 July

I am beginning to write again. I interrupted myself through lack of will. As a matter of routine I should force myself to write a few lines here every day.

22 July

Maeterlinck reads me his *Sept Princesses.*[2]

Yesterday saw Bruges and Ostend. Such boredom, such a lugubrious fatigue strikes me as soon as I am in a new town that I can think of nothing but the desire to get away again. I dragged myself through the streets with a real anguish. Even when these things are most worthy of admiration, the idea of seeing them alone appalls me. It seems to me that I am taking from Em.[3] a bit of that delight that we ought to enjoy together. I sleep every afternoon to be able at least to dream a little. Or else I read. The "landscape," instead of distracting me from myself, always assumes desperately the color of my lamentable soul.

At Ostend the sky and the sea were gray; dire desperations rained down on the sea. I wanted to lose myself in a sensual emotion and, while watching the downpour, I absorbed ices. I had a fever. My nose bled all day long.

23 July

I saw Bruges again with Mother. I snuggled up in her affection.

Said farewell to Maeterlinck. We were beginning to talk. I regret the things that we might have said to each other. I should like to write him. A longing for laborious solitude is again upon me.

Maeterlinck has an admirable strength.

Alkmaar

. . . A garden of tulips and pink lilies. Neat little lanes between tiny houses. I wandered over the washed tiles, and in front of the painted doors appropriately little girls were washing away spots that could not be seen. Above the roofs ships' masts were moving back and forth, because here the good Lord made the waters higher than the land.

---

[2] *The Seven Princesses,* a play (1891).

[3] "Em." stands for Madeleine Rondeaux, André Gide's cousin, whom he married in 1895.

Brussels, 30 July

Drouin takes the first prize!

Drouin is first everywhere!

Mother wept with joy when I read her his triumphant letter. I am happy. At the hotel this evening I wanted to shout it out to everyone. I am proud of Drouin, and his friendship is one of the most precious things to me. I am happy because of him and I need to write it down: My dear Drouin, I am proud of you.

This same evening I learn of the death of Émile A. He committed suicide; I am sure of it.

1 August

Marcel Drouin has the highest record on the examinations for Normale.[4]

Brussels

Adam and Eve by H. Van Eyck.

Scenes of the Inquisition by Goya, and *Portrait of a Girl.*

The Goldsmith's Family by Govaert Flinck.

These are the three that taught me something. There are others whom I admired more, perhaps, but I got nothing new out of them for myself. These three had a personal lesson for me. I am noting down a few reasons.

Flinck. Disagreeable painting. When we say: "He has character," there is always a touch of spitefulness; because to assert himself an artist is always obliged to break things. Flinck has character. Later he worked to please and was afraid of himself.

Unhealthy faces; hideousness and larvæ; both the artist and the subjects assert themselves forcibly. Rheumy eyes, without lashes (very noticeable, this last touch) and red. Gaudy and willful colors (the child's blue dress). Denuded faces, but excellent and powerful relationships between the hair and the features.

Hubert Van Eyck. Girls turn away guffawing and traveling salesmen nudge one another as they pass in front of the *Adam and Eve*. It makes an impression of powerful indecency — first because of the realism that dares to paint everything; second, the impression of types that were never intended to be naked. A shameful nakedness, and aware of its shame; ugly nakedness aware of the cold. Adam after the Fall: "and they saw that they were naked." Whether or not Van Eyck meant to put

---

[4] The École Normale Supérieure for college and university professors. Difficult competitive examinations admit students to the school, after exhaustive special preparation, as holders of the highest government scholarships.

all this into his painting, I cannot say; but he copied nature religiously and just as he saw it, so that his painting suggests all this in spite of him. It is a very religious kind of painting. ECCE HOMO: something very poor, which should be clothed in a hurry because it is ugly when naked. The necessary hypocrisy, or religion: whence the heptatych: the *Mystic Adoration of the Lamb.*

Goya: *Inquisition.* Everything has been said on this subject. *Portrait of a Girl:* I can't understand it at all. I spent an hour in front of it though, for I went back to it every day. Recognized from the end of the hall; and yet I had never seen any Goya, but I knew what it would be like. Manet borrowed a great deal from him. Everything still remains to be said about it.

I ought not to write these utterly objective notes in this notebook, but I have made these paintings mine. They enriched me considerably.

On the way to Nancy. Friday, 7 August

This morning, although with hardly any hope left, I ran once more to the Dinant post office, where finally I find a letter from the man of integrity, the letter I have been so long expecting. . . .

Afterward, on the way back, I was as if drunk, and in spite of myself I shouted with joy. Little girls turned around to look at me and were amazed to see anyone so happy.

I really needed that letter. As my spirit is accustomed to be in moments of silence, it has been crushed by doubt and mad restlessness these last few days.

And now, suddenly, I am happy, I am happy! Oh, how everything takes its coloring from us!

Han Grottoes

This very moment I have finished reading *War and Peace.*

Begun the first day of the trip; finished the last day. Never, I believe, have I lived so completely in books. In fact, I haven't traveled. The other day, in the famous grottoes, I couldn't even look around me; I was thinking of Schopenhauer, who was waiting for me in the carriage, and it annoyed me to have interrupted my reading in order to look at a landscape.

But later on, from all these visions I have glimpsed, I reconstruct in my own manner a few necessary landscapes.

My mind was quibbling just now as to whether one must first be before appearing, or first appear and then be what one appears. (Like the people who first buy on credit and later worry about their debt; appearing before being amounts to getting in debt toward the physical world.)

Perhaps, my mind said, we *are* only in so far as we *appear.*

Moreover the two propositions are false when separated:
1. We *are* for the sake of appearing.
2. We *appear* because we are.
The two must be joined in a mutual dependence. Then you get the desired imperative: *One must be to appear.*

The appearing must not be distinguished from the being; the being asserts itself in the appearing; the appearing is the immediate manifestation of the being.

But, after all, what does all this matter!!?

Saturday, 8 August

Schopenhauer's utterly empirical ethics (*Foundations of Ethics*) gets on my nerves. In truth, it is not an ethic but a psychology: the analysis of the good motive. An ethic must be *a priori.* And I can't really understand why he should so violently attack the Kantian ethics on the ground of a *petitio principii* when his own are full of such errors. To begin with, what philosophy does not eternally beg the very principles on which it is based?

4 September

Not a word, not a name left in my head. Feel oneself to be monotonous and vague like an abstraction. And spend a half-day aimlessly dwelling on some paltry emotion.

Feel oneself to be poor in spirit and not be ashamed of it.

8 October

More than a month of blanks. Talking of myself bores me. A diary is useful during conscious, intentional, and painful spiritual evolutions. Then you want to know where you stand. But anything I should say now would be harpings on myself. An intimate diary is interesting especially when it records the awakening of ideas; or the awakening of the senses at puberty; or else when you feel yourself to be dying.

There is no longer any drama taking place in me; there is now nothing but a lot of ideas stirred up. There is no need to write myself down on paper.

My cousins have left. I hardly dare confess my joy at being alone. On my return from Honfleur my mind was delightfully active and my thoughts amused me more than what I was reading. I have now gone back to my work and my books. I am serious and almost sad; seeking coziness and, as it were, sluggish with sleep.

My mind is lively and strong. I have begun to struggle again; I should like to struggle constantly. I have picked up *Narcisse* where I left off; I believe I shall be able to finish it.

Soon I shall not be able to bear the presence of others; I'll finally turn into a complete hermit, I believe. I work myself up and become easily irritated in the presence of anyone. The opinion of others matters to me, I believe, even more than ever. I have made very little progress in that direction. I now have about ten friendships that I am always fretting about. You would have to be pretty sure of yourself not to feel the need of constantly proving yourself.

This terrifies me: to think that the present, which we are living this very day, will become the mirror in which we shall later recognize ourselves; and that by what we have been we shall know what we are. And each time I make a decision I am anxious to know if it is the right one.

Uzès, 29 December

O Lord, I come back to thee because I believe that all is vanity save knowing thee. Guide me in thy paths of light. I have followed tortuous ways and have thought to enrich myself with false goods. O Lord, have pity on me: the only real good is the good thou givest. I wanted to enrich myself and I impoverished myself. After all that turmoil I am poorer than ever. I remember my former days and my prayers. O Lord, lead me as thou didst in thy paths of light. O Lord, keep me from evil. May my soul again be proud; my soul was becoming ordinary. Oh, may those early struggles and my prayers not be in vain. . . .

I have lost real possessions in the pursuit of vanities that I took to be serious because I saw others believe in them. I must recover the real possessions. "Hold fast to what thou hast.". . . Yet I knew all these things.

30 December

We are restless only when separated from God, and only in him do we rest, for he is what changeth not.

We must desire only God, for all things will pass before our desire for them is sated, or else they will remain when we no longer desire them.

These false goods deceive us; we cease to seek God because we fail to see that we are poor. We think ourselves rich because they are numerous; we have so many we cannot even count them. . . . There is only one possession that can make us rich: God. And since this possession is unique, we know very well when we do or do not possess it. It is easily counted; it is unique and yet it fills us, and that is why it rests us. O God, when wilt thou fill me wholly?

31 December

When one has begun to write, the hardest thing is to be sincere. Essential to mull over that idea and to define artistic sincerity. Meanwhile,

I hit upon this: the word must never precede the idea. Or else: the word must always be necessitated by the idea. It must be irresistible and inevitable; and the same is true of the sentence, of the whole work of art. And for the artist's whole life, since his vocation must be irresistible. He must be incapable of not writing (I should prefer him to resist himself in the beginning and to suffer therefore).

The fear of not being sincere has been tormenting me for several months and preventing me from writing. Oh, to be utterly and perfectly sincere. . . .

1892

1 January

Wilde, I believe, did me nothing but harm. In his company I had lost the habit of thinking. I had more varied emotions, but had forgotten how to bring order into them. Above all, I could no longer follow the deductions of others. A few thoughts from time to time, but my clumsiness in handling them made me give them up. I return now, with difficulty but also with great delight, to my history of philosophy, where I am studying the problem of language (which I shall take up with Müller and Renan).

3 January

Shall I always torment myself thus and will my mind never, O Lord, come to rest in any certainty? Like an invalid turning over in his bed in search of sleep, I am restless from morning till night, and at night my anxiety awakens me.

I am anxious to know what I shall be; I do not even know what I want to be, but I do know that I must choose. I should like to progress on safe and sure roads that lead only to the point where I have decided to go. But I don't know; I don't know what I ought to want. I am aware of a thousand possibilities in me, but I cannot resign myself to want to be only one of them. And every moment, at every word I write, at each gesture I make, I am terrified at the thought that this is one more ineradicable feature of my physiognomy becoming fixed: a hesitant, impersonal physiognomy, an amorphous physiognomy, since I have not been capable of choosing and tracing its contours confidently.

O Lord, permit me to want only one thing and to want it constantly.

A man's life is his image. At the hour of death we shall be reflected in the past, and, leaning over the mirror of our acts, our souls will recognize *what we are*. Our whole life is spent in sketching an ineradicable portrait of ourselves. The terrible thing is that we don't know this; we do not think of beautifying ourselves. We think of it in speaking of ourselves; we flatter ourselves; but later our terrible portrait will not flatter us. We recount our lives and lie to ourselves, but our life will not lie; it will recount our soul, which will stand before God in its usual posture.

This can therefore be said, which strikes me as a kind of reverse sincerity (on the part of the artist):
Rather than recounting his life as he has lived it, he must live his life as he will recount it. In other words, the portrait of him formed by his

life must identify itself with the ideal portrait he desires. And, in still simpler terms, he must be as he wishes to be.

4 January

I thank thee, O Lord, that the only feminine influence on my delighted soul, which wishes for no other, that the influence of Em. has always guided me toward the highest truths and has always inclined me to studious attitudes.

I take joy in thinking that if she were to return to me I should have no secrets for her.

6 January

I notice this difference between intelligence and wit: intelligence is by nature egotistical while wit presupposes intelligence on the part of the one to whom it is addressed.

Whence I get this: intelligence explains (Taine, Bourget, etc.); wit simply recounts (eighteenth century).

Wit is necessary to a clever talker; intelligence is enough for a good listener.

11 January

I am torn by a conflict between the rules of morality and the rules of sincerity.

Morality consists in substituting for the natural creature (the old Adam) a fiction that you prefer. But then you are no longer sincere. The old Adam is the sincere man.

This occurs to me: the old Adam is the poet. The new man, whom you prefer, is the artist. The artist must take the place of the poet. From the struggle between the two is born the work of art.

20 January

In Uzès again.

You talk; you argue; finally you discover that you are dominated by auditory impressions whereas you are talking to someone predominantly visual. And you thought you understood each other! What a difference that makes! (That among other things.)

Two things provoke each other in me and yet I don't mind: the endless boredom I inspire in myself and my endless love for the pure idea.

This is what must happen. It is a victorious progress; adoration kills the individual. The God takes his place.

I had begun again to work over my mediocre poems of last September. But that bores me. Today I have discovered such rich domains that any joy in producing is canceled by the wild joy of learning. It is a mad lust. Oh, to know. . . .

Easter Sunday

To know . . . to know what?

Still more philology; very little so far. Read some of Goethe's poems; the *Prometheus;* read *La Faustin;* some Banville; *Adolphe.*[1]

I foresee that in a short while I shall hurl myself again into a frantic mysticism.

Munich (second day), 12 May

Learn logic; classify my thoughts. . . . There is an inextricable tangle in my head. Every new thought, as it changes position, stirs up all the others. Nothing is clearly delineated, and this absence of contours, which perhaps makes relationships more noticeable, also makes for a general confusion in which each concept clings somewhat to all the others.

If I do not write any longer in this diary, if I shudder at the thought of letters to write, this is because I have no more personal emotions. In fact, I have no more emotions except those I want to have, or those of other people. On my good days, and they are becoming frequent again, I enjoy an intellectual and nervous exaltation that can be converted, as if at will, into joy or sorrow, without either one being more pleasant than the other. I am like a well-tuned harp, which sings, according to the poet's whim, a gay scherzo or a melancholy andante.

This mental and emotional mood seems to me excellent for writing. I am myself *ad libitum;* doesn't this amount to saying that I can take on the emotions of my characters? The important thing is being capable of emotions, but to experience only *one's own* would be a sorry limitation.

In any event, egoism is hateful. I am less and less interested in myself and more and more in my work and my thoughts. I no longer wonder every day and every hour if I am worthy of my God. But that is a great error; one must be capable of reflecting even the purest things.

Moreover, the judgments of others do not interest me any more than my own. But yes, they do, in so far as they are the statement of a relation between the object and the person who judges it, which permits me to know them both better. But it is enough for me if that other person asserts his judgment; when he tries to explain it, to prove that he is right, he becomes a bore; one can never prove anything. "Judge not." Every judgment bears within it the testimony of our weakness. In my case, the judgments I have to make sometimes about things are as irresolute as

---

[1] *Prometheus* is by Goethe; *La Faustin* (1882), by Edmond de Goncourt; and *Adolphe* (1816), by Benjamin Constant.

the emotions that those things arouse. This explains that boundless uncertainty which upsets my acts when they must be based on a judgment.

I always see, almost simultaneously, the two sides of each idea, and
the emotion is always polarized in me. But even though I understand
the two poles, I also am keenly aware, between them, of the point beyond which the understanding of a mind which takes the strictly personal view, which can see only one side of truth, which chooses once
and for all one or the other of the two poles, cannot extend.

And when I am talking with a friend, I generally am concerned only
with telling him what he thinks, and I myself share his opinion, paying
attention only to establishing and measuring the relations between him
and things. (This is particularly true with Walckenaër.)

But when I am with two friends and they disagree, I remain on edge
between them, not knowing what to say, not daring to take sides with
one or the other, accepting every affirmation and rejecting every negation.

After all, these questions of psychology are absurd and petty.

15 May

Disorders of the flesh and perturbations of the soul can go on indefinitely, but they are interesting only so long as you consider these things
important.

A thing has value only through the importance we give to it. We
make the best of a thing when we detach all our thoughts from it one by
one until it finally takes place without stirring up any reverberations in
our soul.

Two really extraordinary faculties of the poet: the permission to
yield to things, when he wants, without losing himself; and the capa-
bility of being consciously naïve. These two faculties can moreover be
reduced to the single gift of dissociation.

The two or three times in your life when you have drunk really refreshing drinks.

*   *   *

Nancy. November

(Military service.) I realize now that I have suffered recently because the various faculties of my soul were not employed in relation to
their hierarchy. The noblest ones were idle. And I know that if I had
been alone I should have made sublime emotions of these purely physical emotions. But I recognized that the others felt sympathy only for the
lower emotions, and I wanted their sympathy.

A body can produce a sound only when it feels around it a possibility of overtones.

I felt sad when I realized that in this environment to sympathize was to lose caste.

I could write of the things round about me; but they are so distorted. . . .

They seem to you distorted because you do not understand them in all their complexity. This is why the poet's work delights you, for it is simpler. By showing only one truth in a work of art he exaggerates that truth. To simplify is to exaggerate what remains. The work of art is an exaggeration.

1893

. . . which gave to my sorry joys, to each one of them, all the bitterness of sin.

. . . and my greatest joys have been solitary and laden with care.

I lived until the age of twenty-three completely virgin and utterly depraved; crazed to such a point that eventually I came to seek everywhere some bit of flesh on which to press my lips.

Leaning together at the window in the evening, we watched the tints of the sea become more delicate and more mauve. The twilight was spreading.

15 March

. . . and my soul, ever more inclined to adoration, became daily more silent.

. . . the saddest of my thoughts.

17 March

I like life and prefer sleep, not because of its emptiness, but because of its dreams.

Spain

Bullfights.

To kill someone because he is angry is all right; but to anger someone in order to kill him is absolutely criminal.

The bull is killed in a state of mortal sin. He has been forced into that state. He himself only wanted to graze. Etc.

Paris, end of April

A perfect knowledge of one's strength, and then see that it is all put to use.

Do not read any more books by ascetics. Find one's exaltation elsewhere; admire that difficult joy of equilibrium, of the fullness of life. May each thing yield all the life possible in it. It is a duty to make oneself happy.

We shall no longer ask God to raise us up to happiness. Why, indeed! We know very well that *I* am weak.

(Too many things in that sentence. Let's not deny anything. Let's go on.)

And now my prayer (for it still is a prayer): O my Lord, let this too narrow ethic burst and let me live, oh, fully; and give me the strength to do so, oh, without fear, and without always thinking that I am about to sin!

It now takes as great an effort to let myself go as it used to take to resist.

That ethic of privation had so thoroughly established itself as my natural rule of conduct that the other is now very painful and difficult for me. I have to urge myself to pleasure. It is painful for me to be happy.

". . . Sometimes he contemplated his virgin body, smooth, however, and ready for love; then he longed for a woman's caresses before all the bloom of his flesh should fade. He longed to be younger and of a much greater beauty, thinking that between two creatures love has the splendor of their bodies." (*Tentative amoureuse.*[1])

They awaited the evening, seated in the grass doing nothing; then, when finally the light had become softer, they continued their way slowly. . . .

. . . blossomed forth like islands, corollas, stemless flowers, rocking on the waters.

An easy ethic? . . . Indeed not! it had not been an easy rule that had until now guided, sustained, and finally depraved me. But I know that when I begin to enjoy those things which I had forbidden myself as too beautiful, it will not be as a sinner, secretly, with a bitter foretaste of repentance; no, rather without remorse, with vigor and joyously.

Free oneself finally from dream and live a vigorous and fulsome life.

29 April

Oh, how I have breathed in the cold air of the night! Oh, windows! and, because of the haze, so like springs of water did the pale rays flow from the moon that one seemed to be drinking. Oh, windows! how often my forehead has cooled itself at your panes, and how often, when I have run from my too burning bed toward the balcony, my desires have evaporated like fogs upon seeing the vast calm sky.

Fevers of bygone days, you wasted my flesh mortally; but how the soul exhausts itself when nothing distracts it from God!

---

[1] *The Attempt at Love,* by André Gide (1893).

4 May

I must have a notebook to go to the Louvre and study the history of painting more seriously than I have hitherto done. Admiration need not be lazy. I should like to study Chardin as an interpreter rather than as a critic; not indulge in style; make amazed observations; then explain these things to myself. There is always something to learn by assuming before someone great an attentive and devout attitude.

5 May

This morning, having arisen at five o'clock, I worked as I used to do. But the morning should not be devoted to production; it is better adapted to philology and the study of foreign languages.

Really there would be some joy in feeling robust and *normal.* I am waiting.

9 May

When you go to Henri de Régnier's in the evening, you find him seated in an armchair turning his back to the lamp that lights his book. Nothing more studious and charming than Henri de Régnier with a book; he reminds me of the time when nothing distracted me from my readings. How different all that is now!

Saturday

Played Schumann and Chopin to Pierre Louis; played until evening.

Yport, Saturday

. . . and those white flowers, whiter in the shadow, still whiter in the night, shone against the dark grass of the lawns. The fine gravel of the path shone too; we followed the path between the fragrant lilacs and as it plunged under the huge trees. Then the stagnant water of the pond beckoned to us and we kept on walking. Finally the moon, which we preferred at the moment suspended in a foggy sky as if swimming, appeared among the branches. And, dreaming already, we returned to the house to sleep.

28 May

We shall not lose any of our anxieties. Their cause is within us, not outside us. Our mind is so constructed that everything unsettles it, and only in solitude does it find a bit of tranquillity. Then the thought of God troubles it.

What I like in the work of art is that it is calm; no one more than I has longed for rest, nor has loved unrest more.

I spent a whole period of my youth trying to prove to others the emotions that I should have felt if that effort to prove them had not killed them all.

3 June

Useless to write one's journal every day, every year; what is important is that at a certain period of life it should be very compact and scrupulously kept. If I stopped writing it for a long time it was because my emotions were becoming too complicated; it would have taken me too long to write them down. The necessary simplification made them less sincere; it was already a literary restatement, something that a journal must not be.

My emotions opened up like a religion. Impossible to express better what I mean, although later on this may seem to me incomprehensible. This is the tendency toward pantheism. I don't know whether or not that will be my final destination; I think rather that it is a passing phase.

3 June

I am becoming so accustomed to the Laurens family that I am almost frightened, so indispensable do I feel them becoming to me. For me they are a family of the elect, and with them I live in a dream world of delights.

. . . I wanted this year to strain powerfully toward joy and to give myself up to life, which I had persuaded myself was good.

My constant question (and it has become an unhealthy obsession): Could anyone love me?

Just now at last a storm after three months of drought. I came in to watch the rain fall, as an odd sight. I no longer enjoy describing what I see; that spoils it for me. I prefer simply to observe things, knowing that nothing is ever lost and that every impression can be found again at the moment when one needs it. I should like to enjoy things even more fully. I want in a short period of time to come to know very different forms of life and, in each one, to encounter that unrest excited by a longing for the preceding form. I know that in a short time I shall hurl myself into austere tasks and work at all hours of the day. Just now, in spite of all my desire for study, I am not yet allowing myself to work. All day long I read, I go for walks, I seek pleasure; at night I go out again; I am thirsty and I quench my thirst, and all this is very new to me. At night I sleep almost out of doors, so wide open is my window; the moon comes in to awaken me and I am not annoyed. It is so hot that one could easily sleep naked under the moonlight. Upon waking in the morning, one sees an invariable magnificence, and branches under the blue sky. Every day I go out to eat a sherbet, as others would go to a lecture course;

and I often go very far to get it and to work up a thirst first. And afterward I feel tortured as by a burning sensation and study my thirst patiently.

Moreover, I know that this manner of life is bad and that the writer must refuse himself to things, but today I enjoy convincing myself of the contrary and creating future sufferings for the time when I shall no longer satisfy myself. And again, other lives! other lives; all that we can live of them, *ourselves*, and (knowing that this is a mistake) all the emotions we can taste for the sake of recounting them.

La Roque, 14 July

I shall remember that then, as last year, I read Tacitus as I walked along the avenue of pines and distant landscape (that admirable thirteenth book in which Nero gradually loses his softness and his inborn fears). Nature, all around, seemed imbued with a horrible and dull sadness.

The cultivation of my emotions was bad; the Stendhalian upbringing is unfortunate and dangerous. I have lost the habit of lofty thought; this is a *most regrettable* thing. I live in a facile manner, and this must not go on. Everything in life must be intentional, and the will constantly taut like a muscle.

Yet I do not regret having changed my method for a year; but one must always come back to oneself. No, I do not regret it; I know that everything can be turned to advantage, provided one is conscious about it. *And I have lived much. But one must certainly pull oneself together.*

August

Nothing matters; I am happy. I am completely happy even so. That is enough. . . . And I shall have known sorrow.

Honfleur, on the street

And, at times, it seemed to me that others, around me, were alive only for the purpose of increasing in me the feeling of my own personal life.

The great works of silence.

Wait for the work to become silent in you before writing it.

"Serious. . . . One must always come back to this word when discussing him," said Fromentin speaking of Ruysdael. And I like Delacroix's remark: "The work contains a seriousness that is not to be found in the man."

Before leaving I reread all of my journal; I did so with inexpressible disgust. I find nothing in it but pride; pride even in the manner of expressing myself. Always some form of pretentiousness, claiming either

to be profound or to be witty. My pretensions to metaphysics are absurd; that constant analysis of one's thoughts, that lack of action, those
rules of conduct are the most tiresome, insipid, and almost incomprehensible things in the world when one has got beyond them. I could
never get back into certain of those moods, which nevertheless I know
to have been sincere. To me this is all over, a closed book, an emotion
that has cooled off forever.

Reacting against all this, I have come to wish not to be concerned
with myself at all, not to worry, when I want to do something, whether
I am doing good or evil, but simply to do it, and the devil take the consequences! I no longer want strange or complicated things at all; as for
complicated things, I don't even understand them any more. I should
like to be normal and strong, merely not to have to think of these things
any more.

The desire to compose the pages of this journal deprives them of all
worth, even that of sincerity. They do not really mean anything, never
being well enough written to have a literary value. In short, all of them
take for granted a future fame or celebrity that will confer an interest
upon them. And that is utterly base. Only a few pious and pure pages
satisfy me now. What I dislike the least in my former self are the moments of prayer.

I almost tore it all up; at least I suppressed many pages.[2]

. . . how dull those marvelous seaweeds become when you take
them out of the water. . . .

I shall have to translate *Heinrich von Ofterdingen*[3] without delay.
I have also thought of *Peter Schlemihl*,[4] which is so little known, and La
Motte's *Undine*.[5] Then some Italian, perhaps Petrarch. See if a play by
Calderón could be adapted.

The source of our laughter is a feeling of atrophy, of a thing that
could be, but is not, full. We are lifted up, on the other hand, by a recognition of fullness. Everything has an inherent possibility of fullness.

At the Louvre . . . and seeking in each of the paintings that modi-
cum of life which remains after the brush has left them forever. And the

---

[2] Since then I have almost entirely burned the first journal (1902). [A.]
[3] A novel by the German romantic poet Novalis (Friedrich von Harden-
berg).
[4] A novel, also known as *The Man without a Shadow*, by the German
Adelbert von Chamisso.
[5] A fairy romance (1811) by the German poet and dramatist, Friedrich
de la Motte Fouqué.

one that stirred me most today is neither by Rembrandt nor Vinci; it is Titian's *Man with a Glove*, which moved me to tears. Decidedly it would seem that the intensity of the life it contains constitutes the value of a thing. Whether that life, moreover, is the life of the artist or that of the subject.

Giving exactly what others expect of you is very astute when you wish to arrive; otherwise I consider it rather cowardly, like everything that is too easy.

One ought not to have any personal sorrows, but rather espouse those of others . . . so as to be able to change them frequently.

Ibsen's *Ghosts* made a great impression upon me at this new reading; I read the play to my mother and Aunt Henry. But one must be careful not to make too much of the element of scandal. It is by pushing things rather than by colliding with them that one sets them in motion. We must always take into account the inertia of both souls and bodies. By colliding one often breaks, and that's the end. One must stir rather.

La Roque

I wanted to suggest, in the *Tentative amoureuse*, the influence of the book upon the one who is writing it, and during that very writing. As the book issues from us it changes us, modifying the course of our life, just as in physics those free-hanging vases, full of liquid, are seen, as they empty, to receive an impulse in the opposite direction from that of the liquid's flow. Our acts exercise a retroaction upon us. "Our deeds act upon us as much as we act upon them," said George Eliot.

In my case I was sad because a dream of irrealizable joy was tormenting me. I relate that dream and, isolating the joy from the dream, I make it mine; my dream has broken the spell and I am full of joy.

No action upon an object without retroaction of that object upon the subject. I wanted to indicate that reciprocity, not in one's relations with others, but with oneself. The subject that acts is oneself; the object that retroacts is a literary subject arising in the imagination. This is consequently an indirect method of acting upon oneself that I have outlined; and it is also, more directly, a tale.

Luc and Rachel [6] also want to realize their desire, but while, by writing mine down, I realized it in an ideal way, they, dreaming of the park that they saw only from the outside, want to go in materially; when they do, they experience no joy. In a work of art I rather like to find transposed, on the scale of the characters, the very subject of that work. Noth-

---

[6] The protagonists of *La Tentative amoureuse*.

ing throws a clearer light upon it or more surely establishes the proportions of the whole. Thus, in certain paintings of Memling or Quentin Metzys a small convex and dark mirror reflects the interior of the room in which the scene of the painting is taking place. Likewise in Veláz-quez's painting of the *Meninas* (but somewhat differently). Finally, in literature, in the play scene in *Hamlet,* and elsewhere in many other plays. In *Wilhelm Meister* [7] the scenes of the puppets or the celebration at the castle. In *The Fall of the House of Usher* [8] the story that is read to Roderick, etc. None of these examples is altogether exact. What would be much more so, and would explain much better what I strove for in my *Cahiers,* in my *Narcisse,* and in the *Tentative,* is a comparison with the device of heraldry that consists in setting in the escutcheon a smaller one *"en abyme,"* at the heart-point.

That retroaction of the subject on itself has always tempted me. It is the very model of the psychological novel. An angry man tells a story; there is the subject of a book. A man telling a story is not enough; it must be an angry man and there must be a constant connection between his anger and the story he tells.

All my efforts this year have been directed toward this one hard task: to free myself at length from everything useless and narrow with which an inherited religion had surrounded me to limit my nature, without however repudiating any of the many elements that could still improve and strengthen me.

Perhaps, rather than Petrarch, I should translate the *Vita Nuova* of Dante.

The Christian soul is always imagining battles within itself. After a short time one never can understand just why. . . . For, after all, the vanquished is always a part of oneself, and this makes for useless wear and tear. I spent my whole youth in opposing two parts of myself which perhaps only sought to come to an agreement. Through love of strife I fancied struggles and divided my nature.

13 September

Goethe. Do we now say, then, that happiness can be achieved through suppressing scruples? No. Suppressing scruples is not enough to make one happy; it takes something more than that. But scruples are enough to keep us from happiness; scruples are moral fears which our prejudices prepare for us. Each one of us is a misunderstood harmony;

[7] A novel of biographical interest by Goethe.
[8] One of Edgar Allan Poe's *Tales.*

you think you can separate yourself, go your own way, and immediately you oppose yourself to yourself. A soloist must play in the same direction as the orchestra. (Study that idea.) Scrupulous souls, timorous souls that oppress themselves. They are afraid of joy as of the blinding quality of a too dazzling light.

> *Proprium opus humani generis totaliter accepti est actuare semper totam potentiam intellectus possibilis.*[9]

RULE OF CONDUCT

Originality; first degree.

I omit the lower degree, which is mere banality; in which man is merely gregarious (he constitutes the crowd).

Therefore: originality consists in depriving oneself of certain things. Personality asserts itself by its limitations.

But, above this, there is a still higher state, to which Goethe achieves, the Olympian. He understands that originality limits, that by being personal he is simply anyone. And by letting himself live in things, like Pan, everywhere, he thrusts aside all limits until he no longer has any but those of the world itself. He becomes banal, but in a superior way.

It is dangerous to try to achieve too early that superior banality. If one does not absorb everything, one loses oneself completely. The mind must be greater than the world and contain it, or else it is pitifully dissolved and is no longer even original.

Whence the two states: first the state of struggle, in which the world is a temptation; one must not yield to things. Then the superior state, to which Proserpine, who always remembered having taken the pomegranate seeds, did not attain; which Goethe entered at once and hence, refusing himself nothing, could write: I felt myself god enough to descend to the daughters of men.

At the Laurenses' house, Yport

Tonight there is such a storm that I have had to get up, forsaking sleep. It is not yet five o'clock; the night is extremely dark and the rain is streaming down outside. The upstairs room where I am, in the tower, has eight windows, and the wind is shaking each one of them. In a moment I shall go and look at the sea. Indeed, it is a terrifying night; you don't feel properly sheltered, and you can imagine an even stronger wind breaking the windowpanes and blowing the door in. You can imagine the roof of a house suddenly carried away and see the family un-

---

[9] "The particular function of the human race taken as a whole is to employ constantly the full power of the possible understanding."

der the open sky, in the dark, standing between the trembling walls of
a house that is on the point of giving in. I visualize especially the father
leaning with all his strength against the door, in the beginning of the
drama, to keep the wind from entering. . . .

I have come to consider the days of restlessness, of scruples, and of
self-denial as overclouded days on which the sun cannot shine through,
on which the past lives more fully than I myself in the present moment; as days of weakness, guilty because of their listlessness.

The Christian religion is above all consoling; it is beautiful especially for this reason. It is not an explanation of things; it is something
better. The explanation would touch only the head, and men would
merely understand.

But this religion consoles us for an evil that it does not claim to suppress; it is understandable that certain people have preferred to be simply happy. Others wanted to suppress the cause of all sorrows; this was
more difficult: great souls wore themselves out in the attempt. Goethe
preferred to pay no attention to it; to achieve happiness he turned away
from misfortunes. At first one holds this against him because one thinks
it was easy, but it is easy only for dried-up souls (and they have no happiness in them). Goethe was not such a soul and he did not do what he
did out of harshness. He thought that the sight of his happiness would
contribute more to the happiness of others than hard and painful struggles against their misfortune.

Mozart's joy: a joy that you recognize to be lasting. Schumann's joy
is feverish, as if it came between two sobs. Mozart's joy is made of serenity, and a phrase of his music is like a calm thought; his simplicity is
merely purity. It is a crystalline thing in which all the emotions play a
role, but as if already celestially transposed. "Moderation consists in
feeling emotions as the angels do" (Joubert). To understand that remark completely you must think of Mozart.

The thought of joy must be my constant preoccupation.

I wrote last year, in Munich (this is a detached page that I have just
found): "There are not so many important things. I could make my happiness of so little; together with plenty of the pride that comes from depriving myself of the others. The other things! When I have had time
to realize their vanity, I shall withdraw into study. In a short while, but
first I want to exhaust their bitter taste so that later on no desire for them
will come to disturb my quiet hours."

It is now more than a year since I wrote those sentences, and since then the things that I then scorned, as I approached closer to them, appeared to me more attractive and more beautiful. And it is for them that, seduced, I now launch out into travel.

Montpellier, 10 October

Christianity, above all, consoles; but there are naturally happy souls who do not need consolation. Consequently Christianity begins by making such souls unhappy, for otherwise it would have no power over them.

Whereupon, ceasing to call my desires temptations, ceasing to resist them, I strove on the contrary to follow them. Pride seemed to me a less desirable thing. In that splendid egoism full of religion, I now saw, perhaps wrongly, only restrictions and limitations. Self-abandon struck me as a superior wisdom; it seemed to me that I would find in it greater profit for my soul. This was, I am well aware, still a form of egoism, but a newer, more curious form and one that satisfied in me more potential powers. I maintain that expression: satisfy potential powers; this had now become my rule of conduct; I wanted to live powerfully. O beauty! O desires! How skillfully you distracted my soul! That was the time when every smile diverted it; I used to smile myself and was never serious; I abhorred sorrow and protested against my inclinations toward sympathy. What more need I say? What I had begun with effort a charm or habit made me continue without restraint. Yet the habit of asceticism was such that in the beginning I had to force myself toward joy and it was with difficulty that I smiled; but how short a time those efforts lasted! Was I not following, meanwhile, perfectly natural laws? This occurred to me from the fact that, to live happily, I had perhaps only to let myself go. I say "perhaps" because I am not quite sure; yet I had the naïveté to be amazed at first; wasn't this exactly what I had wanted: simply to let myself go? . . . I was like a sailor who drops his oars and lets himself drift; at last he takes the time to look at the shores; while he was rowing he saw nothing. My will, so constantly stretched taut, relaxed at present without any function. At first I experienced a mild discomfort; then even that disappeared, melting into the infinite charm of living, and of living carelessly. This was the great rest after the long fever; my former anxieties became incomprehensible to me. I was amazed that nature was so beautiful, and I called everything nature.

A ride to the pass of Anterne. The head of the gray horse grazing the meadow scabious.

Emerson, to be read only in the morning.

DETACHED PAGES

Man! The most complex of creatures, and for this reason the most dependent of creatures. On everything that has formed you you depend. Do not baulk at this apparent slavery, and understand that the more numerous are the laws that intercross and overlap in you, the more exquisite they are. A debtor to many, you pay for your advantages by the same number of dependencies. Understand that independence is a form of poverty; that many things claim you, that many also claim kinship with you.

That one thing, whatever it may be, is not made for another thing, whatever it may be. Each act must find its justification and its end in itself and not be self-interested. Do not do good or evil for the reward, or the work of art with an ulterior motive; do not make love for money, or a struggle for life. But art for art's sake, good for the sake of good, evil for the sake of evil, love for love, the struggle for the struggle, and life for life. Nature takes a hand in the rest, and the rest does not concern us. All things are linked and subordinated in this world, this we know; but doing each thing for its own sake is the only way to justify its value.

I want to speak here of life for life's sake and cry out with the pious Lavater: "Beloveds, let us live, oh, as much as possible!"

"Hold that fast which thou hast."

We possess nothing but the feelings that things have given to us, for which gift those things were lent to us. Things and creatures are only a means to us, only an instrument of emotion. Our error consists in attaching ourselves to them. We never really possess them. Hold that fast which thou hast; and add: prize only what thou hast.

Things are the interpreters of God. In time they pass and the meaning of his words remains. We are capable of longing for them just as, alas! we long, after hearing very dear words, for the irreplaceable voice that spoke them. Beauty of creatures and things and of countries: intonations of God's voice.

"Do you see that wrinkle?" I asked him; "it comes from a horrible fatigue. And the fatigue is the result of my freedom. Freedom of action is all right when a powerful desire, a great passion, or an unflagging will directs it. But not this: having given an equal freedom of the city to all my desires, having welcomed them all with open arms, I now find that all of them at the same time claim the place of honor. I now firmly believe that man is incapable of choice and that he invariably yields to the strongest temptation. Even renunciation is a temptation of pride, or else it's the passion of love. A little less understanding of all the other things (which I am not doing), a little less attraction toward them, makes action easier; and even the most voluntary act is merely a concealed surrender to an inclination. Etc.

Oh, if only my thought could simplify itself! . . . I sit here, sometimes all morning, *unable* to do anything, tormented by the desire to do everything. The yearning to educate myself is the greatest temptation for me. I have twenty books before me, every one of them begun. You will laugh when I tell you that I cannot read a single one of them simply because I want so much to read them all. I read three lines and think of everything else . . . (in an hour I shall have to go and see Paul and Pierre; good Lord, I almost forgot Étienne, and he might have been hurt; on the way I ought to buy some cuffs; and Laure is expecting me to take her some flowers . . .). Oh, my time! my time will be frittered away like this until death. If only I could live on some foreign shore where, the moment I stepped outdoors, I could delight in the sun, the wind and the infinite horizon of the sea! . . . Perhaps I ought to go out. My head is tired; a short walk will cure me. . . . But I had promised myself to spend an hour at the piano. . . .

Ah, a knock on the door! Someone is coming to see me. Good Lord! . . . (Saved; this is at least an hour lost!) Happy, I exclaimed, are those whose every hour is filled in advance and who are obliged to go *somewhere*. Oh for a pair of blinders!

Let us beware, Nathanael,[10] of all the instruments of happiness. And above all let us not choose them. To begin with, you cannot choose, but it is dangerous even to think you are choosing, since in order to choose you must judge, and judging always presupposes . . . ; besides, etc., etc.

FOR THE USE OF M. D.

Means of enticement and instigation to work.

1. Intellectual means:

(a) The idea of imminent death.

(b) Emulation; precise consciousness of one's period and of the production of others.

(c) Artificial sense of one's age; emulation through comparison with the biographies of great men.

(d) Contemplation of the hard work of the poor; only intense work can excuse my wealth in my own eyes. Wealth considered solely as a permission to work freely.

(e) Comparison of today's work with yesterday's. Then take as a standard the day on which you worked the most and convince yourself

[10] The character whom Gide addresses in his *Nourritures terrestres* (*The Fruits of the Earth*), which appeared in 1897,

by this false reasoning: nothing prevents me from working as much today.

(f) Reading of second-rate or definitely bad works; recognize the enemy and exaggerate the danger. Let your hatred of them urge you to work. (Powerful means, but more dangerous than emulation.)

2. Physical means (all doubtful):
(a) Eat little.
(b) Keep your extremities very warm.
(c) Do not sleep too much (seven hours are enough).
(d) Never try to urge yourself on at the moment of writing by either reading or music; or else choose an ancient author and read, with the proper attitude of piety, only a few lines. The ones I choose in such a case are always the same: Virgil, Molière, and Bach (read without the aid of the piano); Voltaire's *Candide;* or, for quite different reasons, the first volumes of Flaubert's *Correspondance* or Balzac's *Lettres à sa sœur.*

In my room a low bed, a little space, a wooden upright with a broad horizontal board elbow-high, a small square table, a hard straight chair. I create lying down, compose walking up and down, write standing up, copy out sitting down. These four positions have become almost indispensable to me.

I should not cite myself as an example if I did not find it very difficult getting to work. I readily imagine that anyone else works more easily than I and tell myself that, consequently, anyone else could have done just as well what I have done; this allows me the better to scorn. I have never been fundamentally convinced of my superiority over anyone else; this is how I succeed in reconciling a great deal of modesty with a great deal of pride.

(e) Be well. Have been ill.

In the workroom no works of art or very few and very serious ones: (no Botticelli) Masaccio, Michelangelo, Raphael's *School of Athens;* but preferably a few portraits or death-masks: Dante, Pascal, Leopardi, the photograph of Balzac, of . . .

No books other than dictionaries. Nothing must distract or charm. Nothing must rescue you from boredom except your work.

Never indulge in politics and almost never read the newspapers, but never lose an opportunity to talk politics with anyone whatsoever. This will not teach you anything about the *res publica,* but it will inform you admirably as to the character of the people you talk with.

Imagination (in my case) rarely precedes the idea; it is the latter, and never the former, that excites me. But the latter without the former produces nothing but a useless exaltation. The idea of a work is its composition. Because of imagining too rapidly so many writers of today create ephemeral, poorly composed works. With me the idea of a work precedes often by several years its *imagination*.

As soon as the idea of a work takes on consistency — that is, as soon as the work organizes itself — the elaboration consists in little more than suppressing everything that is useless to its *organism*.

I am aware that everything that constitutes the originality of the writer is added unto this; but woe to him who thinks of his personality while writing. It always comes through sufficiently if it is sincere, and Christ's saying is just as true in art: "Whosoever will save his life (his personality) shall lose it."

This preliminary work, then, I perform while walking. Then it is that the outside world has the greatest hold over me and that distraction is most dangerous. For since work must always be natural, you must develop your idea without tension or violence. And sometimes it does not come at once. You have to wait. This requires infinite patience. It's no good to seize hold of the idea against its will; it then seems so surly that you wonder what attracted you in it. The preferred idea comes only when there is no other idea in its place. Hence you can evoke it only by thinking of nothing else. At times I have spent more than an hour waiting for it. If you have the misfortune, feeling nothing coming, to think: "I am wasting my time," it's all over and you *have* wasted your time.

1894

Thursday evening, dinner with Henri de Régnier at Rouart's house. I brought some photographs. The three of us spent the evening in the rue de Lisbonne studio. Henri de Régnier told about Casanova's *Memoirs* and Richter's *Titan*.

Friday, lunch with Henri de Régnier at the Soufflet. In the morning, visit to Aunt Claire; bought some books under the Odéon arcade. Henri de Régnier accompanies me to rue de Commailles; I read him the beginning of *Paludes*.[1] Talk about Biskra.

Saturday, left in the morning for Lausanne.

Neuchâtel, end of September

The most beautiful things are those that madness prompts and reason writes. Essential to remain between the two, close to madness when you dream and close to reason when you write.

It seems to me that *Paludes* was the work of an invalid, judging from the difficulty I have in getting back to it now. This is a proof, in the reverse, that I have now recovered; lyric enthusiasm does not leave me an instant and the hardest thing to write is this work, so voluntarily narrow. In short, I no longer suffer from the state of mind that forced me to write it; it has become a sort of disinterment.

Neuchâtel

Even here autumn has its charm. This evening I went up to the woods above the town; I followed a main road bordered on one side by russet lindens and walnut trees. Men were knocking down the walnuts with long poles, and an odor of sodium iodide came from the husks that children were trampling on the ground. A strong warm wind was blowing. Near the woods some men were plowing. As they passed, people hailed one another aloud and it seemed as if you could hear the children's songs from a greater distance than usual. I thought of Cuverville and La Roque[2] and of my regret at not being there. I thought that at that same hour my family were looking likewise at the beautiful edges of the woods and were slowly returning home. The lamp is already on their table, the tea, the books of others. . . .

---

[1] *Morasses*, Gide's first *sotie*, or satirical work, published in 1895.
[2] Two properties in Normandy belonging to Gide's family on the maternal side.

I am going to pick up Leibniz where I left off; for the last three years he has been my regular autumn reading. First I read all the little treatises and some of the letters; then the first part of the *Théodicée;* now I have begun the *New Essays.* For two autumns I also read Fichte; shall I have the time this year? I took with me, just in case, *The Doctrine of Science.* Every autumn likewise I read Dickens, Turgenyev, or Eliot, but especially Dickens, whom I like to read more than anyone else at the end of the day, on my return from a long walk in the woods; then in slippers beside the fire while drinking tea and always in that same big green armchair at La Roque.

And the sound of the dinner bell, and the shadow cast by my mother seated reading at the big table. . . . Is all that over?

Every year at this time a refrain of all my old devotions and ardors is reawakened; I become a good boy again.

I have ordered from Germany a little volume of Lavater. Why is he not better known, that so ardent and so affectionate spirit of whom Goethe said that he was "irreplaceable," and whom the invalided No-valis read in his last years? At the beginning of Tieck's preface stands the following, which I should set at the opening of my translation:

"I say it on each of my birthdays; I think it each day of my life: to meditate upon myself is the life of life, and we devote so little medita-tion to this subject! How rarely we create our life for life's sake" (un-translatable; the original says: *Wie selten machen wir unser Leben zum Leben!*).

And this for my volume of poetry:

"Let us, O beloveds, live as much as possible."

I am unwilling to understand a rule of conduct which does not per-mit and even teach the greatest, the finest, and the freest use and de-velopment of all our powers.

Neuchâtel, October

Biography of Lessing. Voltaire seems to have acted shamefully to-ward him; nothing before had ever so sullied that figure as the story of the Saxon notes. Lessing's arrival in Leipzig is charming: at seventeen he had lived only through books, and that lively and worldly society amazes him; he is a scholar, not a man, and his knowledge embarrasses him. He is Peter Schlemihl without his shadow; he hardly dares bow to people. He came to study theology; he learns to fence and to dance.

I must copy these admirable words of his:

"What constitutes the value of a man is not the truth he possesses or thinks he possesses; it is rather the sincere effort he has made to win that truth. For it is not by possession but by the pursuit of truth that man increases his powers and perfects himself. If God held enclosed in his right hand all of Truth and in his left hand the eternal aspiration toward the Truth (with the certainty of never attaining it), and if he said to me: 'Choose!' I should humbly seize his left hand, saying: 'Give, Father, for pure Truth is intended only for thee.'"

Truth belongs to God; the idea belongs to man. Certain people confuse ideas and truths. "Is it not true that truths are posterior to the ideas from which they are born?" (Leibniz: *New Essays.*)

13 October

"There is not a single temptation that God has sent you which is not human. And God, who is just, gives you also the strength to overcome them." Thoughts are temptations; they are the temptations that come to us from God; they are born of the very pursuit of God. They are the temptations that we must overcome since they can be overcome. The other temptations (better named desires), which do not come from God but rather, when we are looking upon God, come to assail us from behind and turn us away from his contemplation, are not, I·think, all capable of being suppressed. I do not understand how it could be good to seek too arduously and too long to stifle all of them; at least to seek it longer than is appropriate for a certain exercise of the will, and even that only during youth, for otherwise they would concern us too much and take on too much importance. You cannot get rid of them; the soul that at first gained strength in doing so is later exhausted in the attempt. They are natural desires, and when the young soul has resisted them long enough to be justifiably proud of itself, it should apply itself to silencing them or to taking advantage of them, for there is advantage in desires and advantage in the satisfaction of desires. But it is not good to excite desires by a too long resistance to them, for the soul is thereby unbalanced.

That is at least what I think today. One must at any price manage to free one's soul. The noble soul deserves higher occupations. I know that there are very noble souls that the love of God has burned deeper than any other desire; it would seem that that angelic ardor had absorbed the other flame, but then one is burned up too swiftly and the reason remains stunned. Sometimes it is a madness; more often an ignorance. I used to wish for such a madness, but I do not want it now. I want to honor God with every part of me, to seek him everywhere and suppress nothing with a view to a partial exaltation. It seems to me that to do so amounts to inadequate praying. Prayer is praise of God; our whole life is that constant prayer, and I wish to know no other; it can be inspired by love, by distress, or by humility. I should like it to spring only from love. Distress and humility come from a faltering reason; I no longer want reason to be silent so that the heart can speak. And my heart will speak none the less. My reason is called to honor God like all the rest of my being. Is it not inherent in God and does it not approach God in silence?

And it is my reason that God tempts; that is his manner of talking to it. If it were not tempted, my reason would think that God had fallen silent. In the horror of inactivity it would contrive to tempt itself, which is a way of tempting God.

O Lord, I must hide this from everyone else, but there are minutes, hours even, when everything in the world strikes me as without order and lost, when every harmony that my mind has invented disintegrates, when the very thought of the pursuit of a higher order is a bore to me, when the sight of poverty upsets me, when my old prayers and my former pious melancholy rise into my heart, when the passive virtue of the humble man again seems to me the most beautiful.

O Lord, give me the strength to reveal my thought to others only as serene, admirable, and mature.

At certain moments I tell myself: I shall never find my way out. One cannot get out. O Lord, teach me!

But this outcry springs from a temporary rule of conduct.

Religious doubts: mediocrity. The description that others have given me of their doubts has always bored and embarrassed me. Such doubts are born of a diffident mind that thinks one can lose sight of God as soon as one ceases looking in the direction of Mecca.

To create an antagonism between two parts of your nature, to make of yourself an enemy of nature, can perhaps flatter pride and contribute to poetry, but it is not *reasonable*. A clear understanding of God makes one want to follow the direction of things, the direction of oneself. That is much more difficult than resisting the current and at least calls for more wisdom. It presupposes intelligence, which is in no wise necessary to resistance. And serving God without intelligence (when you have intelligence) amounts to serving him with only a part of yourself.

Laws and rules of conduct are essentially educative and hence provisional. All well-understood education tends to the point where it can do without them. All education tends to negate itself. Laws and rules of conduct are for the state of childhood; education is an emancipation. A perfectly wise city or state would live and judge without laws, the

norms being in the minds of its Areopagus. The wise man lives without
a rule of conduct, according to his wisdom. We must try to reach a
higher immorality.

Certain people confuse ideas and truths (see Leibniz: *New Essays*).
Truths are always good, and ideas often dangerous to display. It might
be said that the idea is the temptation of its truth. It is not good to tempt
others; God sends each one of us temptations according to the strength
of the individual; it is evil and unwise to offer people temptations they
cannot overcome. This is why awkward teaching is to be feared, why
we must not shout out our ideas, for fear that a weak man may hear us.

Truth can be told to all; the idea, in proportion to the strength of
each.

In every relationship lies a possibility of influence.

God the rewarder, the just supervisor. . . . It is good for the soul
still in its youth to learn that you cannot lose sight of God wherever you
turn.

Possibility of distress: the soul that thinks it has not adored properly.
(*Mort de Mlle Claire*.)[3]

To know God is to seek him. "You would not seek me," Pascal makes
Christ say, "if you had not already found me." This is because, once
perceived, we always have an ever greater need to find his adorable
presence everywhere. I want to know God only in the study of all things.
What others call "gratitude" I think is my admiration. And that admiration, which I wish to be ever more enlightened, gave me the love of
duty. The laws of nature are those of God: happy is he who can know
them and follow them; what has he to do with commandments? The
tables of the law are eternal, for they are within us. Moses breaks the
tables and they nevertheless continue to exist. The man who willingly
submits to them is the wise man; nature makes fools submit. Everything that you do out of duty, your forehead wrinkled with fear, I wish
to do out of love, smiling with love, smilingly. And I love God because
he is within me; I admire him because he is beautiful; for God is everything, and everything is beautiful to him who can understand.

I tell you all this — which seems to me an excuse for not kneeling on
a prayer-stool. But beautiful, strong souls do not need so many words.
Their adoration is a joyful exaltation, so natural that it does not even
bring the name of God to their lips. Yet they are not arrogant; they are

---

[3] Later became *La Porte étroite* (*Strait is the Gate*) (1909). [Note by
the French editor. Such notes will hereafter be indicated by an E. in brackets.]

submissive; they are pious if you call piety the feeling of a willingly accepted dependency, an obedience to the most spiritual laws.

My soul: a drill-ground.
The effort of virtues and vices. Be Lynceus.[4]

The history of the past is the story of all the truths that man has
released.

Take upon oneself as much humanity as possible. There is the correct formula.

---

[4] A reference to Lynceus, the watchman on the tower in Goethe's *Faust,*
Part II, who possesses the gift of joyful acceptance and was to become a symbol in the *Nourritures terrestres* (1897).

1895

Three quarters of life are spent in preparing happiness, but it would be wrong to believe that on that account the last quarter is spent in enjoying happiness. We have got too deeply into the habit of that kind of preparations, and when we have finished preparing for ourselves we prepare for others, so that the propitious moment is put off beyond death. This is why we have such a need to believe in eternal life. A great stroke of wisdom would be to realize that true happiness can do without preparations, or at least it wants only an intimate, personal preparation.

Man is extraordinarily clever in preventing himself from being happy; it would seem that the less able he is to endure misfortune the more apt he is to attach himself to it. (Once more be it said I am speaking only of other men, having always found it very easy to be happy since I have always held my happiness absolutely independent of things.)

Men are unhappy through lack of faith or through egotism. But how make them realize this? That a soul could claim to be at one and the same time religious and unhappy is an absurd invention. Yet I can understand how Christianity often leads to that, and it is a very noble form of Christianity that focuses on the solidarity of Christ's suffering (the Gospel of St. John certainly does not contribute to this).

Very few souls realize that one can save oneself from egotism by another love than that of creatures (by the pure love of God).

Sin is bad especially because of the horror or love of sin that it leaves us.

Our deeds attach themselves to us like the flame to phosphorus. They constitute our brilliance, to be sure, but only in so far as they consume us.

Can this be realized? Every sensation is of an infinite *presence*.

Suppress in yourself the idea of merit. It is a great stumbling-block for the mind.

To get outside my passing concerns I am reading Rod's essay on Goethe. Nothing has ever served to calm me in life so much as the contemplation of that great figure. (Moreover Rod's article is no good.)

The only good in patriotism, it seems to me, is the vanity of emulation it communicates to certain minds, otherwise too numb.

Suppress the idea of greater or lesser merit. Your admiration for others will be diminished, but also your admiration for yourself, which is a good thing. And your admiration for God will be increased correspondingly; that is, for the sheer beauty of the act without concern for its difficulty, just as you admire the work of art. Besides, every beautiful action is enviable; rather than congratulating the doer, I could understand envying him.

Succeed in doing through a sense of duty what another would have done through love. The love of God must always dominate the love of man.

The greatest nobility of life is obtained not through love of others but through love of duty.

LEAVES GATHERED BY THE WAYSIDE

I

15 December (1895)

Viale dei Colli, San Miniato in the most radiant weather. A sky now but softly overcast, now almost all azure, which deepens toward evening because of the abundant mists: the whole city melts in a golden bake-oven. The roofs are plum-colored; the Duomo with its campanile, the tower of the Palazzo Vecchio rise above the rest; the hills seem remote; the high mountain opposite Fiesole stands out. The wonderful Arno appears in places, as it enters and leaves the city. The sun is setting, bathing with soft and veiled glory this whole scene that we can see from the marble terraces of the cemetery, framed in by mortuary cypresses, almost black, severe and most appropriate to Florence.

16 December

Race through the corridors joining the Uffizi to the Palazzo Pitti; the wonderful Palatine Gallery. The head of the young man on the left in Giorgione's *Concert* is made of a marvelous substance. All the tones are melted and fused to form a single, new, hitherto unknown color at any given spot on the canvas — and all so closely linked together that you could not take anything away or add a single touch. Your eyes follow the forehead, the temple, the soft approach to the hair, without finding any trace of a joining; it all seems a melted enamel that had been poured in still liquid form onto the canvas.

In front of this painting you think of nothing else, and that is characteristic of a masterpiece: be exclusive; make any other form of beauty seem inferior.

Beautiful hills along the Arno from San Miniato to those opposite the Cascine. I am becoming more and more familiar with their contours of stern softness and their hues of green and gray. ,

On the edge of the Arno I like to observe at length the powerful wave made by the rolling water of the weir; the weir is on an angle in the river so that the water piles up rather on one side. Against the wall is a fold that hollows out the wall's edge; the water then rolls over itself like a propeller, forming a constant unmoving wave. Wonderful to look at that fixed form with a fleeting and fluid matter always passing through it. In the sea, on the contrary, a drop of water remains motionless, or at least returns to its original place, and it's merely the form of a wave that moves forward.

A small lock on the side under an arch-shaped projection forming over the water a sort of balcony where I lean; a water ladder, doubtless, for small boats — and, depending on whether the lock is open or closed, the height of the river is modified.

The water is always yellow and clayey, but without any bubbling, any foam on the surface. It flows, swiftly at the weir, on an almost sharply inclined plane, smooth, without a snag, all of a piece and regular. It glides.

Already the Arno has gone down considerably and this morning the mud-sifters reappeared — marsh workers who fill their flat boats with shovelfuls of silt dug up from the bottom or low shores of the river.

The day before yesterday, toward the end of the night, a violent storm burst out. Squall, hail, dumbfounding flashes of lightning and deafening thunder — nothing was missing — not even the full peal of the pre-Christmas bells which ring out toward dawn, desperately bewildered in the vast transport of the tempest, yet whose sound seems angelic in the early morning.

I expected on awakening to find a sky of washed azure; I see clouds and more clouds — a dramatic sky of deluge.

Last year I didn't fully understand Fra Angelico; I seemed to find in him only a wholly pious, moral beauty, and his painting seemed merely a sort of means, the most efficacious possible, of praying. The story of Savonarola, which concerned me at that moment, struck me as the story of the "iconoclast" in its most fearful aspects and I was unwilling to admit that a work of art could have issued from the convent of San Marco. I must confess now that certain works of Fra Angelico are delightful. To be sure, he oversubordinated line to the form. The form was a means of expressing the soul, and the soul a praise of his God — and color a mere addition, a filling-in of the forms — but he colors minutely and smoothly every space and fortunately did not consider too pagan the joy he evidently took in the childlike arrangement of his colors.[1]

Looked at the Raphaels of the Tribuna; shadows consist too often for him in a simple darkening of the lighted parts and have no special quality. The pleasure of modeling comes above all from a horror of sharpness, from a need to round the contours without hiding them, and perfection consists in achieving a gradual shading off from the light to the less light to the dark. It has nothing in common with the perfection sought by the colorist — Venetian or Spanish, Dutch or English — always more restless, more difficult, and more debatable. Giorgione, often even more than Titian, painted each passage with a color that seems peculiar, *unique,* though always of a homogeneous quality and participating at once in the adjacent color.

19 December

Santa Maria Novella. Unbearable guide whose information is self-evident in the paintings themselves. No emotion whatsoever. I cannot understand the enthusiasm people show for the Spanish Chapel. Everything in it is very odd, but nothing is worth admiring. The difficulty has been overcome only at the expense of beauty.

Pretty-pretty frescoes, and already in the florid style, but full of exquisite grace, in the right-hand choir chapel. They are by Filippino Lippi; on the right, a dragon exorcised; on the left, a resurrection (story of St. John the Evangelist). Very soft figure of the young man whom the dragon's breath causes to faint away. The group surrounding him is very fine — the Negro King. . . . Beautiful group of women likewise in the resurrection scene; but these frescoes are not worth the admirable ones of Ghirlandajo decorating the central chapel.

After lunch the young Roberto Gatteschi comes to call and we go out together. He tells me of the novels he plans to write and talks very intelligently about them. It is to be a series forming a cycle in which he will defend crime. The first will defend (or at least will relate) incest; the second, murder; the third, theft. Incest alone is composed; it is the story, modernized, of Amnon and Tamar — which he did not know, moreover, and which I read to him from the Bible. He will tell especially of the progressive disgust and hatred following the possession and this will form the important part of the book. . . .

[1] Absurd judgment. I blush as I reread it today. Fra Angelico is not only a "delightful" painter; he is a great painter. (1902.) [A.]

26 December

This morning at the Museum of Santa Maria dei Fiori and at the National Museum. Looked especially at Donatello, whom I admire above all. At this exhibition of his work, originals or casts, you feel such an extraordinary and such a victorious struggle against the antique tradition. . . . Amazing preference for the male body and odd understanding of the forms of the child. That little *Amor,* one foot half raised over a snake that the other is crushing — the short legs still weighed down, deformed by the badly tied breeches, which are falling down and half uncovering him, the belt remaining around his waist — as if for an ornamental complication; the awkward and charming gesture of his little arms in the air.

The ornamented nudity of his *David;* the flavor of the flesh; the disappearance of the muscles between the bone structure and the total expression; emaciation, greenness — the set purpose, etc. Return to it as to a subject of study.

28 December

Saw this morning Roberto Gatteschi, who tells me of his desire to establish an international review, of his volume of poetry, of still another, of his novel.

He would like a preface by Coppée; but he is intelligent and if he talks of Coppée this is because he is ill informed. In Paris he would certainly belong to the *Mercure.* . . .[2]

When you talk to him of the French writers he knows, he cites Daudet, Coppée, Bourget, Zola.

After dinner I joined Roberto Gatteschi at the Arena, where we were to find d'Annunzio. The latter arrives around ten o'clock, and an hour later we leave the circus with Orvieto, who introduces me to his friend. Together we go to the Gambrinus; d'Annunzio indulges with obvious greediness in little vanilla ices served in small cardboard boxes. He sits beside me and talks gracefully and charmingly without, it seems to me, paying any special attention to the role he is playing. He is short; from a distance his face would seem ordinary or already familiar, so devoid is he of any exterior sign of literature or genius. He wears a little pointed beard which is pale blond and talks with a clearly articulated voice, somewhat cold, but supple and almost caressing. His eyes are rather

---

[2] *Le Mercure de France,* a literary review (at first monthly, then fortnightly) founded in 1890 and edited by Alfred Vallette. It published all the vigorous young writers and introduced many foreign writers to France. The whole symbolist school rallied around this eclectic periodical, which soon became one of the leading influences in French letters. In 1893 it founded a publishing house by the same name, which was for many years to issue Gide's books.

cold; he is perhaps rather cruel, but perhaps it is simply the appearance of his delicate sensuality that makes him seem so. He is wearing a black derby, quite unaffectedly.

He asks questions about French writers; talks of Mauclair, Régnier, Paul Adam — and as I say to him laughingly: "But you have read everything!" "Everything," he replies gracefully. "I believe one has to have read everything." "We read everything," he continues, "in the constantly renewed hope of finally finding the masterpiece that we are all awaiting so eagerly." He does not much like Maeterlinck, whose language strikes him as too simple. Ibsen displeases him by "his lack of beauty." "What do you expect?" he says as if to excuse himself; "I am a Latin."

He is preparing a modern drama of classical form and observing the "three unities.". . . With Herelle, last summer, he followed the coast of Greece in a yacht and "read Sophocles under the ruined gates of Mycenæ.". . .

. . . And when I express my amazement that his great erudition allows him so sustained and so perfect a literary production — or that his work as a writer leaves him the time to read so much: "Oh," he says, "I have my own method for reading quickly. I am a terrible worker; nine or ten months in the year without stopping I work twelve hours a day. I have already produced about twenty books."

Moreover, he says this without boasting at all and quite simply. In this way the evening is prolonged without difficulty.

30 December

After lunch we return to the Bargello. Wonderful *David* of Donatello! Small bronze body! ornamented nudity; Oriental grace; shadow of the hat over the eyes, in which the source of his glance is lost and becomes immaterial. Smile on the lips; softness of the cheeks.

His small delicate body with its rather frail and strained grace — hardness of the bronze — the figured armor-plate on the legs covering only the calf and permitting the thigh to rise from it more tender by contrast.

The very strangeness of that immodest accouterment, and the taut nervousness of the little arms, which hold either the stone or the saber. I should like to call him up before me at will. For a long time I observed — trying to memorize, to retain within me those charming lines, that fold of the abdomen immediately under the ribs hollowed out when he breathes, and even that leanness of the muscle joining the top of the breast to the right shoulder — and that somewhat broken fold at the top of the thigh — and that extraordinary flatness of the loins immediately above the sacrum. . . .

What can I say of the bust of Niccolò da Uzzano? When I look at it I prefer it even to the *David*. He has more life in him now than he once had and his lips are worth all his words. These two works are the most beautiful, and immediately afterward come the little bronze *Amor* and the *Zuccone* of the Campanile, of which, alas, one can see only the bust here. Verrocchio's *David* is admirable too.

31 December

O little cloister of San Marco, I should have wished you full of roses.

. . . Return along the shores of the Arno — setting sun; water losing itself in golden sands; in the far distance, some fishermen; the smoke rising from the roofs, at first gray, becomes gilded when the sun touches it. That radiance lasts for a long time; the roofs near San Miniato, the white walls of the villas become the color of unripe apricots; the cypresses around them seem all the darker. The fall of the Arno has as it were some mother-of-pearl glints of an extremely pale green and, lower down, of that same color with a tint of orange.

The fishermen in the distance are carrying their bow-nets and returning to their boats. . . . The wonder of these lengthening days. . . .

Obsessions of the Orient, of the desert, of its ardor and its emptiness, of the shade of the palm gardens, of the loose white garments — obsessions in which my senses stampede, my nerves become exasperated, and which, at the beginning of each night, make me think sleep impossible.

A few admirable evenings, golden and ashen pink. . . . The shores of the Arno spread apart as they leave the town and uncover themselves. There are poplar woods on the left; on the right, clumps of reeds and the dark gardens of the Cascine. The poplars are leafless; the whole golden sky passes through them and the light is softened by them. From the shore sandbanks stretch out to the middle of the river; the fishermen and the bare-legged sand-diggers get into flat-bottomed boats, step into the water, and load the boats with the silt and sand of the shore. Opposite the Cascine, on the top of the hill, a sort of church among dark cypresses.

Em. somewhat tired. Bad overcast weather. I go out a bit toward evening and shadow a couple of fellows who intrigue me. In *Valentin Knox* [3] I shall speak at length of that mania for following people.

In the evening we play parlor games. Em., too ill to take part, went to bed after dinner. And all evening long I suffer because of not having remained with her and think, each time that the door is opened or that someone shouts too loudly, that the noise will waken her and increase

---

[3] A book that Gide projected but never wrote.

her sick headache. At the end of the evening, around midnight, an almost irresistible melancholy takes hold of me because of the lack of seriousness of all this and because Em. is not with me. I should have liked to leave and never did I so long to return to her. I thought also, amidst the laughter, of Paul's and my so calm and solemn vigil two years ago at Biskra. I wondered how I had formed such a definite decision not to have any personal melancholy and if it really was so definite. Instead of these dances and shouts, at this approach of the New Year, which we like to treat as especially impressive, I longed rather for communal prayers, for a service of divine worship, or merely for a serious vigil. Horror of everything that is not serious — I have always had it. What was Em. thinking of all alone, during this same time? . . .

6 January (1896)

I have been talking of hygiene with d'Annunzio. He tells me that he has never known insomnia, or at least never had to suffer from it. Fencing and riding keep him from it. He fences a great deal and often rides. Tomorrow he is to go to Vinci, Leonardo's village; it is a pilgrimage, he says, and invites me to accompany him. If I were not such a poor horseman, I should have taken pleasure in riding with him. Talking of irony, he says that he cannot endure it, that in using irony you oppose yourself to things whereas it is only through love that you penetrate them, and that that is the essential. . . .

With his meals he drinks only water; this is a hard worker's practice. On the other hand, he says that he drinks ten to twelve cups of tea a day. This morning, excusing himself for coming to the table in riding-habit, his elegance, his suave assurance, and his unselfconsciousness were charming.

Rome

This afternoon visited the horrible bulk of St. Peter's. I see Rome through Stendhal, despite myself. I have found the secret of my boredom in Rome: I do not find myself interesting here.

In Rome, saw especially the Palatine, the baths of Caracalla, the Sistine Chapel — but decidedly I do not like Rome.

The small bronze *Boy with a Thorn in His Foot* at the Capitoline Museum (the one on the right) near a statue of the *Diana of Ephesus* is a wonder beyond compare. I do not believe I prefer any ancient work to it — not even the *Niobe* of the Beaux-Arts or the *Sleeping Faun* in Munich. (I have since seen the extraordinary *Mercury as a Fisherman* of Naples.)

The very substance of bronze, smooth and polished like jasper, almost black, seems to lend to the contours a more intentional and durable decisiveness; no flabbiness in spite of so much grace; and the amazing slimness of this body which has not yet reached the age of puberty does not make one regret that the forms are neither more childish nor more fully developed.

Naples, 29 January

Under this full moon the night, although vaporous, is so clear that one can just make out Capri almost floating and, higher than you think, the horizon of the sea. The classic Vesuvius has on its slope a sort of burning scratch and I should like to see at close range what fiery abysses or what white-hot rocks create at a distance that red sizzling that looked to us, the first evening, like a whole village on fire.

This landscape provokes its own music, open like itself, of bright laughter and born without any laborious period of gestation.

I am surprised to meet as far north as Naples that odd Oriental song, begun on too high a note, which rushes oddly down to the tonic in two parallel phrases, turned out as if between two tones, spasmodically stressed and suddenly stopping as if choked off.

Naples

Capri floats mysterious on the transparent waters. I like sea grottoes. Those on Belle-Isle were certainly moist! The Morgat grottoes were mottled. But I do not like the Blue Grotto; those reflections of a frozen color, not azure but indigo, seem to have been imagined by a god without any sense of color. I was in a hurry to get out. On the other side of the island, another, less frequented grotto was exquisite; small; a narrow corridor with three entrances; the light is so refracted that only the green rays penetrate and the water is so loaded with them that it has a sort of phosphorescence. Any object that is plunged into the water is enveloped in a pale green flame; hands bathed in it are colored green like the skin of Pierre Louÿs's nymphs.

This soil breathes love more than any other, and the two beautiful American women in Florence to whom I introduced d'Annunzio wept as they talked of it, out of longing and desire. Certain people have come here for a week who have never been able to leave.

One of the friends of Miss Magonicle married here and has never since paid any attention to his own country. The Capri girls have many opportunities to become ladies. American men are abundant and Germans superabundant. To me Capri is unbearable, or almost, despite its admirable rocks; I prefer to see Capri from Naples, floating like a vision on the sea.

Yet it is here rather than in Florence that I should have wished to meet those two beautiful Americans, one reading Marlowe and the other the quatrains of Omar Khayyám. And I should have preferred them to give us here, as they did when d'Annunzio came to see them, those grapes gathered on the island, dried in the sun, and then rolled in small packets and enclosed in vine leaves saturated with rum. This makes little packets the color of cigars whose dry and unattractive envelope preserves the grape's sugar and juice.

From La Cava a road rises into the mountains. The network of branches and vine-shoots above the road makes you imagine the wonderful spring seasons ornamented by these trellises suspended in the clear air on slight elm trees and frail poplars. The woods that we go through are already flowering with purple crocuses.

The Benedictine cloister is half sheltered in the rock; after having visited the rooms of the library one goes down to the cloister, where the daylight, falling from high above because of the rocks that dominate and enclose it, seems faded despite the full afternoon sun. Very humid mosses clothe the walls and water constantly trickles down. Everything seems to crumble with a white and green decay. Still lower, receiving its air and light only through a vent opening into the cloister, the much vaster crypt stretches out. An unreal light of limbo softly bathes the asymmetrical pillars; an infinite, profound stillness. The monk leading me lights with a little lamp the piles of skulls and bones; some of them are velvety white.

Then, between two rows of massive pillars, a row of six open sarcophagi, tight against each other and filled to the brim with bones.

Farther on, some rather good frescoes by a pupil of Giotto.

Left Taormina for Catania. Amazing countryside of blackish vegetable-mold and lava, where grow, in the scoria, common asphodels.

Syracuse

See Syracuse in the summer. Then the papyrus of the two banks of the Cyane join together, say our sailor guides, to form above your boat a filigreed vault. The flat boat bumps the shores, tears up the weeds in the shallow water, drags the roots along with a rustling sound. The very low sky pulls the clouds down to earth. The boat goes slowly back upstream.

The spring is surrounded by papyrus formerly planted by the Arabs; I imagine the approaches to the great African lakes as differing very little from this. This spring is at the bottom of a deep basin. Rather thick, the water seems strangely blue. Great azure fish are swimming in it; I should like to throw in a ring. . . . I think of the swimming-pools of Gafsa, those pools of warm water where huge blind fish, supposedly left by the great Tanit, brush against the swimmers and one can see blue snakes wriggling over the tiles on the bottom.

Latomie; closed gardens; caves; orchards in a deep quarry; delicate trickling of the fountain of Venus; liana. This is where prisoners were locked up, in these abandoned quarries. The thick, heavy, moist air was horribly loaded with the scent of orange-flowers. We bit into not quite ripe lemons; the first unbearably acid taste gradually disappeared, leaving only an unbelievably delicate perfume in the mouth. This is a scene of rape, of murder, of abominable passion, one of those subterranean gardens of which Arabian tales speak, in which Aladdin seeks fruits that are precious stones, where the Calender's cousin shuts himself up with his sister and mistress, where the wife of the King of the Islands joins at night the wounded black slave whom her enchantments keep from dying.

Greek theater seen at night at the hour when the moon rises. Above it is the avenue of tombs leading to fields of asphodels. I have never seen anything more silent.

II

February–March

In the autumn, three years ago, our arrival in Tunis was marvelous. Although already considerably spoiled by the wide boulevards cutting through it, it was still a classic and beautiful city, harmoniously uniform, whose whitewashed houses seemed to light up from within at night like alabaster lamps.

As soon as you left the French port, not a single tree was to be seen; you sought out the shade of the souks, those great covered marketplaces, vaulted over or covered with cloth or planks. They received only a reflected light that filled them with a special atmosphere; these souks seemed a second underground city within the city, about as large as a third of Tunis. From the terrace where Paul Laurens used to go to paint, you could see from there to the sea only a broken stairway, white terraces cut by courtyards like ditches, in which the boredom of the women languished. In the evening all the white was mauve and the sky was the color of a tea rose; in the morning the white became pink against a pale-purple sky. But after the winter rains the walls have a green mantle, for mosses cover them, and the edge of the terraces looks like the edge of a basket of flowers.

I missed the white, serious, classic Tunis of that autumn, which made me think, as I wandered through its regular streets in the evening, of the Helen of Part II of *Faust*, or of Psyché, "the agate lamp within her hand," wandering in an avenue of tombs.

Trees are being planted now on the wide streets and squares. Tunis will be more charming as a result, but nothing could disfigure it more.

Two years ago the rue Marr, the Place des Moutons were still such that one didn't know where one had been set down and that not even the farthest East or the most central Africa would have had, I believe, a more stupefying taste of the exotic. A very different form of life and completely realized on the exterior; very full, ancient, classical, established; no compromise yet between the civilizations of the Orient and ours, which appears ugly, especially when it tries to repair something. Sheets of iron or zinc are replacing little by little the screens of reeds as roofing for the souks, and street-lamps distribute the light by fits and starts on walls formerly bathed in the even light of the moon — on that vast Place des Moutons, without sidewalks, silent and wonderful, where two years ago in the warmth of full moonlight nights camels and Arabs used to come and sleep. The door of a mosque would open; some Arabs grouped around a lantern would come out, stop in the street, and sing a monotonous religious chant.

Now sidewalks have been laid in the souks. In one of the finest alleyways the base of the little columns that support the vault is buried. Twisted, green and red colonnettes with a massive and figured capital. The vault is whitewashed, but barely lighted. Even on the most radiant days these souks are always half-dark. The entrance to the souks is marvelous; I am not speaking of the portico of the mosque, but of that other narrow, withdrawn entrance shaded by a leaning jujube tree which makes a sort of prefatory shade for the dark little alleyway that turns sharply and is lost to view. But the jujube tree, covered with leaves in the autumn, hasn't any yet this spring. This is the beginning of the saddlers' souk; the alley turns, then continues indefinitely.

In the perfumery souk Sadouk-Anoun still sits cross-legged in his little shop, a mere recess in the wall, with its floor elbow-high and cluttered with flasks; but the perfumes he sells today are diluted. On my return to Paris I gave to Valéry the last two authentic bottles, which I saw Sadouk-Anoun fill, using a pipette, with essence of apples and, drop by drop, precious amber. He no longer wraps them up today, now that they are half-filled with a commoner merchandise, so minutely with virgin wax and white thread and doesn't make me pay so dearly for them.

Two years ago, with Laurens, his meticulousness had amused us; it seemed to give their proper value to things. With each added wrapping the perfume became rarer. Finally we stopped him, for our purse would not have sufficed.

I also sought in vain that dark café where the only habitués were tall Negroes from the Sudan. Some of them had their big toe cut as a sign of slavery. Most of them wore, stuck in their turban, a little sprig of white flowers, of fragrant jasmine, which intoxicates them; it falls along the cheek like a curl of the romantic epoch and gives their face an expression of voluptuous languor.

They like the odor of flowers to such an extent that often, not able to smell them strongly enough, they insert the crushed petals in their nostrils. In that café one of them would sing, another would tell stories, and tame doves would fly about and perch on their shoulders.

Tunis, 7 March

Little children see this, laugh, repeat the obscene mimicry of Caracous. Difficult exercise of the mind; but let the mind make itself over until it considers such things natural.

The French don't go there; they wouldn't know how to; they are little shops without any exterior attraction; you slip in through a low door. The French generally go to the near-by barkers, who make a great noise and draw only the tourists. The Arabs are not taken in and know that it is not much, this dancing cardboard horse, this camel made of wood and cloth that dances also, very amusingly indeed, but in a manner that has nothing intrinsic about it. But, right near, there is a traditional Caracous shop, classic, simple, as simple as can be, with an admirable stage convention that allows Caracous to hide in the middle of the stage, between two policemen who are looking for him, simply because he lowers his head and cannot see them. And the children accept, understand, and laugh.

If anyone wanted to revive our dramatic art that M. de Goncourt is insisting on killing, he could very well learn that art from Caracous and our old Guignols.

CARACOUS. A small oblong room, street-stall in the daytime, which collapses at night; a small stage is set up with a curtain of transparent linen as a background for the shadows. Perpendicular to the stage are two benches along the walls. They are for the distinguished members of the audience.

The middle of the room fills up with very young children who sit on the ground and jostle one another. Everyone eats a quantity of melon seeds dried in salt, such a provocative delicacy that my pocket is emptied of them every evening, but I refill it in the morning for two cents. It is true that I give many of them to children.

The oddest thing here is the recesses in the wall, or very uncomfortable bunks like terns' nests, to which you pull yourself up and from which you fall out rather than get down. They are rented only for the whole evening to young habitués. I came back here many evenings; there was almost always the same public, in the same seats, listening to the same plays, and laughing at the same places — like me.

The actor who provides the voice for these shadows is excellent.

CARACOUS. Another shop; Sudanese. Where the Sudanese go the Arabs do not go if they can help it. Consequently you see nothing but Negroes here. But this evening I find Fedor Rosenberg here too. The play has not begun yet. (The intermissions are always much longer than the play, which lasts only a quarter of an hour.) One Negro is shaking castanets, another is beating on an oblong drum, and the third, an enormous fellow, is wagging his head in front of Rosenberg. Seated almost at our feet, he sings, improvising a monotonous ballad in which he says, in so far as I can understand it, that he is very poor, that Rosenberg is very rich, and that Negroes always need money. And since he looks rather fierce and the Arabs claim that one can never trust the camel, the Negro, or the desert for long, we make haste to show how generous we are.

CARACOUS. Another shop. Here the play is merely a pretense for assignations. Always the same habitués, from one evening to another, under the benevolent eye of the proprietor. A strangely beautiful child plays the bagpipes; everyone gathers around him; because of him; the others are his gallants. One of them plays that odd drum in the shape of a vase, the bottom of which must be of donkey's skin. The piper makes the café what it is. He seems to smile at everyone without favoring anyone. Some of them recite verses to him or sing them; he replies, approaches, but most often, I think, it does not go beyond a few caresses in front of everyone. This shop is not a brothel, but rather a court of love. At times one of the children gets up and dances; at times two of them together, and then the dance becomes a sort of broad mimicry.

The play itself is almost always obscene. I should like to know the history of Caracous. He must be very ancient. I have been told that he came from Constantinople and that everywhere except Constantinople and Tunis the police would have forbidden his appearance on the stage; he appears only at the time of Ramadan. For forty days everyone fasts from sunrise to sundown; a complete fast — no food, or drink, or tobacco, or perfumes, or women. All the senses held in check all day take their revenge at night and everyone has as good a time as possible. There are certainly other, very religious Arabs who spend the night, after a very frugal meal, in meditations and prayers, just as there are others who continue to have a good time even by day. But that is frequent only in the big cities contaminated by the French; the Arabs ordinarily practice their religion very scrupulously.

This last evening I wanted to visit again, before fleeing, all the rarest and strangest things that Tunis had shown me. I shall remember having followed for some time that army band returning to its barracks, very loud, always in tune, fine and victorious, while in spots along the shore and the French boulevards fireworks turned the foliage of the false pepper trees into a fabulous pink filigree.

Just a few Arabs turned to look as the band passed; the shrill music of their cafés continued.

Many of them recall, I suppose, the day when for the first time that band entered their conquered city. I wondered if their attitude toward the French was still exclusively one of hatred.

I sought dissipation along the rue Marr, but I should have gone to the Halfaouine. A Moorish café was rather large and attractive, but they just barely accepted me there. The French never go there. The gaiety of the Halfaouine attracts them and the other quarters remain quiet. A rather old Negro began to dance grotesquely to the strains of a bagpipe, to the rhythm of a drum.

Following the dark boulevards, I returned to the Halfaouine. No great crowd; nothing particular. Toward the end of the evening I found Rosenberg again in the same Caracous shop where I had taken him the first day. He too understands the advantage of returning regularly to the same places, to see not many faces, but to become very familiar with them. The Arabs become accustomed to you, you begin to seem less foreign to them, and their cycle of habits, at first disturbed, resumes its course.

El Kantara

We arrived here at the end of the day, a radiant day. Athman had arrived in the morning, had slept a bit in the middle of the day, but had been waiting for us at the station for an hour. That hour seemed long to him. "And yet," he told me, "I thought to myself: now it is only an hour; before it was a whole year."

Three burnooses; a white silk gandurah lined with blue silk and edged with pink; his coat of blue cloth, the enormous brown cord turban clasping the fine white cloth that falls from it, brushes his cheek and floats loose under his chin. This headdress metamorphoses him; last year he was still wearing the child's simple chéchia; at the age of seventeen he wanted the man's complicated turban.

Athman has spent all he had for his "costume," dressing himself up for this reunion. Without his greeting I should hardly have recognized him.

Evening fell slowly; we went through the pass, and the fabulous Orient calmly appeared to us gilded by the sun. We went down under the palm trees, leaving Athman on the road to wait for the carriage that was to follow us. I recognized all the sounds — of the running water and the birds. Everything was just as before, calm, and our arrival changed nothing. In the carriage we followed the edge of the oasis for some distance. On our return the sun was setting; we stopped before the door of a Moorish café, the hour of Ramadan being past. In the courtyard, near us, some camels in heat were fighting. A keeper was shouting at them. The flocks of goats were returning; their hasty feet still made, as last year, the sound of a sterile shower.

From all the houses of gray earth a slender vapor arose, a blue smoke that soon enveloped the whole oasis and made it seem remote. The sky to the west was a very pure blue, so deep that it seemed still saturated with light. The silence became wonderful. You could not even imagine any song breaking it. I felt that I liked this landscape better than any other, perhaps; here more than anywhere else nature encourages contemplation.

Biskra

Yesterday we were in the gardens; we followed the paths that first led us to N'Msid then to Bab-el-Derb. We reached the old fort and returned by way of Sidi-Barkat. The walk was a long one and Em. was tired out by it. Athman was with us and Fedor Rosenberg; and Larbi accompanied us. We had coffee at the entrance to N'Msid in front of the bed of the Oued and the mountains of the Aurès.

I do not like this landscape so much as, on the other side, the vague expanse of the desert. Playing dominoes with us, Larbi constantly cheated and was charming. I am expecting Jammes with a delightful impatience. The earth here speaks a different language, but one that I understand now.

My room last year, on the ground floor of the hotel; with my window open, I was separated from the outside only by the balustrade; with a jump one could be over it. Sadek, Athman's big brother, and several others from the old Biskra would come and rest in my room, during Ramadan, before returning to their village. I had dates, cakes, syrops, and jellies. It was night; Sadek played the flute and it was easy to remain silent for a long time. At night I closed only the blinds. All the sounds from outside came in, and each morning they would waken me before dawn and I would go to the edge of the desert to see the sunrise. At that moment would pass Lascif's flock, made up of the poor people's goats; since they had no garden, they would entrust their goats to him every morning and Lascif would lead them out to graze in the desert. He would go knocking from door to door before dawn; each door would open and let pass a few goats. As he left the village he had more than sixty.

He would go off very far with them, toward the Hot Fountain, where the chokeweeds are and the euphorbiaceæ. There was also a huge ram on which he sometimes rode, he told me, when the way was difficult, or else to pass the time, for he did not know how to play the flute. One morning when he had left without passing under my window, I went to the desert to meet him. I like the desert enormously. The first year I feared it somewhat because of its wind and sand; moreover, having no destination, I didn't know when to stop and tired myself quickly. I preferred the shady paths under the palms, the gardens of Ouardi, the villages. But last year I went for long walks. I had no other aim than to lose sight of the oasis. I walked; I walked until I felt infinitely alone in the plain. Then I began to look about me. The sands had velvety patches in the shadow on the slope of their hillocks, where insects' footprints could be seen; colocynths were wilting, tiger-beetles were running over the sand; there were marvelous rustlings in each breath of wind and, because of the intense silence, the most delicate sound could be heard. At times an eagle would fly up from the direction of the big dune. This monotonous expanse seemed to me each day to contain a more apparent diversity.

I knew the keepers of nomadic flocks; I used to go to meet them; I talked with them; some of them played the flute. Occasionally I would sit for a long time near them without doing anything; I always took along a book, but almost never opened it. Often I did not return until evening. But Athman, to whom I spoke of these excursions, told me that they were unwise since prowling Arabs frequent the approaches to the oases and rob foreigners whom they know to be incapable of defending themselves; it would have been normal for them to attack me. Thereafter he wanted to accompany me, but since he did not like walking, my expeditions became shorter, then ceased altogether.

Athman reads like Bouvard and writes like Pécuchet.[1] He educates himself with all his might and copies anything that comes his way. He prefers Hérold's *La Joie de Maguelonne* to my *Tentative amoureuse;* he finds the *Tentative* badly written. "You use the word *grass* too often," he told me.

I give him *Les Mille et Une Nuits.*[2] One evening he takes the book to Bordj Boulakras, where he sleeps, to read it with his friend Bachaga. The next day he doesn't come until ten o'clock, still heavy with sleep; he and his friend read the story of "Aladdin and the Wonderful Lamp" until two o'clock, he says, adding: "Oh, we spent a very good nocturnal evening!" To him *nocturnal* means when you stay up late.

At the end of the oasis, on the deserted ruins of the old fort near which we are passing on this moonlight night, white-robed Arabs, lying on the ground, are talking in low voices and one of them is whispering on his flute. "They are going to spend a nocturnal night," Athman

---

[1] A reference to Flaubert's *Bouvard et Pécuchet* (1881), which satirizes the stupidity of the philistines.

[2] *The Thousand and One Nights* in the translation by Dr. J. C. Mardrus.

explains, "telling each other stories." In the summer no one would dare to lie down in this manner; the scorpions and the horned vipers, hidden in the sand during the day, come out and prowl after dark. Farther on we leave the carriage; there are no more palm trees; the night seems to enlarge the desert, which is full to the brim of blue patches of light. Even Jammes was silent. And suddenly Athman, inspired with lyricism, throws off his burnoose, fastens his gandurah, and turns cartwheels in the moonlight.

Athman has found some collection or other of "Lives of Famous Men" and now, on the subject of camels, quotes Buffon or Cuvier, never talks of friendship without naming Henry IV and Sully, of courage without Bayard, and of the Big Dipper without Galileo. . . .

He writes to Degas upon sending him a walking-stick made of a palm stem: "What I like about you is that you do not like the Jews and that you read the *Libre Parole*[3] and that, like me, you consider Poussin a great French painter."

Jammes amuses himself by letting Athman read these lines, which he improvises while waiting for the carriage that is to take us to Droh:

> *My dear friend Athman,*
> *the trees that bear almonds,*
> *fig trees and black-currant bushes*
> *are made to be sat*
> *under when you are tired.*
>
> *You sit without stirring,*
> *your eyes tight closed.*
> *You are happy lazy.*
> *Below the garden you hear*
> *the clear water singing*
> *like an Arab woman.*
>
> *You are so happy being lazy,*
> *your eyes tight closed*
> *as if you slept,*
> *you are so happy, Athman,*
> *in utter laziness*
> *that you think you are dead.*[4]

[3] *La Libre Parole* was a newspaper founded in 1892 by Édouard Drumont, author of the sensational book *La France juive*, to spread anti-Semitism. Its subtitle was "France for the French."

[4] *Mon cher ami Athman,*
    les arbres qui ont des amandes,

Since Jammes has been here, Athman has been spending day and night writing poetry. The thing he insists on most is that the rhyme be very rich. He doesn't mind going as far as punning to achieve his effect. Occasionally he turns out something striking:

> *Under the palms no concerts are heard. . . .*[5]

or this:

> *. . . He who has known love*
> *Has indeed drunk the bitter water*
> *And time no longer touches him.*[6]

He continues to read *The Thousand and One Nights* assiduously, knows by heart the story of Aladdin, and has begun signing his letters "Athman or the Wonderful Lamp."

Jammes has given me his walking-stick. It is made of ironwood and comes from the "Islands"; it amuses the children hereabouts because its handle is a greyhound's head. It is polished like jade and yet so crude that you would think it had been carved out with a knife. I have never

----

les figuiers et les cassis
sont pour être assis
dessous quand la fatigue est grande.

On reste sans bouger du tout
en fermant les yeux.
On est heureux paresseux.
Le jardin, on entend dessous
l'eau claire qui chante
comme une femme arabe.

On est si bien être paresseux
en fermant les yeux
comme si on dort,
on est si bien, Athman,
dans la paresse grande
qu'on croit qu'on est mort.

[5] *Sous les palmiers, il n'y a pas de concerts. . . .*

[6] *. . . Celui qui connaît*
L'amour a bien bu l'eau amère
Et le temps ne l'intéresse plus.

seen anything so odd. Verses are written in capital letters lengthwise in
the wood, such as these charming ones:

> *A squirrel had a rose*
> *in his mouth; an ass*
> *called him mad.*[7]

And these that he used to write at the top of his letters:

> *A bee sleeps*
> *In the briars of my heart.*[8]

Touggourt, 7 April

An Arab well-maker is being decorated today.

Before the drilling companies and artesian wells, the Arabs had well-
makers. The artesian layer is sometimes found as deep as seventy-five or
even eighty-five yards under the surface. And men go down there.

They have been trained in childhood for this painful trade, and yet
many lose their lives. There are three layers of earth and two layers of
water — the first stagnant and the second seepage that wells up — to go
through before reaching the artesian layer. Then the water often gushes
forth clear and plentiful, but almost always laden with sodium and
magnesium. The effort put forth by those diving well-makers to work
under the water is incredible; this one was one of the bravest, it appears. They have to build a watertight well or passageway in the middle of the water, in which to work and dig deeper. And they have to do
this twice over, through the two liquid layers, laying a channel for the
clear water, which must rise through the stagnant water without coming into contact with it.

This very day, in one of those rectangular wells formed of the trunks
of palm trees, we saw a man go down, hanging from a rope, to a depth
of sixty-five yards to repair some damage.

That is why the Arab well-maker was decorated; this evening he
went mad.

The layer of stagnant water at Touggourt is almost on the surface.
Instead of the beautiful running waters of Chetma or the moving canals
of Biskra, here there are stagnating, stinking ditches full of filthy weeds.
Yet there is also a river running through the oasis, nicely divided for the
sake of the palms. At the bottom, amid the weeds, water serpents
slither.

---

[7] *Un écureuil avait une*
rose à la bouche, un âne
le traita de fou.

[8] *Une abeille sommeille*
Aux bruyères de mon cœur.

The oasis is surrounded by the sands; yesterday a frightening storm raised them. The horizon seemed to rise up toward us like a blanket you pull up in bed. You could see nothing and could hardly breathe.

Not far from the town is a poor cemetery that the sand is slowly invading; one can barely make out a few tombs. In the desert the idea of death pursues us, and, strange to say, it is not sad. At Biskra, behind the old fort, in the very center of the oasis, the rains have furrowed the old cemetery and, since the dead are buried directly in the earth, the detached bones are in spots as plentiful as stones.

The sandstorm lasted until evening; at sunset we went up to the minaret. The sky was the color of ashes, the palm trees were dull; the town, slate-colored. A great wind blew from the east like a blast of divine malediction such as the prophets announced. And, in that scene of desolation, we saw a caravan start out.

The Oulad dance better here than in Biskra and are more beautiful; indeed, this is the only place I have seen them dance well. We returned here, never tired of that grave and languid dance, almost entirely done with the arms and wrists, very decorous; dazed, almost exhausted by that insistent, rapid, diminishing, intoxicating music which stirs you to ecstasy and will not stop when you leave it — which still obsesses me, certain evenings, just as the desert does.

I should have enjoyed spending the night on the square where the caravans were camping. Brush fires were burning; around them Arabs were talking in low voices; others were singing; they sang all night long.

Athman tells me the story of Uriah's wife.

According to the Arab tradition, it was while pursuing a golden dove from hall to hall in his palace that David, whom he calls Daoud, finally reached that upper terrace from which he could see Bath-sheba.

Athman relates: ". . . the Jew told him that Moses was right and that God would receive first the Jews, then the Arabs, and perhaps even the Christians. The Christian told him that Christ was right and that God would take unto himself the Christians, but also the Arabs and even the Jews. The Arab told him that Mohammed was right and that God would admit the Arabs into his paradise, but that he would close the door on the unconverted Jews and Christians. And when he had heard all three, he hastened to become a Mussulman."

The Christians have seniority over the Mussulmans, who say (and enjoy telling me) that if a Christian pronounces before death the credo of Islam: "God is God and Mohammed is his prophet," he enters paradise before an Arab.

"The Roumis," [9] they also say, "are superior to us in many ways, but they are always afraid of death."

Touggourt, 9 April

Arabs camped on the squares; fires being lighted; columns of smoke almost invisible in the evening light. We were at the top of the mosque when the muezzin came up to chant the call to prayer.

The sun set as if for ever on the vast exhausted plain. The sand, all day lighter, has become darker than the sky.

We had suffered all day from the sun, and the freshness of evening was a delight to us. Children were playing on the square and dogs were barking on the terraces of houses. Above us the voice of the muezzin filled the little cupola on the top of the minaret. His voice, prolonged on a single note, seemed the reverberation of a great bell; then it stopped, so suddenly that it left a void in the air.

The caravans were setting out, slowly, and our soul was filled with excitement and anguish not to know the end of their interminable wandering.

Because of the extraordinary drought all the livestock died this year, and meat has become so scarce that people are reduced to eating camel. On the way out of town you can see, under a little roof of dried palms, one of those enormous animals cut in pieces, a mass of purple flesh, which is covered with flies as soon as no one drives them off. The flies in these districts are as numerous as the posterity of Abraham. They lay their eggs on abandoned carcasses of sheep, horses, or camels rotting in the sun; their larvæ feed freely there, then after their transformation fly to the towns in swarms. You swallow them, you breathe them, you are tickled, driven crazy, beclouded with them; the walls vibrate with them, the butchers' and grocers' stands are crawling with them. At Touggourt the merchants have little palm whisks and try to drive them over to the neighbors. At Kairouan there are so many that the best thing is to pay no attention to them. The merchants drive them away only when a customer asks to see the merchandise. Our carriage, when we arrived, was enveloped in a cloud. At the hotel the plates and glasses were protected by metal covers that are taken off, or raised rather, only to eat or drink.

M'Reyer, 11 April

Amazing salt lakes bordered with mirages. From the top of a sandy hill, after the immense expanse of the desert, one thinks: "Look! the sea!" A vast blue sea dotted with small boats and islands, a sea that you fancy to be deep and that refreshes your soul. You approach, you touch

---

[9] Arab name for Christians.

the edge, and that blue suddenly disappears, for it was merely a reflection of the sky on a white salty crust, which burns your feet and hurts
your eyes, splendidly dazzling. Fragile, it gives way under your steps,
since it is nothing but the thin surface of a sea of moving mud in which
caravans are swallowed up.

At that officers' mess the army doctor next to me interests me with
what he says of the south. For a long time he lived at Ouargla. He had
even been at El-Goleah and remembered the soldiers marching in the
sand. Often in those moving sands, burning and vibrating in the steady
sunlight, a sort of odd dizziness would seize them because of constantly
feeling the earth give under their feet; even when they stop, the un-
steadiness continues and the earth still seems to flee them. Occasionally
in the middle of the horrible sands they would encounter a narrow vein
of limestone, something compressed and hard, just wide enough for
each soldier in turn to place both feet on it for a second and pull himself
together on a resistant surface.

To punish a soldier they make him "follow"; to march at the tail of
the contingent is killing. Those in front cannot worry about the strag-
glers; at times some drop out . . . who lose their footing, fall, are swallowed up by the desert. The last ones run along in the stifling dust raised
by the battalion and, on this soft earth, still softer for having been
trampled by the others, if they lose their footing they are lost; they
watch the others disappear in the distance and the hawks that fly behind the marching battalion stop, wait, and then approach.

In this sand, often, gypsum crystals, thin pointed fragments, shine
like mica; on the road to Droh we found some stones that, when broken,
were transparent on the inside like glass.

On the road to El Oued we gathered some of those strange mineral
flowers which are called "desert roses" and which, gray like the sand, are
a bit of conglutinated sand.

Biskra

The sounds of the Negro drum draw us. Negro music! How often I
heard it last year! How often I got up from my work to hear it! No tones,
just rhythm; no melodic instrument, just long drums, tom-toms, and
castanets. . . . *"Florentes ferulas et grandia lilia quassans,"* [10] castanets
that in their hands make almost the sound of a downpour. In a trio they
execute real compositions; uneven rhythm oddly cut by syncopated
notes, which drives one mad and sets every muscle in motion. They are
the musicians of funereal, gay, and religious ceremonies; I have seen

---

[10] "Shaking flowering branches and tall lilies." (Virgil: *Bucolics,* X, line
25.)

them in cemeteries feed the frenzy of the professional mourners; in a Kairouan mosque exacerbate the mystic rapture of the Aïssaouas. I have seen them beat out the rhythm for the club dance and the sacred dances in the little mosque of Sidi-Maleck. And I was always the only Frenchman to see them. I don't know where the tourists go; I fancy the paid guides show them a trashy Africa in order to protect the Arabs, who like calm and secrecy, from intruders. For I have never met a single one of them in the neighborhood of anything interesting; nor even, and fortunately, but very rarely in the old villages of the oasis where I used to return daily until I no longer startled anyone. Yet the hotels are full of travelers, but they fall into the trap set by the quack guides and pay dearly for the falsified ceremonies tricked up for them.

There wasn't a Frenchman last year, either, at that extraordinary nocturnal celebration which I witnessed almost by chance, attracted merely by the sound of the drum and the ululation of the women. The celebration was in the Negro village: a dancing procession of women and musicians was going up the main street preceding torch-bearers and a group of laughing children who were leading by the horns a huge black he-goat covered with jewels and stuffs. He had bracelets on his horns, an enormous silver ring in his nostrils; he had necklaces around his neck; he was clothed in a piece of crimson satin. In the crowd that was following I recognized the tall Ashour; he explained to me that the ram was going to be slaughtered during the night to bring luck to the village, but first he was walked through the streets so that the evil spirits of the houses, which remain on the doorsteps, could enter into him and disappear.

Negro music! How many times, far from Africa, I have thought I heard you and suddenly there was re-created around you the whole south. In Rome for instance, Via Gregoriana, when the heavy wagons, going down in the very early morning, used to wake me. Their dull bounces on the paving blocks would deceive me a moment in my half-sleep and then leave me distressed for some time afterward.

We heard the Negro music this morning, but it was not for an ordinary celebration. They were playing in the inner courtyard of a private house, and the men at the entrance wanted at first to keep us out until some Arabs recognized me and protected our entrance. I was amazed at first by the large number of Jewish women gathered there, all very beautiful and richly dressed. The courtyard was full; there barely remained place enough in the middle for the dance. The dust and heat were stifling. A great ray of sunlight fell from the upper opening, whence, as from a balcony, were leaning clusters of children.

The staircase rising to the terrace was also covered with people, all attentive, as we too immediately became; what they were watching was terrible. In the center of the courtyard a large copper basin full of water.

Three women got up, three Arab women; they took off their outer garments for the dance, undid their hair in front of the basin, then, bending
forward, spread it on the water. The music, already very loud, swelled.
Letting their wet hair fall over their shoulders, they danced awhile; it
was a savage dance involving the whole body. If you have not seen
it, nothing could give an idea of it. An old Negress presided, who kept
jumping around the basin and, holding a stick in one hand, occasionally
struck the rim. We were later told, as we were beginning to understand,
that all the women who danced on this day (and sometimes, so numerous are they, on these two days) were, whether Jewesses or Arabs, possessed of the demon. Each one in turn paid to have her right to dance,
and the old Negress with the stick was a famous sorceress who knew
the exorcisms and was able to make the demons pass from the bodies of
the women into the frequently renewed water. As soon as it was impure
it was thrown into the street. She who told us all this was the beautiful
Jewess Goumarr'ha, who did not like to talk about it, because of a re-
mainder of belief and something like shame to confess that last year she
too, her body horribly knotted with hysteria, had taken part in the
dance "hoping to find some relief for her suffering." But afterward she
had been much more seriously ill, and her husband, learning that she
had danced at this gathering of witches, had beaten her steadily for
three days to cure her.

The dance became animated; the women, haggard, wild-eyed, seeking to lose consciousness of their flesh, or better to lose all feeling, were
reaching the crisis in which, their bodies escaping all control of the
mind, the exorcism can operate effectively. After that instant exhaustion,
sweating, dying, in the prostration that follows the crisis, they were to
find the calm of deliverance.

Just now they are kneeling before the basin; their hands clutching
the rim, and their bodies beating from right to left and forward and
backward, swiftly, like a furious pendulum; their hair whips the water,
then spatters their shoulders; each time they jerk forward they utter a
low cry like that of woodsmen chopping; then suddenly tumble backward as if they had an epileptic fit, frothing at the mouth, and their
hands twisted.

The evil spirit has left them. The sorceress takes them, lays them
out, dries them, rubs them, stretches them, and, just as in a treatment
for hysteria, seizing them by the wrists and half raising them up, presses
with her foot or her knee on their abdomen.

There took part today, we are told, more than sixty. The first ones
were still twisting about when others rushed forward. One was short
and humpbacked, wearing a yellow and green gandurah, unforgettable;
her hair, black as ink, covered her completely.

Some Jewesses danced too. They sprang in disorder like delirious teetotums. They made only one leap and fell back immediately, dazed. Others held out longer. . . . Their madness communicated itself to us; we fled, unable to stand it any longer.

Biskra

"Who invented music?" Athman asks; I answer: "Musicians did." He is not satisfied; he insists. I reply seriously that God did. "No," he says immediately, "the devil did."

And he explains to me that to the Arabs all musical instruments are instruments of the devil except the two-stringed viol, whose name I cannot remember, with a very long neck and a sounding-box made of a hollowed-out tortoise. The street singers, poets, prophets, and tellers of tales provide their own accompaniment by playing this viol with a little bow, and they often play so suavely that, says Athman, "a door of heaven seems to open."

Those singers, those poets intrigue me. What do they sing? And the goatherds, interrupting themselves with their flute? And Sadek with his gusla? And Athman himself, alone or with Ahmed, each on his horse at Touggourt? At times it is a sort of dialogue; I listen but cannot make out a single word. Athman, whom I consult, answers: "No, they are not words at all; it is simply poetry!" By insisting I succeed, these last few days, in getting him to transcribe and translate some of these songs. They are the very ones, unwritten, that the street singers sing, seated on the ground or at the door of a café, and that a group of silent Arabs surrounding them listen to, or that they sing to themselves in the solitude of long marches. I don't know if they will please anyone who doesn't know this country; I hardly dare say that I consider them very beautiful and that I think the oral tradition of that Arab poetry, whether ancient or modern, worthy of attention by students of folklore. Perhaps next year I shall try to gather a little collection of these songs for publication. Here are two of them; I give them here just as Athman gave them to me, merely correcting the spelling:

For two years I have ceased making love and called myself religious.
I made my trip to the North; I found Baya at the celebration.
She put on the comb and the ear-rings,
And the dagger, with the mirror. . . .
Her hair falls on all sides,
Weighted with gold, well arranged.
No one can buy her.
Nothing but she or I. . . .
The girls asked for some coins;
And I was weak (for I am poor).

Tomorrow I shall sell a few sheep
For the beauties with their neat rings.[11]

✳

Today as she passed she turned away;
With a golden belt, the fringes, on her thighs, hanging.
What makes me suffer is her own white gown.
I shall spend the whole night running
And I am the one who makes her dogs bark.[12]

> *If Ramadan*[13] *were a man,*
> *I should myself break his legs;*
> *But Ramadan came from God;*
> *You and I accept his sufferings.*[14]

---

[11] *Deux ans j'ai cessé de faire l'amour et j'ai dit être religieux.*
J'ai fait mon voyage dans le Nord; j'ai trouvé, dans la fête, Baya.
Elle a mis le peigne et les boucles d'oreilles,
Et le poignard, avec la glace . . .
Ses cheveux tombent de tous côtés,
Pesés avec de l'or, bien arrangés.
Personne ne peut l'acheter.
Rien qu'elle ou moi . . .
Les filles ont demandé quelques pièces;
Et moi, faible (je suis pauvre).
Demain je vendrai quelques moutons
Pour les belles avec leurs bagues soignées.

[12] "Love is very difficult among us," Athman says in explanation of this line, "because the women are guarded by dogs and by the whole family." [A.]

[13] Ramadan is the forty-day fast, a fast of love as well as of food and drink. [A.]

[14] *Aujourd'hui, en passant elle s'est détournée;*
Avec une ceinture d'or, les franges, sur les cuisses, pendantes.
Ce qui me fait souffrir, c'est sa propre robe blanche.
Je passerai toute la nuit en courant
Et c'est moi qui fais aboyer ses chiens.

> *Si Rhamadan était un homme,*
> *Moi-même je lui casserais les genoux;*
> *Mais Rhamadan est venu de Dieu;*
> *Moi et toi nous acceptons ses souffrances.*

LITERATURE AND ETHICS

What in relation to fields we call rotation of crops we call the "cyclic phase of the manic-depressive psychosis" in a man.

Everything that has ever happened within us, even if only once, can reappear, time aiding and the will not intervening. (There is never, in the realm of morals, any definitive victory.)

The only things we are sure of never doing are those which we don't understand. The self-confidence of your virtue annoys me because it is made up of incomprehension. I am not speaking of the intelligence of the brain, mere logic, which understands nothing but relationships among symbols; I want nothing to do with it. We understand only what we are capable of doing; thus in nature objects vibrate at the approach of sound only when they themselves, touched by a shock, are capable of producing sound. And I do not say that they will necessarily ever produce it; but this is the source of their indulgence, their excuse for a possible eventuality.

Nihil humani a me alienum puto.[15]

"There are no crimes, however great, that on certain days I have not felt capable of committing," Goethe said. The greatest minds are also the most capable of great crimes, which they generally do not commit, because of wisdom, because of love, or because they would limit themselves by so doing.

Doctrine of sin: being capable of all evil and committing none; that is the definition of good. I do not like this merely negative exercise of the will. I prefer that blindness to evil should result from being dazzled by the good; otherwise virtue is ignorance — poverty.

I can no more be grateful to God for having created me than I could hold it against him for my not existing — if I did not exist.

Et sic Deus semel jussit, semper paret.[16]
God "who is faithful." The miracles are God's acts of disobedience.

---

[15] The famous line from Act I of Terence's comedy: *The Man Who Punished Himself:* "I am a man: I consider nothing human as foreign to me."

[16] The exact quotation reads: *"Ille ipse omnium conditor et rector scripsit quidem fata, sed sequitur; semper paret, semel jussit.* — He himself, author and ruler of all things, wrote the fates, but he also follows them; he obeys forever, and yet but once ordained." (Seneca: *De Providentia*, V, 8.)

To try to prove that God exists is just as absurd as to assert that he does not exist.

For our assertions and our proofs will not create him . . . or suppress him.

I prefer to say that since there is something, it is God. To explain him means nothing to me; he explains himself through all Nature; that is his way of existing.

Prayer is the oratorical form of the soul.

It is a disturbing thought that man needs a tradition, a history, to understand an eternal God. The history of God can only be the history of what men have thought him to be.

As soon as a man has a thought he writes a whole volume not so much to explain it as to excuse himself for having it.

John the Baptist is Christ's oratorical preparation of the audience.

I have always found my happiness in simplifying everything by ever greater generalizations — so as to make my possession as truly portable as the cup with which Hafiz intoxicates himself.

Make a rule of paying attention in each creature only to the unique and different element, of which the common matter is merely the too massive support.

"Paganism" leads to peace only if you presuppose above all those rival gods a single power to dominate them.

Happiness lies in a recognition of agreement rather than of strife. And even if each of the forces of nature in turn struggled against all the others, it would be impossible for me not to conceive a higher unity presiding over that very struggle, starting-point of every division, in which each soul can take refuge for its own well-being.

One ought never to buy anything except with love. Anyone whatever, anything whatsoever, ought always to belong to the person who loves it best. Bread to the most hungry man; the sweet to the one who prefers it or who has already supped. You can explain the drunkenness of the masses on these grounds: they drink to forget that they haven't what they desire; moreover, the drunkenness of the upper classes can be explained in the same way. Drunkenness is never anything but a substitute for happiness. It amounts to buying the dream of a thing when you haven't money enough to buy the dreamed-of thing materially. The bottle that gave drunkenness is worth the Wild Ass's Skin as long as you are drunk. The terrible thing is that one can never get sufficiently drunk.

He thought: the world could have had a different history. The surface of the earth might have been covered otherwise. If the world had never had any other inhabitants than creatures like me, it would have had no history.

I hate all careers that owe their existence only to the spitefulness of men.

In this whole comedy the important acts stand at the two extremities: birth and death. Of one we are not yet aware; of the other we are no longer aware. And it is even likely that as soon as you are buried, you do not remember dying. We are aware only of the death of others – because it makes our life easier.

Individual characteristics are more general (I mean more human) than ethnical characteristics. To restate this: the individual man tries to escape the race. And as soon as he ceases to represent the race, he represents man; the idiosyncrasy is a pretext for generalities.

Honnêteté. All that this word contains.[17]

Synthesis must be preceded by analysis; and analysis, a need of the human mind, springs from an awareness of complexity. And awareness of complexity can become a passionate stupefaction.

That strange weakness of the mind which constantly makes us doubt that future happiness can equal past happiness is often our only source of suffering. We attach ourselves to the outward show of our mourning as if it were fitting to prove our sorrow to others. We seek memories and ruins; we should like to relive the past and long to continue our joys after they are squeezed dry.

I detest all melancholy and fail to understand why confidence in the beauty of the future does not prevail over adoration of the past.

Do we not resemble those people of the seashore who every evening weep over the sun that has set in the sea and cry for a long time before the ocean, facing the west — even after the renewed sun, behind them, is rising?

---

[17] The word has the various meanings of "honesty," "integrity," "civility," "propriety," "modesty," and "respectability." *Une femme honnête* means "a respectable woman," but *un honnête homme* meant "an all-around man" and represented an ideal for the classic age.

"This island, called *Savu* by the natives, is little known." (Cook: *Voyages.*) If it were not known at all, it would have no name.

Curious habit that men have of baptizing plots of ground, and especially that island. They baptize it only on the day when they think of leaving it, and for the sake of others.

". . . Either suffer, or die. — *Aut pati, aut mori.* It is worthy of your hearing to ask you to understand basically the complete force of these words . . . you will agree with me that they contain, in abbreviation, the entire teaching of the Son of God, and the whole spirit of Christianity."

And further on: "There is nothing more contrary than living according to nature and living according to grace." (Bossuet: *Panégyrique de sainte Thérèse.*[18]) So much the worse!

"The ego is hateful," you say. Not mine. I should have liked it in another; should I be hard to please simply because it is mine? On what worse ego might I not have fallen? (To begin with, I am alive, and that is magnificent.)

I pity you if you find something to hate in yourself. I hate only such sorry ethics. If I like my ego, do not think for a moment that I like yours any the less, or that this is because of my more or less happiness.

But you are alive too, I believe, and that is magnificent.

The history of man is that of the truths he has set free.

In saying this I do not mean — please do not misunderstand me — to look upon truths as a small number of elect whose setting free or rather whose choosing would be a way of recognizing their right to reign over us, so that their freedom would be bought at the price of ours.

No, let's drop the word *Truth*, which might lead one to believe that the despotism of certain ideas is legitimate. Instead of Truths, let's say Ideas. And let us call Idea any perceived relationship; if you wish to speak metaphorically, it is the refraction in a man's mind of an effective relationship. The number of Ideas is infinite like the number of relationships, or almost.

In order not to suppress in my own mind every reason for existing and for enjoying existing, I rather like to consider humanity as the accomplishment of the possible relationships. The almost infinity of possible relationships assures humanity of an almost infinite life. The accomplished relationships constitute the history of the past. That is a finished thing and, whether or not it produced a happy result, you cannot retouch it. The slightest idea of today needed the almost infinity of

---

[18] "Panegyric of St. Teresa," one of Bossuet's sermons.

relationships that came into play yesterday. At least in this way you are finally rid of them.

Thus humanity gradually frees itself. But so gradually that it is not aware of the process.

And yet don't go believing in progress except for this reason:

Any locomotion whatsoever, even that of a crawfish, can only be imagined as moving forward, and even if you turned all your faces toward it, the past would none the less go off into the past. What is done is not to be redone.

But to believe that humanity has an end outside itself and not projected by itself would be madness and chasing after a shadow. Man's progress takes place only within himself and has not the victorious significance that you attribute to it.

Ossa collapsed on Pelion, and heaven cannot be scaled. Moreover we should not find in heaven an exclusive gathering of Truths seated on thrones with little corners reserved for us to sit on.

The gods, if they existed, would see our endless struggle as children on beaches amuse themselves with the relative advances of the waves. One is coming; oh, progress! It rises; it overruns and submerges everything; it leaves a froth and withdraws; another follows and rises a bit higher — oh, progress! it's a tide. The tide recedes; the next day it wins over a few more inches of beach — oh, progress! just think how far it will go tomorrow! But the day after tomorrow the equinox is passed and the sea goes down — but continues to be in stress and slowly nibbles away the land.

Time and space are the stage that the innumerable truths have set up with the aid of our minds, and we act upon those boards like willing, convinced, devoted, and voluptuous marionettes. I don't see anything in this to be upset about; on the contrary, I prefer this understanding of my role; and, after all, even if everything motivates that role, each one of us invents his own.

You will learn to look upon humanity as the staging of ideas on earth.

Our sole value is one of representation.

They suffered from the burden of themselves and did not know how to get rid of it. Charity did not tempt them. The individual became unbearable to them, and others even more than themselves. No longer wanting to attend to themselves, they certainly did not want to attend to others. But attend to what, then? What to cling to?

This tormented them so long as they thought ideas subordinate to men. But as soon as they realized them to be sovereign, they attended only to ideas and forgot themselves in doing so.

To exist or to be aware of their existence, things need us; and without us they remain in a state of expectation. This gives man a restless uneasiness: the pressure within us of all that has not yet been and that wants to be, of all the unknown calling for its little moment of thought, seems to beg existence of us, because everything must come to this — as if there were some pleasure in telling oneself that one has existed, after one has ceased to exist.

Inertia of matter. Slowness before the idea has passed through it.

Theory of the book: dead letter? A bag of seeds.

Elasticity! Of all inertias the worst! hypocrisy of immovable matter; it seems to yield, giving an illusion of victory and successful effort, but it returns as soon as you let it go; it was only deferred inertia. Matter that seems plastic, allowing us to exhaust our efforts on it. To prove your possession of what stupid memory do you return, after we had modeled you according to our whims, and rearrange yourself according to your original lines that we wanted so much to forget, that we shall never be able to forget then? Elasticity! matter's crude memory, deferred inertia, apparent docility. . . .

Elasticity surrounds us; what in the immaterial world we call retroaction is merely that — but with infinite complications — until matter itself becomes completely impregnated with it, changed by it.

Repartee: infinite receptivity of matter; porousness.

Social question? Yes indeed. But the ethical question is antecedent.

Man is more interesting than men. God made *him* and not them in his image. Each one is more precious than all.

It is easy to consider the soul as that particle of soil in which many different plants grow and so many insects live. There is superabundance, there is struggle; there will therefore be suppression. It's too much; it's too much! If you do not tear out this one, it will stifle that one. If you tear nothing out, nature will take care of the struggle.

In studying the question of the *raison d'être* of the work of art, one is brought to the conclusion that the justification, the symbol of the work, is its composition.

A well-composed work is necessarily symbolical. Around what could the parts group themselves? What could guide their arrangement except the idea of the work, which creates that symbolic arrangement?

The work of art is the exaggeration of an idea.

The symbol is the thing around which a book is composed.

The sentence is an excrescence of the idea.

Theory. Things are perpetually in a state of disequilibrium; hence their dispersal.

Equilibrium is perfect "health"; what M. Taine calls a happy accident, but it is physically unrealizable because of what we were saying; realizable only in the work of art. The work of art is an equilibrium outside of time, an artificial health.

I will maintain that an artist needs this: a special world of which he alone has the key. It is not enough that he should bring *one* new thing, although that is already an achievement; but rather that everything in him should be or seem new, seen through a powerfully coloring idiosyncrasy.

He must have a personal philosophy, æsthetics, and ethics; his entire work tends only to reveal it. And that is what makes his style. I have discovered too, and this is very important, that he must have a personal manner of joking, his own sense of humor.

CHRISTIAN ETHICS

It is true that all do not equally have to fight in order to conquer themselves and die to themselves — says the *Imitation of Christ* (I, xx, 4). I now believe, if not that it is useless to "conquer oneself," at least that after winning a certain number of victories youth must come to an end and, by means of intimate and perpetual peace treaties, prepare what we call maturity. In like manner, among states, we see classical periods rise only at the end of internal struggles. Then the various forces, educated by these struggles, instead of antagonizing one another, can find employment on the frontiers and permit a blossoming of harmony within the community.

Excellent article by Fouillée on Auguste Comte. I copy from it: ". . . Since there is no limit to free inquiry, Protestantism created a limitless, hence indefinite, hence indefinable religion, which would not know, if free inquiry should introduce atheism, whether or not atheism is a part of Protestantism; a religion that does not know where it stops or where it is heading. . . . All free thought being implied in free inquiry, therefore all free thought, all philosophism, all intellectual anarchy were contained in Protestantism as soon as it ceased to be a basic Catholicism."

"Und alles ist Frucht, und alles ist Samen." [19] An idea continues to be a living force so long as all the nourishment in it has not been used up in phenomena. Christianity will lead man farther; man can rely on it even more. But first Catholicism, then Protestantism, after having been expansive formulas, long ago became restrictive formulas; hard sheaths and shells in which the mind is cramped. To put oneself in tutelage is a plaintive need of the mind; guardianships must not be denied or suppressed too soon. The weak mind would suffer too much and would deform itself too easily. But any formula whatever of any religion whatever can only be considered as destined to disappear. No one has ever ruined more of those worn-out formulas than did Christ.

Christianity can indeed nourish still more anarchies (these in their turn can only be considered as provisional experiments). But it must free itself now from the formulas in which, like torrents of lava, it is congealing on the surface.

I am amazed that Protestantism, while rejecting the hierarchies of the Church, did not at the same time reject the oppressive institutions of St. Paul, the dogmatism of his epistles, in order to derive from the Gospels alone. We shall soon come, I believe, to isolating the words of Christ in order to let them appear more emancipatory than they had hitherto seemed. Less buried, they will appear more dramatically, finally negating the institution of the family (and that will serve as authority for suppressing it), taking man himself out of his environment for a personal career and teaching by his example and his voice not to have any possessions on the earth or any place to lay one's head. Ah, my whole soul longs for that "nomadic state" in which man, without hearth or home, will no more localize his duty or his affection than his happiness on such creatures.

No matter how much I read and reread the Gospels, I do not find a single word of Christ that strengthens, or even authorizes, the family and marriage. On the other hand, I find some that negate them: It is "because of the hardness of your hearts . . ." says Christ, speaking of the old educative laws of Moses on divorce, which those on marriage implied. The recruiting of each disciple is a carrying off from his family; out of filial respect one of them wants, before following Jesus, to bury his father: "Let the dead bury their dead," the Master says to him. "Who is my mother? and who are my brethren?" he replies when told that his mother and brothers have come to see him, and indicating all those who are listening to him, he adds: "Behold my mother and my brethren!"

"Woman," he says to his mother who continues to love him with a

---

[19] "And everything is at once both fruit and seed." (Schiller: *Die Braut von Messina*, III, 5.)

special love — "Woman, what have I to do with thee?" Then later, from the cross, as if fearing to have saddened her and as if to show her what widespread and constantly available affection for one's neighbor is to replace localized affection: "Woman, behold thy son!" he says to Mary while pointing to John, and to John as he points to Mary: "Behold thy mother!" That some should see in this the beauties of adoption, I have no objection, for it, too, ruins the family; the tearful union of two griefs, I still have no objection, but then let me see in it also the possibility of immediate consolation, suggested by him who said: "Let the dead bury their dead"; grief suppressed, made impossible by a perpetual chain of adoptions.

Finally, did not Christ frequently assert that whoever did not leave everything to follow him would not enter the kingdom of heaven? And indeed it must be understood that one cannot follow Christ without abandoning everything one has. Will it be said that the family is not a part of "everything one has" to him who also said: "I am come to set a man at variance against his father, and the daughter against her mother," etc. . . . For "he that loveth father or mother more than me is not worthy of me. . . . I came not to send peace, but a sword." And elsewhere: "And every one that hath forsaken houses or brethren, or sisters, or father, or mother, or wife, or children, or lands, for my name's sake, shall receive an hundredfold." Endless broadening of the object of love as soon as the family is negated.

DETACHED PAGES

MEDITATION I (*outline*)

I reread Pascal's admirable passage: "The example of Alexander's chastity has not made so many continent men as that of his drunkenness has made intemperate ones." Etc. . . .

This is the thought that has inspired the frequent attempts to hide the feet of great men. But why should I care on what level their feet rest? Their feet are beautiful. And, indeed, that is not even the question; head and feet belong to the same man; there are secret relationships between them. Who can say whether I may not lose everything by trying to abstract the greatness alone — that is to say, by considering only the emotion or the thought and not the organ that produced them, the fruit without the tree that bore it? The great man's greatness does not lie solely in his head; if he carries his head higher, this is because his whole body is taller.

Moreover, this metaphor is deceptive. There are so many ways of being great; there are so many ways of being beautiful. There are so many ways of deserving men's interest.

Ugly sentiments are feigned sentiments. We discover, but with difficulty, that there is perhaps not a single one that cannot be . . . etc. The
most modest flower, when cultivated, reveals a particular kind of beauty.

MEDITATION II (outline)

The value of ill health.
(See Pascal: *Prayer for the Proper Use of Ill Health.*)
Ill health a source of unrest.
You can expect nothing from "satisfied people."
Great invalids: prophets, Mohammed, St. Paul, St. John (does M.
Jules Soury think that he can today diminish the divine importance of
Christ's words by making him out to be tubercular and subject to hys-
teria?), Rousseau, Nietzsche, Dostoyevsky, Flaubert, etc. . . . sick he-
roes: Hamlet, Orestes, etc. . . .
The need of ill health that antiquity felt.
System of compensations (hardly understood at all). Homer's blind-
ness; story of Orpheus (save for another place); he sang only out of
pain and suffering; possessing the *reality* of his love, he was silent.
Whence his songs *seemed* sad; because they are the expression of desire and not of possession. In *reality* they are not sad, but simply recount
the *absence* of . . . (too subtle; must be elucidated).
The vast sickly unrest of ancient heroes: Prometheus, Orestes, Ajax,
Phædra, Pentheus, Œdipus (Œdipus deserves a place by himself, in
the meditation on the theater: antipodal to Macbeth).
Apropos of Homer, recall the blinding of nightingales, a much more
satisfactory explanation than the system of compensations. Eyes closed
to the real world. The blind nightingale sings better, not from regret,
but from enthusiasm.
Ill health offers man a new restlessness that he is called on to legiti-
mize. Whence the value of Rousseau, as well as of Nietzsche. Without
his poor health Rousseau would merely have been a boring orator in
the manner of Cicero.
The illusion we enjoy as to the health of great men: see Molière,
Racine, etc. . . . The writer who has said the best things on this subject is precisely the one who is generally cited as the model of the
healthy man of letters: Goethe. See *Faust* (admirable dialogue with
Chiron). He recognized incontrovertibly the advantage in, etc. . . .
see his *Torquato Tasso,* etc. . . .
The famous question as to why Sparta had no great men must come
up at this point. The perfection of the race prevented the glorification
of the individual. But it also allowed them to create the male canon, and
the Doric order. By suppressing the puny, you suppress the rare variety
— a well-known fact in botany or at least in *floriculture:* the most beautiful flowers often being produced by apparently puny plants.

✳

The wonderful thing, on this earth, is that we are forced to feel more than to think.

Conglomeration of absurd sensations during my seasickness on the crossing; impossible to remember exactly, though the most futile sensations stretched out endlessly through the empty hours. But, for instance, certain sounds of the motor recurring periodically at rather long intervals forced me to measure the time by them; and when a new sound would occur I would say to myself and keep repeating until the following sound: "Oh! there is that cake lousy with berries . . ." and in my mind the cake was called a catafalque. At another moment, having had the misfortune to look at a detached cotter-pin dangling at the end of a little copper chain and swinging out of time with the ship's pitching, it reminded me of one of those enormous southern grasshoppers, yellow-green, with long legs, which was busy shining shoes.

And sweating, and almost fainting away, weak as a dying man in one of Edgar Poe's tales — yes, precisely, the unfortunate hero of "The Pit and the Pendulum," think: "Oh, if the port-hole would only open! Oh, open the port-hole!" and not do anything about it, and for whole minutes think of nothing, feel nothing but that: how a little sea air would feel fanning my bruised temples, and feel my volition so far, so desperately far from the wish that for once it is absolutely useless to link one with the other. Oh, misery! And suddenly, stifling, throw myself at the port-hole, clutch the bolts, turn, pull, open, and fall back half dead on the berth, with, stronger than any other feeling, the frightful discomfort of the too cold outside air suddenly freezing my moist hands at the instant when the port-hole opened.

And for a long time remain without even moving a finger, letting the sweat flow drop by drop from my forehead onto the pillow; then think, feel gradually — now frozen by the sea air: "Oh, if the port-hole would only close! Oh, close the port-hole! . . ."

It's not only the nausea, but also the almost total impossibility of swallowing anything solid, one's glands refusing to salivate, one's muscles refusing to swallow; and the mucous membranes of the tongue and the mouth are coated with a sort of salty, insulating secretion.

Manage not to vomit, but only by dint of not eating anything.

※

Sorrento, Villa Arlotta; at Vollmœller's

Who could describe the vividness, the somber magnificence, the order, the rhythmic beauty, the softness of this garden-orchard. . . . I went in under the shade of the orange trees, half weeping, half laughing, and fully intoxicated; through the dense branches one could hardly see the sky. It had rained; the sky was still gray; it seemed that the light came entirely from the profusion of oranges. Their weight bent the branches. The lemon trees, frailer, more gracefully shaped, had less ostentation and greater elegance. At times protective mats above them made an almost dark shelter for them. On the ground, among the trunks whose number, modest height, and oily and polished surface reminded me of the rich pillars in the Córdoba mosque, a thick, unbroken carpet of wood-sorrel of a paler green than lawns, more on the bluish side, more subtle, more fragile. And on the paths of hard black earth, straight, regular, and narrow, where the shade, warmth, and humidity had allowed mosses to creep, one would have liked to walk barefoot.

The garden ended in a terrace, or a cliff rather, dropping straight into the sea. On the extreme edge the orange grove yielded to ilex and pines. A much wider path followed the brink, but in such a way that a fringe of trees rose between the walk and the sea. At intervals, where the rock jutted out, the bold terrace offered a circular bench, a table, a charming spot to rest. On one of these marble benches the diligent gardener had placed some oranges for our pleasure. They were of four kinds: to the largest, almost tasteless, sweet as watermelons, I much preferred the egg-shaped ones with a thick skin; they had an ethereal taste such as I fancy Oriental oranges to have; but I especially delighted in the very small tangerines, hard as lady-apples, with an orangey-green skin of delicate texture that looks like a glove leather. I can't say how many we ate, nor yet, alas, with what (rapture). . . . They satisfied at once both hunger and thirst. From the bench on which we were seated talking, when we threw the skins over the railing, they fell, a few hundred yards below, straight into the sea.

Perugia, February

It was a *light intoxication.* . . . Alas, why is not everyone capable of this delightful ecstasy? This mood is the starting-point for all heroisms. I felt so glorious that a bit of suffering, I believe, would only have exalted me still further. I supervised everything, I presided over everything, but in an impersonal manner; I forgot myself, I was distracted in a vague sensual delight, losing myself absolutely in it.

It is conceivable that all individualism should triumph in this mood since all egotism ends there. Certainly any return to myself, any personal consideration, became not only unseemly, but impossible. In this state I felt just as capable of the noblest deeds as of the worst, capable of any act whatever. And my mind, as if stupefied, was both unable to measure and unwilling to calculate the consequences.

And my mere presence, everywhere, established among all that I saw, heard, and felt a palpitating harmony that broke down my resistance. I was a part of it. . . .

⁂

"Moderation *consists* in feeling emotion as the angels do." (Joubert.)
This is as if you said: Consumption consists in going to spend every winter in the south.

The water that issues from glaciers! nothing could be more turbid; a brew for goitrous people.
The only pure waters gush from the deep earth.

We debated for some time whether Cleombrotus had drowned himself out of despair at not having been present at Socrates' last conversation — or out of haste to know that supernatural felicity that Plato too eloquently described as awaiting him in the other world; and I quoted Milton's lines:

> . . . *and he, who, to enjoy*
> *Plato's Elysium, leap'd into the sea,*
> *Cleombrotus.*
>
> (Paradise Lost, *III, 472*) [1]

It is a greater delight for me to set in motion my body's supple muscles and my senses' voluptuous details than the no less subtle mechanism of my mind.

DIMINUTIVE NOVEL
Precipitate sensuality.
(His haste was such that he scratched his hands on the locks.)

But it was not merely a question of music: the mere sound of a stringed instrument, or of a flute, or of a voice was enough to dominate my thought immediately. Likewise a gesture, a ray of sunlight on the ground, a smile from a human being or from a throbbing nature, alas, more than art, now made my heart swoon completely. So that all the slow preparation, the admirable effort of refinement that, through my ancestors, a whole race had put forth to produce me, bursting its bonds at this point, ended in an after-growth of savagery — just as you see natural plants reappear growing in the ruins of patiently erected palaces.

Compare the clouds that one sees pass over the mountain at El Kantara, then melt into the azure, with the caravans that the desert *swallows up* (or vice versa).

Arrival in Bône.
Heavy perfumes that no breath of air disperses, which spread like a very heavy mist on the sea.

---

[1] Quoted in English by Gide.

I felt that shade simultaneously throughout my body. My bare feet were touching a cooler earth. The less burning air entered my lungs like a wine. My eyelids found acute pleasure in its caress.

Skating. Ice on which no one has yet skated. Cannot be distinguished from the water — treachery — you might even think you were slipping along on the water itself — the sun shining on the ice makes a mirror — and you can see yourself in it — so that through my speed and the angle of my body, combined as I turned, I seemed to myself as if lying in space and looked at myself close by, leaning over the reflection like Narcissus.

Return at evening toward the village, lighted by the setting sun — which gave us immense shadows on the road.

Other tired returns — too late — sun already set — melancholies.

Skating on overflowed ponds, among the reeds — among the tree-trunks.

Skating on canals — not alone — and shout out as you pass very fast: "Look! a gate, a house."

Skating at Versailles to the end of the Grand Canal.

"The most enchanted soil would become hateful to me as soon as I felt that I had put out roots in it." (Dumas *fils*, Preface to *La Question d'argent.*[2])

Human laziness is infinite. It is the triumph of inertia over more delicate laws. It is sometimes called wisdom; it prevents what is coming from arriving too quickly.

Very few people really love life; the horror of any change is a proof of this. The thing they least like to change, with their lodging, is their thought. Wife, friends come afterwards; but lodging and thought involve too great an effort. There you have squatted and there you stay. You furnish the surroundings to your taste, making everything resemble you as closely as possible. You avoid any opportunity for anything to contradict. It is a mirror, a prepared approbation. In this environment you don't live; you take root. Very few, I assure you, really love life.

Listen to people talk. Who listens to one another? The contradictors? Not at all. You listen only to those who repeat your thought. The more it is expressed as you would have expressed it yourself, the more willingly you listen. The skill of popular journalists lies in making the imbecile who reads them say: "That's exactly what I was thinking!" We want to be flattered, not rubbed the wrong way. Oh, how slow is the

---

² *The Money Question.*

succession of time! What long efforts to move from one place to another!
And how we rest between struggles! How, at the least slope, we sit
down!

Determinism and Restraint

I came to a sort of feeling of certainty. Yes, my actions seemed to me
to proceed in a happy and full way and as if from a sure source. Their
beauty would not be visible to me until later. I even quickly convinced
myself that the beauty of my acts, in order to seem perfect and pleasing
to me, must not be prepared by me and must be barely foreseen until
the moment of the act itself. My finest acts, or at least those which
seemed finest to me, are those whose beauty took me by surprise. And
the intoxication that I then felt suddenly filled me with that particular
dizziness which permitted forgetfulness of self, with that strength, too,
which would have made me able to do anything. At such moments I felt,
as if in spite of myself, my whole being stretch, stiffen, harden; I became
harsh to myself and took delight in treating myself very roughly. At
times, convinced as I was that any of my actions would always result in
the greater glorification of my life, I dreamed, almost out of spite, of
letting myself go, of relaxing my will, of giving myself respite and leisure. I never could, and I realized that in me restraint was more natural
than yielding to pleasure is in others, that I was not free not to will, to
relax, and to cease resisting; and I realized at the same time that from
that very absence of liberty came the beauty of my acts.

❄

Paradoxes

Slow evolution: already the intelligence has ceased to seem to me
the pearl of great price for which everything else is sold. The vanity of
understanding everything is just as ridiculous as any other vanity, and
more dangerous than any other. After a short while the thing you least
understand is yourself.

❄

And do not seek to welcome everything; repulse rather. Remember
that the Hebrews killed but did not convert. It is always the enemy that
one welcomes. The Mussulmans know this too; they do not listen to the
thought of others; they resist it. What allows mules to be obstinate is
their blinders. And what will you gain by understanding that all the
rest has just as much reason to exist as you? Understanding is the beginning of approving. To negate with conviction one must never have
looked at what one negates.

❄

(Recollections of the *Affair*.[3]) What constituted Rousseau's strength in his time was that, being the only one in his party, he was able to believe that his party was right. A party is always compromised by *the others;* there are always too many of them; and if there were fewer, the *party* would be too weak.

Yes, Rousseau's strength came from his solitude; for, since there is stupidity everywhere, the danger comes from the fact that one's partisans may exaggerate it; you see that stupidity too clearly and you cease to be convinced. So long as you remain alone on your side, you triumph; the stupidity seems to be all on the other side, and this helps you to get yourself in deeper.

And people think that it is for the sake of meditation that the most convinced theorists need solitude!

No matter: at that time they seemed to lack experience; the Roman experience had become merely historical; it was easy to reason about it. That of the French Revolution is superb. We are still crushed by it.

[3] The *affaire Dreyfus*, the fierce controversy that split France into two camps between the condemnation of Captain Alfred Dreyfus for treason in 1895 and his rehabilitation in 1906.

1902

Each one of us has his own way of deceiving himself. The important thing is to believe in one's own importance.

In front of Henri Albert, Léon Blum, Charles Chanvin, Marcel Drouin (whom I had brought together for lunch), out of vanity I launched a few bloomers. Nothing humiliates me more profoundly, causes me to reproach myself more, or is easier for me to do again. I am no good except when alone. In a group it's not so much the others that bore and annoy me; it's myself.

After lunch the conversation becomes animated; that is to say that several talk at one time. Chanvin, Blum, and Albert do not use the same vocabulary; and not one of them is aware of this. The best thing for the one who is listening then is to be silent, if he doesn't want to have the three others jump on him at once.

The question is to what extent Stendhal loved women, what he wanted of them, and what he actually did with them. Chanvin confused everything by calling "sensuality" what I should call the risqué spirit. One ought to begin by defining one's terms.

In my opinion,[1] Stendhal felt much more interest in than love for women. I can readily conceive of him as proving to himself, at the brothel, that he is not so impotent as his subtlety makes him seem in the company of ladies and actresses.

He makes one recognize his mind to be more beautiful than his body. If I had been a woman, no one would have seemed to me less pleasing to satisfy and more pleasing to put off than Stendhal. To refuse oneself was to "stand up to him"; and in doing so one had the best of him.

Then, abruptly, and as if we already knew it, Henri Albert begins talking to us of Stendhal's syphilis! Then of Flaubert's!! We protest; he insists. . . . Marcel Drouin and I have just read Duclaux's lecture in which it is stated that in any human gathering you can count one syphilitic out of six; and Drouin thinks: "What luck that there are only five of us!"

No warmth, no *charity* in Henri Albert's tone of voice. He talks only of the things he is sure of, and he is sure only of the things he has not invented. You feel that he has not the stuff to make a mistake and that

---

[1] I transcribe this passage although today, 25 March, it strikes me as rather false. I must admit finding in the *Souvenirs d'égotisme* (p. 23): "In ten years I have not gone to the brothel three times." [A.]

if in the morning he puts on patent-leather shoes that hurt him, this is because the pair in which he would be comfortable is not fit to be seen.

5 January

Sometimes the *reality* of an act is perceptible to us only in its consequences. Great crimes have occasionally been committed so easily only because in a sort of dream. Later on, the criminal would have liked to wake up. He would have liked not to have been taken seriously. . . .

7 January

Jacques Blanche, at whose house Henri Ghéon and I are lunching, describes his restlessness to us. He thinks it has reached its pitch; yet it might get worse. The painting he is doing today makes him look with disgust on what he did yesterday; his beggars of Pont-l'Évêque make all the "society people" insipid to him. In England, he claims, this would not be so. And he talks of selling out everything, of dropping Paris and going to live in London, or Pont-l'Évêque at least. But Saint-Martin will not be for rent this year; and he has had no luck in finding another lodging. And we agree with him that his pictures from this summer, perhaps the best that he has done, are only the beginning of something different. . . . Henri Ghéon especially waxes enthusiastic at the idea of a cynical Blanche. He claims that we are largely responsible for this and traces Blanche's cynicism to the period of the Exposition, to our association with him, and to the big canvas in which we are portrayed.[2] I should like to believe it.

In the end Griffin did not sell those *Mercure* stocks[3] that he said he wanted to sell; a reference in his conversation (this evening at the Van Rysselberghes') has informed me. And before I can laugh with him at this change of heart, he manages, as he tells the story, to transform into a premeditated decision what circumstances forced him to do.

It is only because Vielé-Griffin never tells or shows more than the outcome of his indecision that he is able to seem a man of will; but certain little facts betray him.

Talking of his visit this morning to the young sculptor Charmoy, he protests against the work and the man, is unwilling to see in it anything but puffery, *arrivisme*, and pretension; you would think, to hear him talk, that he alone had counterbalanced the others' excessive flattery. But I am free to think that he talked this way out of reaction against

---

[2] This group portrait of Gide, Ghéon, Athman, Eugène Rouart, and Chanvin is now in the Rouen museum.

[3] The young writers who could afford to do so bought stock in the *Mercure de France* when it was incorporated in 1894.

his own exaggerated kindness of this morning. The letter that I have just received from Charmoy encourages me in this interpretation, for he writes still under the stress of the emotion caused by Vielé-Griffin's cordial compliments.

But Vielé-Griffin would not understand that these are precisely the things that make him interesting, intelligent, and likable. Each character can be most attractively approached through its incoherences.

Griffin claims that, on the notice of the *Mercure* stockholders' meeting, an "admirable" misprint had put "genital meeting" instead of "general meeting." This printer's error amuses him hugely and, seeing that it doesn't make anyone else laugh, he repeats it three times (at the Van Rysselberghes').

I have been able to check the story; it is not true.

This Tuesday I have repeated to myself every hour the remark of *Lamiel's* Sansfin: [4] "There are certain days on which I ought to get my servant to tie me to the foot of my bed." I feel myself to be living one of those days. It is not the day to go and fight with the *Revue blanche*.[5] Around six o'clock I go up to the *Mercure*, lose myself for a moment in the crowd, then escape with Henry Davray and together we enjoy in the first office a quarter of an hour's conversation that consoles me for all my foozles of the day.

To collect a modest sum I went to the offices of the *Revue blanche*. Here I am at the cashier's window. I come as a creditor and am received as a debtor. They claim that I owe almost 100 francs. In turn I demand the detailed statement of my debt. I am given a piece of envelope on which is scrawled:

21 cop. China paper *Candaule* [6]	42
6 cop. Holland paper *1001 Nuits*	60
	102
Owed to M. Gide for contributions	17
Owed by him	85

---

[4] *Lamiel*, a novel by Stendhal, published posthumously in 1889.

[5] Monthly literary review founded in 1891 by Alexandre Natanson, which was a leading publication from 1891 to 1900. Though publishing many symbolists (Mallarmé, Régnier, Gourmont, etc.), it was a general review with special interests in the theater, literary criticism, and sociology. Léon Blum began his career as one of its regular critics and Claude Debussy wrote the music column. In 1903 the *Revue blanche* merged with *La Revue*.

[6] *Le Roi Candaule* (*King Candaules*), Gide's play in three acts, telling the story of the King and Gyges the fisherman, was published in book form by the *Revue blanche* in 1901 and presented at the Théâtre de l'Œuvre 9 May 1901.

I stuff the paper in my pocket without saying a word (this was three days ago); but this evening, feeling in good form, I go upstairs to the *Revue* and ask to speak with Alexandre Natanson.

After an exchange of civilities and smiles:

"I was presented the other day," I said, "with this little statement of debt, which I am quite willing to settle, but which I am unable to understand." And I hold out the little scrap of paper. (I had learned my sentence by heart.)

There follows a silly discussion about the copies of *Candaule*, which I was by chance about to pay for a second time. That question clarified, I resume:

"My second amazement concerns the *Mille et Une Nuits*. I never thought for a minute that either you or Mardrus would make me a gift of the edition on special paper; but I am surprised to pay more for it here than I would at an ordinary bookshop. Is this because I am 'one of your authors,' as you say?"

Natanson immediately explains that there is a mistake, that of course the discount will be made, and that I did right to complain.

"You understand," he said, "the accounts are merely approximate, very approximate. Impossible to keep track of individual considerations. So, systematically, the top price is entered everywhere. The accounts are very coarsely made up, you understand. Naturally I can't stick my nose into everything; so each individual has only to lodge a protest. Take for example Mirbeau — you certainly know how definitely he is one of our authors, Mirbeau! Well, he happened to be in exactly the same situation. Since he gets all his books from us, he received a bill the other day for fifteen hundred francs. He protested. Do you know how much his bill was reduced? . . . To nine hundred francs. All you have to do is protest, you see."

"That's all right," I reply, "for those who have Mirbeau's temperament — or mine" (and I emphasize this as best I can); "but there are some who, without suspecting anything, would be capable of paying the full sum."

"Perfect!" says Alexandre. Then, catching himself, he adds: "You understand, if they don't want to pay so much, let them go to their bookshop. Here we don't get the commission. . . . Do you know how many charge accounts we keep?"

"?"

"Twelve thousand! . . ." (I think this is the figure he said.) "Now are you satisfied?"

"No. I should still like you to give instructions to your cashier."

"All right," says Alexandre; "come with me."

We follow the little corridor outside the editorial office. Alexandre opens the second door on the left. This is the business office. At an enormous table covered with papers and ledgers a Jewish girl wearing pince-nez is adding up columns.

"Mademoiselle, this is Monsieur Gide, to whom you will henceforth give the thirty-three per cent discount on all of our books."

He starts to go out, stops, and returns:

"Henceforth you will make the same discount for all those whom we publish."

Then, turning toward me with his crocodile smile:

"Are you happy? . . . Yes? . . . Then so am I. Well, good-by."

My debt, after this little "protest" is lowered from 102 to 50 francs and my credit raised from 17 to 34 after a recheck.

"She had no inclination to make love; what she liked above all was an interesting conversation." (*Lamiel*, p. 131.)

Out of ten moments of joy Stendhal owes nine to satisfied vanity.

8 January

Why do I limit *L'Immoraliste*[7] to three hundred copies? . . . To hide from myself as much as possible the bad sale I know I shall have. If twelve hundred were printed, its sale would seem to me four times as bad; I should suffer four times as much.

Besides, everyone ought to risk a new adventure. I alone can risk this one; everything inclines me toward it; it amuses me; its results will educate me the more because they are unforeseen, and that is the real consideration.

Quietly spent yesterday evening finishing *Lamiel* and meditating. I foresaw that it would be *indispensable* for me to go out. I did not go out, and I am not any the worse off (I even spent a rather good night). Two years ago I should have had to stay out until three in the morning, after having prowled the boulevards from ten o'clock on. I seem wiser; I am older.

10 January

Stendhal's need to write. . . . The need that makes me write these notes has nothing spontaneous, nothing irresistible about it. I have never enjoyed *writing rapidly*. That's why I want to force myself to do so.

10 p.m.

Alexandre S. met on the boulevards. At nineteen he is hardly any less beautiful than at fifteen. Yet he has perhaps lost some of that pale-

---

[7] His tale *The Immoralist*, published by the *Mercure de France* in 1902.

ness, of that delicacy of features, which at first made us take him for Spanish.

I am with Ghéon. Alexandre says as he accosts us: "I have just lost my wife." (The little Aline with whom he had been living for a year.) "We quarreled too much," he adds. And he tells how, on New Year's Eve, when he had been even more brutal than usual, the poor girl, unable to stand it any longer, had fled to a friend's. The other girl, a morphine addict, advised her to take an injection. Did Aline make a mistake in measuring the dose? or did she deliberately increase it? . . . She took so much that an hour later she was dead.

"You must have read it in the papers," says Alexandre by way of conclusion.

I ask him rather stupidly if this saddened him greatly.

"Of course!" he says; "we were very much in love. . . . And besides, now I don't know how to get along."

She used to bring in considerable money since the time when he gave up his original craft as a diamond-cutter. While waiting to make up his mind on a new trade, he dabbles in them all; and God only knows how many there are! Ah, if he only didn't lie, how much one would learn just to hear him talk! . . .

He claims to be completely secure from the police (they almost all say that); and he relates his tricks endlessly. We go into a little café on the boulevard Montmartre and, on the marble-topped table, where he orders a hot milk, I a kirsch, and Ghéon a sort of syrup, he spreads out his papers. His wallet is full of excellent recommendations, letters from jewelers for whom he used to work, etc. . . .

"And look! Search me if you wish; I never keep a paper that might compromise me."

Yet here is a letter from a state engineer, on a mission in Tonkin; a photograph of the engineer surrounded by Tonkinese men and women. Then another letter from the same, which he reads us and for which an anti-administration newspaper would pay dearly. . . . The engineer tells everything they are doing over there and especially what they are not doing; all they are costing the state and the little return they are giving. If I could only have made a copy! . . . In short, Alexandre would like to go and join his friend, whose constant companion he was for over two years. They lived, ate, and slept together. The engineer rarely went out, but he almost never went anywhere without Alexandre, whom he passed off as his cousin. He has been gone six months now.

Then Alexandre tells about last summer, his season at Trouville and Havre. Two women, one in Trouville and the other in Havre, kept him. He spent his days with one, and with the other his nights. Every morning he took the Trouville boat and went to play the races or the casino. Every evening he took the Havre boat back again.

"Ah!" he says, "I had a good time! I led the life of a prince. I had a hotel room, a fifty-franc room. . . ."

One evening, returning to Havre, he found an empty bed; his mistress, tired of waiting for him, had run off with an Englishman.

I ask him what has become of little Auguste, whom, some time ago, he used to introduce as his brother. But he never sees him any more and doesn't seem to enjoy talking about him. "He is in Madagascar," he says. The last time that I saw Auguste myself, he had just got out of the Petite Roquette prison.

Last night Ducoté's last Thursday reception. (He is leaving for Italy.) I get there about ten o'clock, having first stopped in at the Charles Gides'.

Leaving Ducoté's, Charles-Louis Philippe accompanies me. We walk for a long time on the boulevards.

"The thing that embarrasses me when I talk with you," he says, "is that I haven't yet discovered when you find me interesting."

"But precisely when you say such things as that, my dear Philippe."

This morning I was to see Alexandre again. He had invited me to look him up at his lodging, rue de Trévise. The concierge shows an obvious unwillingness to give any information.

"M. Alexandre S.," I asked.

"No, Monsieur."

"I have been told that this is the place."

"This is and this isn't," she replies.

"What do you mean by that, my good woman?"

"That he doesn't live here. He simply keeps some furniture."

"I must talk to him. Where can I find him?"

"I don't know anything about it."

I start away, furious. She calls me back.

"Listen," she says; "if you want to knock at the second door on the left, third floor of the service entrance, you can see whether he is there."

I go up. I knock and wait. I knock again. A quarter of an hour is spent this way. I go away; return; knock again. . . . No one.

And no one at five o'clock either, in front of the Folies, where we had made a vague appointment. No luck! But I should have liked seeing him in his own lodgings.

It is almost five years that I have known Alexandre. How interesting he would be if he didn't lie constantly!

Ghéon's frankness consoles me for all my hypocrisies. He possesses admirable strength and health. Though he restrains me somewhat and delights in making me appear stupid, I take the greatest pleasure in seeing him. If he works very little, at least he reads a great deal. Everything is grist for his mill, and during the last month he has been devouring at random Thucydides, Montesquieu, Marivaux, Stendhal, Sainte-Beuve, and so forth.

11 January

At the shipping office, Place Saint-Sulpice, where I go to make an appointment with Jules Iehl for dinner, I find the two children Juliette and Marcel, whose story he had told us. We walk back for some distance together. The little girl is eight and the boy seven. He was carrying home a litre of red wine and some potatoes for dinner.

While walking I read *Les Hommes de lettres* [8] by the Goncourt brothers.

At the Café Vachette with Ducoté and Chanvin. While waiting for Henri Albert, who is to join us soon, I tell them ten or twelve anecdotes about half a dozen "great men." Poor dear Ducoté becomes gloomy. Then Chanvin speaks up, describing the "treatments" that Carlyle forced on his wife.

"Really," exclaimed Ducoté, "if it takes such oddities as that to prove one's greatness, I wonder what good I am. . . ."

"Good Lord," I say, "now Ducoté is worrying about being too good to his wife."

But my joke does not divert him enough, and for several moments the gentle Ducoté bewails his lot.

12 January

Spent yesterday evening with Jules Iehl. It is the first time I have talked with him alone. Wonderful figure of Iehl, perhaps the most remarkable of this whole "generation" (I mean of this whole group) and I was about to write: of all of us.

Since he works in his office until eight o'clock, I wait for him at the door and together we go to dine in a little restaurant opposite the Café Voltaire.

During the whole dinner, forgetting to eat, he talks. (I have noted elsewhere the tale of his relations with Mme Audoux's niece.)

"But," I say when he has finished, "why don't you write all this down? Just as you have told it to me. . . . It's just as beautiful as *Krotkaïa*. [9]

"Oh!" he replies, "what will you say when I tell you the story of

---

[8] *Men of Letters,* a novel also known by its subtitle, *Charles Demailly* (1860).

[9] A fragment of Dostoyevsky's *Journal* for November 1876, translated by C. Garnett as "A Gentle Spirit."

Madame Audoux? Yes, I shall write that one up, because I played no part in it. It's odd, but I have no desire to write, or more exactly, I *cannot* write a story except when I am out of it altogether."

We talk of death. He says he does not fear it. I tell him of my continual "expectation of the worst."

"I understand that very well," he continues; "but . . . no, I know nothing of that feeling. . . ." He is silent a moment; then softly: "And that's because I have always lived the worst. Yes, the only surprising thing that could happen to me is happiness."

He says this without any pose whatever, just as naturally as he said all the rest.

I have a sort of respect for Iehl. That is to say that I need his esteem.

This Sunday morning the weather is beautiful; I go out at about eleven, take a bus at random, then another one to get closer to the rue Beaubourg. Still full of Iehl's stories, I want to *check* on the places. I arrive at the rue Étienne-Marcel, find the rue Rambuteau, finally the rue Beaubourg, the sorriest and most amusing of streets.[10] But it is late and I can only glimpse what I promise myself to return and see this very afternoon.

At two o'clock received a visit from André Beaunier, who tells me about Petersburg and Moscow.

At three o'clock I return to the Saint-Martin quarter and prowl until nightfall in extraordinary alleyways full of disreputable or shady hotels in which I lodge all the mystery that I should like to know. (Rue de Venise, among others.) Then to the Morgue; wonderful Quai d'Anjou (the Lauzun house, etc.). Quai de Béthune; Notre-Dame. Numbers 1 and 3 on the Quai d'Anjou, that's the house I should most like to live in.[11]

13 January

I bring back to Em. an admirable "Captain Christy," which, all evening, provides as much pleasure as a picture. Calm evening. Em. is reading the Goncourt brothers' *Outamaro*. I play César Franck and then read *Les Hommes de lettres*, in order to learn how not to write.

14 January

The Captain Christy has opened out; very vulgar; absolutely "risen from the ranks," as Em. says.

---

[10] Until 1939 the narrow, filthy streets of the Saint-Martin quarter with their Renaissance houses were among the most picturesque in Paris. This section has now been remodeled.

[11] The Quai d'Anjou and the Quai de Béthune are on the charming Île Saint-Louis, behind Notre-Dame.

We learn of the death of Georges Widmer's granddaughter. She was six weeks old. Em., making a round of visits, informs Mme Walckenaër of the sad news.

"Good heavens! And I have just sent them my card to congratulate them on the birth. . . ."

"But, my child," exclaims another elderly lady paying a visit, "if there was nothing written on it, it can do just as well as an expression of condolence."

Beaunier. His smile, his laugh seem, after each sentence, to beg your pardon. He is one of the most *embarrassed* people I know.

15 January
This morning Léon Blum reads me the first act of his play (*La Colère*).[12]

Today Molière takes his revenge for the fact that Blum has always preferred Marivaux to him.

Finished *Charles Demailly*. It is a hateful book full of remarkable good points.

The word *"naturiste"* is found in *Outamaro* (pp. 112 and 116).[13]

Masaccio is the *"naturiste"* painter (*Italie d'hier*, pp. 111 and 134, written in 1855).

16 January
This morning I feel well; I awake ready for anything; my mind lively, my head clear, and *full of receptivity*. I ought to go and see Roger Marx, but cannot make up my mind to give to others these perfect morning hours. Walk avenue de l'Opéra. Visit to the Louvre (hall of French sculpture). Although my eyes hurt me (because I kept on, last night, reading César Franck with the light in my eyes), I feel a visual appetite that makes of each glance a delight. What I see goes to my head at once. I danced in front of the Houdons, wept in front of the Rudes, pranced in front of the Carpeaux. I should have liked to take Em. back there immediately.

---

[12] *Wrath.* Apparently this play was never either produced or published.

[13] The short-lived "naturist" school began to appear in 1895 as a revolt against the hermetic poetry of symbolism with its back turned to life. Maurice Le Blond and St.-Georges de Bouhélier led the group that in 1897 founded the monthly *Revue naturiste*. But rather than an artistic doctrine they represented an ethic, to which André Gide felt a natural sympathy and was inevitably linked because of his *Paludes* (1895) and *Nourritures terrestres* (1897). Yet he refused, as always, to be classified.

17 January

Fontainas has been suffering from rheumatism for a month. But I just learned this yesterday. I hesitate to go and see him for fear that in return, as soon as I am ill, he may call on me.

In his study, the sweet and stale odor of medicines. Dulled by salicylate, he hasn't been able to do anything for a month, he says. He complains that his brain is still stupefied; this is apparent, moreover; and since he has never been a brilliant conversationalist (nor I either), every few minutes there is a great silence that we break only by the most desperate efforts.

He is getting a novel ready, but excuses himself from talking about it for fear of spoiling it. He questions me about Charmoy, whom Griffin has done anything but recommend to him. I tell him the whole story. He accompanies me to the door. He is enormous and rather bloated. But apart from that, a good fellow; stifled by his own virtues.

Marvelous return from Passy on the river-boat.

The first act of *Alceste* at the Schola. Endless concert. *Alceste* comes too late on the program, when the public is already tired. And I must confess that my emotion is less keen than it was at Cuverville when I played *Alceste* to myself on the piano. The wonderful linear proportion is not sufficiently obvious in the orchestra; one's mind constantly loses the measure and the whole thing becomes a succession of emotions. . . . Gluck loses a great deal in not being acted out. On the stage the acting constantly brings out or recalls the happy proportions of the ensemble, and the harmony is not simply temporal. Gluck's music adds a fourth dimension to the three dimensions of the stage. To sing an aria from Gluck at a concert is all right; but sing a whole act — and I just don't listen.

18 January

I am feeling well. My mornings, my days, my evenings are almost empty; in other words, as full as I could wish of meditation, of work, of reading. I almost never open my piano any more, unwilling to give it only a few minutes each day, and equally unwilling just now to give it any more time. I begin each day by persuading myself that this day is very important; I am easily persuaded of this, moreover. More health, more calm, more clairvoyance. Why should the artist's famous "fatality" always be blind? Oh, clairvoyant fatality! Understand, love, aid the force that drags you on. . . . I eat less, smoke hardly at all, drink almost nothing but water. . . . (Yet last night, about to meet Émile X., I felt so trembling, so full of anguish, that I had to go into a café and drink two glasses of whisky. . . . I could go no farther.)

What an odd winter we are having! So little cold that I expect to see the branches leaf out any day. I must absolutely return to the Louvre this afternoon. Cremnitz told me where I should look for the Clodions. . . . I am reading all of Goncourt at one time; that is to say, I am in the midst of Jules's letters, their *Journal*, and Delzant's study of their work. . . . What vulnerable natures! . . . I have reflected a great deal about them and around them; but to note down, no matter how roughly, what I think would force me to write slowly again, and that is above all what I want to avoid here.

Émile X. used to work in his father's tailoring shop. But for the last two months the fact that they are working on half-time leaves him free almost every day. And every day he spends his whole afternoon at the baths. He gets there at one and stays until seven. Is that why he is as beautiful as a Greek statue? He swims remarkably well; and nothing so much as swimming imposes a rhythm, a harmony on one's muscles, or so hardens and lengthens them. Naked he is perfectly at ease; it is when clothed that he seems awkward. In his workman's clothes I hardly recognized him. Most likely he also owes to the habit of nudity the dull and even luster of his flesh. Everywhere his skin is blond and downy; on the hollows of his sacrum, exactly on the spot where ancient statuary puts the little tuft on fauns, this slight down becomes darker. And indeed yesterday afternoon, in the Praxiteles pose, his shoulder leaning against the wall of the pool, firmly and most naturally planted like the Apollo Saurochtonus, with his slightly snub-nosed and mocking face, he looked like a latter-day faun.

He is fifteen; one sister and one brother; all that remains of eleven children.

At the Louvre, a very long visit to the prints of the Far Eastern Museum; then, going out and entering again through the second court, I look in vain, among the Renaissance sculpture, for the Clodions that Cremnitz told me about. For a moment I loiter in front of the recent acquisitions (two small children's busts by Houdon, a bust in terracotta by Falconet, and, in a glass case, some very interesting clay models by Carpeaux). Then I launch on a tour of discovery in the upstairs rooms, reach the new exhibits of period furniture, and finally in the last of them I descry the *Bacchante* I am looking for, "attributed to Clodion," in white marble rather than terracotta as I expected it to be, standing on a rather heavy "music box" decorated with bronze and black marble. I must confess that the reproduction had struck me as more beautiful than the original. This white marble hardly suits such warm lasciviousness. . . . And, going through a few collections of paintings, I loiter in front of a self-portrait of Géricault that the Louvre has just bought. In the gallery of Greco-Roman frescoes I encounter Vuillard and Vallotton.

Sunday

A trying day, which sets me back. Fortunately I was able to read and write until noon; then little Gérard P. came to lunch, and from then until evening I didn't have a minute to myself.

The hope of a more curious — that is, more indiscreet — conversation made me detain little Gérard until four o'clock. But with him I am like the cat of the fable who wanted to see the other side of the mirror. What seems depth or mystery in him is merely reflection.

Gérard is flabbergasted, on reading Michelet's *Louis XIV,* to learn that the King had so many mistresses. He boasts of not being influenced by anything. "I read this book" (*Les Aventures du Roi Pausole*),[14] he says, "and a quarter of an hour later I don't think about it any more; it's just as if I hadn't read it." He sees this as strength of character; I see it as insensitivity. A superficial relationship with people and things is enough for him. He never longs to say to anyone anything different from what he does say.

I do not expect any great surprises from him; and yet I don't expect much from him.

We go into the Guimet Museum. I had planned to spend the best part of the day there, but Gérard, aided by the absurd Sunday crowd, spoils my pleasure. I merely make a flying visit to make sure that I must come again.

At Jacques Blanche's house. Gradually night invades the huge calm studio.

Blanche tells me of his irritation, at lunch, at hearing that big fool Lebey constantly interrupt Barrès, without every suspecting that what he says interests only himself.

Left alone, Jacques Blanche and I go over our common friends and polish off certain celebrities. We take to pieces Bourget and Wyzewa, whom Blanche depicts moreover as two remarkable minds, "much more remarkable than their books would lead one to believe." That's too bad. Blanche asserts that all the great minds he has known were marvelous conversationalists. Ah, Jacques Blanche, my friend, how little regard you should have for me! You tell me that my way of talking is among those that interest you. I wonder, and have often asked you, what you could possibly find in it, when everything I say interests me so little myself, when, as soon as I begin a story, my only anxiety is to end it as quickly as possible.

---

[14] *The Adventures of King Pausolus,* a risqué, humorous novel (1900) by Gide's early friend Pierre Louÿs.

We talk of the Goncourts:

"According to what I have been able to verify," says Jacques Blanche, "nothing is less true than their journals. Of certain conversations in which I took part, which I remembered perfectly, I was sure of finding in their journals only the least noteworthy bits, and even then often completely falsified. I assure you, Gide, that they didn't know how to listen. There is a paragraph in which they speak of my father and me — why, it's ridiculous; they misunderstood everything. . . . Listen: I remember a wonderful dinner I enjoyed with my father, Edmond de Goncourt, and Sardou. Sardou was in such good form that he was staggering, dazzling; he talked, during almost the whole dinner, about the French Revolution; Goncourt didn't say anything, but kept making indignant gestures at my father; he seemed to be saying: 'Just listen to him! Just listen to him!' That evening we took Goncourt home in our carriage as we often did. As soon as we had left Sardou, Goncourt began: 'No! But did you hear him? . . . And he dares to relate, in front of *me*, Goncourt, the historian of the Revolution, me who — But it was teeming with errors. . . .' And I am certain," added Blanche, "that Goncourt was the one who was wrong; that Sardou was just as well informed as he about the period; and that Goncourt's annoyance came from the fact that Sardou eclipsed him. For at one moment in the dinner, Goncourt having attempted to contradict, Sardou had immediately 'nailed' him like an unprepared pupil. He didn't know how to listen. He didn't understand what was interesting. For instance, I have seen him with Princess Mathilde. The Princess was an astonishing woman; one of the most remarkable dramas I have ever witnessed was going on within and around her. That woman was in love with Popelin, wildly in love; she dreamed, as a way of avoiding a misalliance, of a sort of legitimate concubinage, with all the obligations and all the fidelities of marriage. My father and Goncourt were the only ones she took into her confidence. . . . Well, Goncourt saw nothing, felt nothing, understood nothing in all this; and despite the fact that everything was told him! He was not at all intelligent."

"But," I say, "the words that he puts into the mouths of various people, however false they may be according to you, are almost never uninteresting. Watch out, for the more you reduce his stature as a stenographer, the greater you make him as a writer, as a creator. . . ."

Then we talk of Hugo and, at Blanche's urging, I recite to him several passages from the *Contemplations* and the *Légende des siècles;* but I recite very badly and with a choking voice because he repeated to me a few minutes before the remark of (? — Henri de Régnier I suppose): "Gide does not like poetry." And I couldn't have proved this more conclusively if I had aimed to do so.

Dinner at the Charles Gides'. Returning home from dinner, irritated

and dejected at not having been able to work almost all day, I calm myself by writing these notes.

20 January

This afternoon Charles-Louis Philippe made me drink an accursed
glass of old marc-brandy, which gave me a splitting headache until evening. He is wearing the unbleached white smock worn by grocery clerks
and house-painters; leaving his office at once, he goes down onto the
street without a hat, delighted with any excuse to indulge in a half-
hour's loaf, and hustles me off to the corner pub. He is just right in this
get-up, looking like a man of the people and a wag.

Yesterday F. and he went to visit their "society women." He tells me
how far F. has got with his conquest and says: "The thing that excites F.
the most is that she wears very fine underthings. Yesterday when he
reached the panties and felt that they had lace on them, he couldn't
restrain himself; he became absolutely lyrical."

I show him the amazing passage in the Goncourt *Journal* (Volume
I, page 185, dated 17 May 1857) that was lifted bodily into *Charles Demailly* (I must copy it).[15] "Yes," says Philippe, "it's exactly the opposite
of what we think."

"I think," Philippe said another day, "that we must absolutely look
for something else. . . . Perhaps the sentiment of *justice* will be called
upon to play the same role with us that the picturesque played for the
romantics."

Théo Van Rysselberghe is worn out and irritated by his painting
(*Three Little Girls on a Sofa*).

"But — suppose you let it drop for a while?"

"Impossible! I can't stop thinking about it."

"Well then, work on it madly for a while."

"Impossible! . . . As soon as I touch it now, I spoil it. . . ."

His face is haggard with anxiety.

After dinner Philippe reads us the last two chapters of his *Père
Perdrix*.[16] The next to the last especially seems to us excellent; and
Philippe reads it very well.

---

[15] Gide did not copy the passage, which reads: "One can create only
during the cessation of moral activity. The emotions are contrary to the gestation of books. Those who create must not live. Regular, calm, peaceful days,
a bourgeois smugness, a cotton-nightcap composure are necessary for the creation of the grandiose, the turbulent, the dramatic. People who expend themselves in passion or in the jolts and jars of a restless life will leave nothing to
posterity and will exhaust their life in living."

[16] *Papa Partridge*, published in 1902.

I visit the Edmond R. family, taking roses for Clotilde, who is already unable to get up from her bed. Oh, what a sad visit! Received by the father, I feel as if he doesn't want to let me see Clotilde. He hardly lets me ask for news of her health. And all the time that he is talking to me, affecting a cordial jollity, I imagine what his face will soon be like, covered with tears, and I remember Octave's remark after the death of little Jules, Clotilde's brother: "I saw poor Edmond. . . . It's strange: he weeps like a peasant."

Great disappointment at the Guimet Museum. Second-, even third-class prints for the most part; and most of them without any indication of author or date; no classification at all. How can you find your way about? When the point is that you come here to learn your way about. I spend more than an hour there, though.

On the top deck of the bus that goes from the Trocadéro to the Gare de l'Est I read *Les Frères Zemganno*.[17]

Endless walk along the outer boulevards. . . . I think, or at least I spend plenty of time imagining, but without its sketching itself out, the vague novel I am dreaming of: that is, the *relations* among a dozen characters. But how long will I have the restraint not to talk about it?

21 January

This morning, letter from Marcel Drouin protesting against Philippe's last two articles. He is right. But each one of us, even without knowing it, works on the pedestal for his bust almost as much as on the bust itself. It's a question of placing oneself "in a good light."

Every morning I go to the Louvre, and I am at loose ends every Monday, when it's closed.

Spent an hour or two at J. C. Mardrus's. Mme Mardrus, charming, plays with her rings on the divan where I am half stretched out. J. C. Mardrus, in an old-fashioned dark-blue waistcoat speckled with white, under a vast camel's-hair dressing-gown, wide open, and which makes X. say as he comes in: "What! Are you ill?"

Mardrus relates: "Leaving the café, I meet Henri de Régnier. He *adds himself to me* for a time. . . ."

Mardrus cannot forgive Henri de Régnier for the fact that he is still writing "Schéhérazade."

Paul Valéry's affection; it is childlike and charming. No one understands friendship so nicely or has so much delicacy. I have the greatest affection for him; it takes everything he says to diminish it. He is one of my best friends; if he were deaf and dumb I could not want a better one.

---

[17] *The Brothers Zemganno*, by Edmond de Goncourt, published in 1877.

29 January

In perfect condition for work, for conversation . . . for anything at all. The annoying thing is that one is in form for everything at the same time, or for nothing. This morning, if I were to shine shoes, every stroke would be a stroke of genius.

At the offices of the *Revue blanche:* Bauer, Capus, Mirbeau, André Maurel, Alex. Natanson, Ghéon.

Bauer talks like a man who owes to his dimensions the respect with which he is listened to. He ends each one of his sentences, looks now at one, now at another, and directs his words to each one of us specifically. His hand stresses his words with gestures, but his fingers stick tight together as in a mitten; his eye likewise remains expressionless.

Capus talks intelligently, distinctly, in half-sentences that are enough.

Mirbeau is excessive, brutal, and succulent like his articles, and stupid like them.

The *Mémoires* of Cardinal de Retz. It is a long time since I have tasted such a joy. Strange style that seems made up entirely of substantives and verbs, and that walks on its heels. Related at one and the same time to Montesquieu and to Saint-Simon, but with more tight elegance than the latter.

1 February

Yesterday, with Em. to the Anatomical Museum and the Museum of Paleontology; pursued by the remark of the Goncourts: "At the Jardin des Plantes . . . very little outlay of imagination on the part of the Creator. Far too many repetitions of forms among the animals." (*Journal*, I, p. 231.)

The pettiness of a mind can be measured by the pettiness of its adoration or its blasphemy. Truly, those minds understood nothing about God. This ceases to be atheism and becomes sheer stupidity. Fancy being disappointed at not finding more absurdity! Seeking, and regretting not finding, a greater number of forms where those that exist *suffice;* where adaptation tends toward simplification, toward an ever greater partial standardization; this is the way beauty is slowly acquired. To be unable to admire economy, the suppression of the useless, as much as one would have admired fantasy, the inappropriate, and the gratuitous. . . . Sure indication of a limited intelligence that perceives only details, does not go beyond them, and, thinking it is composing, merely juxtaposes.

There is nothing more *illuminating* than to go from the hall of paleontology to the hall of comparative anatomy. Why do species disappear? . . . There is always a reason for their doing so. How many odd, irrational, monstrous forms nature originally proposes and later is obliged to drop!

At the *Mercure* a moment to take back Davray's manuscript (translation of Stephen Phillips's poor play: *Herod*, in which the emotions are dragged in only to support the gestures, just as Aaron supported Moses' arms).

Evening with Em. at the Comédie-Française: *Andromaque*. Great disappointment for the overproper Bartet. She remains a lady. The public applauds her scandalously. You feel that what they like in her is not style (about which they know nothing) but gentility. Her virtues are negative. Her value lies in her lack of faults.

Mounet was, most often, excellent.

As for the play, I must reread it at once. I was embarrassed by a sort of tragic persiflage.[18]

The great mistake of actors today, when they play Racine, is to try to emphasize the natural qualities where the art should be emphasized. Suzanne Desprès would like to act Phèdre because, as she says, she *feels* the role. . . . To begin with, it's Racine that one should feel.

2 February

It's less a thesis novel than a period novel that I fear, in what I can glimpse from F.'s recital. Oh, how badly he tells anything, that good fellow!

Quiet day with César Franck, Balzac (*Pierre Grassou*), Retz. Read aloud to Em. Laforgue's *Salomé*.

In the evening went to join Philippe and Chanvin at the Taverne. Dull evening; one of those evenings when, for want of something better to do, you smoke more than you talk.

Admirable views of Paris under the snow.

3 February

Again much piano (5 to 6 hours).

4 February

"There are," de Max tells me this morning, "only three roles in the classical theater that I have always longed to play: Orestes, Nero, and Polyeucte; and three historical costumes I should like to wear: Julian, Heliogabalus, and Henri III."

Decidedly I shall some day write *L'Échanson*.[19] I do not know why procurers have always been treated as monsters and vile creatures.

---

[18] Amusement at later finding this same remark in Voltaire. [A.]

[19] *The Chief Butler*. If Gide ever wrote this work, it has not been published.

Whatever you feel a vocation for seems beautiful. I dream of a wonderful drama on Joseph; and particularly of the prison scene: Joseph between the chief baker and the chief butler.

All along the way I read, I sip Retz's *Mémoires*. The liveliness of this style enchants me. I mark numerous passages, which this evening I read to Em.

5 February

This morning, on awakening, I enjoy seeing myself in the mirror. Good sign. On bad days I look at myself just the same, but my reflection seems odious to me.

My mind feels alert; my fingers are agile and do not retard my thought. On bad days I labor over my handwriting, and its malformation in turn deforms my thoughts. On bad days I don't keep myself from smoking, which gives the finishing touch to my stultification. . . .

From this I derive an argument, and the only one that satisfies me, in favor of my "immorality."

Last Tuesday, likewise, I was "brilliant." I mean that my ideas moved about in a lively way in my head and that I did not attempt to formulate more than one at a time. On bad days they all rush together, become tangled, and I have the greatest trouble untangling them.

And Wednesday, likewise, after an almost sleepless night, I felt clear-headed and alert.

Wonderful compositions for organ (*Three Chorales*) by César Franck, in which I plunge myself over and over again every evening.

Yesterday evening resumed Leconte de Lisle (*Massacre de Mona*); pure and perfect satisfaction.

Ghéon, after having wandered aimlessly for some time around the central markets last Tuesday, ended up between three and four in the morning (his train was to leave at six) in a wretched little café near the Pont-Neuf. Inside there were many pimps and tarts; and this wouldn't have been very odd were it not for the presence in such a group of an elderly gentleman, who would have seemed very respectable if he had not been decidedly in his cups. Very much the center of things because he was buying drinks; talking a great deal, footing the bill, acting as everyone's tool. The others amuse themselves by making him rage, laugh, or cry, according to their whim. At moments he seems to reach a decision, says: "I must be going," gets up, then sits down again, without any more effort of will to remain than to go. He lets them laugh at him, make fun of him, rob him; he protests a minute, then grovels. Around him, as part of the game, one pretends to pity him, another to treat him contemptuously; a prostitute pretends to be in love with him; they take off his hat; they pull his hair. . . . (Ghéon gives a spirited mimicry of the whole scene; at one and the same time he becomes the elderly gentleman, the procurers, the tarts; and since everything is in the way he does it, there is not much to write about it.)

Beside Ghéon a pimp had sat down who showed a great scorn for the others:

"It's disgusting; it's shameful," he said after they had just pinched a few more coins. "And would you believe it, sir, every evening the same scene takes place? Yes, the same scene. That gentleman comes here every evening. And every morning he doesn't get home until about six o'clock, and with sixty francs less in his pocket. It's disgusting!"

"Do you know who your elderly gentleman is?" I asked Ghéon. "He is THE WIDOWER."

Thursday, 6 February

In the morning, work; reading Retz and a few little reviews.

T. quotes admiringly some of Degas's remarks. Apropos of a painting representing, he says, "the princess (??) leaving the abode of her ancestors," by I don't know what painter:

"Do you know why the princess is getting the hell out? . . . Because she can't get along with the background."

Degas said likewise, in front of Besnard's *Arab Stable* (a large painting in which a horse, in the foreground, is rearing up, throwing on the ground a strangely purple shadow): "Do you know why the horse is rearing? . . . Because of the purple."

And T., in an ecstasy of admiration, quoted also, apropos of Gustave Moreau:

"He's a hermit who knows the train schedule," and also: "The lions he paints are chained with watch-chains." Or about Besnard: "He advances under our own power." Etc., etc.

Mme Valéry, exquisite in an Empire gown of moss-green velvet, her hair twice encircled by a ribbon. Very good evening, even though I have it in for every evening that upsets my schedule. You feel Valéry, on such days, to be so much better than he shows himself to be.

Josette Drouin tells us at length about her little niece, eight years old. Strange charm that poverty has for her. Her father, head of a factory, I believe, lets her play with the workmen's children; they are the only children she likes. She is not satisfied to give pennies to beggars; she must kiss and fondle their rags. A Negro juggler had taken his stand on the square; he was so filthy and ugly that everyone fled him; the little girl broke away from her family to cajole him affectionately. Finally, when her mother was dressing for some visit or other:

"Oh, Mamma," the child said, "don't put on your best dress. We are poor."

Friday, 7 February

At the *Revue blanche* around four o'clock I find W., with whom for the first time I make up my mind to have a rather long talk. He is a tall fat fellow, soft all over, with a sickly and rather vulgar appearance. I still can see nothing in him but a reflection and he interests me less when he talks than when he listens. He professes an exaggerated admiration for Fustel de Coulanges. "He is the only one," he says, "who frankly loathes the Barbarians." Useless, with W., to look for the proper tone, for he takes his from me without waiting for me to set it for him. Likable withal, unpretentious and striving more to efface himself than to dazzle, or even to be seen and to please. As a test I take him to see an extraordinary photograph of a Velázquez in Braun's window; a Velázquez in an English private collection that I had encountered only an hour before, when I had stopped some time in front of it; a very special Velázquez, in the manner of the *Christ at the Column*, entitled *The Woman with the Eggs*. The head of the woman is not what I like the most, but rather her hands, the objects in the foreground, the face of the child who has just come in to buy and receives all the sunlight in the shop. Head painted in the Zurbaran manner, without any concessions, without chiaroscuro, without semi-shadows; I mean without modulations or transitions, without any diffidence. . . . W. doesn't seem very impressed.

Saturday, 8 February

At old Papa La Pérouse's. His joy to see me again. He sadly reproaches me for not having come sooner. . . . He comes out onto the stairway with me, awkwardly holds my hand tightly clasped in his, then suddenly, not able to resist any longer, makes me go back up three steps and falls sobbing into my arms.

For not having gone to Petersburg I feel, not so much regret, as remorse. Giving yourself your word to do something ought to be no less sacred than giving your word to others.

9 February

Off for Brussels, with Gérard.

Return on the 12th at six a.m. This evening, the 13th, I find it very hard to pick up this journal again. Yet I should like to continue it until Cuverville. Little habits, such as Nietzsche recommends; but mine are too short-lived. They don't lead to anything good. I have not finished Turgenyev's correspondence; I have not finished Retz's *Mémoires*. . . . My time is cut up into too small bits. I am impatient to get to Cuverville. I am eager to be less disturbed.

On the quay at Antwerp, an endless procession of old horses, obviously going to the slaughterhouse; and as if in the normal course of events.

"What a *hecatacomb* they're going to make!" exclaims little Gérard. He also says *warf* and woof, and so on.

His mother, moreover, says: *pecunary, equalimity, renumerate,* etc.; and since her husband never corrects anyone. . . . Besides, she does not accept being corrected.

It is very adroit to persuade yourself that what bores you educates you.

There is plenty of claptrap in this. And that's what seems to me abominable. Racine is good enough to get along without being played up to the audience. Sardou isn't. The habit of playing mediocre dramatists makes the actor see his contribution as too important. He therefore uses the same artifice in presenting Racine's pure gold as in foisting upon us Sardou's tin-plate.

During the first two acts I was sobbing; I didn't think I could see it through, so great was my emotion. I thought I was admiring Sarah;[20] but I was especially admiring Racine; and there was no mistake about it in the following acts. I couldn't see it through, in fact, but because of my annoyance. As long as she remained in the tone of the first two acts, I was aware only of Racine. But with the beginning of the third there was nothing but Sarah. At the fourth I left. Plastically she was marvelous. And just as she is, despite all her shortcomings, she remains unique, incomparable. What she should have had is a Sardou with the qualities of a Racine; and an intelligent public that would not applaud her when she is at her worst.

Sunday

. . . I have in my body and mind all I need to be, and to keep from being, a "great man." If I only knew how to deceive myself. . . . But I am still looking for maxims. What shall I become at Cuverville?

. . . And with that self-esteem which I had painfully acquired through pride, I was fed up and disgusted. I strained my ingenuity to lose it, and this was not hard. Acquisitions are worth amassing only for the sake of spending them easily later on. I gave myself up therefore to debauch; and indeed it did not displease me to introduce a bit of system into it; I mean to work hard at it. I envied ——, who got nothing but pleasure from it; I also gave myself a lot of trouble.

---

[20] Sarah Bernhardt.

And I did not despise anything in me so much as my self-esteem; I intended to make it impossible and took pleasure in debasing myself. My hatred of all cowardice urged me on. When something within me checked me, I feared it might be fear, and I went ahead. At present I don't give a hang what I am or am not. I don't bother with that.

At La Pérouse's. Received by his wife, whom I had not seen in three years.

A moment later, M. T. arrives, Édouard Gide's piano teacher: full of animation, too young, red-headed, quick on the trigger. He knew very well that La Pérouse was out, and it was clear that he was not coming to see him. He rang three times like someone who was expected.

Mme La Pérouse exclaimed: "Oh! Who's ringing as if he owned the house?"

She went to open the door, and right away, from the hall, in a very loud voice, intended, certainly, for me to hear:

"Oh! how sorry Monsieur La Pérouse will be! Actually he is not coming back until seven thirty. He went to play chess with his friend Monsieur Dauphin, as he does every Sunday."

And, like every Sunday, M. T. seemed to know this very well. I recognized that I was in the way, but Mme La Pérouse began to talk of her grandson Pierre, doubtless eager to form my opinion. She talks endlessly about his studies, develops the reasons for taking him out of the École Alsacienne,[21] "where he was too easily at the head of the class.". . . And all the time that she is talking, M. La Pérouse's sad words ring in my ears, drowning out his wife's; and I saw again that wonderful figure saying to me, in the same calm voice in which he might have said: "It's a beautiful day": "My wife always lies. As soon as she opens her mouth, I think: Come now! Not a word of this will be true!"

Late February

Back from La Flèche.

The mere sight of the grass and the branches, even without leaves, rests me. I have had the keenest pleasure from walking, toward evening, on the uneven streets of the village. . . . Charming garden! How well I should work here, if I were alone!

This big avenue of linden trees inclines me, with Marcel Drouin, to serious conversations. Jeanne Drouin has had the shrubs rearranged;

---

[21] A very strict Protestant school in Paris, which André Gide attended as a boy.

a bed of rosebushes exhibits, in advance of the roses, its shining labels of yellow wood.

There I finish *La Fille sauvage*.[22] How badly M. de Curel writes! I read Saint-Simon all the way back. How Retz and he set themselves off to advantage!

I read as I should like to be read: very slowly. For me reading a book amounts to closeting myself with the author for a fortnight.

Fred Natanson, returning the manuscript of *Saül*,[23] thinks it necessary to add: "Besides, I have never read the Bible." It's odd the way all the educated Jews I know make a point of honor of never having read the Bible. . . . What the devil are they afraid of finding in it? Nothing annoys me more. It's like Schwob spreading papers over his mirrors. And this allows them not to admit their uglinesses; yes, but by the same token they miss their beauties. I must discuss this with Blum.

27 February

At last we are leaving! For the last fortnight I have been very impatient. Today, after last night's heavy rain, the air has suddenly become unbearably warm. Suddenly I long for Naples rather than Cuverville. I shall languish there.

Cuverville, 2 March

Went in the buggy to Beuzeville to fetch the gardener we had sent for. I read, or rather try to read, Balzac's *La Vieille Fille*,[24] but since leaving Paris three days ago, my mind is completely absorbed by the work to be done in the garden and I can think of nothing else.

My *Immoraliste* is already so far behind me that I cannot bring myself to correct the proofs.

3 March

Little Louis M.; very good, but so young! . . . He has just got out of the schools of horticulture, nursery techniques, etc. He is full of the new wine of his knowledge; it is important for him to show what he is worth and that he is not a mere workman but a sort of intellectual. He must have listened to his teachers attentively, for he recites their lessons endlessly. He says "English style" about a park, but Cuverville

---

[22] *The Wild Girl*, by François de Curel (1902), the most ambitious play by this philosophical dramatist, which traces the evolution of humanity through the example of the protagonist.

[23] André Gide's five-act drama about Saul and David, written in 1897 and published in 1902.

[24] *The Old Maid*, one of the stories that Balzac classified among his *Scenes of Provincial Life*.

has only a garden. Everything that is not "English style" is "French style" just as all that is not verse is prose. You can't get away from this, and Louis points out to me that I am asking for things that would not "suit the style." The paths must form a "graceful curve." The part of the garden in front of the house is not to his liking. "Do you wish to keep these little paths, sir?" he asks about the tracks that surround the lawn; and since I like very much those "little paths" that he scorns, I answer rather sharply:

"Of course," and after a pause I add: "But don't get the idea, Louis, that this garden is badly laid out or that it could be made prettier by giving it another character. It has the character of the house."

"It probably belongs to the period," Louis remarks, "when the two styles were beginning to merge."

23 March

The weather continues to be rainy, cold, and forbidding. But I am much better and, again, feel very fit for work.

Study of Schubert's Fantasie in C and Impromptus. I am reading Renan's *Souvenirs* and Stendhal's.

Since we have been here — that is, since the 2nd of March — without even excepting the two days in Paris, I have got up at six o'clock at the latest; almost every day I am at work at five thirty; and sometimes even at five o'clock. The day, according to the weather, is devoted, without a regular schedule, to gardening, reading, and piano-practice. The garden takes (and especially took in the beginning) an enormous amount of time. The drawing-room not being ready yet, Em. remains in the dining-room and I in my study; a fire is lighted in the two rooms and the big stove heats the rest of the house. Then dinner comes; in the evening we bring our lamps together.

25 March

Hellebores, lilies, and tiger-lilies have come from Holland. From seven in the morning until six in the evening I work in the garden without stopping.

27 March

Than that some day a young man of my age and my *worth* should be stirred as he reads me and *made over*, as I still am at thirty on reading Stendhal's *Souvenirs d'égotisme*, I have no other ambition. At least so it seems to me as I read this book.

Of my trip to Paris, too much to be said. Of my return here, not enough. Read a rather long speech by Brunetière on Calvin. We continue reading aloud Tolstoy's *Cossacks*.

Francis Jammes. He feels the need of constantly persuading you (or trying to persuade you) that he is much poorer, simpler, more modest, etc., than he is.

Read aloud with Em. Reshetnikov's wonderful *Those of Podlipovka*. We had just finished Tolstoy's *The Cossacks*. We wanted to read *Tess of the D'Urbervilles*, but dropped it for Michelet's *Revolution*.

Pierre Laurens's summary of *L'Immoraliste:*
"I am ill; woe to me. I am cured; woe to her!"

1903

Cuverville, April

These letters to write exhaust me, wear out my patience; they won't let me work. . . . No friendship matters in such a case; I would throw out the best friend. . . . But I don't. I always write eventually; to have peace, peace with myself; for, so long as I don't write, I reproach myself for not writing. The trouble is that when you write immediately, the one on the other end answers; and yet, until he has answered, I wait for his letter.

May
"This one," says Marius's young wife to Em. as she shows her about her little garden, "Marius told me this one's name: it is called *Rose Thé*."[1]

We are reading aloud *A Raw Youth*. At the first reading the book did not seem to me so wonderful; rather more complicated than complex, more involved than sustained, and, in short, more strange than interesting. Today I am filled with astonishment and admiration at every page. I admire Dostoyevsky more than I thought one could admire.

Yet it is important to know whether what one wants is called philanthropy or literature.

Georges reminded me of Mlle Siller's shocked amazement, two years ago, when she heard me say (to startle her, but in an offhand way): "And to think that if I didn't like literature so much I should already be in the Academy!"

* * *

August, 4 o'clock in the morning
In the train; this side of Rouen; banks of the Seine covered with mist. Early-morning joy. I repeat these words full of savor: early-morning joy. Only the tops of the haystacks in the flat fields rise out of a sea of pinkish blue fog; the air is inexpressibly pure; the sky's azure bathes the earth. My eyes, tired by a sleepless night, are washed in the vaporous surface of the river and drink from the milky slopes of the hills. All the plant-life in nature washes and bathes in the dawn, quickly, before the heat of the day. Here the dew becomes sap; the most seared of grasses becomes green again. If I had lost all I possess, everything I most

[1] *Rose Thé* simply means "tea rose."

cherish on earth, I should be no less happy this morning. I become grass among the grasses and take part in the communion of the awakening.

Even at the moment of leaving her, you were unable to hide your joy from her. Why were you almost annoyed that she could not hide her tears?

In the compartment this jovial priest begins half of his sentences with: "And I beg you to believe that . . ." He also says frequently: "I frankly confess that . . ." but, in this case, he adds: "to me personally. . . ."

The other travelers are certainly conservatives; their glance has a way of saying: "you won't catch me napping."

In the train, after Metz

Sad sky! Landscape bathed in horror! Above the low hill where you can see the shale through the grass, loiters a heavy downpour. Everything that is not green is coal-color. Everything is dripping.

Yesterday, from the emotion of leaving . . . I could have sobbed like a child. It was as if I were traveling for the first time. I was constantly wondering: Have I put myself to rights with my fate? . . . Is it my turn yet? I didn't use to be this way; my violent desires gave me rights over everything. I embraced everything within reach. Today I feel like the child who is acting "like a grown-up."

Weimar

I am always grateful to circumstances when they force me to do something that I should not have done on my own initiative.

Bad Kissingen, 7 August

Oh, full of promise and joy, blue morning sky, Apollo dwells in you and I feel your azure nearer me than your clouds of yesterday were. I am surrounded by it; I prosper in it; it soaks into me to the heart.

If only, in this indifferent crowd, there were some attractive face on which my eyes enjoyed gazing!

Oberhof seems delightful. One would like to bathe in its cascades.

Weimar

Kant's dove. Still better: the kite that thinks it could climb higher without the string. . . . Those children flying kites. . . . Am I amused by them, or are they amused by me? They were seated under this tree, just where I am now writing. Right now they are far away. If only I had dared to sit down beside them! . . . They are coming back. I pretend to be interested in what I am writing; but I am concerned only with them. . . .

Dull hours in the Frankfurt botanical garden. I note these names of beautiful climbing plants: *Rhodochiton volubile* with dark-purple heads; *Mina lobata*, gold and red in color; in the temperate greenhouse: *Lapageria superba rosea*, covering the ceiling; covered with flowers (in August). There is also a white variety. Much more beautiful than the passion-flower.

I could see through his forehead the narrowness of his ideas.

Blond hair; pure blue eyes like a *Vergissmeinnicht*. Though Mme Förster-Nietzsche was expecting me at five o'clock for tea, I tarried with the child, and a still younger child came to join him. We climbed up on a haystack; I hoisted them up onto the top and my clothes were soon full of bits of straw.

Mme Förster-Nietzsche, getting tired meanwhile of waiting for me, had started out in a carriage to look for me. In turn I started with the child to look for her. He accompanied me in the streets; he gave me his hand and talked constantly, in a full and transparent voice, although I understood but very little. When I went into Count Kessler's to pack my luggage (since I was to leave that evening), the child stationed himself, with two little comrades, on the steps of the house opposite; he was waiting; occasionally, from the window, I would wave to him, and he would reply laughing. He refused to believe in my departure, and when I spoke of it, he said: *"Es ist nicht wahr!"* Finally Mme Förster-Nietzsche's big landau called for me; I went down. Mme Förster-Nietzsche was in the carriage. I almost made the children get in. The tall footman covered with braid who helped me into my coat dazzled them; I was aware that they took me for a prince; and when I turned around for a last farewell, I saw my little friend weeping.

Sunday, back in Paris.

1904

At the banquet for Edmund Gosse, Verhaeren is seated between Maeterlinck and Henri de Régnier; Verhaeren to Maeterlinck (in a whisper):

". . . Besides, in my case . . . I can confess this to you . . . in reality, the only writing that interests me is my own."

And Maeterlinck: "That's just like me . . . moreover, even what I write doesn't interest me much any more."

Whereupon Verhaeren, giving a jump: "Oh, just a minute! That's not the same thing at all. What I write interests me passionately — passionately, you understand . . . and that's the very reason why I am no longer much interested in the writings of others."

It is Verhaeren himself who tells this, the next day, in Théo Van Rysselberghe's studio. He adds:

"And a little later Maeterlinck told me also: 'What's more, I now work only out of habit.'"

As soon as we have finished *Michael Kohlhaas,* we launch into *Die Marquise von O. . . .*[1] Certainly I have made some progress. In Latin likewise. This morning I read with a little greater facility some of Pliny's letters and some of Catullus' verses. I want to go back to Sallust as soon as I have finished correcting the German translation of *Philoctète.*[2] What a bore to have to prepare that lecture: "On the theater."[3] And what I think about the theater interests me so little myself! — What I think is so unimportant to me!

With what delight I have taken up Montaigne again! I feel wonderfully well. A good sign: I again wept copiously yesterday as I read the chapter *"Sur des vers de Virgile"*[4] and (it's silly to admit it) the German translation of my *Philoctète.*

Read also, and reread aloud to Em., the wonderful page written within sight of Jerusalem in *Les Destinées de la Poésie,*[5] certainly the

---

[1] These are both stories by Heinrich von Kleist.

[2] *Philoctetes, or the Treatise of the Three Ethics,* drama in five acts by André Gide, was published in 1899 and translated into German in 1904 by Rudolf Kassner.

[3] His lecture *The Evolution of the Theater,* given in Brussels, 25 March 1904, was published the same year. It contains the first mention in France of Kierkegaard.

[4] Montaigne's essay "On some Lines of Virgil" which forms Chapter V of Book III.

[5] "The Destinies of Poetry."

best thing I know by Lamartine (in prose); and in the preface to the *Méditations* the so amusing passage about La Fontaine.

This evening my head is splitting as a result of staying up so late. Came in at two in the morning. That dancing-place where I took Kassner is disgraceful. I took away from there nothing but fatigue and disgust.

At the offices of the *Revue des idées*,[6] where I had gone to inquire about the fate of Marcel Drouin's articles. Dujardin and Gourmont are there, whom I have not seen since . . . (?) Long before meeting Gourmont, I knew, I had a premonition that in his presence I should feel this discomfort, or rather this hostility. He has always been very considerate with me. But what can I do about it? I have read things by him that reveal a keen mind, a solid intelligence. . . . I collect my thoughts, reason with myself, stiffen myself. This time too I wanted to see him again and I approached him beaming with smiles. But I cannot: he is too ugly. I am not speaking of his superficial misfortune; no, but of a deeper ugliness. I declare that I already knew him to be ugly simply from reading him.

And I try to understand a little better the reason for my suffering in his presence. It comes, I think, even upon reading him, from the fact that with him thought is never a living, suffering thing; he always remains somewhere beyond it and handles it like an instrument. His reasonings, for he does reason and very well, are never involuntary. His thought never bleeds when he touches it; and this is what allows him to operate on it so easily. He brutalizes. What a heartless surgeon! And how I suffer in his presence! That abstract matter that he seizes remains so alive in me! I made great efforts to talk calmly with him. Quinton arrived . . . and I left.

The discomfort, the suffering that I experience on hearing them talk does not come only from my mind's difficulty in following them, but also, and especially, from a more subtle cause. There is, for thought too, an appropriate beauty, a grace, the lack of which always causes me a certain uneasiness. In their company I think irresistibly of men who, when lifting weights, exercise only their biceps. I do not like big strong arms, I like a harmony of the whole body. Likewise a certain harmony of the mind. As I grow older I can less easily get along without it.

This evening I reread aloud, for Em., *"Il Viccolo di Madama Lucrezia."* [7] How thin it is! hardly appropriate, and what a secondary quality

<hr>

[6] A monthly review (1904–13), edited by Édouard Dujardin and Remy de Gourmont, which was more concerned with philosophy and the sciences than with literature.

[7] "Madame Lucrezia's Alleyway," a short story by Mérimée.

perfection seems here![8] On the other hand some *excellent* letters to Panizzi.

"The maximum of satisfaction is reached when the final uses of the last objects consumed are equal."

Sentence by (?) that my uncle comments on excellently in his *Traité d'économie politique* (latest edition).[9]

Formulated in this way it is not very clear.

An equilibrium must be established; and the sensual pleasure derived from the object must be at the same degree of dulling and of wear.

". . . since no luminous body has ever seen the shadow of the body that it lights . . ." (Leonardo da Vinci: *Treatise on Painting*, Ch. cccxxviii.)

3 May

Met Blanche in the Luxembourg; I was with Jaloux, who had just arrived from Marseille. Blanche was with I don't know whom.

Every time I meet Blanche, I feel immediately that I am not wearing the proper necktie, that my hat has not been brushed, and that my cuffs are soiled. This bothers me much more than what I am about to say to him.

Have I already noted somewhere the conversation he had with Régnier? I was there and I heard this:

"Oh, my friend, what stunning trousers you have on! Where did you get them?"

And Régnier, considerably irritated, replied with dignity and roguishness:

"From the cleaner's."

De Groux could not swallow (following other grievances) the fact that Léon Bloy should say and repeat to him:

"You must, you see — you must vomit yourself — on others."

For two years, ever since I first heard it, I have been analyzing the meaningless remark of Odilon Redon, that aphorism or axiom which he hands out as advice to the young, that maxim on which his whole æsthetic hangs, it seems: "Closet yourself with nature."

---

[8] I have since reread (Nov. 1909) the excellent *Arsène Guillot*. [A.]

[9] *Treatise of Political Economy* by Charles Gide, published in its original form in 1884.

At the Van Rysselberghes' the conversation turned to children's sayings. Although usually such "bright sayings" tend to set my nerves on edge, I note here those that seemed to me best.

Little Bonnier, when asked what he did in school:

"I wait for teacher to let us out."

Francis Y.'s family tries to move him to pity Christ's sufferings on the cross and to arouse his indignation against the bad men who nailed him there. He looks at the crucifix hanging on the wall, and:

"He wouldn't have held if they hadn't nailed him."

When he was spanked, little Gérard used to say as he wept: "It's a pity!"

Among the most charming sayings are those of little Élisabeth, Théo Van Rysselberghe's daughter. One day she cuts herself and, terrified at seeing her blood flow, runs to her parents screaming:

"I'm losing all my sauce!"

When she was learning to read, they aided her memory in every way possible; they used to say: A for Alice, B for Bertha, T for Théo, etc. When next day, as she repeats her letters, they ask: "T for what?" she exclaimed at once: "T for Papa." [10]

Cuverville

Yesterday at Mont Roti. The children draw me even more than the heath. No real village; just a few houses flat against the hill. The road passes at the foot. Immediately recognized in my pilgrim's cloak, a flock of children escort me and, when I sit down on the heath, form a circle around me. In the folds of my cloak, just as last year, little Joseph snuggles up. That child is frightful; he doesn't even know how to smile. His sister is there, pale and puny; no taller than a blade of wheat. A little brother, who wasn't walking yet last summer, is with them; Joseph used to carry him on his shoulders; his name is René; he achieves the paradox of having an enormous forehead and looking like an idiot; he smiles for anything at all, and as soon as he stops smiling looks deeply serious. The destitution of these children is such that pity doesn't know where to begin; they ought to be completely outfitted from head to foot. (I didn't see the one who looked like a vegetable last summer; he had fallen into the soup and one side of his face had boiled.) I show them the illustrations of a La Fontaine that I had in my pocket; but I don't know how to talk to them.

---

[10] Written later in the margin: At a children's party where each one is asked what he would like to do later in life, little Claude Laurens declares suddenly: "I shall marry a very ugly woman." And, amidst the general stupor, he adds: "To get a good laugh out of my friends." [A.]

On my way back, a sea fog rolled in; in a short while the whole land-scape was covered with it. How beautiful it would have seemed to me if I had not tarried on the heath!

While walking I wrote a note to André Ruyters in a pale-green note-book.

Just now I can see, from the window of my room, the bleak fields under a low gray sky. They are being plowed. Circling crows follow the plow, swoop down, seize the grub-worms. . . . I am sure they are leaving some.

20 August

Marius's young wife died while Jeanne and Mathilde were with her. Marcel and I started out to join them a little later. On the way we talked of other things. At the door Marius, red and sobbing, was a pitiful sight; we embraced him; he held out his knife to me, opened it, and said: "We'll need all the white lilacs you can gather." The old mother kept repeating as she wept: "How fortunate that the ladies were here! What would we have become without them?" Then I was ushered in. The room was tidy and filled with a new silence; near the window Mathilde and Jeanne were folding a sheet; on the bed the dead woman still had a bit of false color in her cheeks, but the hands holding an ebony cru-cifix were made of wax. Propped against the crucifix, a few white flowers.

This morning the priest had brought her the last sacraments; wasn't it enough that she had received communion the day before? She didn't expect to die yet. When she saw the priest come in, she was seized with trembling. "Oh! am I going to die already?" she asked. "My child," re-plied the priest, "this never killed anyone. Besides, God may perform a miracle for you." From that moment on she began to be excited. But Jeanne took her hand and said softly: "Last night I had a beautiful dream, Marie; I dreamed that both of us were in paradise. . . ." That was the moment when she went to sleep; it seemed as if she had been waiting to hear that word before dying.

8 September

Yesterday, at Dieppe with Henri Ghéon, saw Walter Sickert again. He said to me: "Do you remember that the first time you met me you asked: 'I hope it doesn't annoy you that I like your painting?'"

It's quite possible. I imagine that if I were a painter the compli-ments of literary men would be too much to bear.

A childhood recollection of Jean Schlumberger: He was about eleven; in the tub in which he was bathing they put also his little brother Maurice, only five years old. After the bath Jean, now dressed again, thoughtlessly says to his parents:

"It's funny how much more people love each other when they are naked."

After that remark they never let him share his bath.

The number of things that are better left unsaid increases for me every day.

"Perhaps the most extraordinary thing about the need of the extraordinary is that, of all the needs of the mind, it is the easiest to satisfy." (Nodier: *Ossianisme. — Examen critique des dictionnaires.*) [11]

September

A frightful storm raged last night. This Friday I was to cross from Havre to Honfleur, meet Jean Schlumberger, and lunch with him. Thursday evening I send him a telegram to postpone the meeting.

Why weren't we at Étretat last night! Yesterday I thought of it but did not dare suggest it to Marcel and Ghéon. Today Jeanne has to go there; I go with her.

The fishing boats are pulled up in the streets, and on the beach everything has been swept away. The sea, still very heavy, is withdrawing now. Yonder, in the direction of the Chaudron, a swarm of children and women are gathering up the wreckage of bathhouses, boardwalks, and springboards.

The big linden tree in the garden had its biggest branch broken; the whole garden seems devastated as a result; the sea wind has scorched the leaves and the rain rotted all the flowers.

November

Since 25 October 1901, the day on which I finished *L'Immoraliste*, I have not seriously worked. My article on Wilde,[12] my lecture in Germany,[13] the recent one in Brussels (which did not amuse me and which I gave very badly) [14] don't count. A dull torpor of the mind has made me vegetate for the last three years. Perhaps, busy in my garden, in daily contact with the plants, I have taken on their habits. The least sentence costs me an effort; talking, moreover, is almost as painful as writing. And I must admit too that I was becoming difficult: at the least suspicion of a thought, some cantankerous critic, always hiding deep in

---

[11] *Ossianism — Critical Examination of French Dictionaries* (1828).
[12] Written in December 1901 for the first anniversary of Wilde's death.
[13] *On the Importance of the Public*, given at Weimar on 5 August 1903.
[14] *The Evolution of the Theater*, given 25 March 1904.

my mind, would rise up to ask: "Are you sure that it's worth the trouble to . . . ?" And, since the trouble was enormous, the thought immediately withdrew.

The trip to Germany last summer shook off my apathy somewhat; but as soon as I got back here, it took a deeper hold on me. I accused the weather (it rained incessantly that year); I accused the air of Cuverville (and I still fear that it exerts a soporific influence over me); I accused my routine (indeed, it was very bad; I never left the garden, where, for hours on end, I would *contemplate* the plants one after another); I indicted my morals (and how could my utterly stagnant mind have triumphed over my body?). The fact is that I was becoming stultified; no enthusiasm, no joy. Eventually, seriously worried, intent on shaking off that torpor to which was added an unhealthy restlessness, I convinced myself and convinced Em. that nothing but the diversion of travel could save me from myself. To tell the truth, I did not convince Em. I was well aware of this, but what could I do? Go ahead anyway. I therefore resolved to go. I almost killed myself in efforts to justify my conduct; going was not enough for me; in addition Em. had to approve of my going. I hurled myself against a disheartening wall of indifference. No, I did not hurl myself; I sank in; I lost my footing; I was engulfed. I know well enough today and already suspected then the lamentable misunderstanding caused by Em.'s voluntary (and yet almost unconscious) — abnegation (I can think of no other word to describe it). It contributed not a little to demoralizing me. Nothing more painful than the exaggeration of my restlessness, of my feelings, etc., to overcome that indifference. Fortunately, the memory of all that is fading now. . . . But if I had to relive my life, I could not see that period approach without anguish. . . .

And all the same, I started out (leaving behind minutely detailed instructions for the setting out of fruit trees that Croux was to send somewhat later). I started out, then (as well as I can remember, the 10th of October), and first took Dominique back to his parents in Bordeaux. I planned to reach Africa by way of Spain; the ships' sailings did not permit this. My horror of ocean-crossings almost made me hesitate; but in Marseille, where I arrived around six in the morning, the radiant weather and the lack of wind made up my mind for me and I reserved my berth for the afternoon of the same day.

I was planning a book on Africa; I had not been able to write it at Cuverville from the very insufficient notes I had brought back from the trip with Em. and Ghéon. I had to see the country again. I set out with the intention of writing from day to day. Considerations, reflections, all that can be added later; what cannot be recaptured or invented is the sensation.

It is from this trip that I brought back the notes that I put together (almost without changing a word) on my return to Cuverville.[15] Em. joined me in Algiers more than a month after my departure. That month of solitude put me back on my feet; then the calm life that we lived together left nothing but good memories. In Algiers, and during the rest of the trip, I was able to read the first volume of Nietzsche's *Correspondence*, and that book contributed not a little to my equilibrium. In Algiers also I read *Les Vacances d'un jeune homme sage*,[16] a rather ordinary book that had just appeared, and the delightful *Enfant à la balustrade*,[17] which I immediately reread to Em. Then, as soon as we reached Biskra, we began *Der Geheimnissvoll* by Tieck, which I found in the hotel library. Each of us separately read the dialogue "*Vom Tragischen*," which Bahr had just sent me.[18] In Rome we bravely launched into *Michael Kohlhaas*, which we did not finish until Paris, when we immediately took up *Die Marquise von O.* . . .

We had frightful weather for crossing Sicily and did not see the sun again until Rome. In Naples, or rather at Sorrento, I went to see the mysterious Vollmœller (I have described that visit at some length in a letter to Drouin). In Rome I found Maurice Denis, but Mithouard was always at his elbow and I did not see him as much as I should have wished. On the other hand, I saw Jean Schlumberger every day and, as we treated each other with ever greater confidence, he came to be one of my inner circle of friends.

---

[15] *Le Renoncement au voyage* (*Renouncing Travel*), published in 1906.
[16] *A Nice Young Man's Holidays*, by Henri de Régnier (1904).
[17] *The Child at the Banister*, by René Boylesve (1903).
[18] An essay "On the Tragic" by Hermann Bahr.

1905

Oreste's character: [1] not really virile, but dominated completely by his fate. He needs his crime to motivate his remorse.

He is among those on whom hangs a fatality — that is, who feel they have a mission to fulfill. Born under the sign of Saturn, obviously. Nothing can be done about it. He will accomplish his task to the bitter end, and he knows it. But it will be hard because he has against him *his own nobility* and the responsibility that Greece has conferred on him. Murder attracts him irresistibly and he has a sacred horror of murder. As soon as Hermione suggests it to him, a sudden thrill warns him that this is indeed his fate. It is a thrill of horror; and yet it is almost a thrill of joy.

All this leads, in the last act, to *a sort of wild joy*, of satisfaction, of repose; but of *mistaken repose*. He thinks he has reached haven. The lines here are wonderfully contrived to deceive us: *"Grâce au ciel,"* etc.

The words "happiness" and "unhappiness" can be used almost indifferently here; it's a relaxing of the nerves after the crime as after an ejaculation. Yet a certain restlessness, a need to keep thinking of the crime. . . . When *suddenly* madness and the seizure of epilepsy grip him just as he wants to get away from himself. It's a curtain that falls around him, a twilight curtain that ensnares him as Clytemnestra's net enveloped his father Agamemnon. He will not escape.

It does not seem to me absolutely necessary to bellow the last lines. I can easily imagine Oreste as almost crushed already, still struggling like a wounded bull; rising up for:

"Tiens! Tiens! voilà le coup que je t'ai réservé."

Then, utterly calm and conquered, *waiting for* the supreme suffering: *"Eh bien, filles d'Enfer! . . ."*

The little square near the Invalides, 20 March

Shall I rest in this garden? Yes, I go in and, even if only for a minute, sit down. Already, I remember, I had sat here last year. It was summer; the air was hot; I was perspiring and had a headache. I enjoyed a few delightful moments here. I was on my way to see, or had just seen, Arthur Fontaine. What book was I reading? It is odd that I don't remember. I must not have read much, for I recall the color of the flowers in the bed in front of me; today it is full of daisies. They are the first flowers of the year; they refresh my mind. But M. occupies too much of

---

[1] One of the protagonists of Racine's *Andromaque*.

my thought; everything in my head is burning and tired. How tired I am! How charming are the songs of those birds! How refreshing is this grass!

I read in the *Dictionnaire des biographies* — under Heliodorus: "In the time of Pliny there could still be seen in Rome, on the porticoes of Octavia, Heliodorus' masterpiece: it was a *symplegma;* in other words, a group representing a struggle between Pan and Olympus (?)."

22 March

Eighteen years ago de Max told me: "You smile with your eyes; you will wear out your face."

"What should I smile with?" I asked him, somewhat surprised.

"Merely with your lips," he went on; "just look at me."

"Theatrical smile," I read today in Stendhal's *Journal* (14 July 1804), speaking of Napoleon's smile, "in which the teeth are shown, but the eyes do not smile."

22 April

I realize that my health is better from the fact that the desire and the need to write have seized me again. Not a need to work, which, indeed, has never left me, but that sort of immediate and involuntary transposition of sensation and emotion into words. If I had been alone today, I think I should not have ceased writing all day.

I can barely scribble these few words this evening in bed. On my night-table, Stendhal's *Journal*.

Montauban. — Copied from Ingres's Notes, 1841

"The adolescents on the edge of the painting to set beauty on the right. That beauty which charms and enraptures and keeps one from noticing the details of the human body . . . the limbs should be, so to speak, like the shafts of columns.

"*Thus the masters of the masters.*"

"But," Boylesve tells me genially, "I write just for people like you. What do we want, after all? Three or four thousand readers. . . ."

"That's much too many."

Hendaye

Less fatigued I should probably have devoted, every day, several pages simply to praising this landscape. Yet I was not in love there with anything or anyone; but the azure-tinted light, that indefinable wild scent amidst the thick lushness of spring. . . .

In beach sandals I almost ran all the way to Urrugne. I was holding M.'s letter in my hand. The sun was dazzling. The hour went by and I was still alive. On the heights, along the slopes, asphodels grew abundantly; not that many-branched asphodel of the moors in the Gard region or of the sacred purlieus of Syracuse, but rather bearing its flowers on a single stem like tritomas.

The day before yesterday on the rocks, near Vera, we had gathered some heather with globular blossoms the color of digitalis, almost each one alone on its stem and so large that it seemed to bend the stem down.

On these rocks and on the embankments along the road a vigorous creeping plant with blue flowers (of that deep blue that I had never seen except in gentians, and which Jammes says is a gentian in fact) dots the grass with tiny gulfs of night. One's eye plunges voluptuously into them.

At San Sebastián, on the square, we ordered Spanish chocolate, thick and strongly flavored with cinnamon; it is served in little cups, much too small to my way of thinking. Jeanne claims she cannot endure Spanish chocolate, so she asks for a French chocolate. Almost at once she is brought some of this chocolate; yes, the same. But the cup is much bigger and Jeanne declares it to be excellent. Em. is willing to try the Spanish chocolate, but shudders at the thought of the cakes made of eggs. And since I am irritated to see them both so resigned (or decided) to enjoy this country only through their eyes or, at most, to taste it with the tip of their tongues, I thought as I sank my teeth into that oily, curdled, saffron-flavored paste that I was biting right into Spain itself; it was terrible.

After thirty-five you are easily tempted to ascribe to age the least effect of fatigue, and even to prolong it by refusing to consider it at first as a passing discomfort.

My low physical condition of late (it had lasted for almost three weeks). I seriously began to think that I should never get over it.

Already I had accepted the inevitable, resigned to a half-life; writing had become a chore to which my will alone forced me; life had lost its savor.

Bordeaux

I am writing in order to look as if I were writing, in this small barbershop from which the summer heat is shut out; the physical charm of this hour; the barber's silent bustle; a fly occasionally annoys me.

Sunday

Back from Bordeaux. Arrived this morning at seven. If it were my house in Auteuil, I should return home with greater pleasure. In this

apartment on the boulevard Raspail every book, every new sheet of paper, increases the confusion and disorder. My thought cannot stretch
out comfortably anywhere in it. At eleven o'clock I go out on the boulevards to meet Vollmœller, with whom I have an appointment. He
doesn't improve with use. He has a memory obviously, but he's a fool. I
can no longer afford to take very cheerfully two hours of my precious
time, or give them, simply in order to flatter someone, to "listen to him
with my eyes," as Wilde used to say. It's a kind of flattery in which I
excel when I am not tired.

(He has this advantage: that a conversation with him yields nothing
worth reporting.)

Though this is not premeditated, it is almost impossible for me, as
soon as I am not listening in an impertinent manner, not to listen in a
flattering manner. When you listen this way, it's wonderful how much
stupidity you can draw out of imbeciles; but also how much substance
from intelligent people.

Very happy not to have lunched, I go into the Petit Gallery, where,
for just one day, twenty-five or thirty good paintings are being exhibited
before being put up for sale tomorrow. Some out-of-the-ordinary Re-
noirs, wondrous Monets, calmer but *more straightforward* Sisleys, a
liquid Berthe Morisot. I meet Louis Rouart there; he is afflicted with a
cordial grumpiness and growls his civilities.

Wouldn't it have been simpler and less flat not to have said to him as
I shook his hand: "Glad to have seen you again"? Absurd, but it came
out automatically.

Driving rain.

I reach my house in Auteuil soaked to the skin. Everything about it
seems so small, so small. . . . But Auteuil in the rain, and the gardens
in the neighborhood, drenched, dripping, filled with flowers, seem to me
more charming than ever.

Monday

Yesterday I finished the day at the Charles Gides'. I find myself in a
rather large gathering, but my aunt soon excuses herself and leads me
into the study. Pathetic indictment of her sister, of her son Gérard, of
her husband. She doesn't ask to be advised or approved, but simply to
be listened to.

Gérard comes in; from the pleasure I feel, I realize that I came especially to see him. I want to take him out to dinner. We wangle it
without too much trouble, but to the evident disappointment of his two
girl cousins. Someone or other has claimed that the elder one (at least
the elder one) is in love with him. It could be so. But it could also be
that she doesn't yet know it; she is so natural with him.

Is Gérard in love with Ventura? I try to figure this out during his long conversation with her. I am almost inclined to see in his pursuit of her a mere sport, of which the difficulty constitutes the chief attraction. Yet there is no denying that Gérard has changed, considerably. Even if he is not really in love, at least he wants to please. And he almost succeeds. The look in his eyes, no longer that of a child, has taken on a sort of softness that might be taken for depth.

This morning, long conversation with Bonnier, my architect. You are aware that he is aware that he is talking to a man of letters; when I ask for news of his brother's unfortunate madness, he replies: ". . . We told ourselves: it's the crack — you know — of Arvers's 'Sonnet.'" Doubtless he is thinking of Sully-Prudhomme's "Vase brisé," which Mme de Janzé used to call "the poem of the Vase cassé." ("Oh! Monsieur Manuel," she would exclaim, "please recite to us the charming Vase cassé which you read so well!") [2]

Copeau tells me he is greatly disappointed by Claudel's "Ode"; [3] so far I have not been able to read it attentively. Jammes's enthusiasm got in my way.

Copeau, with a subtle mind like that of a Jew (at first I thought he was a Jew): "I haven't any great fear for you," I told him; "I feel that you are well armed." He smiled. "Yes, I think so too," he replied; "and yet I don't get anywhere. Do you know what I need? A milieu. Yes, I have no milieu."

Read in Stendhal's Journal, that remark would be considered very discerning. Yes, of course you are right. But, in a few months, how the "milieu" can stand in your way! At twenty my youth, my long hair, my sentimental manner, and a frock-coat that my tailor had turned out beautifully made me acceptable in the drawing-rooms of Mme Beulé and the Countess de Janzé. If I had continued to frequent them, I should be writing today for the Revue des deux mondes, [4] but I should not have written the Nourritures. I escaped early from that world, in which, to appear proper, I had to watch myself too closely.

I tried rather hard to direct Gérard toward Liane de L., who would have been an easier conquest than Ventura, but nothing availed; he

---

[2] Sully-Prudhomme's popular poem about the heart that is broken like the beautiful vase becomes ludicrous when the word cassé is substituted for its near synonym brisé. And to confuse it with Félix Arvers's equally popular sonnet about an unavowed love is a real howler.

[3] Claudel's first ode, "The Muses," was published in 1905.

[4] A very conservative literary review, generally considered a steppingstone to the French Academy.

looked upon it as an insult that one should speak to him of anyone else; Maurice S. thinks he is seriously hooked.

Tuesday

This morning, work — or an attempt at work. At two o'clock there came a certain Marinetti, editor of a review of artistic junk called *Poesia*. He is a fool, very rich and very self-satisfied, who has never learned how to keep silent.

Wednesday

Luxembourg Gardens. Nine in the morning. Radiant weather. I wish I had brought a Ronsard. Stendhal seems less good to me than in the rain.

Gérard had come to pick me up at eight o'clock. He would like me to get Ventura for him. As soon as we have taken tea we go out together. Time flies.

While he goes to sign up at the Law School, I wait for him on a bench in the Luxembourg Gardens and savor this quarter of an hour of solitude, which will be, I fear, the best — indeed, the only good one — of my whole day.

Last night at *Les Ventres dorés*.[5] (I had spent the end of the day at the *Ermitage*,[6] with Ducoté, Gourmont, Jacques Copeau, the very likable Verrier, and two unbearable youngsters, one of whom, named D., writes verse, knows Francis Jammes, and looks like a bath attendant.)

Though episodic, the play struck me as excellent, and intelligent from one end to the other. No softness, no trace of sentimentality or of what is called, alas, poetry. Amazing as this may seem, the last act is the best.

Again I take the greatest pleasure in writing, no matter how carelessly, in this notebook. Throughout my various occupations of the day I long to be alone with it.

I see Anthime Armand-Dubois with an enormous wen on his right eyebrow. Barailloul wears a black wig.[7]

---

[5] *Gilded Bellies*, by Émile Fabre, a popular comedy, which opened at the Odéon in March 1905.

[6] *L'Ermitage*, founded in 1890 by Henri Mazel, took a new lease on life in 1897 when Édouard Ducoté became editor. Until its demise in 1906, it was a leading monthly review of symbolist flavor although its contributors (Gide, Gourmont, Copeau, Ghéon, Claudel, Vielé-Griffin, etc.) and illustrators (Maurice Denis, J.-É. Blanche, etc.) considered themselves above literary coteries.

[7] These are both characters in Gide's satiric novel *Les Caves du Vatican* (*Lafcadio's Adventures*), which was not to appear until 1914. In the finished work Barailloul is spelt Baraglioul and Anthime's wen is on his neck.

Gérard has registered; he joins me in the Luxembourg. He counts on my zeal, on my sagacity, on any qualities I may have, to get Ventura for him.

Together we go to the Athénée to reserve a box for this evening.

Thursday morning

Hofmannsthal's visit and walk with him in the Luxembourg.

The role of Esther, in which she was once so perfect herself, is not to Ventura's liking. Today actors — and in this they are like the authors — are not willing that taste should come before what they consider strength.

This is saying a rather simple thing in a very complicated way. Am I tired from last night? . . . though I have been trying for five minutes, I cannot find a simpler way of saying it.

This notebook was begun to teach me to write more easily.

I write this while still in bed and yet the weather is radiant. At one o'clock we leave for Cuverville. Hofmannsthal is to come at ten o'clock and Gérard at nine. As we separated last night: "You have just undone in an hour the work of a month," he told me. Since I understood absolutely nothing in these mysterious words, I begged him to come and explain them to me this morning.

In the train, Thursday

That lady opposite us with the beautiful forehead unmarked by wrinkles, with very black hair already turning gray, who takes out of a little handbag a book in Arabic and reads it without apparently feeling the amazement in my eyes — how I should have liked to strike up a conversation with her! Remarkable resemblance to Augustine de Rothmaler and *spiritual* resemblance to Anna Shackleton.

I recognized (yesterday at the *Ermitage*) in Gourmont's conversation what sets my nerves on edge in his books; when he says, for instance: "I have come to like only the newspapers that have no literature in them," he says it in such a way as to imply: "Oh, I know you are not like that, but that doesn't matter; I am right."

"I shall use to cure you the means that have always succeeded with me," Ventura told Gérard: "allow you to see me often."

What Gérard blames me for is having, by last night's conversation, reawakened in Ventura's mind the image of de Max, which, Gérard claims, was beginning to pale.

Cuverville

I remember the days of my youth when happiness dwelt in my heart like a god.

All morning in the garden. I couldn't get myself to go in and write. I come to lunch intoxicated and Em. says that I "look like a madman." What have I done to look that way? Merely hunted insects on my rosebushes.

Mont Roti

The air was full of a pale blue, which seemed to moisten the horizon like milk. I went over there without pleasure and, without joy, saw again some of those children. The landscape seemed to me beautiful; I savored voluptuously the honeyed scent of the colzas, but suffered from the emptiness of my mind.

14 May, in the train returning from Cuverville

Well, here I am aiding Gérard in his difficult game, merely out of affection, out of a fear of not satisfying the laws of friendship and out of a vain need to remain indispensable. But as soon as I am alone and not constrained by a too eager friendship, I protest and balk at this undertaking, which I can in no way approve and which, with each step, becomes more ruinous.

At the corners of Ventura's mouth two sharp little wrinkles, still almost imperceptible, but which would give me pause if I were Gérard.

I should have liked to speak of Hofmannsthal. It is rather odd that after two hours' conversation with him I should find nothing to set down. . . . And yet I liked him very much. But there didn't seem to be any great element of *shadow* in him nor did it seem to hide any considerable share of the divine. I talk with him all the more willingly since he talks almost all the time. I should take great pleasure in seeing him again.

Tuesday, 16 May

On a bench at the Salon (in the main sculpture gallery) I wait for M. and Ghéon, who are to get here at about ten o'clock. (They are together this morning.)

Having reached Paris the evening of the 14th, I dined with the Charles Gides; talked a few minutes, unsatisfactorily, with Gérard. I cannot hide from him the fact that I do not approve of his adventure. But he is so helpless that I agree to see Ventura again. Where will this all lead him? Certainly not to happiness. He knows it, moreover. But what does that matter! Do we ever really seek happiness? No, rather the free development of whatever is newest in us.

Monday morning I go to meet M., Ghéon, and Jean at the Salon; Gérard wanted to join us, so that our pleasure is spoiled. The five of us move listlessly from room to room. Then a dull lunch. Certainly as far

as being bored goes (which I consider *useless* at any time), I prefer not
to be so in M.'s company. That's a minor crime against the evenness, the
continuity of our joy. I have an ever stronger intention *to give M. noth-*
ing but joy and to receive from him nothing but joy. And I use the word
joy in its fullest and richest sense; I say *joy* here as I might say happiness,
warmth, virtue, health.

And this morning I am writing in order *not* to tire myself or to get
on edge waiting for them, *not* to sadden myself with the thought that
they might be cursing this appointment. . . . Here they are.

Yesterday after lunch Ghéon and I, having left the others, went to
the Whistler exhibit. We prolonged our stay in the gallery almost two
hours, admiring, above all, the last series, that of the figurines in black
chalk set off with pastels, on brown cardboard, and certain houses seen
from the front (the candy shop among others).

Quiet dinner. I read the admirable first act of *Tête d'or*[8] to Em.

This filling of all my time, even when I do so with the most novel
pleasure, exhausts me. I should like some blanks, some pauses, throughout the day. Sensation flows through me; I do not reduce it to thought;
I do nothing with it; I get some profit only from what I have been able
to ruminate.

Auteuil, Wednesday

I expect from this house whatever energy I put into my work, my
genius. Already it houses all my hope.

I saw Gérard only for a minute. He is to see Ventura again this evening. Already he feels better. His whole health hangs on the outcome
of this adventure. He already talks less of getting me mixed up in it.

I am resuming the habit of sleeping an hour in the middle of the
day.

Before going to meet Ghéon and M. at the Place Saint-Sulpice, I
stop at the office of the *Occident* to get Claudel's *Les Muses.*[9] The few
lines that I read while walking seize hold of my thought at once. It is
a shock to my whole being and, as it were, the *warning* that I have been
awaiting for almost a month now.

Hofmannsthal came again this morning; I greatly enjoy seeing him.
He speaks rather loudly and lacks hidden qualities, but the words with

[8] Claudel's tragedy *Golden Head,* with which his dramatic cycle begins. Originally written in 1889 and published in 1890, it was completely
rewritten before 1900.

[9] Claudel's ode "The Muses" was published by *L'Occident,* a literary
review and publishing house.

which he somewhat stuns you are not at all stupid. Suit and necktie in very good taste. He sits down only for a minute, gets up immediately, walks vigorously up and down, stops, starts out again, bumps into chairs and table, smiles, and plays the overgrown child.

Returning home, I stop at the Charles Gides'. I pick up Gérard, who accompanies me home. Ventura is the sole topic of conversation. He is regaining the ground that he had too quickly thought lost.

On my arrival Paul Laurens appears, then his brother. Impossible to talk pleasantly with the two of them together! Pierre's extremism forces me to defend what otherwise I shouldn't care about at all. I have always repented being sincere with him; that's a failing into which I fall almost every time; neither he nor I shall correct ourselves.

This evening I strive to work, but my thoughts have been dreadfully upset; I do not find any one of them in its place.

Read with great interest the chapters on the habits of scorpions in J.-H. Fabre. I should be glad to write a preface for this (Souvenirs ento- mologiques[10] — a rather badly written book however).

Count Kessler takes me to lunch at Armenonville with the Hof- mannsthals.

The culture of these Germans astonishes me. I cannot find it at fault on any point of our literature.

This evening I feel nothing but discouragement and sleep. A read- ing aloud of Wilde's De Profundis, both in German and in English, comforts me somewhat.

Monday

I should like to take in hand all these causes of sterility that I discern so clearly, and strangle them all. I have conscientiously cultivated every negation in me. Just now I am struggling against them. Each one taken alone is easy enough to subdue, but, rich in relationships, it is skillfully tied to another. It forms a network from which I cannot free myself. What good is this journal? I cling to these pages as to something fixed among so many fugitive things. I oblige myself to write anything what- ever in them just so I do it regularly every day. . . . Even here I seek my words, I grope, and I set down your name, Loxias!

Tuesday

I return to the Whistler exhibit with Em. A somewhat less vivid im- pression, but numerous reflections on the methods of suppression in art. Whatever Paul and Pierre Laurens say, I cannot and will not look upon

---

[10] *Recollections of an Entomologist: Instinct and Customs among the Insects.* These volumes began appearing in 1883; the last one came out in 1907.

drawing and color as anything except *means of expression.* The line or
the color that expresses nothing is useless; and in art everything that is
useless is harmful. Etc. . . .

What did I do in the middle of the day? . . . (I am writing this on
Thursday.) Sleep? . . . No! I went to Gilbert de Voisins's house without finding him. I wanted to ask him where one could see Negro or
Spanish dancing, which Count Kessler, his sister, and the Hofmanns-
thals wanted to see that very evening.

After looking in at the *Ermitage,* I joined the German colony in
Auteuil, at the house of the Marquise de Brion. I found myself in a vast
and rather sumptuous drawing-room, where I was at first somewhat uncomfortable at the thought of my soft hat, gray jacket, light-brown
shoes, and absence of collar (the little cyst that has been bothering me
for five days forced me to substitute for the collar a white silk scarf,
skillfully tied and rather prettily fastened by a gold pin that Em. had
lent me). I made every effort of my will to appear at ease, and besides,
with the aid of Kessler's graciousness and that of his sister, I soon became almost natural. Fortunately I was not too tired.

A few supernumeraries arrived.

It was decided that I should join them at the Ritz, where they were
to dine; I preferred to dine alone and not meet them until the dessert.

The evening that we had wanted to be a bit mad turned out to be
utterly dull. After a stupid show at Marigny, we went to Maxim's; getting there much too early, we left at about one thirty before having seen
any of the dances, which certainly began after our departure. All the
necessary elements were there, but, already exhausted by boredom, we
thought only of going home to bed.

Of course each one of us, without letting it be seen too much, felt a
bit annoyed with the others for his own boredom. I am also sure that
Hofmannsthal held me somewhat responsible. His farewells, because
of this, were cold.

Fortunately at Maxim's I had the courage to talk at length with Mme
de Brion, next to whom I sat, so that both of us escaped somewhat from
the general boredom; but it cost too great an effort. She was grateful to
me for it, though, and when we separated insisted greatly and in the
most gracious manner that we see each other again.

I withdrew, tired out from having pretended for two hours that I
wasn't tired.

Thursday

Gérard comes to lunch and tires me somewhat by examining his adventure; he is marking time and analyzing instead of acting. For fear of
losing his hand he dares not risk it. Too bad.

I stay at home to read and work. Excellent reading aloud with Em. of Wilde's *De Profundis* (German text and English text together).

Quiet evening, but I should have preferred it more studious. It all lacks sharpness.

Admirable life of Carlyle (Brenn: *Pages libres*). When reading it I feel myself to be just the way I used to be fifteen years ago. But the *means* are less easy; my ardor more spotty. I still have *this*, but so many other useless things *with it*. Only one thing is necessary? Yes, but provided that it is the *only thing*.

Friday

"That," he said, "is the portrait of a society woman. But do you notice the vulgar hand? Do you know why? It is because it projects forward. Look at a photograph. *I* have noticed it: when a woman puts her hand in front of her, well, just look: the hand appears too big. At once. Manet saw that at once. No, you see, you don't set yourself *in front of* nature but rather *in* nature. Manet *is* Nature.

"And look! That woman in an evening gown — it's living, it's breathing! That breast — you desire that breast — if you love breasts."

These few remarks are uttered, among many others, in front of some wonderful Manets and some Cézannes, by M. Pellerin, whose collection I go to see with Count Kessler.

Thursday

The first really hot evening, after a stifling and radiant day. If I had some book under way, I should write this evening its most beautiful pages. My brain is lucid, not too gay, my flesh is at rest, my spirit staunch. This evening I should be a wonderful lover, and I cannot think of Gérard without pity. I should like not to have met M. before yesterday and not to have spoken to him until today. . . .

If I threw myself from my balcony tonight, I should do so saying: "It's simpler."

I reread some excellent Jules Renard and some of Barrès's *Taches d'Encre*.[11] I had brought a few pages of Goethe's poems with me. Recently I reread in this way, always penetrating deeper into them and ever feeling surer of my liking them, his *Epigrams* and his *Elegies*.

Four years ago on such an evening I should have prowled all night long.

---

[11] A literary "gazette" entirely written and edited by Maurice Barrès in 1884–5, when he was still under twenty-five.

I cannot seriously undertake a piece of work unless I am sure of being able to continue it tomorrow.

(I don't know what these notes will mean to me later on, for most of the time I put into them only a dry indication of how I have spent my time during the day. Yet I do not want to interrupt them; I shall persevere in this method until I leave for Cuverville in a week.)

Wednesday

At my age and after the experiences of G., of R., and of so many others, I am still unable to defend myself against the temptation of a *noble gesture*. Immediately after doing it, I should like to take it back. That's all.

I have just lunched with Félix-Paul Grève; a fatiguing lunch and without any great interest. I come away drunk, having let myself drink and smoke too much during the too prolonged silences. I write these lines while waiting for Bourgerie in the lawyer's office. I have to consult him on behalf of poor dear old La Pérouse, who is worried and would like to add a codicil to his will in favor of his grandson. With all the lucidity of my best days I could not succeed in untangling anything in all this. In the confusion of mind in which I am today, these complicated matters give me an almost physical discomfort; I am sweating; I have a headache; I should like to bathe in the Eurotas.

Francis Jammes, who had entrusted to me his manuscript (*Le Poète et sa femme*) with the understanding that I was free to publish it in this number or the following one, in one or several installments, wrote me, as soon as I was back, that he intended to be published all at one time and right away.[12] Boylesve's article (on Rebell) having arrived, the number goes twenty pages beyond the limit. Verrier, Ducoté's secretary, writes to Francis Jammes that, to their great regret, they will be obliged to cut his piece. Jammes will not hear of it. Let them send the manuscript back to him or else let it appear all together; moreover, he adds, he is fed up with "such higglings." They are forced to make up a number of eighty pages instead of sixty, and this "higgling" costs Ducoté a hundred and fifty francs.

The weather is so hot, so beautiful, that I go out again after dinner, though already dead tired. Yet no restlessness drives me out this evening; I go out "in order not to have a bad conscience later on"; Em. makes this terrible remark as she herself urges me to go out.

---

[12] The magazine in question is the *Ermitage*. Jammes's *The Poet and His Wife*, verse play in three acts, appeared in the issue for June 1905.

First in the Champs-Élysées, marvelous in the neighborhood of the café-concerts; I go as far as the Rond-Point and return by way of the Élysée Palace; the crowd is in a holiday mood, more and more numerous and excited until the rue Royale; the way that the King of Spain will follow from the Élysée is marked by luminous festoons forming above the faubourg Saint-Honoré and the rue Royale delightful triumphal arches. Not able to bear seeing this without Em., I return home in haste to get her; but as soon as I have sat down in the apartment, I am seized with such exhaustion that we put off our walk until tomorrow.

Wednesday

The great disadvantage of this journal is that it constantly pulls me back toward the past. But I am beyond the age at which it was important to learn to appreciate the present. This morning I found every door closed: Welter's, that of the *Mercure*, Péguy's, where I had some business to do.[13] I felt well; I made the greatest mistake in idly sitting down at the terrace of the Café Soufflet, with the excuse of writing to Marcel, and of befuddling my mind with an apéritif that didn't even taste good.

I am writing these lines in the métro, which is taking me to Ducoté's, with whom I am to lunch. I did not write to Marcel. If I had simply sat down on a bench in the Luxembourg, if I had not shadowed for more than a quarter of an hour a decent enough but odd-looking man in rags, I should have been able to enjoy idyllically the warm air and the soft sunlight, keep my mind in that joyful mood, at once calm and irrepressible, that I had as I left the house this morning; I should have done something a little better than to set down dryly the way in which I spent the last three days.

Tuesday, right after lunch, Em. and I go to the Champs-Élysées, where the King of Spain is to pass. Certainly if the King had been less young and less handsome, sobs would not have choked me when I saw him salute the crowd as he passed. His face was drawn; he saluted with a stiff little military salute.

When, two hours later, we saw him return from the Élysée, his smile was very different; his features, now amused rather than contracted, expressed only an amazed and still almost childish joy. Between the two parades we went to see the two Salons. Nothing so demoralizing as those exhibits.

In the evening we drive out in a carriage to see the boulevards and the squares lighted up. Em. returns home; I go back alone toward the

---

[13] The poet Charles Péguy kept a bookshop opposite the Sorbonne, where he published his *Cahiers de la Quinzaine*.

Champs-Élysées, then to the Opéra. No very noteworthy encounter. The air is dusty and full of flames. On the avenue de l'Opéra (which the King is to descend on his way back to the Palace of Foreign Affairs after the gala performance) the crowd becomes thicker and thicker. Finally, with my heart in my mouth, I get away and by a circuitous route reach the Place du Théâtre-Français. Here the crowd is not so thick. It is almost midnight. People come out of the Théâtre-Français. The procession cannot be very slow in coming. I climb up on one of the columns of the theater portico and wait among a group of children. From that spot I heard the bomb very clearly; it made less noise than people said. Several persons near me insisted that it was a firecracker. *I* thought it was a revolver-shot. Again I noticed in me that disinclination to *take the event seriously.* I was highly amused, and even fear of the crowd, which hardly left me a minute, kept all my senses keyed up and made my heart beat joyfully. The next day the papers spoke of an "indescribable tumult" following the report. But I was struck by the complete immobility that followed the detonation. The crowd, for about four minutes, remained as if rooted to the spot with stupor. Then there was a wonderful wave stirred up by a movement of the police. A little later a charge of the mounted police filled me with fear, horror, and a sort of wild enthusiasm. Yet I was completely master of myself, merely embarrassed by the tears that rose to my eyes. But impossible to *take seriously* what I saw; it didn't seem to be real life. As soon as the act was over, the actors would come back and take a bow.

Friday, 2 June

Gérard's intrigue gets on my nerves. I notice, besides, how much my potential of sympathy decreases. Right now, most of the time, when I show sympathy, it is merely to continue a gesture that I unwisely began, but with a secret revolt against myself, and often with a distinct irritation against the object of my sympathy.

Saturday

As soon as I get up, my appointment with Gérard makes me furious. I get there late and fuming. The first thing I do is to cancel the automobile that he hired the day before. At least this returns no less than seventy francs to his pocket. His adventure has no other interest than the fact that it is happening to him.

In the bottom of the glass, after one had drunk, there remained a sort of thick and almost buttery cream that the straws would not suck up. My thirst and greediness overcame my disgust; but for a long time afterward my stomach felt heavy and my tongue as if coated with it. I note this sensation with a minuteness that will seem merely literary to others, but I know very well that my recollection will form around it. I envied the huge glass of very black coffee, foamy on the edges and ice-cold, that Ventura had ordered, in preference to our coffee with cream. The conversation remained dull; each one of us lacked enthusiasm.

Already in the café of the Gare Saint-Lazare, by a childish subterfuge, Gérard and M. had left me alone with her — just long enough to exhaust the *subject* and to long bitterly for them to come back. I am more and more convinced that nothing can be done and am more and more suspicious of the two little wrinkles at the corners of her mouth. *All this bores me terribly.*

From Saint-Lazare we took the suburban train to the woods, then two carriages took us to the Cycle restaurant near the Seine, under rather beautiful trees. I was alone in the cab with Ventura, to whom I have no more to say. I did not feel properly dressed or cleanly shaved; I didn't care whether or not I was attractive. *I was bored.*

I long for solitude and decide to start tomorrow without waiting for Em. I shall sleep Monday at Étretat and Tuesday can receive her at Cuverville.

The air is thick with heat.

Sunday

I am writing in the train which is carrying me off. At last!

Yesterday, important conversation with Gérard, which leaves me satisfied, lightened. When I tell him that Ventura is not very desirable (I mean exciting), he exclaims: "So that's why I have so little desire for her!" Moreover, I exaggerated nothing. The excitement that Ventura causes is entirely cerebral; that's the worst kind, for it can never be satisfied. And then I tell him that Ventura is not "so interesting as all that . . ." etc. . . . . Poor boy! Will he finally get out of his tunnel?

Back home, I wear myself out putting papers in order and packing my trunk. It is like my books, like the least of my sentences, like my whole life: I try to put too much into it.

Monday morning

"You can get anything out of me with a well-turned compliment," said X. What a shame it is that I no longer believe in those I pay myself!

Cuverville

As the convinced Mohammedan cries: "God is God," I should like to shout: "Art is Art." Reality is always there not to dominate it but, on the other hand, to serve it.

Oh, talent! slowly nibbled away.

Tuesday
Schädliche Warheit, ich ziehe sie vor dem nützlichen Irrthum.
Warheit heilet den Schmerz, den sie vielleicht in uns erregt.[14]
(For Barrès.)

It is raining pitchforks. Closeted in the greenhouse with Goethe's poems, surrounded by golden yellow calceolarias, without fever, without anxieties, without desires, I enjoy a PERFECT FELICITY.

June
I find here this notebook abandoned last November. In Paris I left others begun in the interval. One in particular (blue cover) kept conscientiously from day to day, from my return from Hendaye to my leaving for Cuverville.

Today, the 13th of June, on the first day of good weather, I am writing outside, rather uncomfortably seated, and considerably bothered by my dog. Since we have been here, the almost incessant rain, ruining the garden, has helped my work. Every day I have been able to add a few lines to my *Porte étroite*.[15] I prefer such regular assiduity today to the finest inspiration in the world.

Between sessions of work I read German and Italian (*Werther* and the *Vita Nuova*).[16] This morning the manuscript of the translation of *Paludes* arrived.[17]

This evening I finished the first part of *Werther*. I finish also Léon Bloy's *Journal* (*Quatre ans de captivité*)[18] and resume with delight Stendhal's *Journal*. I should like to write an article on Bloy; it seems to me that no one has as yet written about him as he deserves.

Finished reading (day before yesterday) Tristan Bernard's charming book: *Amants et voleurs*.[19]

Thursday, 14 June
Visit to La Pérouse. He asks rapidly for news of me and of others, but doesn't listen to my replies, and abruptly:

"You have to admit that there is something diabolic in the human

---

[14] *Harmful truth, I prefer thee to useful error.*
Truth cures the pain that it may cause in us. (Goethe: *Gedichte, vier Jahreszeiten: Herbst*, 49. In the Weimar edition, Vol. I, p. 352.)
[15] *Strait Is the Gate*, first published in 1909.
[16] By Goethe and Dante respectively.
[17] The German translation by Félix-Paul Grève of *Morasses*.
[18] *Four Years of Captivity at Cochons-sur-Marne* (1905) is the third volume of Bloy's eight-volume *Journal*.
[19] *Lovers and Robbers*.

race. Especially in women. I have just had a frightful scene with my wife. Please excuse me, sir, if I am still all upset by it. Something that I was reproaching her with (in the midst of a discussion), something she did six years ago, she now says no, she never did it. And with the greatest assurance, without blushing, with such a complete absence of embarrassment that I am absolutely flabbergasted. It was all a question of a subscription to a box at the Théâtre-Français."

"Yes," I say, "you have already spoken to me about that incident."

"Well, she denies it now."

"What! She denies having had that box at the theater?"

"No. She denies having asked me to help her pay for it. Really if it were to her interest to say that this armchair, this one here, is a pair of slippers, she would do so; she would maintain it. If God is to judge us according to our intentions — Suddenly I left the room; my hands were clenched: I was on the point of strangling her. Do you know what she said to me? . . . She told me: 'Your grandchildren despise you.'"

"She had lost all self-control and was only aiming to hurt you."

"To hurt me, yes. I am crazy to attach any importance to it. . . . She told me: 'Moreover, Sir, everybody makes fun of you and despises you.'"

Touching his arm, I say:

"You know, don't you, that that is untrue?"

"I know; I know; I am even embarrassed by the affection and respect that some people show me."

"No one," I say, "has greater affection and respect for you than I have."

There followed a long silence. He held my hand in his. We didn't dare look at each other, for neither one of us had been able to check his tears. Finally I risk asking him:

"You were very young when you married her?"

"Yes . . . I was young."

Written a few notes on Bloy. Worked on *La Route étroite*,[20] the correction of *Paludes*. Went back to Baudelaire with the greatest pleasure.

Irony considered as a form of maceration. Very important.

10 July

The Jacques Copeaus left us at eleven o'clock. It is now three. In two hours I myself leave. Tomorrow I lunch at the Van Rysselberghes', go to visit the house again with them, etc. . . . Gérard takes his first law examinations in two days.

The pleasure I derived from talking with Jacques Copeau was very

---

[20] The title of *La Porte étroite* was not yet definitely decided upon. [E.]

great, until the day before their departure. Perhaps I began to suffer a bit then from not daring to talk to him more freely, from the fact that he did not, or could not, invite me to. He excited me to work instead of distracting me. Yesterday I read him what I had written of *La Porte étroite*. I didn't like it a bit: farther on I shall write down the things I noticed. I am almost ready to chuck it all into the fire. Copeau, a very good adviser, is able to see, in what I read him, only the preparation of something better. A few years ago I should have been utterly demoralized to have read, amorphous as they still are, these pages that I thought to be already perfect (or almost). Nothing is created without a divine patience.

Copeau, at twenty-seven, seems ten years older; his overexpressive face is already worn by sufferings. His shoulders are high and hard like those of someone who takes a great deal upon himself. The softness of his voice is at times almost disturbing; he would charm naturally if occasionally he did not try too hard to charm. He expresses himself so well that one is suspicious; his voice takes on just the inflection he wants; his gestures are never involuntary; it took me some time, I confess, to admit that it could all be genuine. One gets to the point of suspecting the sincerity of too impeccable expressions. Everything in him improves when better known, when explained — even if by himself.

15 July

Returned from Paris the day before yesterday. I have lost the key to my little blue trunk in which I had hidden the notebook I am using as a journal.

Rather interesting luncheon Wednesday at Saint-Germain with Van Rysselberghe, Aristide Maillol, Van de Velde, at the Maurice Denises' house.

Maillol talks with animation, graciousness, and innocence. He looks like an Assyrian from Toulouse. If only Mirbeau does not force him to "think"!

Denis is certainly not very happily inspired by Spain. But whereas I react as a Greek, he reacts as a Roman Catholic.

Van de Velde does not like fruit; moreover, he claims never to have eaten any and will not consent to eat what is so beautiful to see. Yet he has it served; at each meal his table is decorated with it, but he doesn't want anyone to touch it; at least he does not touch it himself. Of course he builds up a theory to justify his not eating it; most certainly an æsthetic reason: he maintains that the beauty of fruit invites platonic Contemplation; in short, he does not like fruit.

Cuverville

In the carriage that brought me back from Les Ifs, I thought of writing a "Portrait" of Gérard P. and of sending it to him. It would not be very flattering. Since he has no charity toward anyone else, he might at least see himself clearly. His fatuousness makes me unkind.

Yesterday the 14th of July, very small reward for my bicycle ride in the sun (Étretat). Yet I go back at nightfall to see the fireworks at Criquetot.[21]

The badly handled rockets fall back on the audience.

After the final piece of the display, a lantern parade, then a dance. Had I been more disinterested, I should have enjoyed even more those varicolored lanterns strung across the streets above the eager crowd, appearing vaguely distant in the clouds of smoke that the Roman candles, here and there, both thicken and color with a pink light.

On the stone steps of the town hall the musicians, who a moment ago led the parade, sit down and attack a polka. At moments the individual instruments lose their way; for several measures you hear only a bellowing stressed by an ophicleide that is still beating the initial time, then an abrupt caper on a clarinet. The dancers stumble on the pebbles, for they are dancing right on the square, which hasn't even been swept.

"Come now, gentlemen, no shyness!" shouts meanwhile Monsieur L., the notary and mayor of the village. "Choose your partners."

Only four or five couples risk it. Around them the rest of the villagers and peasants form a circle, surer of being amused by watching the others dance than by dancing.

A few years more and I shall write less good books — which will be more admired because they will be more carefully read.

Today I found out what waiting is; not the impatient waiting that makes the horse froth at his bit, but that horrible anguished waiting in which, from one beat to another, the heart labors as if it had to push aside a blood clot. On the road, right there, on the embankment, under the burning sun, I wait for X.'s wagon to pass by. It doesn't come. It must have taken the other road. . . .

19 July

I still have in me an enormous sum of joy that I have found no way of expending.

---

[21] The 14th of July (Bastille Day) is France's Independence Day, celebrated everywhere with fireworks, parades and street dancing.

Will nothing calm the frightful beating of my heart? The whole summer oppresses it. Yesterday a long bicycle ride, more exalted than crushed by the heat. At the Laurens house a rather warm reception, to be sure — cordial, even friendly. But what can I do about it? Between Pierre Laurens and me I feel a greater distance than ever. All my sympathy is concentrated on Paul Laurens and on his young wife, who strikes me every time I see her as a better and more charming wife. Pierre's conversation, all made up of peevishness, suppresses everything he comes into contact with. In advance I feel his irony ready for any stupidity I might say — which I necessarily say. The only resource with him is to play stupid, to act the fool, to be very careful to say nothing sensible or sincere or that you care about. After an hour of this game I am done in and demoralized in my soul. Yet I am well aware that this hostile mood in him is only a defense; he takes as a personal attack anything around him that succeeds.

Wonderful return. Apparent serenity of the harvest labors in the fields. Solemn approach of evening. I wander like a madman amidst this peace as arid to me as the desert.

31 July

I have gone back to work with a certain regularity, but I make very slow progress. I spend hours on a group of sentences that I shall completely rewrite the next day. The scene in Geneviève's room, in particular, when he finds her kneeling, gave me great difficulty. But I admire now all the things I succeeded in *not saying*, in KEEPING BACK. (I think for some time of the virtue that "reserve" can become in a writer. But who, today, can appreciate it?) I try to consider patience as my greatest quality; in any case it is the one I must above all encourage in me. I write "patience"; I ought to say "obstinacy"; but what is really needed is a *supple obstinacy.*

I have again begun my piano-practice two hours a day (Beethoven's sonatas). Every evening, before going to bed, I read a few pages of Hebbel's correspondence. Interesting indeed, and written in a rather palpitating language, but I have not yet felt him speak to me *directly.*

Read several articles in the recent *Revue des deux mondes,* in the latest *Mercure,* etc. In spite of all the good I heard of it, I got very little pleasure from Georges de La Salle's book on the Manchurian war. Just now I am finishing (in translation) Hugo Ganz's *Russia, Land of Riddles.*

In small doses, for the good of my health, Stendhal's *Journal.*

In the train, 8 August

Left Cuverville this morning.

Gérard asks me if my patience is not taxed by so many people. (We are twelve at table every day.) — No, but only on condition that I can be "polite" only when I want to be. A few dips into solitude are as essential to me every day as my sleep at night. That is the way I smooth out my ruffled nerves. What joy I felt the other evening at my work, in the small room beside the linen-room, after I had left them all together in the drawing-room! My greatest advantage between the ages of eighteen and twenty-three was that I preferred that kind of pleasure to those of society.

My work is hardly getting ahead at all, and will not progress any better so long as I am not convinced that I am writing a masterpiece.

My Aunt Charles Gide has just been very ill; a very bad heart attack; less painful, however, than the one I saw her have one evening in Paris. Gérard, since he has begun emancipating himself, worries her. One must admit that he was not very reassuring. What a look he had the first evening! Apart from the other children, he was pacing up and down the garden; I was giving him the *indifferent* treatment, but eventually I took pity on him; in the darkness I sought him out on the path where I could see the light of his cigarette.

"I ought to be in Paris," he said right away. "Yes, Ventura was waiting for me. For the last hour I have been telling myself that I could be with her. . . . Well, too bad! Tomorrow she leaves for America and I shan't be able to see her for six months." A few steps more in silence; then he continues in a more muffled voice:

"This evening, without any doubt, I would have had her."

"You mean that she was giving up."

"Yes, more than a week ago she had ceased defending herself against me."

"Then you, for fear of not — being up to it, you abruptly sidestepped?"

Gérard (taken aback, sheepish and furious, after a pause):

"All right, yes! . . ."

But right now he is sick at having left just as he was sick at staying.

Marcel is not working and will not work. He rushes ravenously toward every distraction; in my study he has already devoured in less than six days the books I had set aside for three months' reading.

Six years more and he will be ripe for that "Catholic discipline" he spoke of in one of his recent letters. That "discipline" reminds me very much of the Red Cross ambulances. If in spite of everything you tried to go ahead on foot instead of getting someone to carry you. . . .

The day before yesterday, at the graduation exercises, I suddenly ceased being bored when I noticed in the second row a little girl with a gypsy look that I couldn't take my eyes off of. The *conviction* of that little six-year-old. Her laughing eyes in a serious face; square chin, warm color of her cheeks; her hair, badly combed and too full, falls in a mass on her forehead. Compared with her, all the others seemed even more lamentably ugly. She was darkly dressed in a little dress of calico printed with a big plaid, very simple. You could feel that she was the poorest of all; everything combined to make me like her. She recited, then sang — always with the same warmth. That gave me a chance to read her name on the program: she is a little Lemaître.

As soon as the ceremony was over, I saw her rush toward her parents, holding out a little red book and shouting: "Look! They gave me A WHOLE PRIZE!"

In my vicinity people did not consider her pretty; Jeanne particularly went so far as to call her "frightful." And I was foolish enough to be hurt by this!

"It is not enough to be happy; I want others to know I am." So long as you think thus you will not be happy.

Paris, 8 August

Copeau, with whom I was dining, repeated a certain sentence that I supposedly said to him at Cuverville: "Even if the drama were to end in bloodshed, I do not know a single sentiment whose sincerity cannot be questioned."

I did not *acknowledge* that sentence (in the sense of "acknowledging a child"), yet did not disavow it; and yesterday, returning to the subject, I emphasized this: "The sensation is always sincere; it is the only guarantee of the authenticity of our sentiments; our sentiments are guaranteed by their physiological repercussions. Literature and fine arts (in modern times) have, for their own convenience, made man a much more emotional creature than he is, or than he *was* at least, for very soon man began to conform to the image that he was offered of himself."

It is odd how the stock of *Humanity* has risen on the market since the Greeks, or even since Shakespeare. Nothing does more harm to drama than this excessive evaluation. This is quite properly the very subject of my *Sylla*.[22]

---

[22] If Gide ever wrote this work, it has not been published.

Cuverville

Back from Paris, I went up to bed at nine o'clock. The others continued their evening downstairs. Gérard, seated with Mlle R. on the bench under my window, kept me awake for a long time; then the games they got under way in the drawing-room; I was not annoyed by this noise, but I was glad to be alone. I did not mind even the vague hum that came from the drawing-room. The only thing that provoked me was the sudden sound of Gérard's voice, rising above the others, harsh and without overtones.

Copeau was amazed to find that I was still in the midst of Stendhal's *Journal*. There are certain writers that I read as slowly as possible. It seems to me that I am conversing with them, that they talk to me, and I should be sorry not to be able to keep them with me longer.

13 August

Right after *St. Yves* I took up *The Ebb Tide*, then *The Wrong Box*, which I finished today. This last one, which begins in the manner of Dickens and recalls in its best chapters *The Wrecker* or *The Suicide Club*, ends with a rather ordinary piece of humbug. You can't get into *The Ebb Tide* until after the first hundred pages, but suddenly it becomes excellent and remains so almost to the end. In *St. Yves* I liked the *innocence* of the emotions. Today I begin *Kidnapped*.[23]

14 August

Gérard has introduced baccarat here; from nine thirty to ten thirty these last few evenings the quiet atmosphere of Cuverville has been corrupted. Yesterday I held the bank, with a fiendish luck. It rather amuses me to win *against* Gérard. But I should have preferred to win only from him.

Gourmont has published in the *Ermitage* of 15 July some new *"Pas sur le sable."*[24] He certainly hasn't very beautiful feet!

"There are certain things one must have the courage *not* to write," says the first of his aphorisms; this first one ought to spare us many others; we should like him to be more "courageous."

"Rise above yourself to contemplate yourself," he writes immediately afterward. This is because he doesn't seem handsome to himself seen full-face; he hopes to be better in a bird's-eye view. From sentence to sentence he remains ugly; when he talks of women he does so as a repulsive man who has been repulsed and who is taking his revenge.

---

23 Books by Stevenson. [A.] Gide quotes the titles in French.
24 "Footprints in the Sand."

The orderly appearance of my life depresses me. Certain days it seems to me unbearably hypocritical.

I am working now in the attic, where a large table is covered with the pages of my novel. Another, smaller one, in front of the window, stands beside the chaise-longue where I stretch out to read Stevenson. Here I am farthest from the sounds of the garden and of the house. Today it has been raining since I woke up; my only pleasure is reading and trying to work.

21 August

This title: *Le Cône d'ombre* [25] is suggested by a letter from Grolleau, who asks me for a preface to his translation of Wilde's *Poems in Prose*.

22

Marcel explains to me this evening that what keeps him from writing is the almost equal interest that he takes in everything, his lack of any prejudice to urge on others. The minds that are carried away by enthusiasm in one direction have the greatest facility in speaking or writing; when too well balanced, thought prevents us; out of balance, it drags us far afield. It is the party men, necessarily, who talk the most in the Chamber of Deputies.

24 August

Nothing is consistent, nothing is fixed or certain, in my life. By turns I resemble and differ; there is no living creature so foreign to me that I cannot be sure of approaching. I do not yet know, at the age of thirty-six, whether I am miserly or prodigal, temperate or greedy . . . or rather, being suddenly carried from one to the other extreme, in this very balancing I feel that my fate is being carried out. Why should I attempt to form, by artificially imitating myself, the artificial unity of my life? Only in movement can I find my equilibrium.

Through my heredity, which interbreeds in me two very different systems of life, can be explained this complexity and these contradictions from which I suffer.

25 August

Too much novelty dazzles us; we can appreciate in others only what we are able to recognize (just as the Barbarians could make out in the words we spoke only the letters they were accustomed to pronouncing); as for the rest, we do not even hear it. The artists with the most genius are understood only after their savor has ceased to be rare; the new values they brought, not being in circulation, were not quoted

---

[25] *The Cone of Shadow.*

on the market. If you praise so much my article on Wilde (I mean the last one), this is just because I say nothing new in it. My second regular chronicle (of this year) on the other hand awoke no echoes anywhere; the unaccustomed truths I put into it could have been assimilated only if they had been watered down with pages of commonplaces.[26]

Would it not be possible to write a whole volume (and a successful one) on this subject, historically developing this argument that I merely suggested there:

A race as mixed as ours recognizes through their expression the elements that make it up. By an easy imitation, what it first expresses is what has already been expressed in a preceding period. Who dares to assert that the Latin elements are the strongest in our race — and not simply the most articulate, for very obvious reasons? What has not yet been expressed is no less important because it is less precocious. It is merely harder to invent than to imitate. We strengthen ourselves with the past; but where does that get us? Barrès is one such: leaning heavily as against a wall; motionless.

You cannot imagine an author so great that his most banal qualities are not the first to be appreciated. The crowd always enters by way of the "commons" — and most often never gets beyond them.

1 September

I am again losing my footing; I am letting myself be carried along by the monotonous current. A great drowsiness benumbs me from my awakening until evening; games occasionally shake it off, but I am gradually losing the habit of effort. I compare what I am to what I once was, to what I should have liked to be. If only . . . but no, everything becomes soft in such an easy existence. Sensual pleasure permeates everything; my finest virtues are dissipated and even the expression of my despair is blunted.

How can I call absurd a rule of conduct that would have protected me against this? At one and the same time my reason condemns it and calls out for it in vain. If I had a father confessor, I should go to him and say: Impose upon me the most arbitrary discipline and today I shall say it is wisdom; if I cling to some belief that my reason mocks, this is because I hope to find in it some power against myself.

As soon as a healthy day comes along, I shall blush at having written this.

[26] The article on Wilde is the one on *De Profundis* that appeared in the *Ermitage* for 15 August 1905. The "chronicle" is the second of Gide's regular articles in the form of imaginary interviews, which appeared in the *Ermitage* for February 1905. Both are collected in the fourth volume of the *Œuvres complètes*.

2 September

Before closing this notebook and starting out for the south, I want to make a record of the month just past.

Read aloud, with Mlle Siller, the first four acts of Hebbel's *Gyges und sein Ring*[27] and Leopold Andrian's *Garten des Erlebnis*. Derived much good from resuming my reading of Pascal's *Pensées* and *Opuscules* in the Brunschwicg edition (chiefly the *Prières pour demander à Dieu le bon usage des maladies*).[28] Finished the excellent *Kidnapped* of Stevenson. Corrected the proofs of *Paludes* (the German translation by Félix-Paul Grève) and of my *Essai sur Wilde* (English translation by Millard).

Whipped into shape the first forty pages of my novel.

It was one of the emptiest months in the year for me.

3 September

Finished yesterday Hebbel's *Gyges*. There is much to be said about it. What an interesting *parallel* could be written between this play and mine! I think again of the *Caves*, of the *Curieux malavisé*[29] and feel somewhat better than yesterday.

Received this morning a letter from Franz Blei with a telegram from the Vienna theater asking for the right to produce my *Roi Candaule*.

. . . and my will which complains of aging. If the wear were only constant and regular, if it attacked at the same time, and in like manner, both body and soul; but no, it proceeds by leaps and bounds; I am aging in bits, which become an object of amazement and sorrow for all the rest.

* * *

5 September, 4 o'clock

Fantastic glimpse of Lyon, in a sudden awakening, just as we were crossing the Rhone. Vague looming up of the gray shadowy roofs under a sky the color of a rich fruit-juice. An acid coolness fills the air with a taste of red currants, and the Rhone draws through the scene its iridescent reflection of mingled shadow and dawn.

---

[27] This play (1856) deals with the same legend as Gide's *Le Roi Candaule* (1901). When the latter was produced in Berlin in 1908 it was unfavorably compared with Hebbel's work.

[28] "Prayers to Ask God for the Good Use of Ill Health."

[29] Gide had not yet begun writing *Les Caves du Vatican* (*Lafcadio's Adventures*), which was to appear in 1914. *Le Curieux malavisé* (*The Ill-Advised Experiment*) is an episode in *Don Quixote*, which Gide may have planned to adapt.

Then the curtain drops again; I sink back into a sort of torpor, which I try to coax into becoming sleep. But, alas, I have hardly slept a wink all night. My thought, accelerated by the train's speed, delights in wandering madly. As if in spite of myself, I compose and memorize sentences that I intend to write down on rising.

Soon the dazzling blue of the south feeds my early-morning exaltation. I recognize the shadow of the plane trees on the light dust of the roads; the brightness; the crisp trot of the mules. . . .

Yes, a *good sport* (the expression is Em.'s), this is what, despite all the disappointments, I continue to like so much in Gérard. When by an awkward movement during our bicycle ride I caused Gérard to run into Drouin and made them both fall, Gérard merely burst out laughing, whereas Drouin did nothing but grumble.

Les Sources. — Alais. — Malataverne

This morning a slight headache, which I owe to last night's mosquitoes, does not dull the eagerness of all my senses. I smell every flower, lie down in the shade of each tree, become the guest of every house. Everything smiles upon me and I withhold my smile from no one. What need have I of a companion? Thanks to everything, I am delightfully sufficient unto myself. At the age of twenty I didn't know how to be happy.

Nîmes (Les Sources)

I love, in this garden, that dry, resinous smell.

Saturday

I am rereading almost from beginning to end *Le Visage émerveillé* [30] with as much rapture as the first day. What makes a masterpiece is an adaptation or a happy matching of subject and author. And I am inclined to doubt that such a fortunate coincidence will ever occur again in the life of Mme de Noailles. Her very faults, this time, set off, emphasized her good qualities; yes, I like in this book even "the little golden knife against my heart." But henceforth the "little golden knife" will be prejudicial to her.

Mme de R. congratulates me on *L'Immoraliste*, "that book in which there are such beautiful thoughts." Obviously she thinks they are sprinkled on afterward like nasturtium blossoms on a salad. How unculti-

---

[30] *The Awe-Struck Face*, a novel (1904) by the Countess Anna de Noailles.

vated these women of the south are, and how paradoxical you seem to them when you don't disguise yourself considerably!

Gérard was unable to appreciate Em.'s exquisite remark when, speaking of Octave, she said: "You are not grateful to him for the pity he excites in you." He is incapable of judging that type of wit.

Minutes of such excruciating joy that you think they might break the thread of life; then, between two such, the succession of monotonous days, spent merely in growing older.

Cuverville, 2 October
Time flies. The cloudy sky is already filling with winter. My dog is sleeping at my feet. Full of anguish, I sit helpless in front of the white sheet of paper, on which everything might be written but on which I shall never be able to write more than *something*.

I finish the second volume of Hebbel's correspondence (but I began it in the middle, or, to be exact, with the first letters dated from France); continue the reading (methodically for the first time) of Pascal in the Brunschwicg edition. Jacoby's *Selection*.[31] *Histoire de la littérature* (Renaissance) by Brunetière.

7 October
I finish painfully and in haste, skipping many pages, that absurd *Fanny* by Feydeau which I had begun more than a month ago. Nothing prevented this book from being a good book — except its author. The love dialogues already very close to those of Dumas *fils,* and almost as bad. A sort of "belief in love" that is indeed one of the most stupid and ridiculous inventions of our literature.

Feydeau writes: "My teeth were chattering in my mouth. . . ." This is almost as bad as Cousin Br.'s "The wheel went over the thigh of his leg."

Ghéon delighted by *St. Yves* — by the French aspect of that work. "Yes," said Em. about this book, "it is one of the nicest compliments anyone ever paid us."

I find in Gaston Deschamps's latest article: "I should be very glad to find some masterpieces among the innumerable novels that French publishers put on the world market every day. I welcome new names and young talents. And I do not think there could possibly be, through my

---

[31] *Studies on Selection in Man,* by Paul Jacoby (1904).

fault, any unknown Balzac, or neglected Daudet, or unpublished Ferdinand Fabre, or forgotten George Sand. . . ."

And yet he has never mentioned Paul Valéry, or Paul Claudel, or
André Suarès, or Francis Jammes, or me.

Today the big pine opposite the cedar is being cut down. Three men
worked at it all day. This evening the desperate silhouette of its huge
branchless trunk rises like a nightmare against the wonderful pure sky.

17 October

Like a prize fruit, Gourmont is ripening. He is losing his sharpness,
gaining in fragrance and sweetness. His latest writings are full of juice.
(His *"Dialogue des Amateurs"* of 1 October — the beginning of *Ani-
maux et morale chez La Fontaine* — remarkable.) [32] Just one step more
toward autumn and he will be excellent in every way.

3 November

Gourmont does not understand that all intelligence is not on the
side of free thought, and all stupidity on the side of religion; that the
artist needs leisure for his work and that nothing keeps the mind so busy
as free inquiry and doubt. Skepticism is perhaps sometimes the beginning of wisdom, but it is often the end of art.

4 November

Le Dantec, at the Van Rysselberghes', claims to have no visual imagination at all.

"But after all," Mme Van Rysselberghe asks him, somewhat provoked, "when someone says to you: 'House' for example, what do you
see?"

"I see simply H. O. U. S. E.," he replies.

"Come now," she continues, "turn around and, quite sincerely, try to
say something about me."

"What? What do you mean?"

"Oh, anything about me without seeing me; for instance, what color
is my hair?"

"I know that your hair is gray, but merely because we were talking
about it at table; I know it as a fact, but I don't see it."

"Well, something else, then. My height?"

"I *know* that you are small, but only because the last time I was here

---

[32] The "Dialogue" in the *Mercure* for the 1st of October concerned ethics; the first installment of "The Life of the Animals and Ethics in La Fontaine's Fables" appeared in the *Mercure* for the 15th of October.

I noticed that you only came up to my shoulder. I know also that you have heavy eyelids, but this is because they are like my mother's."

I: "Then he did imagine his mother's eyes."

MME VAN RYSSELBERGHE: "It seems that he had heard someone talking about his mother say that one of the characteristics of her face was her heavy lids."

I: "Does he recognize faces without difficulty?"

MME VAN RYSSELBERGHE: "With great ease at a distance of ten years. He even recognizes resemblances."

I: "Then I don't understand. . . ."

MME VAN RYSSELBERGHE (*who is telling all this*): "And as he was leaving, he also said: 'Oh! I have made another discovery: namely, that I don't know anything about art — and that I never have understood anything about it.'"

Back in Paris, 8 November

Met little Louis Rouart, redder and more middle-class looking than ever. As it is a long time since I have seen anyone, my smile suggests an exaggerated joy; he comes along with me. As spotty, as strained conversation as ever; it seems like the spasmodic skirmishes of a fencing bout, but of a bout without courtesy. With the very first words, from the start, he attacks. With him, in spite of myself, I throw up my guard, take on a false, tense attitude, and say nothing natural. What silly things he made me say yesterday! To be sure, I was already tired out by the conversation I had just had with Gérard.

Louis Rouart went with me to Welter's bookshop, where I ordered Nyrop's grammar for André Ruyters. He heard me give the order and thought: three foreign names!! Protestant, cosmopolitan, etc. . . . And as I asked him, on the way out, if he knew that wonderful grammar: "I don't mind telling you" (he in fact told me pompously) "that I never felt the need of grammars to learn French." Nothing could have been more insulting or more stupid. And I, quite dumbly, out of weakness and kindness, bothered to explain that the first volume of that grammar was "above all historical." Absurd! Absurd!

And so on. I drop him in front of the *Mercure* (without going in, for I suddenly remember that Tuesday is Mme Rachilde's *day* for receiving visitors), annoyed with him and even more with myself. But when he speaks of calling on me, I reply: "Yes, do." For, after all, I find him likable. Now I'll never shake him off.

17 November

I am glad that, as soon as I got to Paris, I had to devote myself to that article on the Autumn Salon that Roger Marx had ordered for the

Gazette des Beaux-Arts. It gave me a great deal of trouble; this amounts to saying that it did me a great deal of good.[33]

Reflected at very great length on what "art criticism" can be (and especially on what it cannot be).

Plunged from nine o'clock until midnight in a religious contemplation of some photographs of Polyclitus' works (reading Collignon).[34] Copied from Delacroix's *Journal* a wonderful passage on the "theory of decadence" for little Louis Rouart.

22 November

Last corrections to my article for the *Gazette*. In order not to shock his public, Roger Marx asked me to suppress a coda on Cézanne and Renoir. The coda was rather ordinary, so that I easily fell in with his request; but the article, with its abrupt end, seems ill arranged. The lack of volume of everything I write distresses me, but I can't do anything about it. My great hostility toward prolixity, facile fluency, and patter is the cause of it.

I long for a hidden eloquence.

. . . My mind still anxious at not being able to decide what to tackle. I have before me Collignon's *Sculpture grecque*, Nyrop's *Grammaire française* and the *Histoire de la littérature anglaise* by Jusserand — which all tempt me equally. For each of these works I need a month of unbroken study; my mind is still too restless to choose and to limit me exclusively to my choice. I have left everything in the air: Pascal, Taine's *Correspondance*, Stendhal's *Journal*. These are readings that one can easily drop and pick up anywhere and that I prefer not to read to the end at one time. But one must at least be able to pick them up conveniently at the point where one left them. At Auteuil I am going to have a special shelf where the books I have begun will stand waiting for me; each one will have its bookmark, which I shall occasionally move a few pages. That will allow me, dropping the book and picking it up at will, never to read anything without giving myself to it wholly.

From Athman's latest letter I copy this sentence that Mardrus would not understand and that I should like not to forget:

"I love her very much" (he is speaking of his very young wife) "and *yet I have been able to make her sincere* toward my mother and me; she is very good, and I only treat her very gently like how you treat a child."

[33] Gide's *Promenade au Salon d'Automne* is in the fourth volume of the *Œuvres complètes*, wrongly dated by the editor.

[34] *Histoire de la sculpture grecque* (*History of Greek Sculpture*) (1892–97), by Maxime Collignon, contains photographs of works by Polyclitus, who was, after Phidias, the most celebrated sculptor of antiquity.

23 November

Around four o'clock O. S., a young German, comes to call. I remember, or rather he reminds me, that he is the author of a book (rather mediocre), *Lothar*, which I read or skimmed through last spring on the recommendation of Félix-Paul Grève. I believe I even wrote him a note about it. . . . O. S. not at all unpleasant, but talking too much, like all foreigners (moreover, those who don't talk are even more tiresome). He praises my *Immoraliste*, adding that those who admire it have hardly understood it, that people always speak of me as a lyric writer, failing to appreciate my chief virtue, which is knowing how "to look through the cracks of culture." That's not bad at all!

I have just read, first to myself, then aloud, the extraordinary Sixth *Chant de Maldoror* (chapters i, ii, and iii).[35] How does it happen that I didn't know it until now? I have even begun to wonder if I am not *the only one* to have noticed it. "You feel as you draw toward the end of the volume that he is gradually losing consciousness . . ." writes Gourmont. Let's admit that he *never read* these pages; that is less insulting to Gourmont than to suppose that he read them without noticing them.

Here is something that excites me to the point of delirium. He leaps from the detestable to the excellent. Amazing, the exchange of letters between Maldoror and Mervyn, the description of the family dining-room, the figure of the Commodore, the little brothers, "their caps topped off with a feather torn from the wing of the Carolina fern-owl, with their velvet trousers ending at the knees, and their red silk stockings," who "take each other's hand and go into the drawing-room, taking care to touch the ebony parquet only with the tips of their toes," etc. . . . etc. . . . I must read it all to Copeau. What mastery in the "sheer cussedness" of these lines.

Immediately afterward I reread Rimbaud's *Poètes de sept ans*.[36] Then in Gourmont's book of *Masques* the few pages on Lautréamont and the ones on Rimbaud, which are a painful disgrace.[37] (Those on Lautréamont are sadly insufficient.)

24 November

Morning at the Louvre; delightful morning. I had a little Montaigne with me, but read it only occasionally, while walking, and just enough to fan my mind's joyful enthusiasm. Went into Picard's to buy the *Syn-*

---

[35] By Isidore Ducasse, who took the pen-name of Count de Lautréamont. The now famous *Maldoror*, first published in 1869, was recognized as a work of genius by Léon Bloy and Remy de Gourmont in the early nineties and popularized by the surrealists in the 1920's.

[36] Rimbaud's poem "The Seven-Year-Old Poets" describes the revolts and visions of childhood.

[37] These pages are not found in the recent editions. [A.]

taxe of Haase and a second-hand Cabanis, into which I plunged when I got home.

Various errands. This evening read to Copeau the Sixth *Chant de Maldoror*. Too short day.

25 November

Supper at the Pousset with Mme E., Gérard, and J. S.

I hardly ceased thinking, during the whole listless evening, of the good reading I might have enjoyed, and could not keep myself from showing some resentment toward Gérard. Time, money, thought, he wastes everything to no purpose, without really enjoying it, without any real desire.

Mme E. disappointed me. With the best will in the world I was unable to be as enthusiastic as I should have liked to be. I imagined M. with her, understood why he was not more in love with her, hoped he would be even less so, as if I feared having to measure the quality of his love according to its object.

Yet the evening was not cheerless; I liked her pleasant disposition even though she had no more positive qualities. Not smoking, I was able to remain lucid, and since I was not trying too hard to please, I was able to remain natural. Besides, she helped me to do so and unconsciously I was grateful to her for it.

What a child I remained for a long time, always looking for, even going out of my way to invent, sympathetic points of contact — *in whosever company I happened to be*! It did help me, to be sure, to a more subtle understanding of others, but it also encumbered my life with pseudo-friendships that I have trouble getting out of today. Indulgence toward others is hardly less ruinous than indulgence toward oneself.

Gérard had gone ahead on the rue Godot-de-Mauroy last night — where Jean and I are prowling. Suddenly we hear someone shout from the end of the street: "Stop! Thief!" In the distance we can make out the white apron of a barmaid who is apparently running, and galloping toward us a tall, thin, gaunt silhouette. A butcher-boy suddenly appears near us; sticking out his arm, he knocks down the thief, who collapses on the edge of the sidewalk at our feet and moans: "Oh, you hurt me!" He tries to get up, all covered with mud, but is immediately seized by three big chaps who look as if they are going to crush him; but others intervene, for already a crowd has gathered. "Leave him alone. No! Don't hit him! . . ." A fat mulatto woman runs up who looks to me just like Pierre Louÿs's old Zora. "He took my purse. I had no money in it, but I'd like to have my keys back." All this was said with great dignity. Her heart is pounding; she is also out of breath from running; but she controls herself. Meanwhile the man keeps repeating: "Give me my cap. Give me my cap." It must have fallen on the sidewalk; no one has seen it; it doesn't matter. Various voices lean toward him and, almost in a whisper: "Give back the purse and get out of here quick." The thief looks stunned. He stays where he is. He gave back the purse, I suppose, but I didn't see it. People say to him several times: "Get along; *they* will be coming." The circle that had formed around him opens to let him get away. He goes, very slowly at first; then, at a little distance, he starts running.

We were amazed by the charity of these people. It is true that the poor fellow didn't look very frightening; probably half dead with hunger; later on I reproached myself for not giving him something.

28 November

I have come to hate this apartment, this furniture, this house. No concentration is possible here; I am defenseless against anything, against anyone; the least noise from the street or from within the house reaches me.

It is years now since my head has been warm. I think of that happy fever which, all the time that I was writing *Paludes,* kept my book awake in me.

The reading of Rimbaud and of the Sixth *Chant de Maldoror* has made me ashamed of my works and disgusted with everything that is merely the result of culture. It seems to me that I was born for something different.

But perhaps there is still time . . . perhaps in Auteuil . . . Oh! how I long . . .

1 December

Yesterday I read *L'Église habillée de feuilles* [38] at the Arthur Fontaines' to Raymond Bonheur, Paul Claudel, and the Mithouards. Bonheur had come to pick me up at about three. I had just come in from Gougy's shop loaded down with the fat Plutarch of Amyot, which I dive into at once.

Raymond Bonheur had been at the Frères-Saint-Jean-de-Dieu, where Carrière had just been operated on. He already talks of Carrière in the past tense. He says: "I don't know whether or not you will understand me, Gide, but I used to feel a physical pleasure in Carrière's company; for me he was like a big brother who took a protective interest in me. But I felt with him that warmth, yes, that sensual pleasure without which a friendship means nothing to me. I have never made a great distinction between friendship and love." And when I say something, he

---

[38] *The Leaf-clad Church,* a collection of poems by Francis Jammes published in 1906.

continues: "I am losing a great deal in him. Why, Gide, I have already seen many sad things in my lifetime; but nothing has ever upset me like the look Carrière gave me the morning of the operation."

A little later I learn from Delvolvé, the son-in-law, who sees Raymond Bonheur to the door, that the operation was terrible. "Too risky an operation," says Raymond Bonheur somewhat later; a delicate discretion kept him from giving me the painful details: the tracheotomy, the paralysis of the left leg and of the tongue muscles; even after a fortnight the poor man only partially recovers the use of speech. You feel that Raymond Bonheur would prefer not to talk about these things that Delvolvé, to whom, however, I am almost a stranger, relates. Never did the painful expression of Raymond Bonheur's face, never did the sad, sweet charm of that face seem to me so beautiful; and his hands shaking — I almost said stammering, like his voice — with emotion.

At Fontaine's. Paul Claudel, whom I have not seen in more than three years, is there. As a young man he looked like a nail; now he looks like a sledge-hammer. Not very high forehead, but rather wide; face without subtlety as if chiselled out; bull neck continued by the straight line of the head, through which passion can rush to flood the brain. Yes, I think this is the dominating impression: the head is of one piece with the body. I shall study him more fully next Tuesday (when he comes to lunch with us); I was a bit too concerned with defending myself and only half responded to his advances. He gives me the impression of a solidified cyclone. When he talks, it is as if something were released within him; he proceeds by sudden affirmations and maintains a hostile tone even when you share his opinion.

While I am talking with Fontaine, out of the corner of my ear I hear him proclaiming his admiration for Baudelaire. Mithouard, tactlessly taking up the subject, speaks of Baudelaire's "health," seeing in him above all a "healthy" genius. Is that a necessary prerequisite before he will allow himself to admire him?

"Poe and Baudelaire," declares Paul Claudel with a sort of stifled rage, "are the only two modern critics." Then he praises, most intelligently, the critical intelligence of Baudelaire and Poe, but in terms so close to those recently used, on this very same subject, by Remy de Gourmont that I can hardly keep myself from pointing this out. But I am afraid, at the mere name of Gourmont, of provoking an explosion.

Claudel is wearing a little jacket that is too short and that makes him look even more thickset and lumpish. One's eyes are constantly drawn to and shocked by his necktie, a four-in-hand the color of a locust-bean.

After the reading, as I compare Francis Jammes's series of poems with Verlaine's *Sagesse*, Claudel at once declares that *L'Église habillée de feuilles* is a much finer work, that he for one has "never liked *Sagesse* very much, in which Verlaine's juggling is always apparent and spoils even the best poems."

He talks in a not very loud voice, like a man very much in earnest; I notice once more how unsuitable real passion is to eloquence. Léon Blum, whom I went to see the day before yesterday, talked loud, vigorously and easily; he must have been audible in the next room.

2 December

From Russia the most alarming news, which makes a sort of figured bass to all my thoughts throughout all the day's occupations.

Great crowd at the exhibit of the Cronier Collection,[39] which we first visit in the morning before the official opening and to which we return at about two o'clock with Mme Copeau while Copeau goes back to his work. We had dined with them at the Rome restaurant.

The whole collection has a flavor of the nouveau-riche. After all that had been said of them, the Fragonards and Chardins disappoint me; it is absurd to say that the Louvre has no paintings by Fragonard that are comparable to *The Love-Letter;* charming, marvelous if you will, but not enough so to pay three hundred thousand for it, as the museum is being urged to do. I certainly prefer to it the wonderful *Portrait of the Engraver Schmidt* by La Tour; indeed, it is less the work of a painter than the Fragonard, but yet it is hunted down, dominated, so intelligently and so lovingly! I had a lump in my throat as I looked at that wonderful work. In the middle of the gallery a palpitating *Flora* by Carpeaux, squatting like the one in the tympanum of the Louvre, just as beautiful, perhaps more so, less supple, less fluid perhaps. . . . Nowhere has so much spirit and vigor more nobly excited sensual pleasure.

A wonderful Reynolds.

"An art-lovers' dialogue"[40] in front of Fragonard's *Love-Letter* (heard in the morning, when there were not many visitors): "Did you notice that the same dog is *in mine?*"

In the afternoon could be heard the insolent conversations of a group of sons of collectors, still without any down on their upper lip,

---

[39] The rich art collection of Mr. E. Cronier was put on sale in Paris at the Georges Petit Gallery in December 1905. Its masterpieces of French classical and romantic painting, works by Gainsborough, Lawrence, Reynolds, Romney, and sculptures, tapestries, and porcelains were dispersed.

[40] A reference to Gourmont's regular articles in the form of imaginary conversations appearing in the *Mercure de France* under the title of "*Dialogues des amateurs.*"

calling Fragonard "Frago" and saying: "What *I* like in him, etc. . . . etc. . . ." and this dialogue between two affected and very young men: "But why doesn't anyone do things like this today?" And the other replies with a superior air: "What do you expect, my dear fellow? No one has the time! No one has the time!"

I have just seen again the photograph of the Louvre *Flora;* I think it is more beautiful than the other; it has in addition a tenderness, a certain softness or lack of restraint, that makes the other, in recollection, seem rather dry.

In the evening we pursue our reading of Mme d'Épinay's *Mémoires.* At times we compare Rousseau's text, which, beside the *Mémoires,* seems to have a wonderful fullness and richness.

I note this sentence from the *Confessions:* "In short, however violent a passion I may have had for her, I found it just as pleasant to be the confidant as the object of her love, and I never once looked upon her lover as my rival, but rather as my friend. It might be said that this was not yet love; that may be, but it was more, then." (He is speaking here of Mme d'Houdetot and Saint-Lambert; he might have been speaking of Mme de Warens and Claude Anet.) Interesting comparison to be made with Dostoyevsky's Muishkin in the company of Rogozhin and Nastasia Philipovna in *The Idiot.* The expression of this feeling (which is also the feeling of my *Candaule)* — which I have never encountered *anywhere else* — is of the greatest importance.

Gourmont's article on Rivarol and his excellent *"Dialogue des amateurs";* irritating, exasperating — but excellent.

4 December

Back from La Roque where I had to go the day before yesterday; suffering from grippe, ill at ease, in very bad shape. Freezing trip in a half-heated compartment opposite a thin man with a low forehead and small face who, after having finished reading *La Patrie,*[41] never stopped smoking little cigarettes that he rolled himself. It seemed to me that with each one his forehead became narrower and more wrinkled. He smoked with a sort of systematic rage, not so much, it struck me, from a need as from a desire to stupefy himself. If his face had been a little less unattractive, I could not have restrained myself from saying: "You are killing yourself . . ." and I should have suffered, whatever he might have answered.

I was reading *La Domination* by Mme de Noailles.

At Pont-l'Évêque Édouard was waiting for me. Together we climb

---

[41] A conservative daily paper in which Paul Déroulède wrote regularly.

into his buggy and strike out into the night. The scented air of the country cured me immediately of my grippe and fatigue.

At his house a cold supper that his wife had prepared for me. The old deaf maid sits down in the dining-room near us, clasps her hands on her knees, and falls into contemplation. I feel her eyes weigh upon me.

5 December

Paul Claudel came to lunch. Too short a jacket, aniline-colored necktie; his face still more square than the day before yesterday; his speech both precise and full of images; his voice staccato, clipped, and authoritative.

His conversation, very rich and alive, does not improvise anything, you feel. He recites truths that he has patiently worked out. Yet he knows how to joke and, if he only let himself go a bit more on the spur of the moment, would not be without charm. I try to discover what is lacking in that voice . . . a little human warmth? . . . No, not even that; he has something much better. It is, I believe, the most *gripping* voice I have ever heard. No, he doesn't charm; he does not want to charm; he convinces — or impresses. I didn't even seek to protect myself from him, and when, after the meal, speaking of God, of Catholicism, of his faith, of his happiness, he added as I said that I understood him:

"But, Gide, then why don't you become converted? . . ." (this without any brutality, without even a smile). I let it be apparent how his words had upset my mind.

I should attempt to set them down here if I were not to find them in his *Traité de la co-naissance au monde et de soi-même* [42] that he has just finished. Likewise I should write down the few details he gave about his life if I did not think that life were to become famous.

L'Ode aux Muses, he tells us, begun in 1900, hung for a long time interrupted. He didn't know "how to finish it." It was only in 1904 that he added the invocation to Erato and the end.

"For a long time, for two years, I went without writing; I thought I must sacrifice art to religion. My art! God alone could know the value of this sacrifice. I was saved when I understood that art and religion must not be set in antagonism within us. That they must not be confused either. That they must remain, so to speak, perpendicular to each other;

---

[42] "Treatise of the Awakening to the World and to Oneself," which forms part of the *Art poétique* of 1907. This title, inspired by Bossuet's seventeenth-century *Traité de la connaissance de Dieu et de soi-même* and untranslatable in its subtlety, rests on Claudel's typical identification of the two words *naissance* and *connaissance:* "*Nous ne naissons pas seuls. Naître, pour tout, c'est co-naître. Toute naissance est une connaissance. . . .*" ("We are not born alone. To be born, in brief, is to be born with something. Every birth is an acquisition of knowledge.")

and that their very struggle nourishes our life. One must recall here the words of Christ: 'Not peace, but a sword.' That's what Christ means. We must not seek happiness in peace, but in conflict. The life of a saint is a struggle from one end to the other; the greatest saint is the one who at the end is the most vanquished."

He speaks during the lunch of a certain "frontal sense" that allows us, without reading them, to recognize in advance a good or a bad book, and always warned him against Auguste Comte. I should be more amused to hear him execute Bernardin if he did not at the same time demolish Rousseau. He demolishes many others! Beating about him with a monstrance, he devastates our literature.

(I remember my consternation, at Cuverville, when, pruning and cleaning out a peony plant, I noticed that a branch I had just removed because it seemed to me dead was still full of sap.)

He speaks with the greatest respect of Thomas Hardy and Joseph Conrad, and with the greatest scorn of English writers in general "who have never learned that the rule of 'nothing unessential' is the first condition of art."

He talks a great deal; you are aware of the pressure of ideas and images within him. As, apropos of I don't remember what or whom, I spoke of the weakening of the memory: "Memory doesn't weaken," he immediately exclaimed. "None of man's faculties weakens with age. That is a gross error. All man's faculties develop continuously from birth to death."

He talks endlessly; someone else's thought does not stop his for an instant; even a cannon could not divert him. In talking with him, in trying to talk with him, one is forced to interrupt him. He waits politely until you have finished your sentence, then resumes where he had stopped, at the very word, as if you had said nothing.

He shocked Francis Jammes some time ago (in 1900) when he replied to Jammes's anguish with "I have my God."

(The greatest advantage of religious faith for the artist is that it permits him a *limitless* pride.)

Upon leaving me he gives me the address of his confessor.

He also said:
"I attach absolutely no value to the literary quality of my work. Frizeau was the first one who, brought back to God by my dramas because he saw religion dominating everything in them, made me think: then I haven't written in vain. The literary beauty of my work has no other significance for me than that found by a workman who is aware of having performed his task well; I simply did my best; but, had I been a carpenter, I should have been just as conscientious in planing a plank properly as I have been in writing properly."

18 December

When I don't write is when I have the most to write. If I have a moment's relaxation, I use it to correct proofs, to write letters. I am barely sufficient unto my life. It is not so much the urgency of my occupations as their number and diversity; my mind is completely dislocated by them. My best time in Paris is when I am supposed not to be there. If I cease to write in this notebook for more than three days, it becomes painful for me to go back to it, and the moment I do not pay attention to details, I no longer enjoy noting anything down. Let us force ourselves.

(Raymond Bonheur, whom I saw yesterday, cannot conceive of *forcing* oneself. On the other hand it's my watchword. I want all my branches to be arched, like those the clever gardener torments to urge them to fruit.)

What especially shocked Paul Claudel when, after several years in the Orient, he returned to modern civilization was the waste.

"What!" he exclaimed, "when St. Francis of Assisi found in the mud of a path a bit of crumpled parchment, he picked it up in his hand, smoothed it out, because he had seen writing on it — *writing*, that sacred thing — and look at us, what we do with it today! It really pains me to think of that enormous mass of paper which is covered with printing for one day and then thrown into the garbage-pail. . . . We have not only no more respect for the writing of others, but not even for our own. . . ."

Waste, yes, that is also what spoils for me an evening like yesterday's. Waste of time, of money, of strength — and for what a petty pleasure!

Yet everything would have been all right if it had not been for that sort of obligation we felt (at least some of us) to go and finish out the evening at Maxim's. I had dined (rather pleasantly too) with Gérard and Ventura at the Café de Paris; it was my first time there. We met the J. T. couple and Copeau at the Athénée, where Tristan Bernard's *Triplepatte* was being played. On seeing it again, that delicate play seemed to me even better.

The interest of the evening was concentrated, during the intermissions and after the show (at the Bal Tabarin) on Ventura and Mme T., or rather on their polite attentions (the expression is too weak) for each other. I am merely noting. To relate it all would be too long.

Ventura made the greatest efforts to achieve spontaneity, and she let her pleasure be seen in the most childlike fashion. She was charming, but Mme T. was beautiful; and not only her features; an odd inner flame showed through her cheeks. Etc. . . . There was the episode of the shawl; an Egyptian shawl, a scarf of light material, but weighed down by a great number of silver sequins; when it slipped from Mme

T.'s arm onto the shoulders of the smiling Ventura, the grace and the delicate attention in the gesture could not pass unnoticed, either by Copeau or by me.

Christmas Day

This morning I lug out to Auteuil in a cab a table and two chairs, the first furniture in my new house.

Yesterday Mardrus came to look me up in Auteuil.

Jovially superior, lively as ever, getting on everyone's nerves but mine.

"Georges Louis," he told me, "is a charming fellow; he likes me a lot."

"He is right."

"Yes . . . but he is a very superior person. He esteems me very much indeed! . . . Oh, I don't mean as a poet, but as a man; as a mind, as a political thinker. . . . I am going to start out with the very highest official status! . . . The highest official status, Gide!" he repeats, raising his voice; then somewhat lower:

"They are waiting for the end of the conference, then they let me loose on Morocco!" He bursts out laughing, draws back, repeats: "They let me loose on Morocco!" — and goes away. (Yes, those are his very words, but the intonation is lost.)

Natanson reports to me these sentences of Maillol:

"A model! A model; what the hell would I do with a model? When I need to verify something, I go and find my wife in the kitchen; I lift up her chemise; and I have the marble." All this said with a strong southern accent.

"No, not at all," says Copeau; "you have no need to be afraid. I am satisfied with my happiness and I don't want to change anything about it; the most serious adventures can never draw me away from it more than two or three days. . . . But I am incapable of not holding out a hand to events. Oh, it won't do any good asking that of me."

"Cleave to the dogma; loosen up rather on morality." This is the remark of an influential Jesuit, brought to me by Arthur Fontaine.

Unfortunately Miomandre is here; not at all unattractive — on the contrary — but a bit young, a bit animated; Fontaine stays after him to talk to me about Jammes and Claudel; Claudel is getting married too! As for Jammes, he sends me word that Wyzewa is looking for a wife for him; and since Wyzewa is rather slow about it, he asks me to go and stir him up. . . .

Suarès writes in *Le Prisme:* [43]

"The type of mortification matters little. For instance, no one mortifies himself better, if he considers himself born for love, than in the state of marriage."

---

[43] Some pages by André Suarès entitled *"Profondeurs-Naufrage"* appeared in No. 6 of *Le Prisme* (November 1905), a little review edited and published by G. Jean-Aubry at Havre between June 1905 and March 1906. These pages were later reprinted in Suarès's book *Voici l'homme* (*Presenting Man*).

1906

There are still many things I should have noted in the last notebook; I leave it unfinished in Paris and begin this one on the train taking me to La Roque.

Yesterday, late afternoon at the Mathurins. Georgette Leblanc in *La Mort de Tintagiles*.[1] Small theater entirely filled. Maeterlinck gives me a seat in his box. Opposite us, Mary Garden; to the right, Duse (wonderful face of an *old* woman; not a single inexpressive wrinkle). *Utter lack of interest* of Maeterlinck's face; materiality of his features; a very positive, very practical man of the north, in whom mysticism is a sort of psychic exoticism.

I expected to find Georgette Leblanc terrible and was annoyed with myself for not being more annoyed with her; but no, the lights were dim enough so that we were spared the coarseness of her features and the indiscreet aspect of her whole body. Indeed, I am willing to admit that she set herself off rather well.

Succession of living tableaux in the Burne-Jones or Walter Crane manner. Continual music slowing down the diction and suggesting great depths behind every sentence. This interferes with the action considerably; every word tends to suggest that the action is taking place anywhere except on the stage.

Dinner with the Drouins, Charles-Louis Philippe, and Ghéon. The last-named more *headstrong* than ever. I have already noticed that he is much more intractable when he has just seen Vielé-Griffin. Faced with Ghéon's protuberances, Philippe withdraws into himself. The few remarks he makes are charming.

Back from La Roque.

What a danger! What a danger in concerning oneself with so many things! My mind is quite "deconsecrated."

Em. goes to the Louvre with Olga who is trying to learn, who stands in front of the great works and says facing the Venus de Milo: "What a shame that she's lost her arms!" In the Apollo Saurochtonus she especially admires the lizard.

---

[1] *The Death of Tintagiles*, a symbolist play by Maurice Maeterlinck, first published in 1894.

10 January

Unbearable mental fatigue. Work alone could rest me, gratuitous work, or play . . . I am far from that. Each thought becomes an anxiety in my brain; I am becoming that ugliest of all things: a busy man.

Stupidly missed yesterday the rehearsal of Curel's new play, for which Copeau had given us two tickets.[2]

We have finished reading aloud the *Mémoires* of Mme d'Épinay. Without Grimm she would be easier to bear. Here and there, charming passages; I have noted several. Nothing is up to the first half of the first book.

We try *Le Chevalier Destouches*,[3] but after twenty pages the book falls from my hands. I want to go on with it by myself. I find just as much profit in cultivating my hates as my loves. From one end to the other there is nothing but rhetoric and bluff in that man.

In two evenings we read *La Princesse de Montpensier*.[4] I am too tired to say anything about it. Curious epoch in which the art of writing is confused with politeness, and manners govern the mind above all.

11 January

Radiant weather this morning. The air is dry. I can't recognize my thoughts. I don't feel my age.

We go to the Val d'Aulnay (with the Schlumbergers) to choose an arborvitæ at Croux's for our Auteuil garden.

Copeau in the Van Rysselberghes' box at *Tintagiles* yesterday. (I was not there.) Copeau blubbers, says: "I am falling ill; can't go to the theater any more without weeping." And when Mme Théo asks him what he thinks of the show, he replies, to the tune of *Ça finira mal:* "They are paying too much attention to the little fellow." Then, after a pause, adds: "In fact, that's the big mistake in the play."[5]

15 January

Style: not so much sagacious as prudent; cautious; a man of infinite precautions.

Art would consist, despite the greatest explicitness, in always holding a surprise in store.

---

[2] *Le Coup d'aile* (*The Wing-Stroke*), three-act play that opened at the Théâtre Antoine on 10 January 1906.

[3] A novel (1864) by Jules Barbey d'Aurevilly.

[4] A short-story by Mme de La Fayette, published anonymously in 1662.

[5] Jacques Copeau was drama critic for the *Ermitage* (1904–6) and later for the *Grande Revue* (1907–10).

Again three days of rain. My head is tired, my will restless, and my personality indecisive. Numerous chores make all real work impossible, and that is the only thing that would rest me. I dare not go back to my novel for fear of blunting my emotion and zeal. I have begun studying the piano again, for the good of my health, but not methodically. My handwriting is becoming uglier. I sleep badly; I tremble and twitch the way wild animals do.

We have given up Boylesve's mediocre novel [6] and taken up with trepidation *Pochékonié d'autrefois* by the wonderful Shchedrin.[7]

Friday, at Charmoy's, a strange evening. In the studio, cluttered with huge statues fantastically lighted by a score of candles ingeniously stuck here and there, on the corner of benches, in the folds of the robes of the enormous angels supporting the monument of Beethoven — in that studio, overheated by a little cast-iron stove, José, his wife, and I wait for the Princess de Broglie and Miss Barney.

Around ten o'clock we hear the Princess's automobile, which appears in the blackness at the door. The Princess is wearing an ermine wrap, which she drops into Charmoy's hands. A gown of black velvet covering only the lower half of her body sets off a vast expanse of lustrous skin; the gown hangs from jet straps. Her face is small and tired; her coiffure, almost virginal, strives unsuccessfully to make her look younger. No wrinkles, however, but her features are painfully tight.

As soon as she comes in, she stares at me through her lorgnette, whose gold handle is linked by a small chain to a delicate bracelet of rubies.

Her intention of charming is flagrant.

On the back of a wicker chair, which she considers "not very inviting," a fur is stretched; on the floor a foot-warmer for her little feet, which she also wraps in a shawl. Near her, behind her, Miss Barney takes refuge in an eloquent silence and lets the Princess strut.

Back in France, 30 January. Liverdun

I like this landscape in which the washings of the earth bathe the grass with ochre. Parallel to the train a stream flows evenly; a little higher up, a little farther from us, a canal with a towed boat on it. Beyond the canal the ground rises still more; fields dismantled by the winter; a patch of rocks; then a sky of low clouds. Trees border the canal. Lower down, in the meadows that the stream has just flooded, half-

---

[6] Most likely *Le Bel Avenir* (*The Fine Future*) (1905).

[7] *Bygone Days in Poshekhonie*, first published in French translation in 1892. Poshekhonie is an imaginary region created by Shchedrin to symbolize the backward manorial society that he satirizes.

melted snow and ice mingle in their uncertain white patches, among the clumps of reeds, pale reflections of the sky.

Cuverville, 3 February

Apropos of a very interesting letter from Tahiti published in the *Journal des missions,* I pick up Darwin's *Journal* and reread to Em. the wonderful account of his stay in the South Sea Islands.

I continue the reading alone.

It is a long time since I have read with such a healthy appetite and at the same time with so much gluttony. Each new idea drawn from my reading, as soon as it enters my head, links up with something; it seems to me that I was waiting for it; its place was ready.

I recall certain readings in my childhood, so voluptuously penetrating that I felt the sentence almost physically enter my heart. This evening I again felt that marvelous sensation.

I had stayed in the garden until five o'clock, pruning my rosebushes with Mius under the flurry of snow; came in chilled to the bone, inebriated by the clear air. How beautiful the livid, slate-colored sky was above the russet hill and the leafless trees of the avenue!

In the greenhouse an *Iris tuberosa* offers me a delicate green and black flower. In the garden almost all the hellebores are in flower.

9 February

I finish the *Mémoires de deux jeunes mariées.*[8] A confused, pasty book; throughout the book, the lineaments of a masterpiece. Singular *pressure* of the subject. Balzac — that sort of genius he has for making a sudden knot of all his threads; the very first sentence of the book, for instance; that is the sort of thing that only a brain working at a very high temperature can invent.

Genius incapable of criticism. (See the preface to *La Fille d'Ève;*[9] judgments on the novel in the different countries of Europe.)

13 February

I interrupt my reading of Barrès's new book for *Archipel* by Pierre Louÿs:[10] scratch collection of calligraphed commonplaces and stupidities, with suddenly an excellent, peremptory article against the reform of spelling; another, very good, on sports in antiquity.

---

[8] *The Memoirs of Two Brides,* by Honoré de Balzac.
[9] *A Daughter of Eve,* a novel by Balzac.
[10] *Archipelago,* published in 1906.

The Van Rysselberghes, the Jean Schlumbergers, Ghéon, and I come out of the Schola (Monteverde's *Orfeo* very poorly executed). At the Closerie, where we stop a moment, we see at a table in the rear a residue of *Vers et Prose*[11] gathered around Paul Fort and his wife, B. R., and several others unknown to me. Handshakes. R. begins an enormous compliment directed at me: "I thank you, Gide . . . I thank you for the beautiful pages of *Vers et Prose* that you permitted us to read." Nothing is so silly as the expression of a man who is being complimented. One must avoid it. And as he insists, quoting me: "I don't know where to place in my sentence this monstrous toad. . . ." I interrupt him abruptly with: "Well, I am glad it has found a place in your mouth." It came out in spite of me.[12]

For the past three days I have been packing my books with the enthusiasm of a vandal. As my bookshelves progressively empty themselves I feel my brain being aired out. At one and the same time I feel the intoxication of a sort of havoc and the joy, as I arrange the books in their baskets, of neatness and precision, of ingenious juxtaposition.

1 March

Finally I am back again at my work, and nothing separates me from it any longer. Finished, yesterday and this morning, bringing my correspondence up to date. Began piano-practice again. Received my writing-paper. Received the copies of *Amyntas*.[13]

2 March

Read Hugo's astonishing essay on Voltaire.

---

[11] *Vers et Prose*, a literary quarterly edited by the poet Paul Fort from 1905 until 1914, was founded to publish the works of the surviving members of the symbolist movement and their disciples. Such writers as Maeterlinck, Verhaeren, Barrès, Régnier, Claudel, Jammes, Moréas, Louÿs, and Gourmont appeared regularly in its pages, and it contributed to the discovery of younger writers like Guillaume Apollinaire, Jules Romains, and Georges Duhamel. The following writings of Gide were published in *Vers et Prose: Bou Saada* (1905); *Alger* (1906); *Poésies d'André Walter* (reprint, 1907); *Le Retour de l'enfant prodigue* (1907); *Bethsabé* (1909); *Feuilles de route 1895–1896* (from the *Journals*) (1911); *Proserpine* (1912).

[12] Gide's description of the toad occurs in his *Alger*, published in the fourth issue of *Vers et Prose*, which had just appeared. In French "to swallow a toad" means "to pocket an insult."

[13] The volume *Amyntas*, published by the Mercure de France in 1906, contained "*Mopsus*," "*Feuilles de route*" ("Leaves Gathered by the Wayside"), "*De Biskra à Touggourt*," and "*Le Renoncement au voyage*."

3 March

I do not yet use all my time effectively. A slight dizziness when faced with too many empty hours; I must invent some landmarks. This evening I read Hugo's *Villemain* to Gérard.

6 March

Yesterday evening read to Copeau all I have so far written of *La Porte étroite*. I had dined at his house; in the afternoon I had taken him my *Amyntas* at Petit's; then the swimming-pool; then the *Ermitage*. It was beautiful weather; I felt very well.

After dinner Copeau first reads several passages of *Amyntas* to his wife; then, taking the book from his hands, I read the passage about the flute, Droh, etc. . . .

Mme Copeau leaves us alone; I take my manuscript out of its envelope. The reading, rather well begun, sinks into a mire of ennui. Lamentable impression, not so much on Copeau, perhaps, as on me; moreover, he already knew almost all of it. I resented that sort of cowardice which had made me have recourse to him before having obtained more. How much work still ahead! I must start it all over again. Excellent profit from the evening. Copeau, a good doctor, without cruelty, with even too much indulgence, but yet strengthening my impression with his. And already I know him too well to be ashamed of showing myself to him without having dressed up more.

This morning I send an express letter to Rouart to refuse his luncheon (at Prunier's with Albert Sarraut and Michel). I hurl myself into work.

Rouart comes after me and drags me off. Unbearable lunch at which no one talks anything but politics and at which I pretend to have some ideas on the question. Toward the end the conversation becomes somewhat livelier on the subject of the Inventories.[14] Albert Sarraut talks rather well.

At three o'clock I get away.

I had the stupidity to go and see Blanche this afternoon. The indignation that I feel toward him makes me believe in eternal life. Impossible to work after that, or even to play the piano. I must go out and get a change of air. There is not a single thought in my mind that does not rise up in revolt.

---

[14] According to the law of 9 December 1905 concerning the separation of the churches from the state, the religious establishments were suppressed and a double "descriptive and qualitative inventory" was ordered made of all the properties owned or controlled by each establishment.

Ingenious in spoiling the happiness of others, not exactly through ill will, but through an inability to understand any other form of happiness than that which his fortune would allow him to enjoy — in short, through an incapacity to achieve happiness himself. I fancy that he seeks it rather in a convenient use of things than in a self-determina·tion; he is an extraordinarily dependent creature. He naturally look⸗ with pity on the happiness of others. He says, or seems to say: "Oh heavens! how can you consider that as happiness? In your place, I . . " and instead of pitying, he advises.

Tuesday morning

I derive from the excellent *Vie de Poussin* by Paul Desjardins [15] a calm health. For several days now Gérard and I have been getting up at six (he leaves for his factory at seven thirty). Bach has taken the place of Chopin, and Pascal the place of Montaigne. I have sent off almost all my copies of *Amyntas*. My novel is slowly taking form in my head again; I no longer see it as a matter of expressing emotions very clearly, but rather of accumulating little facts to "inform" or animate the characters.

I thought I knew Pascal; every day I am discovering new things in him.

Em. returned yesterday from Cuverville. At eleven o'clock I am at the Gare Saint-Lazare. The suburban train gets us here by midnight.

Impossible to find the key to the wardrobe. Em. insists that she put it in her basket, on top of four dozen eggs. Naturally, the eggs having moved, the key — heavier than they — must have slipped to the bottom. We burrow with great care for fear of breaking the eggs. We bring up a pair of gloves, a veil, a pair of scissors, a handkerchief, what else? and ten boxes of matches! [16] But no key. We decide to take the eggs out, one by one. Each egg is wrapped in tissue paper which we remove. The egg is cool in one's hand, clean, and dull off-white in color. In Eugène Rouart's cloisonné bowl, so blue, so green, they make a marvelous still-life. Now it is one o'clock in the morning; the basket is empty, the bowl full; we admire the effect. But no key.

---

[15] *Life of Poussin*, published in 1903.

[16] I must note here the story of the boxes of matches.

"Why, of course," says Em., "I bought them at Criquetot. Do you know that in the country they are only a penny? Berthe filled her suitcase with them."

"But, my dear, these are sulphur matches! You must have taken them for safety matches. Look, smell it." And I light one of them under her nose. Em. chokes a bit and exclaims:

"Oh! the robbers!" [A.]

I use the very best technique with Gérard: I act in such a way that he advises and teaches me the right way of working. He cannot do so without working himself. We are both up at six o'clock. In his case I recognized as no good the system that consists in first getting rid of the small undergrowth — back letters, reading of the newspaper, tidying up — on the theory that then your brain is completely free for the *real* work. One must begin with the real work. One must attack it directly, without delay, deliberately, and bring to it one's greatest and freshest energy.

This morning very beautiful letter from Claudel. Excellent, stirring letter from Mauclair, to which I feel like replying at once.

Friday

Gérard — a creature without courage. Then he should have more gifts.

Saturday, 17 March

Came home furious last night (at a quarter past one) from an absurd evening at the Odéon. It was the opening of *Glatigny* by Mendès. Gérard dragged me to it on the excuse of seeing Ventura play (in very ordinary fashion) a tiny role; she was on the stage only a quarter of an hour. What a deadly evening! Steady chatter on the part of the actors. Rhetoric and loquacity.

In the box, the Jean Schlumbergers, Jacques Copeau, and, after she has removed her make-up, Ventura. Gérard keeps moving about.

This morning my head is splitting. It takes all the joy of this radiant weather to set me up again.

Sunday, 18

I finish slowly, as slowly as possible, Paul Desjardins's salutary book on *Poussin*, copying several passages. I order his book on *La Méthode des classiques,*[17] which Maurice Denis recommends. (He lunched with us Monday.) I wish Maurice Denis were less easily satisfied with himself. But a little anxiety would deprive him of a great deal of health.

He tells of Henri Matisse going to show Rodin his drawings and leaving the master's studio furious because Rodin had said to him: "Fuss over it; fuss over it. When you have fussed over it two weeks more, come back and show it to me again."

He speaks of Simon, Cottet, Dauchez; Jacques Blanche's *self-assurance* impresses them all. Unfortunately.

Clara Ungerer comes to dinner. Very pleasant evening. But which I should have spent even more pleasantly at the piano or with a book.

---

[17] *The Method of the French Classics* is the full title of this book, published in 1904.

Tuesday

Coutard comes to lunch. Slightly bloated; very much the "just back from America" look. I shall not help Gérard to detach himself from him. It will come by itself, and the movements of Gérard's vanity would lose some of their interest for me if I pulled the strings.

Immediately after lunch I rush to meet Ghéon at the Monet exhibition. Together we go to the Société Nouvelle [18] to see Copeau.

(Amazing bust by Rodin.) At the Salon des Indépendants we discover in the crowd Garnier, Mourey, Guérin, Rouart; and Retté, utterly drunk, staggering about supported by a very young man, shouting my name from one end to the other of a large gallery, who says: "I am a bit drunk," and belches in your face. Verlaine drunk was *tremendous*. Drunk, Retté seems more insignificant than ever; he is merely revolting; no one pays any attention to him.

Saw nothing but very ordinary things. But how can one listen, caught in that ignorant throng? How can one loyally give one's attention to anything? Vauxcelles's article that was being sold at the entrance is idiotic.

20 March

Impossible not to go to the Louvre today. For the past week this has been an unsatisfied need. And I was angry with myself because at first the Poussins seemed to me dull. It wasn't until I saw them *again,* after going all around the gallery, that they lighted up. I admire that sort of awkwardness, of heaviness in the execution. No manual dexterity; no dash; in no other artist perhaps has the head so completely dominated the craft.

On my way out I stop in front of two paintings by Jean Boulogne called Valentin (1591? to 1634?). I must see them again. The *Judgment of Solomon* is an almost pathetic work and one of the most disconcerting I know.

21 March

Patiently I am making progress in the *"Apologie de Raymond de Sebonde."* [19]

Certainly the *secret aim* of mythology was to prevent the development of science.

---

[18] A Belgian literary review by this name was published at the time in Mons; it may have had an office in Paris or this may refer to some "Société Nouvelle des Artistes Décorateurs."

[19] "The Apology of Raymond Sebond" (as the title is generally given) forms chapter twelve of the second book of Montaigne's *Essays.* As the most coherent statement of Montaigne's skepticism, it stands at the center of the edition of 1580.

24 March
I do not admit that anything should be prejudicial to me; on the contrary, I want everything to be useful to me. I intend to turn everything to advantage.

25 March
The inside of Gérard's head — clear, sonorous, and frigid — like a room without furniture and without a fire. . . .
This morning, between my pen and my brain, no haze intervenes.

28 March
From little Gérard's presence here I have now gained about everything that I could hope to gain. It is to be feared, if he stays too long with me, that I might become a Christian again. I am too keenly aware of the use he might derive from practicing certain maxims of the Gospels, and I cannot restrain a *profound* indignation upon seeing him squander without beauty a moral patrimony that generations have striven, *with abnegation,* to build up for him. (That seems almost to come from an article by Claretie; but if I begin trying to write "elegantly," I am lost.)

His monstrous fatuousness is unhealthy; one would like to treat it like a cancer, but perhaps without any greater hope of curing it. Perhaps he owes to his very constitution his inability to prefer any pleasure to that of vanity. He is bored.

He claims that he is better now; my fear is that he really believes this. Yet no, he cannot be taken in by this superficial semblance. Indeed, after an hour or two of calm work he still recaptures that clear complexion which I often think lost forever. . . . An hour later, his cheeks redden again, take on that dreadful brick shade; the look in his eyes becomes heavy, closed. . . . How can you then distinguish him from any other dissipated wash-out? He frequents them assiduously; that is in fact his environment; even his fatuousness brings him closer to them; that is the only milieu in which his remaining distinctions are legal tender.

29 March
I reread my old letters to Em. that I have brought from Cuverville. In vain I seek in them some material for my novel. But in doing so I lay bare all my intellectual flaws. There is not one of them that fails to annoy me.

30 March
Gérard. — He has his good qualities nevertheless; he had his virtues. I liked many things in him.

What do natural gifts matter to me in someone who is unable to ripen them?

I watch, not without interest, the slow transformation in his mind of the image he had formed of me.

The delightful first hours of work in the morning are claimed by all my pursuits: piano-practice, dead languages, reading, correspondence, notes in this notebook; so that they are often broken up and I disperse unsystematically the most valuable moments of the day.

3 April

This evening I sob as I finish the wonderful *"Souvenirs d'Hôpital"* by Lucien Jean.[20]

Three times today, while talking to Leclerc, the secondhand-book-seller, I yielded to impulses of vanity and ostentation — for the least of which Lafcadio would have buried the blade of his knife in his thigh.[21]

How beautiful the weather was this morning!

4 April

Heredia's library and a part of Verhaeren's are being sold a week apart. I go to the first day of the first sale and to the second sale. Between them a severe grippe keeps me in the house.

In the auction-room I dispute a few books against Pozzi and Hanotaux. (In another notebook I shall set down my purchases in detail.) Most of the books are pushed 'way beyond their value. You let yourself be enticed into pursuing books that you only half want or perhaps don't want at all.

I had promised myself to get hold of a Desbordes-Valmore in the hope of then giving it to Marie de Régnier. I still remember the day when, alone with her in her father's study, she recited to me *"Les Roses de Saadi."* [22]

Kept in the house by grippe.

---

[20] "Recollections of the Hospital," character sketches by Gide's friend, appeared in the *Ermitage* in February and March 1906.

[21] The hero of *Les Caves du Vatican* (*Lafcadio's Adventures*) punishes himself for each show of vanity by jabbing his knife into his thigh. The book was not published until 1914.

[22] Henri de Régnier's wife, herself a poet, was the daughter of the poet J.-M. de Heredia. "The Roses of Saadi" is one of the most famous of the poems by Marceline Desbordes-Valmore.

5 April

Wasted two hours at the Auteuil races for ten minutes of adulterated emotion. I haven't the habit of such paltry pleasures. My demoralization came especially from having paced the public enclosure over and over without meeting a single person with whom I wanted to talk or go to bed.

6 April

In Heredia's big copy of Ronsard I discover the wonderful ode *"Contre Denise, Sorcière."* [23]

7 April

Read without much profit Sainte-Beuve's double article on Grimm.

Before he left for the south (he is taking a three-day motor trip with Pierre Espinas) I again had a talk with Gérard. I like the way he disarms me with a few words and makes me aware of all the affection that, despite everything, I still have for him.

I have already said that he is (to me especially) the consummate type of the flatterer. Let me explain myself: in his presence I am grateful to myself for all the emotions I feel. Yes, every time Gérard leaves the better role to me. It's a pity that the play is not more amusing.

8 April

Ghéon came after me yesterday after dinner. I go with him on the boulevards and don't get back to Auteuil until two o'clock. This morning I get up slightly tired, but my mind clear, ready for work, and voluptuously active.

I finish Sainte-Beuve's poor article on Grimm, take a few notes on Barrès, then go walking through the gate to the Bois, taking along Montaigne and Flaubert's letters to his niece. I am writing these lines seated on the first empty bench. It is beautiful weather. The air as you breathe it is delicious.

For the last three days the sky has been clear. The air is still rather cooler than warm. I delight in every little thing assiduously.

Went to see Jacques Blanche yesterday. "What beautiful weather!" I couldn't keep from saying as I came in. But he immediately replied: "Oh! how can you say that? It's frightful weather. You call 'beautiful' the only weather I can't endure." Such remarks strike me as blasphemy. I should never go to see Blanche except when it's raining.

He wants everything, around him, to share his gloom.

Wonderful letter from Raymond Bonheur in reply to mine on the oc-

---

[23] "Against the Witch Denise."

casion of Carrière's death. And this disturbing sentence as a postscript: "I have received a letter from Francis Jammes that will be one of the sorrows of my life."

On each serious occasion Jammes's lack of real kindness is revealed again.

Nevertheless his two books that I received yesterday (*L'Église habillée de feuilles* and *Pensées de jardins*) [24] are full of marvelous pages.

9 April

I reread a few pages of Anatole France. . . .

I should like France more whole-heartedly if certain rash people did not try to make of him a writer of importance. That sets me wondering. I fear that perhaps I have not been fair. I reopen *La Vie littéraire* and especially *Le Jardin d'Épicure*,[25] where his thought is most directly accessible. I read this sentence which I applaud:

"One thing above all gives charm to men's thoughts, and this is unrest. A mind that is not uneasy irritates and bores me."

I am reminded of Goethe's remark: *The tremor of awe (das Schaudern) is the best in man.* Alas! this is just it; no matter how I try, I do not feel any tremor in France; I read France without a tremor.

He is fluent, subtle, elegant. He is the triumph of the euphemism. But there is no restlessness in him; one drains him at the first draught. I am not inclined to believe in the survival of those upon whom everyone agrees right away. I doubt very much if our grandchildren, opening his books, will find more to read in them than we are finding. I know that, as far as I am concerned, I have never felt him to be ahead of my thought. At least he explains it. And this is what his readers like in him. France flatters them. Each one of them is free to think: "How well put that is! After all, I wasn't so stupid either; that's just what *I* was thinking *too.*"

He is well-bred; that is, he is always aware of others. Perhaps he does not attach any great value to what he cannot reveal to them. Besides, I suspect that he hardly exists at all behind and beyond what he reveals to us. Everything comes out in conversation, in relationships. Those who frequent him appreciate being taken right into the drawing-room and the study; these rooms are on one floor; the rest of the house doesn't matter. In my case, I am annoyed not to have any hint of the near-by room in which a crime is committed or of the room in which people make love.

[24] *The Leaf-clad Church* and *Thoughts of Gardens,* two collections of poems published in 1906.

[25] *The Literary Life,* four volumes of literary criticism published between 1888 and 1892, and *The Garden of Epicurus,* a novel (1895) full of random reflections.

10 April
Paul Laurens, who comes to lunch and with whom I spend the whole afternoon, repeats to me Albert's disheartening remark: "Oh, how slow our youthful dreams are in dying!"

Sunday, 15 April
The number is increasing . . . of things that I allow myself to think, that I am less inclined to allow myself to say, and that I do not allow others to say at all; as for example, that the beginning of *Madame Bovary*[26] is very badly written.

Tuesday after Easter
My nerves on edge as a result of the day yesterday when, from nine o'clock in the morning on, I was unable to work, or even to be alone, a single moment.

This morning my work is constantly interrupted by a *mad* anxiety: how did Jacques Copeau get home Saturday night? Already on Sunday I stopped at Georges Petit's to find out about his return. Copeau was not there; I left a note for him, an urgent question. . . . Since then, *nothing*. I shall stop by again this evening.

How *much* I enjoyed going out yesterday with Élie Allégret's four children. I took them to the Jardin d'Acclimatation with Domi. All along the way I had little Jean and the very small André clinging to me. From time to time, suddenly, one of them would squeeze my hand with a sort of rapture. Their affection enveloped me like a perfume. Jean held my right hand and little André my left. The weather was perfect. We saw a balloon take off.

Little Jean. His anxiety; his attention each time he saw me take out money (for the train, the cab, the admission, the tea).

I wanted to repeat to Jeanne a very amusing remark of Eric, Jean's younger brother; I stopped suddenly, having encountered Jean's *anxious* look. Certainly, never having heard his parents call attention to a remark by any one of them (and this is the reason why each of these children talks in such a delightfully natural way), it would never have occurred to him that I was repeating these words because I considered them charming; he feared that they might have been out of place.

A very good shepherd already — "guiding the flock"[27] — he did not think of his own pleasure, was constantly anxious to gather together his little brothers; kept an eye out if one of them strayed; became alarmed if he did not see all of them at the same time.

---

[26] Flaubert's great novel, published in 1857.
[27] Ronsard. [A.]

Wednesday, 18 April
Have found the right paper for writing *La Porte étroite* and begun copying. Three pages.

Monday, 23 April
This morning I put my papers in order, for they had been accumulating in disorder; read the papers of the last few days, took some notes, and clipped some articles. This afternoon, tired out, I slept an hour; read Blum's indifferent short story, back numbers of reviews, etc. . . .
Finished the volume of Flaubert (*Lettres à sa nièce*).

27 April
I cling to my work; but allow myself to be distracted, and, in spite of myself, even seek to distract myself.
Léon Blum's *thought* has lost all interest for me; it has become merely a subtle instrument that he lends to the demands of *his cause.*
It is a long time since I had read any book of criticism that satisfied me as much as this excellent book by Paul Desjardins. After his *Poussin* I am reading his *Corneille* and without any haste to reach the end.

I am rereading *Madame Bovary.* The difficulties that Flaubert plans to overcome are all of the same order, and to reduce them Flaubert always finds the same common factors.

Since yesterday we have adopted a poor black poodle that was starving to death and prowling around our door for three days. His coat is all thick and matted from the plaster debris on which he has been sleeping in the house that is being built next door. At two a.m. Em. makes me go down to see if he isn't barking in the cellar, where we locked him up. I don't think he is intelligent, but he is affectionate.

I have bathed, I have soaped my poor dog in my tub. I hoped that cleanliness would give some luster to his coat! But now he looks more than ever like a blind man's dog. And I who wanted a pedigreed dog, I've got what was coming to me! No matter; it is time to learn once more to prefer the events that choose me to those I should have chosen myself.

Saturday
After a period of passable work, went out to call on the good La Pérouse, whom I knew to be alone that day. I leave him just in time to go and pick up Copeau as he leaves the Petit Gallery and walk home with him, before dining myself at Auguste Bréal's.
Very nice dinner, with the Philippe Berthelots, Moréas, Bonnard, and a sculptor whose name I didn't recognize.

Moréas protests when you speak of his healthy look and declares that he is "very ill." When you look at him more closely, you see in fact that the apparent "health" is only a rather nasty puffiness. He is just the way I have always seen him, scrupulously dressed, careful in his speech, and constantly turning up his mustache with a twist. Every time he addresses me, his big cockatoo eye caresses me in a way that stirs me. I should like to tell him how much I like his poems, but cannot produce the least compliment. He speaks of Victor Hugo with a slightly disdainful arrogance, which, however, is only a pose; he says he prefers Lamartine to him and recites some of his lines, which, picked out in this way and warmed by that brazen voice, seem, indeed, full of ambrosia. He does not talk much, remains unaffected, does not insist on silence all around him, and talks only to a few at a time.

Philippe Berthelot produced, as usual, the easy paradoxes of a superior mind. The ruin of San Francisco is "an unimportant little event"; the eruption of Vesuvius likewise; the May Day strike "exists only in the imagination of the frightened bourgeois"; the Bonmartino trial is "a very banal news item, which attracts a little more interest than the usual news items only because the names are Italian." And so on. Moréas inclines somewhat toward this failing too, which belongs to three fourths of the literary men and intellectuals of today (Paul Valéry, Gourmont, Vielé-Griffin — I have chosen the most dissimilar men). There are few failings more tiresome to me.

Monday
Yesterday at about six there came back to see me that preposterous little fop named R. L., whose intrigue finally succeeded in slipping a rather long essay into the *Ermitage.* Yet he is not stupid, nor unpolished; but I consider it impertinent that at the age of nineteen he should make me read his sixty pages without having read a single one of mine. He comes to me not because he is drawn, but simply to push himself and because he has understood that I could get him into the *Ermitage.* I shall have it out with him if he returns.

2 May
Jammes writes me on sky-blue paper a typical parish priest's letter, in which he reminds me of Pourceaugnac's doctors trying to persuade him that he is ill.[28] Perhaps I am about to enter paradise, but not through the door he thinks. "You seem to me restless," he says, "like a cork bobbing on the water." I am restless when I can't work as much as I want.

(I am keeping the draft of the letter I am writing him.)

---

[28] In Molière's comedy ballet *Monsieur de Pourceaugnac.*

Yesterday went out at about two. Went to Albert's.

His wife opens the door, shouts from the bottom of the stairs leading to the studio: "Papa! it's André," then goes upstairs with me and settles down in our conversation, in our intimacy, which she hinders, which she makes impossible. And all during the two hours I stay, she doesn't budge once. It's this way *every time* I go to see Albert. With her there, we talk about almost everything that we would talk about without her . . . but not in the same way.

And I feel that Albert is fed up with this. Timidly, giving some excuse or other, he accompanies me into the hall, then onto the landing, and whispers as he leans toward me: "I can never be alone any more," and I see an old man's big tears, which he hastens to rub away.

When both of them came to Auteuil, Em. taking charge of his wife, I had been able to remain alone with him for some time. Then it was that he repeated the heartbreaking sentence with which his father's will ended: "My dear children, above all don't have any ambition." And Albert added lugubriously: "He knew that we were not up to it."

And I wonder what a come-down Albert's father had made too when, toward the end of his life, he used to weep silently in the evening, with his back turned to the lamp, while his wife, beside him, read the newspaper or embroidered and Albert, out of respect for his father, pretended not to see.

3 May

Through excessive turbulence, I cannot succeed in imposing a method on myself, not that I am unwilling to submit to it, but my body constantly revolts against what my mind proposes.

What is the good of my resolution to get up at dawn when I haven't been able to sleep all night? or to stay up late when I can't keep my eyes open? I am forced to fool myself and to take advantage of the good moments as they come.

Finished Paul Desjardins's study of Corneille. Excellent. A trifle long.

Em. was to leave for Cuverville yesterday; but I felt so bad that I asked her to put off her departure one day. After lunch, taking advantage of the sudden soft weather, we went out into the Bois de Boulogne and, skirting the embankment of the fortifications, reached La Muette and the avenue Henri-Martin. Went up for a moment to call on Aunt Charles; Gérard had warmly proposed coming and keeping me company during Em.'s absence; I had to tell him, as decently as I could, that I preferred solitude.

Worked in desultory fashion until dinner.

After dinner, read to Em. the first few pages of *La Porte étroite.* Certainly the description of the garden is good — but the rest of it . . . ?

I finish reading to myself *Les Secrets de la Princesse de Cadignan,*[29] which we had begun reading aloud.

4 May

After a night of frightful insomnia, got up this morning more excited than tired.

5 May

Stayed so long at Aunt Charles's that I missed a wonderful sunset. As soon as I come in at rue de la Tour, she begins talking of her troubles. She is ill, yet talks only incidentally of her health and interminably of Gérard.

"What did he do yesterday? He drank six cups of coffee. He opened his law book and closed it saying: 'Oh! I can't work today.' He thumbed through the *Revue des deux mondes,* then dropped the issue on the table with the remark: 'Nothing interesting.' Finally he went out, suddenly, as if he couldn't resist any more. Where was he going? . . . Even his father, André, even his father, who never pays attention to anything, asked: 'What's the matter with him this evening?' "

I hoped to find him at rue de la Tour, where I arrived in time for dinner. He is dining at Robert Burnand's. Very eager to see him, for he had seemed to me to be falling back into the dumps the day before yesterday, I get away from my aunt's without dining and am off to catch him at rue de Varenne.

In the métro wrote a scene of my novel; read some of *Le Mémorandum* (the second one) by Barbey. Wonderful the way he makes use of the *intoxication of sobriety.*

Gérard, who disposes of the will of others even more easily than of his own, decides that I shall go with him at midnight to meet Copeau in Roggers's dressing-room. I raise as objections my fatigue and my need to work, but to no avail; and, indeed, discovering that *The Wild Duck* is being played at Antoine's theater, to which I should not have felt like going but for their urging, but which I do want to see, I walk along the boulevards with the young men (they leaving me for *La Dame de chez Maxim's*[30]).

I planned to stay only a moment at Antoine's, drop Gérard, Roggers, etc. . . . but that strange play gripped me just as on the first seeing. I am unable to leave.

In the local train taking me back to Auteuil.

This is, I believe, the first time I have ever ditched anyone. I was to

---

[29] One of Balzac's novels that he classified among the *Scenes of Parisian Life.*

[30] *The Lady from Maxim's,* a popular light comedy by Georges Feydeau, first played in 1899. *The Wild Duck* is, of course, Ibsen's famous play.

meet Gérard at midnight in front of the Renaissance and go in with him to meet Copeau and Roggers. Feeling tired and losing interest in the acting (since the actors, eager to maintain the unity of their roles, showed no originality), I left during the first quarter of the fourth act, then hesitated as to whether or not I should wait for Gérard. First I took a bus for the Gare Saint-Lazare, then another for the Renaissance, and finally a third for Saint-Lazare again, my fear of supping with Gérard and Roggers together winning out. Then the fear of being no good for work tomorrow, my stinginess in regard to time, strength, and money, then my boredom, then, above all, my horror of seeing Gérard think that he can make a plaything of my will.

Sunday

Got home last night at half past twelve; went to bed at once. Slept fairly well, got up soon after seven; bathed; wrote to Gérard; answered Jammes; and rewrote from memory (I rather like that kind of exercise, but it took a bit too much of my time) the letter that motivated the one I receive from him this morning.

The story of how that article was still-born is rather comical.

I am making progress in *Le Mémorandum* and am more amused than I like to admit to myself by the unbrokenly stilted quality of its style, which makes all others seem *pasty*.

Go out to lunch with the Ducotés.

Impossible to go on this way; I must see a doctor. This frightful fatigue has eventually given me a sort of fear of all manifestations of life. This evening, after dining at my Aunt Charles's, I come home at nine o'clock, my head heavy with fatigue; not worth anything. Am going to bed.

Monday morning, 7 May

I am suspicious of the *genuineness* of a feeling the moment that feeling can be of advantage to me. That is what made me side-step the Jammes article. But the story is rather comical (unfortunately I have not kept all *my* letters). That article would have been of great value to me; but I should have owed it to a misunderstanding. I am beginning to believe that I have even more pride than vanity — and terrifying reserves of malice against myself.

This need of mortification is worth meditating on.

✻ ✻ ✻

10 May

I chose this very small notebook in order to be able to put it into my pocket. I like having it on me, busying myself with it anywhere whatever, just as abruptly as I am doing today while waiting my turn at the barber's. The other one, too large, permitted too much affectation.

I must hasten to Cuverville in a couple of days. That thought is enough to disorganize my days. Spent all of yesterday and all of the day before on errands. Having finished the Oxford notebook and not yet having this frightful little one, I have noted nothing since the 7th; moreover, I've done nothing worth while; my relaxed mind has drifted aimlessly. I must decide to go and see a doctor. I should have made up my mind to do so three or four years ago. I have resigned myself too long to being tired and to getting along on a reduced vigor. Absurd! What do I care about the severity of a regime if it allows me to work more! What have I produced up to now compared with what I should have produced? For the last four years I have been floundering and marking time.

. . . .

Sunday

Reached Cuverville yesterday. The weather is so beautiful that this day is related to the happiest days of my childhood. I am writing this in the big room above the kitchen, between the two open windows through which the sun's warm joy surges in. Nothing but my tired reflection in the mirror hanging above my table is an obstacle to the fullest development of my happiness. (I need to learn all over again, and methodically, how to be happy. This is a form of gymnastics, like exercise with dumbbells; it can be *achieved*.) My feet are in the sunlight, wearing green and blue list slippers. The warmth enters into me, rises within me like sap. In order to be utterly happy the only thing necessary is to refrain from comparing this moment with other moments of the past — which I often did not fully enjoy because I was comparing them with other moments of the future. This moment is no less full of delight than any other moment of the future or of the past. The grass of the lawn is deep like the grass in a churchyard. Each apple tree in the farmyard is a thick mass of blossoms. The whitewashed trunks prolong their whiteness right down to the ground. Every breath of air brings me some perfume, especially that of the wistaria, on the left, against the house, so loaded with blossoms that one can hear its bees from here. A bee has come into this room and won't leave. The light envelops each object as with honey.

Yesterday before sunset I had just time to visit the garden thoroughly. The big apple tree leaning toward the tennis court, smiling and rustling in the last rays of the sun, was becoming pink. A frightful shower, a few hours before, had submerged the countryside and purged the sky of all clouds. Every bit of foliage was brimming as with tears, particularly that of the two big copper beeches, not yet copper-colored, but transparent and blond, which fell about me like soft hair. When, going out by the little door in the bottom of the garden, I saw the sun again and the luminous cliff in front of it formed by the grove of beeches, everything struck me as so affectionately beautiful, so new, that I could have wept with joy. With me tears are not the privilege of sorrow, but also of admiration, of emotion, of a brusque and violent sympathy, of excessive joy. I cannot remember ever having wept, since childhood, for a personal sorrow, and yet I weep so easily; in the theater the mere name of Agamemnon is enough: I weep torrents. From this physical accompaniment my emotion derives the guarantee of its authenticity.

The violence of this emotion had all but overwhelmed me. On going in I had a rather sharp headache and immediately after dinner, heavy with sleep, went to bed.

Read before going to bed the biography of Athenaïs (Eudocia) and a few lines of Tacitus.

Read this morning a few chapters of Tacitus (beginning of Book XI), then began writing before going down to the garden.

I know that, outside, a vegetative lethargy seizes me and that, if I let myself go, I am lost to work.

Sunday, 3 o'clock

After lunch, went to sleep for an hour (read the indifferent article by Deschamps on Ferrero); woke up, my head swimming from the buzzing of the bees. A swarm, escaped from Frémont's, had got into the dining-room chimney. This young swarm, which Frémont wanted to capture, was still uncertain and you could see it, as if elastic, above the top of the house. Burning a little paper in the chimney drove it away and it lighted in the lawn on one of the lowest branches of the cedar. Mius, his wife and his three not very handsome children, F., and Em. were watching; I joined them. The shrill swarm, dazed with sunlight, surrounded the branch, a moving cloud that gradually became tighter and denser. Soon a large number of bees, some of them fixed directly to the branch and others clinging to the first ones, formed a sort of gourd, growing, swelling, lengthening out as we watched, then occasionally letting fall on the lawn what looked like thick tears of burning pitch.

Frémont, the farmer, then set out to fetch his hive. When he returned, Mius was setting up the stepladder; the swarm had not moved. Frémont measured the distance from the ground to the branch and cut a forked pole exactly of that length, to which he attached the hive. The bees stirred a bit; that is, there took place on the surface of the swarm a sort of sudden evaporation, when he brought up the ladder and climbed onto it to fix the forked pole against the branch. Finally everything was so well arranged that, the weight of the forked pole and of the hive bending the branch slightly, the whole business came to lean against the ladder and was supported there, the hive forming a cover over the swarm and protecting it from the sun. To give even more shade, an umbrella was opened over the whole thing, supported half by the branch, half by the ladder, in an equilibrium so precarious that the least breath would have upset it; but the air is so calm today that in the distance the upper branches of the avenue can hardly be seen to tremble.

I left the scene, crushed with sunlight. I am writing these lines on the path in the flower garden, of which the part next to the vegetable garden is in the shade. Opposite me, above the dark curtain of Portuguese laurels, I see the top of the house wall where the big firs are already throwing their shadow. On my left, in perspective, the line of espaliers; above them the bright red of the new tiles; the branch of a big snowy apple tree springs out and waves in the joyous blue.

6 o'clock

We have had tea. I read aloud to Em. the first pages of the *Voyage d'un naturaliste*,[31] then, sitting on a folding chair down in the vegetable garden, after having read some amusing articles by Ernest-Charles, I am letting myself be voluptuously soaked up by the evening.

8 o'clock

Frémont, who was waiting for the cool of the evening, has come back carrying a forked pole at the end of which, like a sort of broom, he has stuck a bunch of elder leaves. The odor of these leaves, crushed under foot and then dipped in a pail of water, is supposed to be very unpleasant to the bees: "It is like poison to them," he explained. Having, therefore, raised the forked pole under the swarm, he waited about half an hour until the smell of the elder leaves forced the bees into the hive. But to no avail. Night was falling. He had either to give up the swarm or to hurry. I advised cutting the branch; Frémont had been careful not to suggest this. Mius went off to fetch a huge hand clipper. Frémont, up on the ladder, held the branch with both hands, above and below the swarm. A towel had been stretched on the grass, the hive had been placed on the towel, not flat on the ground but raised, leaning against a plank so as not to cause trouble for the few bees that had already settled in it. With one stroke Mius cut the branch. Everything proceeded in the best manner possible and Frémont, by raising the hive, was able to slip the branch with its swarm between the hive and the towel.

But when everything was over, Frémont noticed that he still had on his shirt-sleeve (he had taken off his coat) a rather viciously active squadron of bees. The most amusing — I was about to say the most

---

[31] *Journal of a Naturalist* by Charles Darwin.

piquant[32] — aspect of the whole business was formed by the efforts and odd movements of Mius and Frémont to get rid of the last bees, fortunately somewhat numbed by the night. Each of them had wrapped his head in a white cloth: the masquerade effect of those two men jumping about and gesticulating in the growing darkness considerably amused the maids and the children, and since no one was stung, the general good humor contributed to everyone's individual joy (or everyone's individual good humor contributed to the general joy — and so on — ridiculous sentences).

In bed before ten o'clock, I still read in bed some of the *Mémorandum*. Sleep interrupted by rather long stretches of insomnia, during which my imagination gets excited and suggests absurd subjects of worry.

Awakening without any feeling of freshness; but I get up in a fairly good mood.

The sky, pure again now (it is two o'clock), was filled with cold fog this morning.

We send a telegram to Albert to urge him to come and rest here a few days.

Until lunch, correspondence and a short walk in the garden, during which I remove the caterpillars from the rosebushes.

Stretched out on my bed, read the article by Brisson on Labiche and, in this connection, reread *La Station Champbaudet*[33] — ineffably stupid. Then, to put me in the right mood again, reread immediately afterward the last two acts of *The Wild Duck*.

Read for three quarters of an hour to Em. some of the *Voyage d'un Naturaliste*, but I do not know whether or not I can continue this reading, which, to begin with, takes me too far afield from the thoughts that would nourish my work, and moreover fills me, fills both of us rather, with a sort of almost intolerable anguish.

Went out; should have walked; but am again absorbed by the garden, where I spend my time in transplanting the winter cuttings from the rosebushes and in trying to understand the nature of the amorphous animal that is called in this district "gray worm," which this year is eating up all our salad greens, our strawberry plants, etc. . . . I spend an hour on this. There is a high wind. I am writing this in the avenue. I go back in to work. How late it is already! in the day and in my life . . .

---

[32] In French *piquer* means "to sting."
[33] *The Champbaudet Station*, a comedy by Labiche.

Tuesday

Never a man, I shall never be anything but an aged child. I live with all the incoherence of a lyric poet, but two or three ideas, crosswise in my brain and rigid like parallel bars, crucify every joy; everything that would like to try its wings at random runs into them.

Written a rather important letter to Jammes; read some Montaigne.

After lunch worked on my novel; [34] I go to enormous efforts to roll that mass a bit forward, not because it is so heavy, but because there is no place to grip it.

Took tea with Em.; read Darwin aloud for an hour.

Around five o'clock I go to the Criquetot fair. Medium-sized crowd, in which the fear of not speaking to those who recognize me and of speaking to those who would not recognize me makes me slip along like a thief behind the booths. A few gypsy wagons with a dozen very ugly and very poor children. Came home terribly depressed.

It is frightening how much I have aged recently. Certainly something is not right inside me. It is impossible to age more rapidly or to be more aware of it. I cannot yet take this seriously, believing in a passing fatigue. Already I experienced this hideous aging last year, at the same time of year.

Wednesday

Strange drowsiness of the mind and of the flesh. Lethargy. After a great effort, this morning, to wind up my first chapter (and I do not succeed) I plunge into reading (Dostoyevsky's *From the Notes of an Unknown Man*).[35]

Excellent reading of Darwin (aloud). The moments spent with Em. (particularly in the garden) are extraordinarily pleasant. Her affection, her charm, her poetry envelop her in a sort of effulgence in which I warm myself, in which my fretful mood melts.

After having labored over it for several hours, suddenly my work deciding to progress toward evening, I make up my mind to remain here one day more.

Thursday

No, Albert's health worries me too much. I leave, in a hurry to see him again. He can no longer digest anything but eggs; here are two dozen gathered this morning on the farms.

---

[34] *La Porte étroite* (*Strait Is the Gate*).

[35] Two short stories by Dostoyevsky, "An Honest Thief" and "A Christmas Tree and a Wedding," bear the collective subtitle: *From the Notes of an Unknown Man.*

The weather is cold and rainy; I should leave Cuverville without regret if I were not leaving there Em. and some roses ready to open.

Although I was a rather chronic invalid, these three days spent with her were close enough to happiness.

Friday, 18

Returned to Paris last night.

Finished the Dostoyevsky in the train.

Today saw Charmoy; talked for a long time with a very real pleasure. Happy to see him working.

He claims to be subject, for some months now, to sudden blushings, so embarrassing in society that he no longer *dares* go out. Hence he is forced to live a hermit's life.

"They are," he explains, "the blushes of someone who has just lied. What do you expect the person with whom I am talking and who sees me blush in this way to think of me? Recently I changed color in this way because of something Bartholomé said to me, because of a question, and I felt so embarrassed that I didn't dare reply. I who just a few years ago had such nerve! The other day, at de Max's apartment, I blushed twice like that; everyone saw it. . . . But, would you believe it, I blush even when alone with my wife. Oh, it's hereditary; my father or my grandfather (?) was that way; his unsociability went to the point where he had all his meals served in his room."

Saturday

Prolonged insomnia. Keen suffering in my pride; it could even lead to madness if daylight did not come soon enough. Yes, that position was easy enough to take; it is cruelly painful to maintain.

Ægri somnia.[36]

Artisan of my own suffering!

When I am *well* again, I shall blush at these confessions. Let's get to work.

Headache; sort of screen between me and *thoughts.*

Oh, really, can't I demand more of myself?

Monday

Terrible night; I had stayed up until one o'clock hoping that fatigue would win out over insomnia. After a rather good session of work I go to bed with a calm head. Impossible to sleep and progressive *cooling off* of my whole body in spite of the pile of blankets. In vain I rub myself; I put on woolen knee-pads, I pull the coverlet over me. I ought to be stifling, but I am shivering.

---

[36] "The dreams of an invalid," from Horace: *Ep. ad Pisones,* 7.

Around three o'clock I go to sleep and am awakened before seven
—apparently not too tired, but vulnerable in every regard, at the mercy
of the least *vexation*. And it is precisely this morning that I receive from
Jammes the most insulting of letters. And one from little Louis Rouart,
so frightfully pugnacious (under cover of the nicest affection) that I
must spend the whole morning replying to it. (It is all about the article
that the *Occident* has asked him to write about *Amyntas* and in which
he wants to show that . . . etc. . . . etc.—thus falsifying utterly the
meaning of my book, of all my books, of myself. . . .)

After lunch, to rest myself, I receive Paul Valéry's visit. Charming
visit, but it leaves me exhausted.

Spent a vast amount of time replying to Louis Rouart.

He is one of those creatures who do not think they are being frank
unless they are being brutal.

25 May

Anguish—bewilderment.

I interrupt this journal; dreadful fatigue.

. . . .

Leaving for Geneva. I am going to get the advice of Dr. Andréæ.

. . . .

*   *   *

20 June

As I was about to leave Copeau after having lunched with him, "Oh!"
I said suddenly, "look at that elderly gentleman over there in front of
Marpon's bookstall" (this was beside the Turkish baths); "he is the one
you have often heard me speak of, my old piano teacher, La Pérouse."
He was standing there without moving any more than a wax figure; his
face had the color of wax; certainly he didn't dare touch the books. I
left Copeau and approached my revered teacher. I remembered what
he had said the next to the last time I had gone to see him:

"I am slipping; I am slipping rapidly. I used to be a good walker;
now, with great effort, I walk only very slowly. It seems to me that I am
going through the same movements as I used to, but I notice that all
the others pass me; once upon a time I was the one who passed them,
and without any effort at all. . . ."

4 October

Sudden departure from Cuverville for La Poissonnière, in answer
to a sad letter from Albert that Em. brought back from Criquetot yesterday evening. Walk last night, together, in the garden full of moon-

light and shadow, late, after the others had gone up to bed. It is so warm that we are not even wearing coats. My heart is affectionate and ready to melt. I wish so much that Albert would not die in despair.

René wanted me to invent some fairy-tale to explain my arrival. What a mortal fear of hurting one another in that family!

I arrive. Albert is there in bed, waiting for me.

"Oh, why did you come?" he exclaims, smiling. I sense that he is almost embarrassed not to be more seriously ill. I embrace him.

"But your letter frightened me, old man. I have come to reassure myself."

He takes my hand and squeezes it softly.

"I should have done the same."

Tired out from trying to sleep, he gets up; he wanders along the deserted corridors. In vain he seeks the sleep that would be his salvation. His thought flutters within him like the sail abandoned by every propitious wind. And while the night wanes, he listens to his strength ebbing slowly within him.

15 October. Back in Paris

Traveled with a seventeen-year-old tramp, the son of a Douai tinsmith who had come to Havre to ship out as a cabin-boy. The ship for which he had a recommendation had left for Brazil a month ago. After vain attempts to sail on other ships, he was getting ready to return to his home town.

I fear that Paris will delay his return. He has eighteen francs in his pocket, to which I add two francs to pay the cab that will take him to "a friend of his parents, a warrant officer who lives Place de la République." His parents do not expect his return. And I am aware that he is rather amused to arrive alone and free in Paris with twenty francs that will be stolen at his first stop. I do not leave him until I have seen him get into his cab.

Curious, the psychology of the vagrant. I should have great difficulty in defining it, yet I glimpse the rather special nature of the mania. Violently interested by that youngster (especially compared with the few other tramps I have already met). I am beginning to grasp the essential common features. But still impossible to define exactly.

Tuesday morning at de Max's. I find Lugné-Poë there; as always, seeming at one and the same time both querulous and ferocious; the manner of someone whose feet have been trodden on. He has no sooner left the room than de Max exclaims: "And now that the humbug of Paris has left, my friend, I am the most unhappy man on earth. X. shot himself in the chest last night."

Friday morning

Read an hour of *A Gentleman's Nest* [37] in my bath, as d'Aurevilly used to do.

Fauré is asked about the tempo of his *Clair de lune:*
"That depends on the voice," he replies. "When I don't like it, I speed up the movement."

At times I annoy Marcel and disconcert him by my too hasty and as if unconsidered approval. Nothing makes him more wary in regard to me; I should be careful of this.

23 November

It hurts me to write Jammes so flatly. But what else can I do? . . . His nose is no longer susceptible to anything but incense.

Cuverville, 27 November

Croquignole, which I read yesterday, makes *La Turque*, which I am reading today, seem even weaker. [38]

It's a wonderful thought that there is probably not a woman in Paris who, when she is applauding Rostand, does not think she has more taste than the Englishwomen of Elizabeth's time, for example. Every public has the Shakespeare it deserves.

---

[37] A novel by Ivan Turgenyev.

[38] *Croquignole*, a novel by Charles-Louis Philippe, and *La Turque*, a novel by Eugène Montfort, appeared almost simultaneously in late 1906.

1907

Yesterday evening, family dinner at the Charles Gides'.
First Jeanne, then Gérard, tell me of Arthur Fontaine's visit to Briand
to get me a decoration. M., Briand's chief private secretary, told them on
Saturday. Since M. knows nothing of Fontaine's friendship for me
(which, moreover, would seem inexplicable to him), M. will certainly
think that I have started a campaign, and yet I knew nothing about it.
This is profoundly distasteful to me, and I was unable to eat all during
the dinner.

M. does not like me; he doesn't hide his scorn and aversion for everything I write. He suffers in his affection for Gérard, and especially in
his vanity, that Gérard prefers my society to his. Gérard does not hide
his scorn from him. M. thinks that my company can only harm Gérard,
and when Dr. Andréæ, who knows me well, convinced Gérard's mother
to put the youth in my care last spring, M.'s disapproval became passionate.

M. is not exactly a hypocrite; yet he plays an underhand game. He is
small. I am suspicious of small men. For a long time I have been telling
Gérard he must be afraid of M. Some day I shall try to sketch this small
character, held upright by moral principles so as not to lose an inch of
his height. He appears full of affection, of responsiveness; but one always
feels that he hasn't much to expend. Perfect type of climber. He succeeds by means of patience, of minute economy, of hygiene. He succeeds in everything. Forever up to his best, he considers his constancy as
wisdom and calls virtue the lack of turbulence of his desires. But enough
about him.

I have wasted my morning in writing him. Then went to the G.'s to
show Gérard a rough draft of a letter, which he has the good taste not
to consider excellent. It was merely a question of making M. understand
that I had nothing to do with Fontaine's initiative. It was especially a
question of not seeming annoyed that he, M., had known about it even
though it did not succeed. Eventually I understood, as a result of re-
copying and beginning this letter over again, that, in order to achieve
this last point, the best thing was not to write anything; and finally I
threw everything into the fire.

Lost about three hours over that letter, four even if I count the time
spent at the Ch. Gides'.

The Marcel Drouins came to lunch; around two o'clock, leaving
them, I dozed for an hour. But lost the advantage of this sleep by still
concerning myself with that exasperating letter to M. Other letters ab-

sorbed my remaining patience. It was no good to try to read or work.
. . . After dinner, picked out the piano and violin sonata that Magnard
has just sent me.

The best moment of the day is the half-hour I spend in my tub (in
d'Aurevilly's manner) calmly finishing Ferrero's first chapter (*Antony
and Cleopatra*).

2 January

Visit of Giovanni Papini, the editor of the review *Leonardo*. Younger
than I had thought, with an expressive and almost handsome face. A bit
too irrepressible, yet not so much so as the other Italians I know. Too
full of compliments, but seems nevertheless to think a part of what he
says. Like all the Italians I know, has too high an idea of his own importance; or at least shows it too much; or in a different way from a
Frenchman's. If he only knew how hard it is for me to take myself
seriously! . . .

After Papini has left, I read three chapters of Ferrero; and after dinner, a fourth.

The important thing for me now is not so much what I read as how
I read it, the attention that I bring to it. I must struggle by every means
against the breaking up and scattering of my thought. It is for *this reason* likewise that I have harnessed myself to this journal again, without
any great pleasure, but as a means of getting myself into the spirit for
work. But what can I dare to hope for if, as soon as I begin working
again, sleep again quits me?

3 January

What a happy period it was when, master of all my hours, I had so
well arranged them that each one was completely filled, when not even
the least quarter of an hour went by without carrying its weight of accomplishment! My whole work was arranged in advance; before going
to bed at night, I knew what I should do the next day; one occupation
rested me from another. I liked the restraint imposed by that method
and kept utterly faithful to myself by living up to my resolutions.

Perhaps I could not have continued without some artificial tense-
ness. . . .

5 January

Wrote nothing last night. Read nothing. Is that why I slept better?
In bed soon after dinner, I succeeded in almost filling that vast cup with
sleep and in emptying it without coming up for breath too often. I get
up this morning with my head solidly set on my shoulders.

Very tiring day yesterday. The weather was fine. I should have liked
to ride my bicycle to the Latin Quarter, where I had business to con-

duct; but unsure of any place to stand my cycle safely, I had to be satisfied with the top deck of the street-cars. First stop at the *Mercure*. I am trying to get a tobacconist's license for Emmanuel Signoret's widow; I have already spoken of this to Fontaine; the request that she must send to the Ministry will be approved by several carefully chosen signatures; and Vallette and I decide on this choice. Mme Signoret will never know how irksome these proceedings are to me.

I reach the rue d'Assas by crossing the Luxembourg. Since I have been paying more attention to people, I pay less attention to nature. About ten years ago every shadow, every light would have vibrated within me. Yet I did see the early iris shoots. . . .

Excellent lunch at the Jean Schlumbergers' where I am served at dessert with that wild-rose jam which strives so savagely to seem Oriental and which I already liked at Braffy.

At two o'clock, call on Léon Blum. A very pleasant thing about him is that he always receives you as if he had seen you the day before. Conversation flourishes easily between us. His book on marriage must be finished in a month.[1] He is writing it almost as fast as his pen can function. I am not sure he is wrong. The artist in him hasn't any great value, and his sentence, like Stendhal's, does not need to go out of its way to achieve anything more than the mere movement of his thought, which flows from his mouth or his pen at once abundant and clear — clearer, to be sure, than abundant, without any noticeable *Schaudern* — but, as a consequence, easily and completely expressible; having a beginning and an end and always properly clothed. You cannot imagine a more exact, clearer, more elegant, easier summary than Léon Blum can give, on the spur of the moment, of an event or a book or a play. What an excellent committee chairman he must be in the Conseil d'État! Oh, if politics did not bend all his thoughts, what a keen critic he would be! But he judges things and people according to his opinions and not according to his taste. He has less confidence in his taste than in his opinions and prefers to distort the former rather than to seem to contradict himself. You can't be always quite sure that he likes everything he says he likes, but you can be sure that he thinks he likes it and knows why.

Monday

The disorder in my mind reflects the disorder in my house, where every room remains "at a standstill."

Last night I went to bed, without writing anything, at eight thirty, crushed by the need for sleep. But I couldn't go to sleep. . . . Impossible to decide whether or not to leave for Berlin; impossible to decide even whether or not I want to go. Let myself be taken there? Yes, per-

---

[1] *Du mariage* was in fact published in 1907.

haps. At least my indecisive character has this advantage: that it is ignorant of regrets. This lack of decision is both an effect and a cause of my fatigue. . . . Perhaps it would be better, then, to stay in Paris.

I shall leave to my friends the trouble of explaining my apathy as disdain and pride.

Only when I see de Max ill and discouraged do I become aware of the great affection I have for him. The day before yesterday in his dressing-room his tragic face seemed overshadowed by fatigue. Forced to act despite a slight overflow of synovia that prevents him from climbing the forum steps, he complains moreover of laryngitis; I confess that I never find him better on the stage than when he cannot use his whole voice. The impossibility of bending his knee also makes him discover several handsome gestures that his lyricism alone would not have invented.

This afternoon, brief attempt at work; finally I decide to go and call on Thadée Natanson. Thanks to an error in the address, I ring at his brother's; hearing my voice, he comes running and immediately his effusive cordiality submerges me. He treats me with a sudden intimacy unencumbered by esteem, which, indeed, is his way of dominating. Despite his smile, his face expresses through his most affable manner only a calm ferociousness. He shows me his paintings, a Monticelli portrait, above all, that is really a remarkable work; then the panels of the dining-room "all carved in solid wood" — then takes me away in his carriage, expressing the hope that I may have some favor to ask him, "he would be so happy to oblige me." Going down the Champs-Élysées, he stops so that I can admire the former Dufayel mansion, which he has just bought and in which he is having a theater cut out "in depth" — a house on which he is spending seven hundred and fifty thousand francs — which, as he says, "is not a trifle." Moreover, extremely obliging. But with him I don't know what role to act — and yet cannot be natural.

Wednesday, 9 January
Good work after lunch and a short siesta. Correcting the translation makes me examine closely my *Prométhée* and feel with joy, and in detail, all the qualities of my style.[2] In the whole book there are not four sentences that I should like to change. I greatly admire the work of the Tharaud brothers on their *Dingley*, of which I am reading the excellent rewriting. But to what an extent this reworking several years later

_____
[2] *Le Prométhée mal enchaîné* (*Prometheus Ill-Bound*) of 1899 was translated into German by Franz Blei.

amazes me and remains foreign to me! I cannot, I have never been able to, rewrite a sentence later; all the work that I put on it must be when it is still in a molten state; and each sentence strikes me as perfect only when retouching has become impossible.

Maurice Denis is putting the finishing touches on his decorations for Roucher's anteroom. I like seeing him in a smock like an ordinary workman. . . . He is softening the oversuave pinks of his clouds, sobering down and toning up his harmonies. This will never be one of his best compositions, but there are successful bits in the foreground. Will Maurice Denis now learn to work a little less facilely? . . . But his facility, after all, is but one of the signs of his health.

He is getting ready to accompany me to Berlin for the opening of my *Roi Candaule* and tells me his joy in the most charming way. I cannot say that my feelings for Maurice Denis are very lively and yet his cordiality and esteem are always very pleasant to me. His health comforts me, and his rather crude but never unintelligent judgments. If I had nothing but friends like him, my sensitivity could find expression only in my books; but at least I should *write* those books.

I meet Thadée Natanson at the Sickert exhibit, where, awkward and lumpish, I do and say the wrong thing; a flatterer in spite of myself like someone who, recognizing his remarks to be without savor, sugars and sugars again to give them at least some sweetness. The Walter Sickert exhibit is gloomy to the point of defying the public; and I like this. Absurd conversation with Thadée. Through fatigue I let myself say the sort of things that, if written, I should cross out in shame. I assume in his eyes the appearance of "complaining" (the appearance people least forgive — which I forgive myself least). So why should I speak of the silence surrounding me to someone who, if he had three lives, could never understand that I am the one *who created* this silence around me. I tell Thadée that not the *Ermitage,* nor *Vers et Prose* nor the *Occident,* all friendly reviews, has said a word about my *Amyntas.* I should have liked him to understand that I did *not want* any articles where praise was almost obligatory. But Thadée begins at once to console me! I leave him to ruminate at length the sort of anguish in which you are left by the awareness of having put yourself in a bad posture. I say "bad posture" since the *beauty* of this attitude will matter only if I have the courage (and the strength) to maintain it consistently. And I am wrong to speak in this connection of an *attitude* without adding immediately: *natural,* for it is only when I deviate from it that I deform myself and shrivel up; and I never deviate from it except when I am tired.

Bad sleep last night. I endlessly chew the cud of these thoughts like a betel nut whose bitterness will never be exhausted.

But as soon as I feel better I again understand that I must never let up in my harshness toward myself, never move backward or recant, but rather plunge farther along my path, austerely and fiercely.

Having said this, I go and rest a moment at Copeau's, through the need of seeing my image again in a somewhat flattering mirror.

Work after dinner; I finish going over the translation of *Prométhée*, decidedly much less good than it seemed at first. Read aloud an act of Ford's *The Broken Heart*.

Saturday

Quite calm and studious day, which would have been perfect if only I had been able to sleep last night. In the evening, continued the reading of Ford aloud. Interesting chapter by Hello on Shakespeare in his *Plateaux de la balance*.[3]

Sunday

Ended the day yesterday at the Variétés, where Lavallière, Brasseur, and Prince laboriously exceed their qualities in *Miquette et sa mère*.[4] Max Dearly on the other hand attenuates his buffoonery and shows himself to be an excellent actor. My fatigue exaggerates for me the play's mediocrity. The authors understood only too well that with today's public they didn't have to go to any great pains. At times, however, a cleverly turned scene, a single line, shows that with a little effort they could have made it better and satisfied people of good taste also.

Ghéon, who knew we were at this theater, suddenly appears at the end of an intermission. I drop the play to talk with him until his train at twelve twenty-five.

Ghéon, noisier and more brilliant than ever, affirmative, dazzling, just as I like him — but I know only too well, alas, that this brilliance is merely a passing reaction to his dull stagnation at Bray. He tells me that he is now painting, that he is doing nothing but painting. "I am turning out some excellent things; I'll show them to you. And what gives me the most pleasure in it all is the conviction that the Vuillards, the Roussels, and many others who used to charm us . . . well, old man, nothing is easier." In short this encourages him to appreciate more and more line, composition, decorum, restraint. So much the better.

He shouts all of this out on the boulevards, making everyone turn around. Wearing his cloth cap, completely wrapped up in his sheep-

---

[3] *The Pair of Scales* (1880).
[4] *Miquette and Her Mother,* a three-act comedy by Robert de Flers and Gaston de Caillavet, which opened at the Théâtre des Variétés in November 1906.

skin, he looks like a perfect old soak. This is the way I like him; this is
the way he is *himself*.

I am to meet him Tuesday at the Bach concert.

Pierre Louÿs was too Ionian and I too Dorian for us to agree.

Charmoy has returned very ill from a visit to the madhouse of . . .
(Nemours, I think). De Max had already given me bad news of him. A
card invites me to go to his studio and see the busts of Nietzsche, Beethoven, and Zola. In his studio there is a crowd, but Mme de Charmoy
is receiving alone; she tells me that José has been in bed for a week and
asks me to go and see him. They have left their apartment on the im-
passe du Maine, probably too expensive. I reach 91 rue de Vaugirard,
in front of a regular slum stairway. On the second floor the key is in the
door, for there is no bell on the landing. A sort of dark anteroom, then
the room in which Charmoy is lying. A lot of photographs trying to hide
the ugliness of the walls. A bare box-spring under a mattress in a corner; a bedspread of the most ordinary kind, a blanket of a sort of brown
rep. In the room, forming a semicircle around the bed, a rather faded
girl with the face and headdress of a young page by Carpaccio, a lawyer, an unknown man, then, enormous, cutting off all the light from the
window, Jean de Bonnefon. On José's bed some mimosa branches,
which he is ruffling with his bloodless hands; his velvet jacket suits his
excessive pallor. I sit on the foot of the bed, where are piled up a feather
muff, an umbrella, and some coats. Jean de Bonnefon's speech has
more flavor than his writing; he didn't bore me a single moment.
Soon he yields his place to Mlle Anne Sée and to the female doctor
Contat.

Charmoy talks of the madhouse and gives me a desire to go there
with Dupouey, who has just returned.

On my way home I stop in at the Drouins', where I find Jean Schlumberger. He comes to the house at dusk and stays to dinner. I force myself to play him Dukas's variations and succeed in not getting too excited over the first ones.

This clerk in Durand's would reconcile me with humanity. With the
few hints I give him he finds in the Peters collection the Bach Fugue in
B minor on a theme by Albinoni, which poor old La Pérouse would like
to have and which I shall be so happy to take to him. I receive the music this evening on getting home — exhausted, I don't know just why, by
my visit to *Vers et Prose*, where I went to return to Paul Fort the proofs
of the *Poésies d'André Walter*, which he is republishing.

Too tired to go to the Laurenses' as I wanted to, I go home, read
Dingley, and perfect my playing of some Debussy compositions.

Wednesday

Came home exhausted yesterday, incapable of writing a line.

Had gone to see Ghéon (after a visit to my Aunt Charles Gide, just back from Switzerland) at Copeau's. He shows us his water-colors, which reveal him to be obviously very gifted. Together the two of us go to see again the exhibit of gloomy and powerful Sickerts. I accompany him to the Bach concert (*"Brandenburg" Concerto,* wonderful).

Today visit to the madhouse of Ville-Évrard — whence I do not get back until eight o'clock. Too long to relate here.

Thursday

Barrès's formal reception into the Academy. For the first time in my life I enter the small enclosure. Paul A. Laurens, at whose house we had lunched and who is with us, withdraws before the mob.

Why speak here of what all the newspapers will be full of? We leave before Vogüé's speech.

Barrès wears the frightful uniform as elegantly as one can. Of all of us he has changed the least. How I like his thin face, his flattened-down hair, even his common accent! What a flat speech he made! And how I suffered from the touches of cowardice, the flatteries, the concessions to the opinion of his audience, which are perhaps natural to him (I mean for which he probably did not have to distort his thought, but which met a too easy applause here); and also his thrust at Zola!

I was not the only one to notice the care with which, praising the family of Heredia, he said nothing of the sons-in-law.[5]

Will no one bring out with what strange and crafty cleverness this master sophist enrolled in his camp, in order to praise them, those two uprooted masters: Leconte de Lisle and Heredia? (And Chénier! and Moréas!)[6]

Left the Academy quite demoralized with fatigue and melancholy. Another day like this and I shall be ready for religion.

At Charavay's, who is going to sell them the day after tomorrow, skimmed through a packet of letters by Flaubert. His frankness and

---

[5] Barrès was elected to the chair vacated by the death of the poet José-Maria de Heredia. The daughters of the poet all married writers: Hélène first married the novelist Maurice Maindron and then the critic René Doumic; Marie became Mme Henri de Régnier; and Louise, after her divorce from Pierre Louÿs, became Mme Gilbert de Voisins.

[6] With his long novel *Les Déracinés* (*The Uprooted*) in 1897, Barrès became the apostle of stability and conservatism symbolized by the individual's roots in his provincial earth. Gide's *Nourritures terrestres* in the same year preached the necessity of fleeing all such restrictions, and his review of *Les Déracinés* in the *Ermitage* for 1897 clearly voiced this ideological conflict.

guilelessness rest me. Among many insignificant notes, a few pages suddenly show him as he is, admirable. His handwriting is much less attractive than Baudelaire's, of whom I also see a few pages.

Went to thank Charmoy for the interesting time I had yesterday on his recommendation. A large group in his studio, where he himself is receiving today.

Return by métro; stop at the Drouins'; I get home almost devoid of energy.

As I am leaving the métro, two fellows accost me and introduce themselves: Ibels and some Spanish painter. Having nothing to say to them, I leave them after having listened to their compliments. I give every appearance of separating from them, and then find myself right beside them while waiting for my streetcar — but do not recognize them until the car is leaving (yes, the very men I had just been talking to) — and then only because Ibels tips his hat to me very ostentatiously. How could I convince anyone that there was no impertinence or intention not to recognize them in this, etc. . . . ?

Em. wonders whether she would like to see me (and whether I can see myself) pronouncing a speech in my turn in the Academy.

"I certainly am not heading in that direction, my dear. I am less and less attracted to gatherings in which I am not allowed to snort as much as I want."

That remark of Barrès's against Zola, as I reread it, makes me even more angry. There is some spiritual baseness in never exaggerating anything but profitable opinions.

Saturday

After lunch, at the Van Rysselberghes'. Maurice Denis comes in and in a burst of laughter sweeps away all the arguments I had been building up against going to Berlin. Impossible to resist his cordial assurance.

Sunday

Departure for Berlin with Maurice Denis.

Berlin. The Museum

In the same gallery:

Michelangelo: *John the Baptist,* very Donatello, excessively youthful; mannerism without mawkishness, strangely long neck, frail torso; in the gait more rhythm than direction. In his left hand he holds a honeycomb and with his right hand he is raising to his mouth something bitter that puckers his mouth.

Wonderful work; greater perfection but perhaps not greater beauty than in the little sketch of an Orpheus [Apollo (?)] hardly as tall as a gladiolus, which, even in the still thick marble, is palpitating with glorious life. He is holding the lyre with an arm folded flat against his left side; with his other arm he is leaning against what is about to be the branch of a tree. By Michelangelo likewise a very small bronze under glass, among other Renaissance figurines, has kept the charm of softened wax. A mere torso of the Crucified Christ.

Gallery 30

GALLERY 30.

Domenico Veneziano:

Head of a woman, seen in a perfect profile against a background of blue sky, probably repainted, standing out against the delicate and rather pale tone of the face. The nape of the neck completely uncovered in the manner of a Piero della Francesca; dress of brocaded silk, indiscreetly sumptuous.

Pollaiuolo:

A little David, with nothing remarkable about the painting, but creating a rather odd impression. The folds of his cloak, the corners of which are caught in his belt, raised almost immodestly, uncover the legs painted with a nervous and very elegant line.

Verrocchio:

A Madonna and Child. As usual with him, he indicates shadows on flesh with a monotonous darkening.

A little sacred wood, almost symmetrical, yet full of mystery and charm, where a Christ child and a John the Baptist just a little older meet. Near them some does come down to drink; wild anemones sparkle against the very dark green of the grass. And not far off, St. Joseph and Mary are coming forward. (This is attributed to some pupil of Filippo Lippi.)

Dierik Bouts:

Magdalen anointing the feet of Christ. She is on the far left of the painting. At the corner of a table Christ, together with three disciples, is eating bread and fish. A donor, kneeling in the right corner, balances the Magdalen.

A very beautiful crucifixion by Dierik Bouts also.

CARPACCIO	1470–1522
TIZIANO	1477–1576
TINTORETTO	1519–1594
VERONESE	1528–1588
(*Strange gap. Look into it.*)	
TIEPOLO	1696–1770

G U A R D I   1712–1793
C A N A L E T T O   1720–1780

1 February
Back from Berlin on 30 January. Miserably wasted the first two days. Yesterday I catch hold of myself and do not go to bed before having written the beginning of *L'Enfant prodigue.*[7]
This morning I forbid myself to go out. I begin by working. This is the way to do, and any other system is absurd. A still very distracted afternoon, but not without interest. Useless to go on noting my occupations and encounters. I must record here my "concentrations" and not my distractions. On the way, read with great profit the beginning of Dupouey's *Vie de Rossetti;* alas, badly written.

6 February
Have forsaken this notebook the last few days, but for the sake of work. I am composing an *Enfant prodigue,* in which I am trying to make a dialogue of my spiritual reticences and impulses.
This morning, from Claudel, a letter full of a sacred wrath, against the epoch, against Gourmont, Rousseau, Kant, Renan. . . . Holy wrath no doubt, but wrath all the same and just as painful to my mind as the barking of a dog is to my ear. I cannot endure it and cover my ears at once. But I hear it nevertheless and then have trouble getting back to work.

9 February
Valéry will never know how much friendship it costs me to listen to his conversation without an outburst. I go away black and blue all over. Yesterday I spent almost three hours with him. Afterward nothing was left standing in my mind.
Going out with me, he accompanied me to the Bois de Boulogne. I had taken my skates, which had been lying in a packing-case for the last ten years, and, to my surprise, I didn't find them too rusty on the ice. Valéry did not leave me an instant; I suffered to see him waiting for me, so that I hardly skated at all. Leaving there with him, I abandoned him in front of the Charles Gides', where I went up to get news of Gérard.
And, of course, impossible to work this evening. After such a "conversation" everything in my head is in a state of havoc.

Valéry's conversation throws me into this *frightful* alternative: either consider everything he says absurd or else consider absurd every-

---

[7] *Le Retour de l'enfant prodigue* (*The Prodigal's Return*), a short prose poem, is one of Gide's most beautiful works. It was first published by *Vers et Prose* in 1907.

thing I am doing. If he suppressed *in reality* everything he suppresses in conversation, I should no longer have any *raison d'être*. Moreover I never argue with him; he merely strangles me and I struggle back.

Didn't he declare to me yesterday that music (he is sure of this) was going to become purely imitative; or rather, a more and more precise notation of what speech cannot express, but without any further æsthetic aim: an *exact* language?

He also says: "Who is concerned today with the Greeks? I am convinced that what we still call 'dead languages' today will fall into putrefaction. It is already impossible to understand the emotions of Homer's heroes. Etc. . . . etc. . . ."

After such remarks my thoughts take longer to rise up again than grass does after hail.

12 February

Little by little I am finishing the *Fils prodigue* — but today I break away from it to reply to the letters from Berlin. Blei and Grève are sniping at each other over my *Saül*, each one thinking he is winning out.

My conduct is simple enough if I follow a straight line. But I am risking a lot. Yet this doesn't matter; I am swaggering and to preserve my attitude am about to lose my situation. I am keeping a copy of my letters, which I went to read to Marcel Drouin this morning.

Yesterday went to see some paintings with Rouart. Very beautiful Gauguins, Van Goghs, Cézannes. But I was rather tired by my irritating day before. I had thought I had to go to see *Notre-Dame de Paris*, as a tribute to de Max (in the role of Claude Frollo). I had made an appointment with Jean Schlumberger to help me endure the play. But he hadn't been able to come.

During the first half-hour the artifice and absurdity of the play give me a desire to slap my neighbors; I think I can put up with only an act of it. But I can see de Max only between the ninth and tenth tableaux. He is good, moreover, giving a semblance of existence to that odious, declamatory puppet. I leave immediately afterward, unable to endure any more.

16 February

Again tired; it is better then to stop writing than to force myself. What I should like to break off is not my work but rather the varied daily occupations. Reread last night what is written of *L'Enfant prodigue;* there is very little to change and certainly I am satisfied with it.

Spent an hour with Suarès's book, exasperated by the pathos and false sublimity of his mind. Religious boosting. What do I care that his book was finished on Good Friday? And what does he mean by "was finished" in speaking of a book of this sort, which is merely a collection of random papers?

I like only the passage on Goethe and Pascal; Suarès says in it, and very well, excessive things, which first seemed right to me; but as I reflect on it now, I feel sure that his opinion of Goethe is the *easiest* one to have, the opinion that I myself have gone through; and that it is only since I got beyond that opinion that I really began to advance in culture.

If I spend a few days without playing my piano, the most beautiful page of music finds me without the sentiment to play it. The sentiment returns with my fingers' dexterity. Importance of the instrument; as soon as it is a good one, you discover in yourself some new skill in using it. A good pen is responsible for a fourth of my genius.

Perhaps the function creates the organ; but later the organ invites its functioning.

21 February

Another attack of vanity at the Charles Gides', just now. An outburst of boasting (about the playing of my plays in Germany) for which Lafcadio, that evening, would have given himself a real stab in the thigh. And in front of Gérard! How often I have chosen my cruelest lancet to open such an abscess on him! And how easy it would have been for him today to do the same to me! I appreciate his kindness in not doing so.

But as I left the Charles Gides', my head seemed in a vise just as when I should like to eat my words.

No matter how ridiculous my behavior is in this regard, I can explain it: when I feel that I do not have sufficient prestige, I try to force it, going about it as best I can with dreadful awkwardness, which would take that prestige away from me if I had it; whereupon I insist, exaggerate everything, and lose everything.

Fortunately, most of the time, scorn and contempt spare me such confusion. The mere feeling of dignity ought to protect me from it at all times.

Departure for Cuverville. 22 February

Robidet, the keeper, tells Édouard while they are out hunting:

"Ah! Mlle Marie" (our old maid) "was a very witty person! One morning as I was coming into the kitchen, she beckoned me to follow her: 'M'sieur Robidet, just come and look at this,' she says. She leads me to the foot of the kitchen stairs, where the shoes to be shined are lined up on the last step: 'Just take a look at the shoes of the master's friends!' Then she shows them to me: one was missing a heel, another had lost a piece of sole, another was coming unsewed at the end . . . Ah, she was very witty, Mlle Marie!"

16 March

Finished *L'Enfant prodigue* a few days ago. As soon as I had suddenly glimpsed the composition of the poem in Berlin, I set to work at once; for the first time the writing followed the conception immediately. I was afraid, if I brooded over it any longer, of seeing the subject expand and deform itself. Moreover, I was sick of not writing anything, and all the other subjects that I am carrying about with me offered too great difficulties to be treated at once.

So that I have hardly spent a fortnight in elaborating and writing that *Enfant prodigue*.

I spent a week correcting it. Between Drouin and Copeau, like *L'Homme entre deux maîtresses*,[8] I really enjoyed this job of perfecting and polishing.

I read today in Brunot's *Histoire de la langue française*: [9] "Corneille and Racine were subject to the rule; they did not create it. If later on, through the influence of their genius, they became stylistic authorities, yet in their lifetime they humbly corrected themselves, the first to please Vaugelas, and the second out of respect for Father Bouhours, official arbiter of style." (Preface, p. xv.)

Yet I don't know if I am doing right in yielding to Copeau on this point: he claims that *lui parler* is incorrect. Indeed I find nothing in Littré to authorize it, and still there is no other means of expressing this relationship: "Quiconque veut parler au Père doit *me parler.* — *Je lui parlais* fort aisément sans toi."

None the less I correct it.[10]

March

Yesterday went to hear Father Janvier at Notre-Dame. We had dined with Rouart. Notre-Dame, badly lighted, disappoints us, but not Father Janvier, to whom we listen to the very end without being tired or bored. Constant political allusions help him to give color to his speech. A few seats in front of us, Boni de Castellane listens to the explanation of his duties. Subject of the sermon: Error — sins through ignorance. Necessity of *informing oneself;* that is to say, of learning to know *Truth.* Ah, how beautiful it is! Let's rush out and imprison Galileo!

---

[8] The reference is to La Fontaine's *Fables,* Book I, 17: *The Middle-aged Man and His Two Mistresses,* in which the man is torn by the need of satisfying both at once.

[9] *History of the French Language,* an authoritative scholarly treatise.

[10] "Whoever wants to speak to the Father must speak to me. — I spoke to him quite easily without you." The text of *Le Retour de l'enfant prodigue* has: ". . . et qui veut comprendre le Père doit m'écouter. — Je l'entendais très aisément sans toi."

22 April

I have just suffered a little illness that kept me in bed twelve days, and I am surprised that I do not feel weaker after the long diet that the doctor imposed on me. (Typhlitis — but I am not convinced I really had it; my illness consisted chiefly in this twelve-day fast.) Read *Le Faucon* in La Fontaine and in Boccaccio; some of Rabelais's *Quart Livre; L'Anneau d'améthyste,* which confirms me in my judgment of Anatole France, and *Putois* even more so; some of the *Cent Nouvelles nouvelles;* some Lanson, etc. . . . Saint-Évremond.[11]

Now I am correcting for Claudel the proofs of *Connaissance de l'Est.*[12]

I wanted to go back to writing *Ajax,* but, upon examining the *subject* further, I fear not being able to explain, even to excuse, Ajax's gesture without the intervention of Minerva or of madness; I should need the two together: practically absurd (it already is sufficiently so) and, ideally, wonderful (it isn't at all so). — Nothing to be done about it.[13]

Received a great abundance of visits the last few days, from which I could not protect myself.

The first time I went out, the day before yesterday, was for the Maurice Denis exhibit. The great praise he is receiving had made me expect more from it. Decidedly be cautious where there is unanimity of praise. . . . But those who were praising in this case felt a little in arrears regarding Maurice Denis.

In Brisson's regular article in *Le Temps* a letter from Bernstein that gives rather accurately an idea of his worth. What an infirmity not to understand the æsthetic value of the *honnête homme!* [14] But Bernstein writes: "We are tourists feverishly seeking the picturesque." Whence, in his plays, that æsthetic vantage-point of the Buttes-Chaumont.[15]

23

Excellent exhibit of Cross, at which I regret not seeing Cross himself, whom I should have enjoyed congratulating.

---

[11] "The Falcon" is one of La Fontaine's *Tales* which he imitated from Boccaccio's collection; the "Fourth Book" of Rabelais is the one describing the first part of Pantagruel's travels; *The Hundred New Stories* is a fifteenth-century anonymous collection of erotic tales borrowed from the *Decameron* and medieval fabliaux; Gustave Lanson's is one of the most authoritative histories of French literature; Anatole France's *Amethyst Ring* (1899) is a novel, and his *Putois* is a tale.

[12] *Knowledge of the East* (translated into English as *The East I Know*).

[13] Gide did in fact abandon his play *Ajax* after writing but one scene of it.

[14] The seventeenth-century ideal of the respectable, all-around man.

[15] A populous section of Paris.

24

I go to consult Marcel Drouin about the Claudel proofs I am correcting. Wonderful *Connaissance de l'Est,* which I am rereading with close attention. Certain less ample, less inspired chapters still do not mar the book; a large number of them are of the loftiest beauty.

Spent some time also on the edition of Signoret, which the *Mercure* has agreed to bring out for the support of the poor widow. Some of these poems (almost all the last ones) are among the most dazzling and stately that I know. And, indeed, it is not enough to speak in this manner: to tell the truth, in our whole language I do not know any more beautiful ones.

25

Luncheon at the Ch. Gides' with Mme de Watteville. Great moral "distinction." But is a bit too much convinced that real poets never go to the toilet. Greatly admires *L'Intelligence des fleurs.*[16] And so on. . . .

30 April

Go to get Gérard for I had promised to go with him to see Fabre's *Timon* at Gémier's theater. Costly evening without any advantage. Yet the play is more interesting than I had hoped. De Max good; very good even in the ironic parts of the third act.

Weakness of going with Gérard to see him after the show. We stop for a drink at the terrace of a café with the ordinary, nauseating company that de Max drags along with him. Ventura suddenly appears. Gérard's anger at being "forced to see her again." No interest. Annoyance that this lost time causes me. I hope this will do for a long time.

Never yet has the stupidity of a conversation made me suffer so much; and even more the obliging smile I forced myself to assume.

"A peasant sees a parrot perched on a hedge; wants to catch it, and when he takes off his hat to net it, the parrot says: 'Hello, Jacquot.' Whereupon the peasant, embarrassed, says: 'Oh, excuse me, sir, I thought you were a bird!'"

"I adore that story," exclaims the girl, laughing conspicuously every time de Max says anything.

I set down here, however, this bit of "social gossip" which young Nau is spreading abroad and which is of much finer quality:

"Two tiny urchins are gallivanting on the avenue du Bois. A sumptuous victoria passes. 'Do you see that woman?' asks the elder; 'well, yesterday I could have screwed her.' 'Do you know her?' — 'No, but I had a hard on.'"

---

[16] *The Intelligence of the Flowers* is a rather naïve work by Maeterlinck, published in 1907.

Delighted Marcel, to whom I told it this morning. "Wonderful il-lustration of the distinction between the English *can* and *may*," he said.

1 May

I am well; am happy. Again I know that indefinable *moral sensation* which gives me a light step: I am borne.

2

Bad day after a bad night. Nervous exhaustion; dispossession of my-self. Loss of strength and loss of time.

3

Morning spent with Wojtkiewicz and his charming compatriot Jo-seph Retinger (and Druet) chasing from station to station and office to office looking for some crates containing ten canvases that S. is sending from Cologne.

16 May

Back from Cuverville, where we spent three days. I had, before leaving, written a preface for the Wojtkiewicz exhibit. Who else would have done it, once Maurice Denis had withdrawn?

Copeau, very cleverly, gets a picture of his sold by exclaiming in front of the "collector": "If I had been Gide, I know that this is the one I should have chosen!"

Perplexities as I correct for Claudel the proofs of *Co-naissance au monde et de soi-même:* so often grammar and syntax are intentionally outraged that I fear, at times, taking for an error some deliberate anom-aly. But what can be said for *plus ou moindre?* [17] Religious certainty gives this robust mind a deplorable infatuation. Perhaps it is impossible to write quite correctly without some fear of making a mistake.

17 May

I was on my way out; I was going to see Philippe Berthelot to ask his advice about the presentations of *Le Roi Candaule* at Cracow that Wojt-kiewicz had told me about; at the gate I am caught by Jaloux, who has just got in from Marseille, and Miomandre, who is piloting him in Paris. The latter dressed all in gray, sparkling, light, full of verve. Jaloux a bit dull and his mind as if it had the snuffles, yet very likable. It was easy for me to continue on my way, even with them; I did nothing of the sort. A sort of dizziness upset my will in a minute and the brakes loosened: at once I am given over to all the vagrant impulses of curiosity and van-

---

[17] "More or lesser."

ity . . . to all those little nameless stimuli which are generally kept coiled up, but which sometimes, in me, a nervous lapse releases . . . in short, a state of complete anarchy and, if the word did not annoy me so much, I should say of "irresponsibility." I who this very morning was congratulating myself on feeling well. Oh, how far I still am from the truth! (Yet one must understand and admit that certain natures are deformed by lack of constraint. I am not saying this for myself, for I have always known it, but rather for Fontainas, Jammes and the Belgian School.)

I take hold of Jaloux and Miomandre, then, and bring them home. Here we are in my study. It appears that I have nothing to say to them, nothing to learn from them. I have, however, read Jaloux's book and didn't find it at all bad; but when I try to talk to him of it, I get all wound up in restrictions to prove at one and the same time my frankness and the delicacy of my critical taste. Then, I don't know how or why — through the same absurd fatality that makes Muishkin approach the fragile vase he is afraid of breaking — I bring up the subject of Suarès (a dangerous subject on which I know that we shall not be able to agree). The letter I have just written to Mauclair about Suarès is in my pocket; I have kept it for three days since I don't know his address, which Miomandre gives me at once. I am unfortunate enough to be somewhat satisfied with this letter, and especially with having dared to write it. I am seized with an itch to show it to them. Come on, I can't resist any longer. Besides, the envelope isn't closed. Fully aware of my error, of my mistake, holding in a trembling hand this sheet that I read stumbling over each sentence, I read it. I read painfully, my forehead covered with sweat, *forcing myself*, interrupting myself, looking closely for the disastrous effect of the reading, altogether lucid and conscious; then I resume, I go on. . . .

I have slept on it; I am still sick about it. The least unfortunate result of this mistake is to keep me now from sending the letter. But the greatest harm it causes me is to fill and becloud my whole mind for so long.

I am writing all this down as a lesson to me; but what I should do is to strengthen myself against myself. For I already knew my failing well; and that absurd need heedlessly to hand myself over disarmed to anyone whatsoever.

Sunday

The mere recollection of my stupidity of the day before yesterday is enough to scrape on my heart as with a knife.

Read yesterday Upton Sinclair's *King Midas;* very bad, quite outside literature.

The Charles Gides and the Drouins come to lunch. The least society, even the most friendly, gives me a real nervous upset; obliged to limit myself to silence as a child is limited to bread and water; I seem gloomy as soon as I cease being peppery; and I long for solitude.

22 May

Last night Strauss's *Salomé*. Ghéon repeats to us the remark of Mme Strauss (as reported by Vielé-Griffin), commenting on the fact that Parisian audiences do not sufficiently applaud her husband's work: "Well, it's about time that we came back here with bayonets." Perhaps apocryphal. . . .

Abominable romantic music, with enough orchestral rhetoric to make one like Bellini. Only the parts filled with comic (the Magi) or morbid relief, Salomé's hesitations when Herod wants her to dance for him — almost the entire role of Herod, show a remarkable ability. Lasserre notes the same excellence of comic truculence in Hugo — likewise in the *Meistersinger* — same causes. And same causes of the shortcomings: lack of discretion of the means and monotony of the effects, annoying insistency, flagrant insincerity; uninterrupted mobilization of all the possible resources. Likewise Hugo, likewise Wagner, when metaphors come to mind to express an idea, does not choose, does not spare us a single one. Fundamental lack of artistry in all this. Systematic amplification, etc. . . . A shortcoming that it is not even interesting to examine into. One might better condemn the work as a whole and wait for the bayonets, because such an art really is the *enemy*.

Lunched at the Tour d'Argent with the Van Rysselberghes, Count Kessler, and Rodin. We talk to the last of his "start." For a long time, to earn his living, he makes "Carrier-Belleuse" of terracotta.[18] It is one of these poor insipid things that Druet recently exhibited in his window.

With *The Bronze Age* he arouses a protest; he barely avoids a trial with great difficulty (he is accused of having exhibited a mere cast of a man). But at that moment some friends group around him to defend him. That is when he leaves Brussels for Paris.

"How old were you then?"

"FORTY-FIVE."

This dominated my day.

24 May

Yesterday cycled to Saint-Germain, where I went in the hope of seeing Maurice Denis — but he is not at home any more on Thursdays.

---

[18] Decorative statuettes so named for the popular French sculptor Albert-Ernest Carrier-Belleuse, who multiplied them to satisfy the bourgeois public.

First I had gone to Bagatelle (exhibit of portraits – a very beautiful one by Courbet – a very odd one by Monticelli – almost all the rest very ordinary) – visit to the rose-garden.

Lunched in a low-class restaurant at Suresnes. Took the train as far as Marly. Interesting route to Saint-Germain, which I repeat (after having rung at Maurice Denis's house in vain) in the hope of getting to Versailles. But I start out wrong and first go to Saint-Cyr.[19]

Visited the two Trianons, which I didn't remember well. Didn't take much interest in the "visit of the apartments."

Very tiring return. Having got out of the train at Bellevue, I get lost in frightful sections, cobbled roads on which the bicycle is impossible; take the train again from Bas-Meudon to Javel; get home early enough to take a delightful shower.

But today is a day without any good in it. Loss of time; correcting proofs of *L'Enfant prodigue* – which I go and return to *Vers et Prose* right after lunch.

To the Colonial Exposition at Saint-Mandé by métro. Endless trip; great fatigue. Terrible fit of the blues upon hearing Arab music again, even though it was very nondescript, at that very nondescript exposition.

Crossing all of Paris in the métro, I end the day at the Sudanese village in Neuilly.

16 June

Arrived yesterday evening at Cuverville, at ten p.m. because of a delay in trains. Having missed the connection at Les Ifs, we had to go to Havre, where we dined while waiting for the evening train. I haven't had the heart to chat with this notebook the last few days. Suddenly one morning, spells of giddiness seized me again, and for fear of falling back into last year's sorry state of cerebral fatigue, I interrupted almost all work.

Then a flood of chores carried me to 15 June like a half-drowned man who, to save his breath, is satisfied to float. Yet, between going down the first and second times, I succeeded in writing the first scene of *Ajax*. Vast disgust with almost all the literary production of today and with the "public's" satisfaction with it. I am ever more convinced that to obtain a success *beside* one of these successes could not satisfy me. It is better to withdraw. Know how to wait, even if I have to wait until after death. To long for lack of recognition is the secret of the noblest patience. In the beginning, with such remarks I used to feed my pride with words. But not any more. The height of one's pride can be measured by the depth of one's scorn.

---

[19] Saint-Germain, Suresnes, Marly, Saint-Cyr, and Versailles are all within a few miles of Paris.

Théo, the perfect friend, finally pulls me out, I hope, of the morass into which Bonnier had thrown me. Really! on certain days I could have packed up and left this house unfinished where my time, money, patience, and enthusiasm are being exhausted. . . . Everything is progressing better now; I don't give up hope of seeing it just about finished this autumn, before having completely ruined myself on it. I hardly know how I shall be able to pay — or at least how, after having paid, we shall be able to live.

Read Lasserre's book with the greatest interest at first, then not without irritation as it continued.[20] Is it because they stand at the beginning? — but the first chapters seemed to me by far the best. The thought is not too bad, but the expression is feverish, careless. Today the desire for perfection seems merely to embarrass all those to whom it is not a joke.

Blum's book *Du Mariage* is occasioning much comment. The dialogued commentary of Marcel Drouin and Fontaine, at a certain tea at the Lerolles', struck me as far above the ordinary; a book is certainly not negligible when it makes people talk so well. But the constant, the sole avowed preoccupation with *happiness* in this book shocks me none the less. I am far from convinced that in the easiest and least costly understanding of his satisfactions man becomes most worthy of love and admiration. And what of woman!! The finest feminine figures I have known are resigned; and I cannot even imagine being charmed and not being aroused to a slight hostility by the contentment of a woman whose happiness did not involve a little resignation.

Dined *quattro giorni fa* at R. N.'s on my way back from a visit to Maillol at Marly. Very pleasant dinner, like all the dinners at the charming R. N.'s house; with a fat idiot whom I had already met through Rouart and who is named — no one knows why — Victor. His outthrust jaw prolonged by a sort of goatee makes him look as if he had just come down from the Ægina pediment. He grits his teeth and clenches his fists as he talks; he impresses himself as a wild man and puts frenzy into his utterance of the most stupid aphorisms. He says: "Art? It's a vice." Emits a whistle: "I, for instance, the day before yesterday I bought all at once forty Valtats: it's a vice!" He also says: "Catholicism has made of this world a vast hollow top." He has his own ideas on religion and, after dinner, enlightens me on metaphysicis, or rather on theology. He says: "The Greeks! The Greeks!" and that is enough. At table could be heard already (but since he was speaking to the ladies, there was a shade of irony in his voice): "The nature of religion . . . yes! . . . or the religion of nature . . . one or the other . . . or perhaps a bit of

---

[20] Pierre Lasserre's major work, *Le Romantisme français*, appeared in 1907.

both. . . . Don't you think so, Madame Gide?" And my wife pretended not to hear.

And this pig is a painter. He paints on wood because his frantic brush-strokes would go right through the canvas. With this detail I leave him.

I let him believe that I am much like him. (He says: "The Church," then adds, so that you will be sure of understanding: "Ecclesia!" He says: "What we need today is a cult — *cultus*, rites . . ." then, doubtless failing to find the Latin word or the Greek word, he is satisfied with repeating and rolling the *r* a bit more: "*Rrites.*")

22 June

For the fourth time I take up again from the very beginning this miserable book, over which I have labored so much already. The great improvisers of today would call this impotence or mania. Today I am almost at the point where I could agree with them. Yet toward the end of the day, after a great effort, I think I have set the amorphous mass in motion again.

The piano came yesterday. Good study of Chopin's wonderful preludes, which I am reviewing all together.

Every time that "success" has approached me, I have made faces at it.

Already in '91, I remember: I was with Pierre Louÿs; we met Retté at the d'Harcourt, where we had gone for dinner, I believe. The latter begins an elaborate praise of *Les Cahiers d'André Walter*,[21] which has just appeared and which he "has just finished reading." I can hear his sentence: "It is one of the twelve (or twenty) important books that have appeared since . . ." At these words I get up to hang my coat a bit farther away, leaving Retté with half of his compliment unspoken. When I sit down again, Pierre Louÿs leans toward me and says in my ear: "My boy, when someone compliments you, you could at least listen. It looks as if compliments drive you away." This was true. It still is today. Too much pride perhaps; also fear of blarney. Flatterers catch on at once and don't let themselves get caught again.

On 29 June, in reply to a note from Marcel Drouin about Blum's book, I had written this — which I later considered it wiser not to send him:

"Yes, Blum's book can do harm. . . . People will seek in it not a 'new light' on a question which belongs, I should say, more to the field of ethics than to sociology — but rather an *authorization*. As for me, I first read the book very hastily, then, embarrassed at hearing everyone

---

[21] André Gide's first volume.

talking about it and being too uninformed to say anything myself, I re-read the book carefully; and was able to tell Blum himself how foreign to me was a point of view that proposes 'happiness' as an aim, limits happiness to the bedroom and claims to furnish a recipe for capturing it.

"However typical and well presented all the observations of this book are — which seems a clever preface to the whole Jewish theater of today — they utterly overlook the value of resignation and restraint and imply the monstrous argument that the tree never produces so much or such fine fruit as in *the state of nature*."

I am merely a little boy having a good time — compounded with a Protestant minister who bores him.

* * *

16 October
I begin today because I should have more trouble beginning tomorrow. Returned to Paris yesterday, lunched at Copeau's, who dragged me off, immediately after the meal, to the dress rehearsal of *Monsieur Codomat* [22] at the Théâtre Gémier.

Copeau had to lend me a collar; I still looked like a rustic; none the less, this sudden plunge into the world of Paris after the warm bath of autumn down in the country stirred my blood most pleasantly. Alone I should have flinched, but Copeau gave me assurance. I even let myself be introduced to Bréval, who "had been wanting to meet me" for a long time. Found nothing moreover to say to her, nor she to me. She remained hidden in the shadow of her stage-box; very much sought-after however; somewhat worn face, but rather tragically beautiful. Said without difficulty or regret the flattest banalities; to enliven my wit, I should need a real desire to please, and not to stop there. (What Stendhal would have said or done . . .) Shook a rather large number of hands, of which I recognized only about half. B.'s little brother is turning into a big fool. One is amazed always to be meeting Mendès; he seems to be amazed that I do not speak to him. Franc-Nohain introduces to me his very nice young wife; the three of us talk of dear old La Pérouse. This summer, invited by his old friend Dauphin (Franc-Nohain's father-in-law) to come and spend a few days in the country, he, who for the last thirty-three years has not left Paris, makes up his mind, gets to the Gare du Nord without having looked at the train schedule, waits for an hour and a half for a local train that takes three hours instead of one, arrives when he is no longer expected and hence finds no one at the station, gets an old woman to lead him through the woods to the Dauphin property, where she leaves him at the gate; look-

[22] Play by Tristan Bernard.

ing for a way in, he sees a sign "wolf traps," so that, terrified, not daring to go any farther, he was about to retrace his steps when, unexpectedly meeting his friend, he is nevertheless able to spend almost an hour with him.

Before Tristan Bernard's play, a device for stage machinery by Lorde on the disaster of Martinique. A rather well-arranged volcanic eruption in the first act, which, however, as a result of the bad functioning of the ventilators, fills the theater with smoke (subject of conversation with Mégard). Last act with literary, moral, and anti-religious pretensions. The public, which feels the show rising a peg, applauds and is in raptures. It is almost nauseating.

Tristan Bernard's play is one of the best I have heard in some time. Perfect acting by Gémier, moderation, effects obtained quite naturally by the construction of the characters. Perhaps even a little overdelicacy, little details, a certain groping in the indication of the characters. If Tristan Bernard had been a little more sure of writing a really good play, he would perhaps have dared to paint more broadly. — None the less, I left delighted and eager to go back with Em. and the Drouins.[23]

17 October

Alone with the aged Augustine in the big Auteuil house. Terrible weather; all the paths in the garden are rivers of mud; the wind is whistling under the doors and shaking the windows.

Lunched with the Théo Van Rysselberghes. Did some errands. Went to chat at length with poor old La Pérouse; then to the pool. Picked up Copeau as he left the gallery, went a long distance on foot with him. This evening, after dinner, wrote some letters. Too tired to chat at length here. But I am well, and this fatigue is the promise of a good sleep.

18 October

I am writing on Anna Shackleton's little table, which was in my room at rue de Commailles. This is where I used to work; I liked it because in the double mirror of the dressing-table, above the shelf on which I was writing, I could see myself writing; after every sentence I would look at myself; my image spoke to me, listened to me, kept me company, kept me in a state of fervor. I had never since written at this table. These last few evenings I have been recapturing my childhood sensations.

Went to see de Max this morning as I left the bank. (Money questions that used to excite me now depress me; I gave a few orders almost at random to satisfy a finicky need for excitement.) The visit to de Max

---

[23] (Written in the margin.) I have since seen the play again with a Gémier altogether spoiled. [A.]

produced nothing. — In the afternoon slept, wrote to the Sorma. Did some errands. Met Marcel at the dentist's door and returned to Auteuil with him. This evening worked on *La Porte étroite.*

20 October

Yesterday spent almost the whole afternoon writing to Haguenin about the staging of *Candaule* in Germany. Last year he had asked me for some bibliographical details to furnish the substance of an article; I am sending them to him. Dined at Paul Laurens's after having spent some moments with Copeau.

I am keeping this journal without pleasure, as an exercise and without any care for the interest I may ever take in rereading it.

This morning I go to meet Dumont-Wilden (whom I do not yet know) at the Salon d'Automne. Four times I bump into Sert, infinitely anxious to know what people think of his painting.

Very joyful meeting with Charles Chanvin, whom I hadn't seen in five years. No embarrassment; a totally unaffected pleasure.

The Maus, always the same, cordial, frantic, and vain. How beautiful the Carpeaux are!

Very nondescript and very expensive lunch at the restaurant on the corner of the Champs-Élysées and the rue — (Montaigne or avenue Matignon?) with the very likable Dumont-Wilden.

Visited, without learning anything, the Italian pointillists or divisionists. Returned, worn out, for a short nap and work.

24 October

Again snowed under. Worked yesterday from morning until two o'clock on a letter to Haguenin intended to facilitate and favor his zeal. He talks of presenting my work in Berlin. He talks well. I am beginning to be tired *of not being;* as soon as a great enthusiasm does not sustain me, I struggle. Wounded vanity has never produced anything that matters, but at times my pride suffers from a real despair. And I live certain days as if in the nightmare of the man who was walled up alive in his tomb. Frightful state, which it is good to know, to have known. I shall write about it later when I have got out of it.

No news from Berlin, where they *must* play me before the 28th.

I think of Keats. I tell myself that two or three passionate admirations like mine would have kept him alive. Useless efforts, I feel at times all *wilted* by the silence.

Late October

Called to Pau for the death of Marcel Gilbert.

"My dear friend," Claudel would say to Jammes, "when, after having lived for many years in the love of God, I succumbed as you know to the love of that woman, it seemed to me that, leaving a pure mountain lake, I was plunging into a foot-bath."

19 November

Saw Jammes at my brother-in-law's funeral, then again at Orthez. I had to "lead" the mourning with Léon Cafford. Very dignified, very beautiful ceremony; simple ritual music, which I much prefer.

At the end of the Mass a woman of the district, a *sister*, knelt at the railing separating the choir from the congregation; the priest covered the stone railing with a cloth and then held out the host to her, which she took with wonderful devotion. I thought at first that a beautiful local custom invited her to receive communion for all of us, and with my whole soul I shared in her gesture. I learned later that everyone was permitted to partake of that communion at the end of the Mass; the following day thirty received communion after another funeral Mass. How much more eloquent than such a group that beautiful isolated figure!

Saw Eugène Rouart and recovered down there at Bagnols my unrest, my curiosity, my rapture.

For the last week and more I have had a typewriter, having found in Pierre de Lanux someone with the need to be a secretary. Whence discipline, zeal, and regularity in my work, and general raising of the moral standard. While I am writing this, the machine is producing four copies of *La Porte étroite*, which I am actively concerning myself with correcting. I have spent a fortnight more on the first chapter, but it now satisfies me.

Read very little, my mind occupied almost exclusively by my book. This is also what made me forsake this journal. Once again, for several days, I got stuck in the first chapter.

André Ruyters came to live here a week. He left every morning at eight for his bank and returned only for dinner. One evening after dinner we went to meet Ghéon, Copeau, and Jean Schlumberger at the Pousset on the boulevards. After some hesitation Ghéon took out his manuscript (the first hundred pages of *L'Adolescent*); [24] gathered in the back room of a very ordinary pub, despite the noise near by, we devoutly listened to the even, average voice of the novelist Ghéon, so different from the Ghéon who wrote *L'Eau-de-vie* and *Le Pain*.[25] — Excellent impression on us all.

Five days later, meeting of the same group in Auteuil without Copeau. After many a reservation I launch into the reading of *La Porte étroite*. Very imperfect reading at first, since the first two chapters are

[24] Henri Ghéon's first novel, *The Adolescent*.
[25] Two plays, *Brandy* and *Bread*.

still pastily amorphous in spots; rather dull reading all together. . . .
What causes so much trouble in writing this book is also what causes
them (I am thinking chiefly of Ghéon) considerable trouble in listening to it: it remains an anachronism amidst everything that we are thinking, feeling, and wanting today. But despite this, I cannot not write it;
and from this crushing trial I issue, after all, less depressed than
strengthened.

8 December

Stendhal's correspondence.
Stendhal has never been a real sustenance for me, yet I constantly return to him. He is my cuttlebone; I sharpen my beak on him.

La 628, E 8.[26] People talk of Mirbeau's psychology and of Zola's naturalism or realism because both of them discuss shamelessly what used
to be hidden. One must admit that they talk better about these things
than about all the rest — than about what everyone discusses. The most
successful pages are those in which he keeps closest to the tone and gait
of conversation; certain ones, in this regard, are almost perfect; he never
rises above them. He gets angry and becomes enthusiastic, one never
knows just why, but sincerely, I believe, and like a child; he likes to get
angry; it is the best in him. He writes in the heat of passion without reflecting, notes his quakes like a seismograph. The satiric spirit completely prevents the development of the ironic spirit in him.

Gourmont's Dialogues des amateurs. The desire to prove himself intelligent makes him constantly talk nonsense. I can well imagine that
he impresses and why, and that many readers don't dare resist for fear
of thinking themselves less intelligent than he. Nothing so stupid as that
fear of being taken in! I have seen the sorry fruits of it in Georges Rondeaux and in Gérard.
He speaks of literature and in general of "the things of the spirit"
with a rather great competence and a taste that is most often delicate
(excellent, for instance, his dialogue on romanticism and Lasserre) —
but as soon as he deals with alcoholism, virtue, depopulation, criminal-
ity, etc., he puts forth nothing but monstrosities and shows that he has
never known life except through books.
"It must be rather hard, all the same, to go off to prison when you
haven't deserved prison."
"And when you have deserved it, is it any less hard? And does one

---

[26] Mirbeau's novel by this title recounts a motor trip that serves as a
pretext for a review of the author's opinions. The title comes from the license-
plate of the car.

ever deserve it? What do guilt and innocence depend on? On mere chance," etc., etc.

There is someone who really takes a superior point of view! And are these considerations really involved? Rightly or wrongly society establishes rules outside of which the citizen is recognized to be answerable to the law. If these rules are arbitrary, what does it matter? That the man who escapes them is an innocent man, a martyr, a saint, or a fool is not the question, and Gourmont talks of this with the *superiority* of Molière's *bourgeois gentilhomme* saying of the dancers after the minuet: "Those people certainly put on quite a jig." — But, as a child, did he never play? Didn't his heart ever overflow upon hearing himself falsely accused of *having cheated*? Or did he already reply to his playmates: "What is cheating? Does one ever *cheat*?" etc., etc. But the truth is that he never had any playmates and that he never played except alone.

12 December

Again my mind is disjointed, upset; my flesh weak, restless, wildly listless. My whole organism is like those oversonorous houses in which from the attic can be heard everything that is going on in the kitchen and in the cellar.

Valentine came to spend six days with us; her presence has certainly contributed greatly to setting my nerves on edge.

13 December

Frightful, wonderful squall all night long. My mind seems to be lifted up by the wind — carried off like a kite — a kite on the end of a rubber band.

I find and reread a letter from Paul Claudel (1899): "Your mind has no slope," he said to me. That is just what is needed. No praise is more precious to me.

Gourmont — a desperately opaque soul.

Absence of sympathy = lack of imagination. This goes well with ignorance of dizziness; but Gérard doesn't know that this comes from his inability to imagine what he does not feel. This is what is often called *sang-froid;* merely impotence of the imagination. The most gifted natures are perhaps also the most trembling.

1908

Yesterday the *Aulularia* [1] at the matinee at the Odéon. De Max, who for the first time attempts what is generally called "an ironic role," is excellent. But a bit too much attention to details. I doubt if he will ever reach that simplification, that "powerful erosion of the contours," which Nietzsche speaks of, and without which there can be no perfect work of art. He confronts the critics with all his pride, but forgets it when he faces the public. That public — and I mean chiefly the public in his dressing-room — helps to falsify his taste beyond recall.

In his dressing-room yesterday a half-dozen insignificant young whippersnappers. Fortunately there was also José de Charmoy. And Bréval also, whom I recognize only in the course of, and thanks to, the conversation. She does not take offense at this and talks to me very cordially of Copeau.

Last night, the opening of *Candaule* in Berlin; this morning I receive the following telegram from Haguenin:
"Well acted Gurlitt (Nyssia) [2] very good great success for half of the audience the rest recalcitrant."

The day after the opening the press launches its attack. Barnowsky (the manager of the Kleiner Theater), terrified, hastens to cancel the play.
Great exchange of letters with Haguenin, who shows on this occasion a devotion that embarrasses me. An excellent article by him in the — (?) attempted to prepare the public. The critics stifle any inclination the public might have had to applaud.
I fear that the playing of *Saül* may be dreadfully compromised. . . . We made a bad start. I have kept a copy of my letter to Haguenin. I should like it to be published, if ever . . .
Try to be proud rather than ambitious, that is the whole secret. I am beginning to think, moreover, that one suffers more from justified accusations than from those one doesn't deserve. To be told that I speculated on . . . to be called a pornographer, a boulevardier, a writer of farces; to be accused of imitating Maeterlinck! or Donnay, of whom I have never read anything!! Really, the blows fall wide of the mark.
Not a single critic who fails to drag out Hebbel; probably the same

---

[1] The famous comedy by Plautus.
[2] Gurlitt is the actress who played Nyssia, the heroine.

critics strangled him when he was alive. They are all vying with one another in their insults; terrifying monotony of these articles, only the first of which I read entire. One of them begins thus: *"Le Roi Candaule* had a dazzling success in Paris. [!] This does not surprise us . . . etc. — *eine solche Schweinerei . . ."* etc.

16 January

Met de Max at the skating-rink; motionless amidst the skaters, dejected, his eyes lack-luster; surrounded by agile swallows, he looked like a dismal stilt-bird from the swamps. White gloves, gold bracelet, otter jacket, derby hat. . . .

"You seem very melancholy?"

"I often look like that," he replies.

A few good skaters, but they all look like flunkies.

Translation of Dostoyevsky's Correspondence in the *Mercure.*

I had asked Roucher to save for me the article in the *Grande Revue;* with the Signoret preface and this new study, I am going to be thoroughly distracted from my novel.

21 January

I go to Marcel Drouin's and he helps me read the German clippings until dinner. Yesterday, 20 January, I received my *hundred and fifty-third* clipping (*Candaule* was played on the 9th) — *every one* of them insulting, dishonest, stupid, unspeakable — with the notable exception of the two articles by Haguenin in the *National Zeitung* and the *Zeit.*

(I have since received three excellent magazine articles; others will be coming along.)

Copeau comes to dinner; after dinner Marcel comes to join us and we spend our time until one in the morning making up, out of quotations, a *letter from Germany,* which I copy out Sunday morning, go and read to Copeau Sunday evening, and take to the *Mercure* Monday. I think it is . . . just right.

A bit more courage, joy, *pressure* these last few days. If only I could sleep! Already I consider myself *almost* satisfied with these broken-up nights, if my numerous awakenings are without anguish and do not interrupt sleep too long.

I have slept better, having gone to bed two nights in succession at eight thirty like a child; but force myself to this! . . . regularly. . . . Give up all evening work, all reading! . . .

25 January

Inquiry conducted by the *Berliner Tageblatt.*

On the occasion of the twenty-fifth anniversary of Wagner's death they are interested in sounding out "the leading artistic and intellectual figures of all Europe as to their opinion of the influence of Wagnerism, especially in France."

I reply:

"I hold the person and the work of Wagner in horror; my passionate aversion has grown steadily since my childhood. This amazing genius does not exalt so much as he *crushes*. He permitted a large number of snobs, of literary people, and of fools to think that they loved music, and a few artists to think that genius can be acquired. Germany has perhaps never produced anything at once so great or so barbarous."

26 January

Yesterday, having arrived too early at Mme Brandon's, I spend three quarters of an hour waiting for the stroke of four in the Trocadéro Museum. In just the right mood for criticism and contemplation. Got a great deal out of it.

Got less from my visit to Mme Brandon; in less than five minutes eight people arrived; the inanity of the conversations was terrifying. Moreover Mme Brandon hardly talked with anyone but me. And as I got up to leave: "The people with whom one enjoys talking are so rare . . ."; the expression of the others as they heard this compliment.

Left to meet Copeau at the Pousset.

The *Phalange* banquet.[3]

I had promised Copeau not to separate from him, but unfortunately this was not possible. The embarrassing honor of seating me on the right of Royère was paid me (on his left Vielé-Griffin, then Gustave Kahn). It would have been hardly decent to refuse and I could not have done so without too many explanations. On my right Robert de Souza, then Ghéon, then, as the table turned a corner, Han Ryner, Apollinaire, Copeau, Jean Schlumberger, then about thirty people unknown to me. In all we might have been a hundred and fifty. — Pleasant room on the first floor of the Cardinal. Passable food; but a nervous tension makes me incapable of eating. . . .

Interrupted story. Useless to relate it in detail. Very much amused and attracted by Apollinaire's face. At the moment of the toasts a young fool who is not given the floor when he wants to recite some of Royère's poems goes off in the wings and breaks the mirror in a private dining-room. "Very Dostoyevsky," says Copeau, with whom I walk home. Jean

---

[3] *La Phalange*, a literary review edited by Jean Royère from 1906 to 1914, published the second-generation symbolists, many of them also contributors to *Vers et Prose*. It was in this review that the great critic Albert Thibaudet, later associated chiefly with the *Nouvelle Revue Française*, began his career.

Schlumberger is with us; Ghéon had to take his train at eleven. Vielé-Griffin and Robert de Souza take us to the Weber, where the evening is prolonged until after midnight. It is one thirty when I get home.

Abominable night; not able to fall asleep a minute. If anyone catches . . .

27 January

My temperament, most deplorably, revolts against any restraint, any rule that my mind would like to impose on it. What can I do against insomnia, or that nameless nervousness that stands in my way? Do I know in what mood I shall awake tomorrow? Can I dare to sit down to work after a night of anguish with the same heart that I would if I were rested? I dream, I have always dreamed, of a method that, regulating even my fancy, would permit me to get the maximum out of myself; and here I must make that method over every day. Yesterday if I had not slept for two hours in the afternoon, I should not have been able to last until evening. — And so on.

28 January

Good enough night and, consequently, good enough work this morning (preface for Emmanuel Signoret) — so that I can allow myself to practice the piano again for an hour. I had resolutely given it up for almost two months, my weak work being jealous of it.

Jammes, at lunch today, tells us the remark of a little girl cousin of his wife who, at nine, used to say:

"I am not so much angry with the Protestants as with Calver and Luthin."

After lunch he reads me some excellent *Poèmes mesurés.*[4]

2 February

Hateful night; did not stop *talking*, interminably remembering a lot of nonsense (the obsession of bits of sentences, and words, that one repeats idiotically, irresistibly, I don't know how many times) and reading new texts that I was inventing! Besides I was frozen despite the hot-water bottle and a pile of blankets. I probably had caught cold yesterday; a sore throat and pains in my intestines; but my nerves amplify everything. Then, without taking any exercise, I had remained working all day or almost. . . . That is not yet possible for me.

3 February

I reread the necrological article by Francis Jammes on Charles Guérin (*Mercure*, 1 April 1907). He has never written anything worse.

---

[4] *Measured Poems.*

I do not like his citing Henri de Régnier as a model of dignity when a few months earlier he was calling him a whippersnapper.

"Seizing with his delicate fingers the wings of a sphinx that had taken refuge on a street-lamp." I am absolutely sure that it was not a sphinx. — Why? — Because a sphinx's wings do not fold back and because sphinxes do not light on things. . . . And besides who cares!

6 February

This most recent clipping from a German newspaper sums up so well the stupidity of all the others that it is the only one I wish to retain and therefore I set it down here:

"In Hebbel's play," the article begins, "Candaules is a barbarian king and Gyges is a cultured Greek; in M. Gide's playlet, on the other hand, Gyges is the barbarian while the cultured man is Candaulus. . . . These few words should suffice to show that M. Gide has not understood the subject at all."

8 February

Verhaeren comes and reads me some wonderful passages from his *Hélène*.

Debussy was being spoken of.
"He is so softly affectionate," said Mme X.
"Oh no, madame! he is cuddly," Mme Debussy corrected.

12 February

One more clipping from Germany; it says:
"*Hebbels Auffassung steht für unser Empfindung ebenso hoch über der Gides, wie etwa Kleists Ausgestaltung des Amphitryons Stoffes über der Molières*" (*Bühne und Welt*, Berlin).[5]

Radiant weather; an azure we had forgotten during the last three months. My mind full of gaiety, I go to return the Signoret proofs to the *Mercure* and get tickets at the Odéon for tomorrow's lecture (Moréas on *Electra*); I walk back with Henry Davray to his new apartment on the rue Servandoni. Go to take his ticket to Eugène Rouart, at the Ministry. It is too late to return home — besides, it is too beautiful. I go to lunch alone (for one franc seventy-five, tip included) in the little restaurant on the Square Sainte-Clotilde where Ghéon and I lunched a month ago. Then obliged to drop in at the École Alsacienne (for the purpose of paying an old bill), I go up the part of the boulevard Raspail that has been recently cut through, going over fences and wallowing

---

[5] "In our opinion Hebbel's interpretation stands just as far above Gide's as, say, Kleist's handling of the Amphitryon legend above Molière's."

somewhat through vacant lots dug up by the construction gangs, but amused to the point of rapture by the odd aspect of these gutted houses on which the laughing sun sparkles. Old gardens, a well; caged trees, drooping and blackened; ancient courtyards, entrance steps of tumbledown private houses; all this dazzled and looking like a night bird that has suddenly been plunged into the light. How beautiful the day was!

Went to ring at Jean Schlumberger's and he accompanied me for a moment to the Luxembourg while waiting for the school to open. — Old school; courtyard I hadn't entered in twenty years! I hardly recognized myself there or old Papa Braünig, who spoke to me.

Back by métro — and work (Dostoyevsky for *La Grande Revue*).

13 February

Went with Eugène Rouart to hear the lecture by Moréas at the Odéon — which preceded a playing of Euripides' *Electra* in a prose version by Ferdinand Hérold. Numerous friends in the audience created a kind of success for the lecturer, who took three bows. I too applauded most willingly, for it was evident that everyone was applauding the poet of *Les Stances* and *Le Pèlerin*.[6] As for the lecture, it was interminable and boring. Moréas's voice, beautiful in a drawing-room or a café, remained hollow, monotonous and pompous. Having, indeed, but very few ideas, the fear of lacking substance made him embrace as many subjects as possible; he emptied his bag at random, spoke very little or not at all of *Electra* or of Euripides, but of Corneille, Shakespeare, Nietzsche, Malherbe, Aristotle, Otway, Voltaire, etc., etc. — limiting himself, most of the time, to reading old articles from *La Gazette*, which I remembered well enough to recognize sentences and groups of sentences. What in those articles had seemed to be delicate and discreetly phrased did not carry, and with the best will in the world I no longer found any savor in them. Many in the audience opened books or newspapers; some left noisily; people very nearly booed.

We left soon after the curtain went up, exasperated by the pasty elocution and the actors' lack of art.

The *points* in a speech have much to be said for them; need of knowing *how far one has got.*

It is not the subject that Moréas exhausted, but rather himself. One felt that he was saying everything and that, having done this, he had nothing more to say.

14 February

But I didn't know that Molière worked slowly! Very *important*, the remark of Grimarest quoted by Lemaître in his third lecture: "He did

---

[6] *Stanzas* and *The Pilgrim* are the principal works of Moréas.

not work rapidly, but he didn't mind having people think he was prompt."

Andler tells Marcel Drouin that he had the opportunity of reading some letters of Nietzsche, not yet published for several reasons. In them one can see that his course in Basel had no success whatever. One can also see in them the lack of consideration he had for his sister: *"Eine dumme Gans,"* he calls her.[7]

"Those people who have their hind end in the Church and their head in the Academy," says Valéry.

Received (in reply to my letter in which I begged him in the future not to open what was not addressed to him) a letter from Verrier, the faithless secretary of *L'Ermitage*, which is as insolent and witty as the retort of a stage lackey. If I were not twelve years older than he, I should have liked being close friends with the young fellow, but nothing will ever let him suspect this.

Trip to Italy — came back 20 March.
Wrote to Em. every day.

Article on Dostoyevsky (for *La Grande Revue*).
No more interest in keeping this journal.

5 April
Went last night to Wonderland to try to forget for a moment little Louis Rouart's letter, which kept me from sleeping last night. That letter poisoned my day.

How much simpler it would have been to break off completely, a few years ago, when each of us had *noble* (political) griefs against the other. Our friendship remains like those painful consumptives whose life is prolonged by dint of precautions and who go on living only to suffer. That friendship gives me no joy, furnishes me with but few occasions of self-esteem, teaches me nothing, and hurts me as soon as I try to sink it a bit deeper in my heart.

7 April
Lunched yesterday at Albert Mockel's with Stefan George, Albert Saint-Paul, and a rather pleasant young man whom they called Olivier (I never could make out whether it was merely his first name). Wonderful head of Stefan George, whom I have long wanted to know and whose work I admire each time I manage to understand it. Bluish-white com-

---
[7] "A stupid goose."

plexion, skin dull and more drawn than wrinkled, sharply defined bone-structure; impeccably shaved; full, heavy hair, still more black than gray and all brushed back. Hands of a convalescent, very delicate, bloodless, very expressive. He speaks little, but in a deep voice that forces attention. A sort of clergyman's Prince Albert with two clasps toward the top, which opens for a necktie-scarf of black velvet, above and overflowing the collar. The simple gold slide on a ribbon leading to a watch or monocle gives a discreet accent to all this black. Shoes (elastic-sided, I fancy!) of a single piece of leather tightly gripping the foot, which I didn't like, perhaps because I had seen similar ones on Charmoy.

He expresses himself in our language without a single mistake, though yet a bit cautiously, it seems, and shows a surprising knowledge and understanding of our authors, particularly our poets; and all this without self-satisfaction, but with an evident awareness of his evident superiority.

9 April

Excellent visit from Louis Rouart; I go out of my way to note it because of the excessive words written above.

Read Knut Hamsun's *Pan*. Bouquet and flavor, but nothing but bouquet and flavor. The meat is lacking. Miserable awkwardness and insignificance of the dialogues.

Hunger was far superior; or at least, given the special nature of the subject, the deficiencies were less noticeable.

After a very hot day it is cold this morning. I make the big circuit of Longchamp by way of Boulogne. Bleak heights of Suresnes looking as if deflated under the fog, ugly and sunken. . . .

I read a rather stupid article in the *Mercure* (of 16 February) on *Salammbô* and Punic archaeology. "Flaubert's error," one reads, "Where Flaubert goes wrong . . ." I am not convinced that M. Pezard, the author of the article, did not make a greater mistake when he read *Salammbô*. An *explanatory* article on *Salammbô* would be interesting to write.

Last month, in Italy, I just happened to reread that wonderful book, which I had not set high enough in my esteem. Childish perhaps, but with the disarming puerility of a poet; it seems to me that Flaubert, in the texts on which he relies, never sought so much a documentation as an authorization. Through loathing for everyday reality, he fell in love here with everything that differed from it. Does he really believe with Theophrastus that carbuncles are "formed of lynx's urine"? Certainly not! But he is delighted that a text of Theophrastus authorizes him to pretend to believe it; and likewise for the rest.

16 May

Back from Cuverville. Recalled suddenly by the news of the birth of Jeanne's child.

At Cuverville, good work for fourteen days.

Excellent piano-practice (exclusively Chopin: nocturnes, finale of the Sonata in B-flat minor, etc.).

This evening at rue Drouot, for the Kessler sale, directed by Druet. Among those present Mme Redon, Mme Denis, who is taking part in her husband's ascent (the prices have quadrupled in the last three years), and Maus. I sit near Fénéon, not far from Druet himself; not far likewise from Coolus; Lebey comes and sits beside me. We chat and our conversation soon distracts me from the sale. I had noted the first bids; I soon lose sight even of the paintings. And this is why I shall cease going to such sales:

A Bonnard is put up at auction, rather badly put together, but racy; it represents a naked woman dressing and I have already seen it somewhere or other. It climbs rather painfully to 450, 55, 60. Suddenly I hear a voice shout: "600!" — And I am dazed, for I myself am the one who just shouted. With my eyes I implore a higher bid from those around me — for I have no desire to own the painting — but nothing is forthcoming. I feel myself becoming purple and begin to sweat copiously. "It's stifling in here," I say to Lebey. We leave.

Such impulses are absurd. Already a similar experience had occurred to me at the same place. And the most ridiculous thing of all is to be angry with myself afterward; generally speaking, it is only with difficulty that I am *resigned to myself*. (The oddest fact is that the bidding was still this side of 500 francs, so that in rounding out the sum they counted my bid as only 500 francs, as the bill showed the next day; and yet, I am certain, it was 600 francs that I shouted.)

18 May

To thank him for his article on Signoret, I have decided to read Mithouard's *Les Pas sur le sable*.[8] There is no denying that the style is racy. He has only one idea; and the need of constantly justifying it. There is nothing so boring as his continual domination by that single thought. And since he is afraid of boring, he has recourse to a sort of odd humor, which none the less seems rather spontaneous.

As an example of the *proofs* with which he is intellectually satisfied, take this, as early as page 3 in the volume: he relates an ascent in a balloon (in order to prove that one must not lose physical contact with "the earth and the dead"); he describes his sensations of fright, the only ones

---

[8] *Footprints in the Sand.*

he was able to experience, and concludes: ". . . and then this, of whose horror nothing can give an idea: to feel, monstrously in my flesh, the uselessness of my legs. . . ." But, dear Mithouard, in the train, in a carriage, etc. . . .

Already some time ago I noticed, in his *Traité de l'Occident*, I believe, or his *Tourment de l'Unité*,[9] the great number of false quotations. He wrote — thinking he was quoting Bouilhet: "Eternally Virgin from having borne her God" — and in the belief that he was quoting Stendhal: "Love is a promise of happiness," and so on. This derives from the same spiritual shortcoming. I pointed this out to him in Rome, where I met him with Maurice Denis. He excused himself by saying: "I have noted all those things on cards; one hasn't the time always to go back to the sources!"

Oh, the Sources! the *pure* sources![10] But that is precisely just where one should drink and never let one's thirst be slaked by other waters.

Thus, because Mithouard was afraid in a balloon and because he stifled in a mine, he concludes that Ibsen and Tolstoy are not proper reading for a Frenchman.

6 June
Having left La Guimorais (Saint-Malo) at eight in the morning, I reach Trégastel at eight in the evening. Went to pick up my mail at Saint-Coulomb. Lamentable letter from Fedor Rosenberg telling of the death of their little Sonia.

"I should so much like to know, Mummy . . . just what do people call an *idyll*?" she asked on her last day.

Got a real sunburn over almost my whole body by letting myself brown on the beach yesterday.

Four hours to kill in Rennes. Read some Bergson in the train.

Found at the Rennes fair a Pushkin, with which I immediately delight myself; *Boris* is more beautiful than I remembered.

Emotion of my arrival at Trégastel — an emotion such as I no longer thought my *age* capable of feeling. I cycled almost all the way from Lannion to Trégastel, the wagon with my suitcase following at some distance. Radiant evening; light, almost cold air. The sun is on the point of going down as I enter the courtyard of the hotel.

. . . As a reaction I have plunged deeper into Pascal; sketched out two important dialogues of *La Porte étroite*. Went swimming every day.

---

⁹ *Treatise on the Occident* and *The Torment of Unity.*
¹⁰ In French the word *source* means both "source" and "spring."

Returned strengthened, but after three days in Paris have lost almost all the advantage. Fortunately we are staying here only twelve days.

Cuverville, 22 June

Sublime style — direct emanation from the heart; it is only through *piety* that it can be achieved.

27 June

One can find in them (letters to Mlle de Roannez) [11] very fine arguments, even in favor of the Pope; ardent arguments, the only ones that persuade (see Letter VI, Brunschvicg edition) — and that leave me shaken.

"He ardently delighted in this outrage to flesh, the enemy. . . ." (Suarès: *Visite à Pascal.*) [12]

It doesn't seem to me that Suarès is following Pascal at this point. The Jansenist feels a loathing for sin, not for the flesh, and imagines the flesh itself not necessarily as a sinner but as a victim.

He speaks readily of an "innocent body" that death "afflicts." He considers it possible to have "peace between the soul and the body" and sees nothing wrong in seeking to flee a death that would destroy that peace (letter on the death of the father).

And finally he writes (first letter to Mlle de Roannez) the strangest sentence: "God never forsakes his own, not even in the sepulcher, where their bodies, although dead in the eyes of men, are more living before God because sin has ceased to inhabit them." It must be remembered that the Church teaches the resurrection of the flesh.

28 July

A week's stop at Bagnols-de-Grenade.

Reading of Bergson — which I didn't carry very far (*L'Évolution créatrice* [13]). Capital importance of this book, through which philosophy can again escape.

That our intelligence cuts out of the outer continuity surfaces on which it can operate; that the rest escapes it; that it takes account only of those fragments. . . .

Amusing, these poems of Valery Larbaud. [14] As I read them, I see that in my *Nourritures* I should have been more cynical.

[11] By Pascal.

[12] *Visit to Pascal.*

[13] *Creative Evolution.*

[14] *Poèmes par un riche amateur* (*Poems by a Rich Non-professional*) were attributed by Larbaud, when they first appeared in 1908, to an imaginary South-American millionaire named A. O. Barnabooth.

Speaking of Valery Larbaud, Philippe said to Ruyters:
"It is always a pleasure to meet someone in comparison to whom
Gide seems poor." [15]

18 October

Visit of the Paul Laurenses from 2 October until the 12th.
I returned from Paris, where I had spent a week. Painful fatigue,
which continues even after the Laurenses have left. Yet I finish *La Porte
étroite* on the 15th — and on the 16th shave off my mustache. Shocked by
the lack of expression of my upper lip (as if something that has never
yet spoken could suddenly become eloquent). How old I seem! "My
poor André!" exclaims Em. on seeing me, and: "You must see your mistake." (I do not see it so readily.)
Prodigiously beautiful, warm weather for the last three weeks at
least. I return to Paris tomorrow.

24 December

Alexandre Natanson comes to pick me up at about two thirty to take
me to the studio of the young Polish sculptor Nadelman.
He takes only a cursory, if not hostile glance at Piot's fresco. We get
into a sixty-horse-power auto that he is trying out; we reach the rue
Boissonnade.
I am going to set down some of his sentences; but the tone of the
voice is needed; the intonation seems to add to each remark: "That's
the kind of man I am!"
"When I leave you I must go to Billancourt," he says; "yes, to inspect
a jam factory. It's an absolutely new process. They make jams . . ."
"Without fruit?"
"No, but they don't cook the fruit; they freeze it; at a hundred and
six degrees below zero [centigrade]. I tasted one the other day — a
strawberry; extraordinary; as if it had just been picked; yes indeed; no
difference at all."
"And you are going to finance the enterprise?"
"Oh no! . . . and yet I don't really know. With me you can't ever
tell; with me you can be sure of only one thing: that I'll never be concerned for long with the same enterprise. . . . But do you know that
people like me are very valuable! *I am responsible for a vast circulation.*
. . . For instance, I keep in my list of securities only the bad paper:
whatever I can't sell. . . . Oh, I have enough to paper my bathroom
with it! Occasionally my brother Thadée gets angry with me: 'But why
do you load yourself down with such no-good investments that will only

---

[15] Charles-Louis Philippe lived in near poverty; Larbaud inherited a fortune accumulated from mineral springs at Vichy.

cause you trouble?' I answer him: 'Calm yourself; they won't cause me any trouble.' It's very simple: I never get worked up about anything."

In Nadelman's studio and while he was talking, Natanson occasionally leaned toward me and said very rapidly in a whisper:
"Charming nature, hasn't he?"
Very cordial with me, besides. Insists that we should make a new appointment; and when I tell him that for the next fortnight I am going to be very busy: "But right after that, then!" and he shakes my hand without saying good-by.
Interesting; uninventable — and, as Albert used to say of Cousin Isabelle: "You ought to spend some time with her!"

1909

The vicar of Cuverville comes to see poor Mius, who is starting his twelfth week in bed. Typhus has successively attacked all his organs; he is, as they say hereabouts, "very low." Just as he thought he was over it and already could see himself on his feet again, phlebitis set in — which he calls "feeblitis."

"Well!" says the priest, "I have an idea. Joan of Arc has just been canonized; there's a saint that hasn't been used much yet or too much bothered; we shall do a novena for her. . . ."

At this poor Mius is delighted. At the end of the novena the priest comes to see him. The very day he should have been cured, his second leg is attacked. "Oh, how taken in the priest was!" the good man writes us.

"You understand," explains the priest, "there are so many saints; each one has his specialty; Joan of Arc's wasn't yet known; we had to try her out; we made a mistake . . . well, we shall look elsewhere."

A few days later, on market-day, Juliette Mius meets an old neighbor.

"If you had only told me this earlier! I have just the thing for you. For a swelling there is only one; I already prayed him for my man."

"What is his name?"

"St. Hydropique." [1]

"My child, you must have made a mistake," the priest says to Juliette. "You must have misunderstood your friend. St. Hydropique does not exist. It is doubtless St. Euterpe that you mean. I was thinking of him. By the way, he is the patron of Cuverville. I am inclined to think that he will be particularly interested in you."

2 March

Departure for Rome at the height of rapture.

* * *

Monday, 25 or 26 April

Preview of the Nadelman exhibit at Druet's. (Élie Nadelman is the young Polish-Jewish sculptor to whose lair Alexandre Natanson took me, as I related last winter.)

But at that time I did not say enough about Nadelman; Natanson's importance eclipsed him. Rather well-tempered nature, however! Natanson kept him alive until he could "launch" him. In exchange for the

---

[1] In French, *hydropique* means "dropsical."

living, Nadelman made statues for him. These are the ones that are being exhibited now, together with numerous preparatory sketches. Nadelman draws with a compass and sculps by assembling rhombs. He has
discovered that each curve of the human body is accompanied by a
reciprocal curve opposite it and corresponding to it. The harmony that
results from these balances resembles a theorem. The most amazing
thing is that he nevertheless works from a model. He is young and has
time to return to nature. But I am frightened by an artist who starts from
the simple; I fear that he will end up, not with the complex, but with
the complicated.

Nadelman went through six years of dire poverty; isolated in his
den, he seemed to live on plaster; Balzac might have invented him. I
find him yesterday, in a little blue suit he is doubtless wearing for the
first time, talking with a very vulgar and very ugly woman whom he introduces: it is Mme X. She says, pointing to the rhomboidal back of one
of the statues:

"That, at least, is living! It's not like their Venus de Milo! What do I
care whether she's beautiful or not? That, at least, is a real woman! It's
living!" And there is precisely no epithet less applicable to Nadelman's
art — which is still only a technique, and rudimentary at that. Most
likely Stein likes it because it can be grasped without effort. Stein is the
American collector, a great buyer of Matisses. Nadelman's exhibit has
hardly opened, but he has already bought two thirds or three fourths of
the drawings; at what price? I don't know this; but in the office of the
gallery I witness this little *genre* scene: Druet takes out from under a
table a plaster head, or at least the outline of a head, without eyes, nose,
or mouth; in short, about as well formed as a baby chick on the third day
the hen has been setting.

"How much do you want for it?"

"What! You are exhibiting it?" (I can understand the surprise; even
in our era that unformed thing is not exhibitable.)

"No," says Druet; "I am keeping it in reserve; I don't want to be
caught short."

"Well, I don't know . . ."

"Make up your mind. I'll act as the auctioneer. . . . Come on, now:
one! two! three! . . ."

"Two hundred francs!"

"Oh, it's too much! it's too much!" says Druet, taken aback that the
other has entered so well into the spirit of his role. And Nadelman in
turn:

"Well then, set a figure yourself. Come on: one! two! . . ."

"A hundred francs! That is enough."

And Druet leaves with the head.

14 May

Yesterday, Thursday, Francis Jammes and his young wife came to lunch. I went to meet them at the train from Soissons. I found Jammes grown stout, looking very life-of-Reilly as a result of his marriage. "Doesn't he look happy!" says Ginette. Obviously he has found the life for him.

At his request I had invited the Lacostes, Arthur Fontaine, Bonheur, and Ruyters. The lunch went off very well.

After the coffee, Jammes read us some *"Proses sur Bernadette"* which he gave in part to the *Figaro*, then a *Lettre à P. C. Consul*, which he is putting in the hands of the *N.R.F.*[2]

"An all the more magnificent work since you are named in it," he had written me a few days before.

He leaves the others a moment, goes up with me into the library, and there, with a great sigh:

"You are certainly lucky not to have any disciples! I don't know how you manage. . . ."

"They are the ones who wouldn't know how to manage it."

Then suddenly:

"I am afraid that Bonnard will begin to cut the ground out from under me."

Blum said to me: "Ernest-Charles always insists on my finesse and discrimination" (we were talking about an article in the *Grande Revue* concerning the republication of the *Nouveaux Eckermann*[3]). "He would like to get me accepted as the Jules Lemaître of a generation of which he would be the Brunetière."

4 July

Going through Paris for the review copies of *La Porte étroite*, I stop at the Valérys' to get news of Jeannie Valéry, on whom there was some question of operating. Degas is with her and has been wearing her out for more than an hour, for he is very hard of hearing and she has a weak voice. I find Degas has aged but is just like himself; just a bit more obsti-

---

[2] The "Prose Lines about Bernadette" concern his little neighbor Bernadette Soubirous, later sainted; the letter was addressed to Paul Claudel. This is the first mention Gide makes of the *Nouvelle Revue Française*, which he founded with Copeau, Schlumberger, Eugène Montfort, and others. After the first number had appeared, in November 1908, a quarrel eliminated Montfort from the board and a new initial number appeared in February 1909. From then until 1940, the *N.R.F.* under the successive editorship of Copeau, Jacques Rivière, and Jean Paulhan, but always reflecting the influence of Gide, was the leading literary periodical in France, if not in Europe.

[3] Blum's *New Conversations of Goethe with Eckermann*.

nate, more set in his opinion, exaggerating his crustiness, and always scratching the same spot in his brain where the itching becomes more and more localized. He says: "Ah, those who work from nature! What impudent humbugs! The landscapists! When I meet one of them in the countryside, I want to fire away at him. Bang! Bang!" (He raises his cane, closes an eye, and aims at the drawing-room furniture.) "There ought to be a police force for that purpose." Etc., etc. And again: "Art criticism! What an absurdity! I am accustomed to saying" (and in fact I remember hearing him say exactly the same things three or four years ago) "that the Muses never talk among themselves; each one works in her domain; and when they aren't working, they dance." And twice more he repeats: "When they aren't working, they dance." And again:

"The day when people began to write *Intelligence* with a capital *I*, all was damn well lost. There is no such thing as Intelligence; one has intelligence of this or that. One must have intelligence only for what one is doing."

9 July

At La Roque; I dismiss Robidet and, after an hour's conversation, succeed in making him sign a formal renunciation of the house, of which, in a moment of great stupidity, I had given him undisputed use. Most probably Robidet's misappropriations were even more serious than I had even been able to imagine, to judge from his collapse when I began to accuse him. He, usually so wordy, did not even try to defend himself. I was well aware that my great advantage when facing him was that he believes me to be *good*. All the time that I was talking to him I had much more disgust than pity for him; how had I been able to put up with him so long?

I find it hard to imagine his return home, the evening spent with his "housekeeper" and his daughter. . . . What did he say? What did he tell them? Did they get angry that he signed so easily? . . . Oh, how weak the imagination feels before what reality must have been! . . . Yet that was the best chapter of the novel. . . .

11 July

Georges does not like *La Porte étroite;* he prefers my other books to it; and he is free to do so; but he begins to be wrong when he reproaches this one for not having the qualities that made up the charm of some of the others; I try to make him understand that the important thing, the hard thing, was precisely not putting in here those qualities which were not the ones suited to this novel.

"In everything excellence is as difficult as it is rare." (Last words of Spinoza's *Ethics*.)

Cuverville, September and October

Criticisms of *La Porte étroite*. — It is hard for them to admit that these different books cohabited, still cohabit, in my mind. They follow one another only on paper and through the great impossibility of letting them be written together. Whatever the book I am writing, I never give myself to it utterly, and the subject that claims me most insistently immediately afterward, develops meanwhile at the other extremity of me.

It will not be easy to trace the trajectory of my mind; its curve will reveal itself only in my style and will escape most people. If someone, in my latest writing, thinks that he can finally seize my likeness, let him be undeceived: it is always from my last-born that I am most different.

Letter to Lucien Rolmer (stupid article) — he praised *L'Immoraliste* at the expense of my *Porte étroite*.

"Obviously it is a great pleasure to be compared to crystal! . . . But what a strange confusion you make between the painter and the model. Because he wrote *The Confessions of a Beautiful Soul* does Goethe seem to you any narrower? — If I were only the author of *L'Immoraliste*, which you admire so much, then it is that I should feel myself shrinking."

In order to describe something well, one must not have one's nose on top of it.

Sunday, 7 November

Ruyters, Philippe, Rivière, Copeau, Drouin, and Claudel have come.
Monday: Steinheil trial with Copeau and Boylesve.[4]
Tuesday: dinner at Claudel's with Philippe and the Frizeaus (much to be said — but no time).

The book now strikes me as a nougat in which the almonds are good (i.e., the letters and journal of Alissa), but in which the filling is pasty, nondescript writing; but it couldn't have been otherwise with the use of the first person, the flabby character of my Jérôme implying flabby prose. So that, all things considered, I think the book well done. But how eager I am to write something different! It will be ten years before I can again use the words: *love, heart, soul*, etc. . . .

Late November

Reading *Arsène Guillot*, first to myself, then, right afterward, aloud to Em. I didn't know anything of the kind in Mérimée. Why isn't it bet-

---

[4] In November 1909, after a year in prison, the beautiful and wealthy Marguerite Japy Steinheil, who had been the intimate confidante of President Félix Faure, was tried for the double murder of her mother, Mme Édouard Japy, and of her husband, the painter Adolphe Steinheil. After a most sensational trial she was acquitted on 14 November 1909.

ter known? Taine himself (preface to the *Lettres à une inconnue* [5]) does not seem to have properly understood or appreciated it, not by a long shot. Yes, it is better than anything that I supposed Mérimée could write. Really first-rate.

3 December

Read this evening *La Partie de tric-trac* [6] — in which I recognize once more that unbearable impression of a successful student theme and of useless perfection which ordinarily irritates me every time I open Mérimée again.

The *subject* is not propounded: A man of honor cheats. That was enough. — But he wins. He wins forty thousand francs. And the man against whom he was playing commits suicide. *There* is something to increase his remorse. But what would he have done if the Dutchman hadn't killed himself? What would he have done if he had won only a little? — *That is what interests me.* And the rest is a mere news item.

What he would have done? . . . He would have cheated again. And that would have been very pathetic. For there is no *essential* difference between the honest man and the knave. And the fact that the honest man can become a knave is both terrible and true. In the path of "sin" only the first step is difficult. And it has already been said that it was easier for a woman not to have a lover than to have but one.

This is the story of Lafcadio.

✳　✳　✳

Dialogue des Amateurs in the *Mercure* of 15 November — in which M. de Gourmont returns to one of his three favorite themes: alcoholism, demoralization, depopulation. He proves (or tries at least to prove) anyone guilty of stupidity who is cautious and frightened, who does not reason as follows: The proof that France is still overpopulated is that one still meets workmen without work. Moreover: "Invasion would probably not do France so much harm as all that. It's only an unpleasant moment to go through," he says farther on.

"The big words must all be soiled," he says in the following number. If that were all he soiled! . . .

Oh, of course, I understand what M. de Gourmont means and agree that it is good to demolish certain idols. But those big words today often seem to me already covered with filth; and often when I seek the "big word," I see only a M. de Gourmont soiling it.

When I cease getting angry, I shall have already begun my old age.

✳　✳　✳

---

[5] *Letters to an Unknown Woman.* "Arsène Guillot" is a story by Mérimée.

[6] Another Mérimée story, "A Game of Backgammon."

Here are the first two issues of a very small, very red review called *Sincérité*. M. Nazzi nourishes it all alone. Who is M. Louis Nazzi? To introduce him to me these sixty pages are not enough. They inform me as to his opinions rather than as to his tastes — that is to say, as to himself. I cannot be interested in the opinions before being interested in the person.

The word *sincerity* is one of those that are becoming harder for me to understand. I have known so many young men who vaunted their sincerity! . . . Some were pretentious and unbearable; others, brutal; their very tone of voice rang false. . . . In general, every young man thinks he is sincere when he has convictions and is incapable of criticism.

And what a confusion between sincerity and cheek! Sincerity means something to me, in art, only when it is consented to reluctantly. Only very banal souls easily achieve the sincere expression of their personality. For a new personality can be expressed sincerely only in a new form. The sentence that is personal to us must remain as peculiarly difficult to stretch as the bow of Ulysses.

THE DEATH OF CHARLES-LOUIS PHILIPPE

No! no, it wasn't the same thing. . . . This time, he who disappears is a *real* man. We were counting on him; we were dependent on him; we loved him. And suddenly he ceases to be there.

On the way to Cérilly

I am writing this in the train — where I am still chatting with him. Oh, already confused recollections! If I did not fix them today, tomorrow, already utterly crushed, I should get them all mixed up.

Saturday evening a note from Marguerite Audoux tells me that Philippe is ill.

Sunday morning I rush to his place, on the Quai Bourbon; his concierge sends me to the Dubois hospital; he is unkown there. I learn that three persons came to ask for him the day before, who went away as uninformed as I. Mme Audoux's card bears no indication. . . . What shall I do? . . . Doubtless Francis Jourdain can give me some news; I write him. The telegram I receive from him on Tuesday morning already deprives me of all hope; I rush to the address he gives me.

At the end of the corridor in the Velpeau hospital a room door remains open. Philippe is there. Ah, what does it matter now that the long windows of that room open directly into a big bright garden! It would

have been good for his convalescence; but already he has lost consciousness; he is still struggling, but has already left us.

I approach the bed where he is dying; here are his mother, a friend
whom I don't know,[7] and Mme Audoux, who recognizes and welcomes
me. I lead her out to the parlor for a minute.

Philippe has been here a week. At first the typhoid fever seemed
very mild and, in the beginning, of so ill-defined a character that it was
treated as a mere grippe. Then, for several days, Philippe was treated as
typhoid cases are treated today; but the regime of cold baths was very
impractical in his little lodging on the Quai Bourbon. Tuesday evening
he was carried to the Velpeau hospital; nothing alarming until Sunday;
then suddenly meningitis sets in; his heart beats wildly; he is lost. Dr.
Élie Faure, his friend, who, against all hope, carries on and will continue
to surround him with care, from time to time risks an injection of spar-
tein or of camphorated oil; but already the organism has ceased to react.

We return to the bedside. Yet how many struggles still and with
what difficulty this poor suffering body resigns itself to dying! He is
breathing very fast and very hard — very badly, like someone who has
forgotten how.

The muscles of his neck and of the lower part of his face tremble; one
eye is half open, the other closed. I rush to the post office to send some
telegrams; almost none of Philippe's friends is informed.

At the Velpeau hospital again. Dr. Elie Faure takes the invalid's
pulse. The poor mother queries: "How is the fever developing?"
Through her suffering she is careful to speak correctly; she is a mere
peasant, but she knows who her son is. And during these lugubrious
days, instead of tears, she sheds floods of words; they flow evenly, mo-
notonously, without accent or melody, in a somewhat hoarse tone, which
at first surprises as if it didn't properly interpret her suffering; and her
face remains dry.

After lunch I come back again; I cannot realize this loss. I find Philippe only slightly weaker, his face convulsed, shaken; struggling with
slightly less energy against death.

❋

Wednesday morning
Chanvin was waiting for me in the parlor. We are led, on the right
side of the courtyard, to a little secret room, with an entrance on an
angle — hiding as if ashamed. The rest of the establishment does not
know of its existence, for we are in a *house of health*,[8] which you enter

---

7 Léon Werth. [A.]
8 In French *maison de santé* is one of the expressions for "hospital."

only to be cured, and this is the chamber of the dead. The new guest is led into this room at night, when the rest of the house is asleep; on the wall a notice specifies: "not before 9 p.m. or after 7 a.m." And the guest will leave here only by way of that low door, the bolted door I see over there at the end of the room, opening directly on the other street. . . .

There he is: very small on a large shroud; wearing a brownish suit; very erect, very rigid, as if at attention for the roll call. Hardly changed, moreover; his nostrils somewhat pinched; his little fists very white; his feet lost in big white socks rising up like cotton nightcaps.

A few friends are in the room, weeping silently. The mother comes toward us, unable to weep, but moaning. Each time another person comes in she begins a new complaint like a professional mourner of antiquity. She is not speaking to us but to her son. She calls him; she leans over him, kisses him: "Good little boy!" she says to him. . . . "I knew all your little habits. . . . Ah, close you in now! close you in forever. . . ."

At first this sorrow surprises one, so eloquent it is; no expression in the intonation, but an extraordinary invention in the terms of endearment . . . then, turning toward a friend, without changing her tone, she gives an exact indication as to the funeral charges or the time of departure. She wants to take her son away as quickly as possible, take him away from everybody, have him to herself, down in their country: "I'll go and see you every day, every day." She caresses his forehead. Then turning toward us again: "Pity me, gentlemen! . . ."

Marguerite Audoux tells us that the last half-hour was horrible. Several times everyone thought all was over; the frightful breathing stopped; the mother would then throw herself onto the bed: "Stay with us a bit more, my dear! Breathe a bit more; once more! just once more!" And as if "the good little boy" heard her, in an enormous effort all his muscles could be seen to tighten, his chest to rise very high, very hard, and then fall back. . . . And Dr. Élie Faure, seized with despair, would exclaim sobbing: "But I did everything I could. . . ."

He died at nine p.m.

At the *Mercure de France*, where the edition of the works of Lucien Jean, for which he was to write the preface, is in abeyance; while I talk with Vallette, Chanvin is writing some letters of mourning. The mother wants to take the body away this very night; at eight o'clock a brief ceremony will gather together a few friends, either at the hospital or at the station. I shall not go, but want to see Philippe once more. We go back there. Léautaud accompanies us.

Here we are again in the mortuary room. Bourdelle has come to take the death-mask; the floor is littered with splashes of plaster. Yes indeed, we shall be happy to have this exact testimony; but those who know him only through it will never imagine the full expression of this strapping little fellow, whose whole body had such a special significance. Yes, Toulouse-Lautrec was just as short as he, but deformed; Philippe was upright; he had small hands, small feet, short legs; his forehead well formed. Beside him, after a short time, one became ashamed of being too tall.

In the courtyard a group of friends. In the room, the mother, Marguerite Audoux (oh, how beautiful the quality of her grief seems to me!), Fargue; Léautaud, very pale against his very black beard, is swallowing his emotion. The mother is still moaning; Fargue and Werth are examining a time-table; it is agreed that we shall meet tomorrow morning at the Quai d'Orsay station for the eight-fifteen train.

❊

Thursday, 8 o'clock

Quai d'Orsay station, where Chanvin and I arrive, fortunately well ahead of time, for there we discover that the eight-fifteen train leaves from the Gare de Lyon. Alas, how many friends, ill informed as we were, will not have time to get to the other station as we do at once! We don't see one in the train. Yet several had promised to come.

All night long it rained and there was a strong wind; now the air, somewhat calmed, is warm; the countryside is drenched; the sky is uniformly desolate.

We have taken tickets to Moulins. From the time-table that I buy in Nevers, I discover that to reach Cérilly it still takes three or four hours from Moulins in a little dawdling train, plus a long ride in the stage-coach; and that the little train will have left when we arrive. Can we make that leg of the trip in a carriage?

In Moulins we get refusals from three hacksters; the distance is too great: we shall need an automobile. And here it is! We light out into the country. The air is not cold; the hour is beautiful. In a moment the wind wipes away our fatigue, even our melancholy, and speaking of Philippe, we say: if you are watching us from some part of heaven, how amused you must be to see us racing after you along the road!

Beautiful country ravaged by winter and the storm; on the lavender edge of the sky how delicate are the greens of the pastures!

Bourbon-l'Archambault. This is where your twin sister and your brother-in-law, the pastry-cook, live. Ah! here is the hearse coming back from Cérilly. . . . Evening is falling. We enter the little village just before nightfall. The auto is put in the coach-house of the hotel where we have left our bags. Here we are on the village square. We are moving about in one of Philippe's books. We are told the way to his house. It is there on the road halfway up the hill, past the church, almost opposite the house of *Père Perdrix*.[9] On the ground floor the shutters of the only window are closed like the eyelids of someone plunged in meditation; but the door is ajar. Yes, this is the right place: someone opens the door as he leaves, and in the narrow room opposite the entrance, between lighted candles, we see the coffin draped with black cloth and covered with wreaths. The mother rushes toward us, is amazed to see us; was her child so much loved! She introduces us to some village people who are there: friends come from Paris on purpose; she is proud of it. A woman is sobbing in a corner; it is his sister. Oh, how she resembles him! Her face explains our friend's, which was slightly deformed by a scar on the left side of the jaw which the beard did not quite hide. The brother-in-law cordially comes up to us and asks if we don't want to see Charles-Louis's room before more people come.

The whole house is built on his scale; because it was very small he came out of it very small. Beside the bed-sitting-room, which is the one you enter, the bright empty room where the maker of sabots, his father, used to work; it gets its light from a little court, as does Philippe's room on the second floor. Small, unornamented room; on the right of the window, a little table for writing; above the table, some shelves with a few books and the high pile of all his school notebooks. The view one might have from the window is cut short by two or three firs that have grown right against the wall of the courtyard. That is all; and that was enough. Philippe was comfortable here. The mother does the honors of the place:

"Look carefully, gentlemen; this is all important if you are going to talk about him."

In the front of the house, the best parlor, in which is collected the little luxury of this humble dwelling: decorated mantel, framed portraits, draperies; this is the room that is never used.

"Even though we are poor people, you see that we are not in dire poverty."

She intends that at the hotel where we are staying we should consider ourselves as her guests as long as we remain in Cérilly.

"Do you want to see Papa Partridge's house?" asks the brother-in-law; "it should interest you."

And we go with him to the last house in the village; but the room in which we are received has been redone. As we are leaving, the brother-in-law leans toward us:

"The man you see over there is Jean Morantin; you know, the *lord of the village*. When Louis spoke of him in his book, people wanted to get him worked up. He said: no, no, I know little Philippe! He's a good boy; he certainly didn't intend to say anything bad about me."

---

[9] *Papa Partridge,* a novel by Charles-Louis Philippe.

We return to the hotel, where we find Valery Larbaud, just arrived from Vichy, and we spend the evening with him.

❋

The funeral takes place Friday morning at ten o'clock. No other friend has come; yes, Guillaumin, the author of *La Vie d'un simple;* [10] he lives on a farm thirteen kilometers from here. We still "hope" for a quarter of an hour more; Cérilly lies between several railroad lines and can be reached from several different directions. Finally the short procession starts moving.

Small gray and brown romanesque church, filled with shadow and sound counsel. The deacon comes toward us where we remain grouped around the coffin:
"This way, gentlemen! Come this way, where we have a big fire."
And we approach a brazier near the apse. Twice during the ceremony the brother-in-law comes toward us; the first time to tell us that Marcel Ray has just arrived from Montpellier with his wife; then, the second time, leaning toward us:
"You should visit the Chapel of the Saints; my brother-in-law spoke of that too in his books."

The ceremony ends; we walk toward the cemetery. The sky is overcast. Occasionally a low moving cloud befogs the distant landscape. Here is the open grave. On the other side of the grave, opposite me, I watch the sobbing sister, who is being supported. Is it really Philippe that we are burying? What lugubrious comedy are we playing here? A village friend, decorated with lavender ribbon,[11] a shopkeeper or functionary of Cérilly, steps forward with some manuscript pages in his hand and begins his speech. He speaks of Philippe's shortness, of his unimpressive appearance, which prevented him from attaining honors, of his successive failures in the posts he would have liked to hold: "You were perhaps not a great writer," he concludes, "but . . ." Nothing could be more stirring than this naïve reflection of the modesty Philippe always showed in speaking of himself, by which this excellent man was doubtless taken in. But some of us feel our hearts wrung; I hear someone whisper near me: "He's making a failure out of him!" And I hesitate a moment to step up before the grave and say that only Cérilly could speak so humbly of Philippe; that, seen from Paris, Philippe's stature seems to us very great. . . . But, alas, wouldn't Philippe suffer from

---

[10] *The Life of a Simple Man.*
[11] The insigne of the Palmes Académiques, a minor distinction awarded by the state.

the distance thus established between him and those of his little village, from which his heart never wandered?

Moreover, Guillaumin follows the other speaker; his speech is brief, full of measure and tact, very moving. He speaks of another child of Cérilly who went away like Philippe and died at thirty-five like him, just a century ago: the naturalist Perron. A little monument on the square immortalizes him. I shall copy the pious and touching inscription:

PERRON

DRIED UP LIKE

A YOUNG TREE

THAT SUCCUMBS

UNDER THE WEIGHT

OF ITS OWN FRUIT

Another side of the monument bears a bronze relief showing François Perron seated under a mangrove dotted with cockatoos in an Australian landscape peopled with familiar kangaroos.

An automobile stops at the gate of the cemetery; it is Fargue arriving just as the speeches are ending.

I am happy to see him here; his grief is very great, like that of all who are here; but it seems, besides, that Fargue represents a whole group of absent friends among the very best and that he comes bearing their homage.

We return to the hotel, where Mme Philippe invites us to dinner; her son-in-law, M. Tournayre, represents her. I am seated beside him; he tells me certain details of his brother-in-law's early childhood:

"Already at the age of five or six little Louis used to play 'going to school'; he had made up little notebooks, which he would put under his arm and then say: 'Good-by, Mamma; I am going to school.'

"Then he would sit down in a corner of the other room, on a stool, turning his back to everything. . . . Finally, a quarter of an hour later, the class being over, he *would come home*: 'Mamma, school is over.'

"But one fine day, without saying a word to anyone, slipping out, he really went to school; he was only six; the teacher sent him home. Little Louis came back again. Then the teacher asked: 'What have you come here for?' 'Why — to learn.'

"He is sent home again; he is too young. The child insists so much that he gets a dispensation. And thus he begins his patient education."

O "good little boy," I understand now what made you like so much, later on, *Jude the Obscure*. Even more than your gifts as a writer, than your sensitivity, than your intelligence, how much I admire that wondering application which was but one form of your love!

We leave.

And during the whole return trip I think of that article which I had promised him to write, that I was getting ready to write, on the appearance of his book, which Fasquelle is to publish any moment now — that article which he was waiting for. I fix the various points in my mind.

Philippe's death cannot make me exaggerate my praise in any regard; at most by bending me more sadly over that stirring figure and by allowing me to study him better (in the papers he left behind), it will strengthen my admiration by sharpening the contours.

Some people only half knew him because they saw only his pity, his affection, and the exquisite qualities of his heart; with that alone he could not have become the wonderful writer that he was. A great writer meets more than one requirement, answers more than one doubt, satisfies various appetites. I have only moderate admiration for those who cannot be seen from all sides, who appear deformed when looked at from an angle. Philippe could be examined from all sides; to each of his friends, of his readers, he seemed very unified; yet no two of them saw the same Philippe. And the various praises addressed to him may well be equally justified, but each one taken alone does not suffice. He has in him the wherewithal to disorient and surprise — that is to say, the wherewithal to endure.

* * *

30 December

Jammes's vanity.

Annoys me like the upsetting of an equilibrium; like something lacking; is permitted him only by an utter ignorance of everything that is not himself. Paying attention to what is not oneself he calls discussing; and naturally he hates *discussion*. Schwob having rashly told him one day that *Jean de Noarrieu* seemed to him more beautiful than *Hermann and Dorothea*, Jammes concluded from this that he is greater than Goethe. The idea never came to him for an instant that those who risk such a comparison consider *Jean de Noarrieu* as Jammes's best work; and what is *Hermann and Dorothea* in Goethe's work? However perfect the poem may be, suppress it and the total work is hardly diminished at all.

"*Jean de Noarrieu*," writes Jammes, "even though I never tried to embody any philosophy in it, is in Schwob's opinion, as well as in my own, superior to *Hermann and Dorothea* — although I have never had the courage to read that work of Goethe."

There is a certain *sincerity* that consists in trying to *see truthfully*, and Jammes will never know that form of sincerity. "If water breaks a stick," as La Fontaine says, his mind never "rectifies" it.[12] I am well aware that it is essentially *poetic* not to allow the reason to intervene too quickly and that often rectifying one's judgment amounts to falsifying one's sensation; but art would consist in maintaining the sensation in all its freshness and yet not allowing it to prevent any other functio. Odd lay-out of that mind! One cannot blame him for anything, so well aware is one that the spirit of inquiry would spoil him. He doesn't seek, either, to see the truth about himself; and besides he would have less genius if he were less convinced of having genius.

I am saying this rather sloppily. Let me sum up: to be a poet, one must believe in one's genius; to become an artist, one must *question it*. The really strong man is the one in whom *this* augments *that*.

------

[12] La Fontaine points out that a stick projecting from water appears broken at the water-line; but it only appears so, and our mind, rectifying the impression, straightens the stick.

1910

T he day before yesterday long study of the manuscripts left behind by Philippe — or at least, more specifically of the *Charles Blanchard,* of which I discover half a dozen versions almost equally good and excluding one another. Yet Francis Jammes will continue to believe that Philippe was good because he "gave his inspiration free rein." Nothing has *taught* me more about the art of writing than these abandoned pages — a great many of which I shall try to publish — probably adding an explanatory commentary to them.

Very much disposed to work this morning; a few intruders upset me. I do not count among the intruders the very likable Pierre Cornu. Ruyters comes to lunch. I have an appointment at two thirty with Copeau at Mirbeau's. We spend about three hours there and come away fagged out, both of us.

We went to Mirbeau's, not for the moderate and tiring pleasure of hearing him talk, but to take him Iehl's novel and to get him excited about reading it. To talk to him about Marguerite Audoux also. As soon as one goes to call on someone to ask him a favor, one spends infinitely more than what one expects of him. By five o'clock we were ruined, fagged out with nervous exhaustion; and we had got nothing for our trouble.

Got nothing but an incoherent series of anecdotes such as Mirbeau excells in telling. About Claretie, about the Baroness de Z., his neighbor and "landlady," about Gregh, about "scholars" whom he claims to ridicule.

"I know one who, for months now, has been preparing a paper. . . . Can you guess on what? . . . On the muscles of spiders! The muscles of spiders! But he has never even seen any spiders. . . . And naturally he is drawing conclusions of world-shaking interest. . . . I know another who brought out in 1900 a study on 'the digestive mechanism in acridians. . . .' Just imagine!"

"Have you read it?" Copeau shyly asks.

"I have read the title, yes. I have seen it. Doesn't that seem preposterous to you? I assure you they are all the same. All the same!" And he walks about the room repeating these words.

Certainly his spirits are rather amusingly colored, but what he exaggerates about everyone is always the most vulgar shortcoming; he ridicules only at the expense of truth. I am inclined to believe that he never recognizes, in anyone, the important particularity. Now he is calling Claretie a bandit, an assassin. "I assure you he is an assassin." In a moment he will speak the same of Descaves. Next it is Charles Morice that he jeers at:

"He had come to see me in the country; the windows of my drawing-room opened on a wonderful panorama; the weather was fine; Morice was seated near the window; I saw him squinting, grimacing, closing his eyes. . . .

"'Monsieur Morice, does the light bother you?'

"Then he, bursting out: 'Oh, if it were only the light! But it's the landscape, Monsieur Mirbeau, the whole landscape! How can you fail to understand that the artist needs to be absorbed in his own thought; he withdraws within himself; he combines things and elaborates a work. Show him nature — and everything is shot! The artist! the artist ought to live in a house without windows!'"

Francis Jourdain, who arrives at this point, tells other tales about Morice, but he talks of him with much more finesse. Unfortunately we are picked up and carried along by this gust of exaggerated disparagement; Jourdain talks of Maillol and refuses to understand, or at least pretends not to understand, some of Maillol's remarks that he relates and that would be easy to explain; even I let myself laugh and tolerate without quite approving the massacre . . . and, besides, trying to make them understand would be so ridiculously useless. And what would be left to keep Mirbeau busy if he didn't lunge at everyone? That is his vocation and his primary occupation. He would fall flat if he didn't imagine himself surrounded by monsters.

Howbeit, I do not find him unattractive; quite the contrary, and contact with him is warming. But nothing to be learned from him. Not even possible to get any precise information from him.

The more intelligent a humorist is, the less he needs to deform reality to make it significant.

6 January

I receive the same evening an effusive letter from Mardrus and an effusive letter from Royère; a few days ago both of them were writing me insults. — Amazing incoherence of certain brains. This evening a mad letter from little Louis Rouart, who longs for my "rapid decomposition," etc.

"You must be very happy," someone said to his wife, "to see him become so religious."

"I! Why, I'm as sorry as I can be!" she exclaimed; "so long as he wasn't religious, I was able to count on religion to improve his character; now I have given up counting on anything."

16 January

Copeau asks me to go with him to the Bibescos'; he is to be introduced to Chaumeix. I overcome my apprehension of the frightful bore that a society dinner is for me and get out of the closet the dress suit dating from my marriage, which I have not worn a dozen times. At Copeau's, on the rue Montaigne, where I go to pick him up, we notice that my trousers are terribly eaten by moths! Laughter and anguish; impossible to show myself this way: the white of my drawers appears in odd patterns; we light on the black felt ribbon of my panama hat and sit down to sew onto the drawers, opposite the holes, little squares and stripes.

I knew from Boylesve that Chaumeix was quite willing to write an article on *La Porte étroite* in the *Débats*, hence I was unable to say three words to him. Nothing freezes me up so much as knowing that my cordiality could be useful to me.

20 January

Pleasant visit from Boylesve; I am well aware that the conversation will not go very far with him, but each time I have greater enjoyment in seeing him. Ghéon is with me and in a moment will go with me to the Countess de Noailles's. We are going to get from her the review of *La Mère et l'enfant* [1] that she has consented to do for *La Nouvelle Revue Française*.

Mme de Noailles is at the hotel (Princess Hotel) on the rue de Presbourg; the windows of her room look out on the Arc de Triomphe. She was expecting us, and this is rather apparent: she is lying on a chaise-longue made up of two armchairs and a stool that all go together, sinuously draped in a sort of Rumanian or Greek robe of black Tussore silk with a broad band of whitish gray, of that soft white one finds in China paper and certain Japanese felts; the chemise floats amply around her bare arms loaded with Venetian bracelets. A scarf wanders around her, the color of the yolk of a hard-boiled, or rather a soft-boiled, egg; the color of dried apricots. Siren, her feet disappear mysteriously under a Tunisian cloth. Her hair is undone, abandoned, and jet-black; cut in bangs on her forehead, but falling as if wet onto her shoulders. She introduces us to the Princess de Caraman-Chimay (?), who trains on me a lorgnette that she doesn't put down during the entire visit.

Impossible to set down anything from the conversation. Mme de Noailles talks with an amazing volubility; the sentences rush to her lips, crush themselves, and become confused in their haste; she says three or four at a time. This makes a very tasty compote of ideas, sensations, images, a tutti-frutti accompanied by gestures of the hands and arms, of the eyes especially, which she turns skyward in a swoon that is not too artificial but rather too encouraged.

Speaking of Montfort in passing, she compares him to a tench with

---

[1] *The Mother and Child*, a book by Charles-Louis Philippe.

big pop eyes and imitates the fish when it comes against the glass of the aquarium. This very striking image makes us laugh, and as later on we allude to it, she becomes quite worried:

"Don't repeat that. Oh, I beg of you, don't say that I said it! You would make me an enemy of him. And I am always promising myself never to say anything bad about anyone!"

Ghéon, very much a wondering yokel just off the train at the Gare d'Orsay with heavy muddy shoes, but, as is customary with him, very much at ease, is much more interested, intrigued, than he expected. One would have to hold oneself very much in check not to succumb to the charm of this extraordinary poetess with the boiling brain and the cold blood.

*   *   *

March–April

I enjoy an empty pleasure in noting in my companion [2] even less gift for languages than I have. In the first restaurant beyond the frontier, when he points on the wine card to a half-bottle of *"cerveza,"* which we decide must be beer,

"Pilsen ó inglés?" asks the waiter.

"My poor fellow, there's no use trying, I shan't understand a word of what you say."

No matter how urgent our curiosity was at Valencia, having arrived in the morning, we think only of leaving by noon.

"But not without having seen the cathedral. . . ."

Guided by our fancy from *calle* to *calle*, we suddenly stumble on it. Copeau, who is smoking a rather good cigar, sends me ahead as a scout to see "if it's worth the trouble of going in." The cigar not being finished when I come out, we go on. . . .

But was it really the cathedral?

I slept like a log. Charming morning! An unknown joy chimes through the town; this is the hour when the flocks go through it; each passing goat ripples off, as he trots, the single note of his little bell. The air is perfumed with azure; the roofs shine. Flee! Ah! flee farther to the south and toward a more total exile. It is on such a morning that the most confident and most daring hope of our soul sets sail and that the Golden Fleece trembles before Jason's eyes.

Elche

Thanks to our Tyrolean cloaks, we are taken here for two Catalan *toreros.*

---

[2] Jacques Copeau. [E.]

Just as some time ago in Seville, the *"círculos"* are what I most wonder at in Murcia. There is one odd thing about these circles, and that is that they are always rectangular. They remind one of the inside of an omnibus with the two sides widely separated. Against the two side walls, two rows of big armchairs face each other. In each armchair a member of the club. Each clubman is smoking a cigar and, on an angle, watching the passers-by. The passers-by, as they pass, watch the clubman smoking his cigar. A large plate glass separates the clubmen from the passers-by; seen from the outside, the club looks like an aquarium. The unpretentious clubs are on a level with the street. (It is a street in which no vehicles pass.) Others, a bit higher, offer the knees of the club members on a level with the eyes of the passers-by. The one who is seated dominates. No books or newspapers or anything served other than the cigars; nor any conversation possible from armchair to armchair because too distant. On the front of one of these aquariums, in which a few turbots are stagnating, can be read: *"Círculo instructivo."*

When you come to Spain hungry for sun and dancing and singing, nothing is so dismal as a movie theater where the rain forces us to take shelter. Singing and dancing, in vain we sought them as far as Murcia. At Seville doubtless they can still be found; in Granada . . . Yes, I remember that in the Albaicin, almost twenty years ago (nothing since, not even the songs of Egypt, has touched a more secret spot in my heart): it was at night, in the vast hall of an inn, a gypsy boy singing; a chorus of men and women, in an undertone, then sudden pauses, punctuated that panting, excessive, painful song, in which one felt his soul expiring every time he caught his breath. It seemed a first draft of Chopin's last ballade; but it remained almost outside of music; not Spanish, but gypsy, and irreducibly so. To hear that song again, ah, I would have traveled over three Spains! But I shall flee Granada for fear of not hearing it again there.

Moreover, frightful weather made us return northward.

To the memory of that evening is attached the memory of a blush.

It was during Easter vacation. I was traveling with my mother. I was a little over twenty; but I reached twenty rather late; I was still soft and new.

For the amusement of a few tourists a manager had organized an evening of dances on the second floor of an outlying *posada*. Already I disliked everything that smelled of artifice . . . but how else could we see those dances? Soon they won't be exhibited anywhere outside of the Paris vaudevilles and cabarets.

Authentic habanera, cachucha, and seguidilla were served up to us that evening. On three sides of the hall straw chairs and benches for the tourists were arranged in double rows. I was seated beside my mother;

we had opposite us about twenty Spaniards and gypsies, of whom six were women; some of them were very pale, the others tanned like the leather of their shoes (I am saying this out of romanticism, but I think that almost all of them were wearing canvas shoes). Each woman in turn got up and danced, alone or with a partner; the chorus of instruments, the clapping of hands, and the voices beat time to the dances. . . .

The show, somewhat dull in the beginning, was warming up. They had reached perhaps the third dance; the one who was dancing it, an Andalusian woman probably, with a pink complexion, was shaking her abdomen and her arms in the manner of Algerian Jewesses and was waving two silk scarves, one the color of a locust-bean and the other cherry-red, which she was holding in her fingers. Toward the end of the dance she began to spin, slowly at first, then faster and faster, first in the center of the hall, then in a big circle, like a teetotum about to fall, along the row of spectators, whom she brushed. At the moment she passed in front of me, slap, I received the scarf in my face and it fell on my knees. I should have liked to think it was through awkwardness and by chance; but no, it was direct, sudden and premeditated, discreet. . . . This is what I must have grasped at the very moment, as I felt a rush of blood dazzling me — for this little wile became clearer in the light of a song that a little seamstress used to sing when she came to work at our house; she used to sing it when she was quite sure my mother couldn't hear her; I have since learned that it was simply *La Chanson de Madame Angot,* "not at all a prude; her speech was lewd," etc. One stanza told of the sultan who "threw her the handkerchief." I was well aware of what the gesture meant; obviously it must have been currently used in certain lands.

Even redder than the scarf, which I hastily hid under my coat, I strove to believe that my mother had seen nothing, though most painfully aware of the possible consequences of my "adventure.". . . Meanwhile the celebration continued. I paid only a mild attention to the dancing of a couple of *gitanos;* but, just as this new dance ended in a delirium and the audience's applause burst out, I was amazed to see the gypsy girl suddenly leave the dance, take a little kerchief from her bodice and throw it not far from us onto the knees of an old dandy who, instead of applauding, was pounding on the floor with his cane. The dandy surely knew the customs, and I didn't lose sight of him for an instant. What was he going to do?

Very calm and smiling, he took the little kerchief, felt in his vest-pocket, took out a silver coin, very ostensibly rolled it up in a corner of the kerchief, made a knot over it, then, from a distance, threw it toward the Spanish girl. . . . Reassured, I took the red scarf out from under my coat and asked my mother for a coin. Now that I was recovering my composure, what vexed me most was that, of the six Spanish or gypsy women gathered in the celebration, the one who had "thrown me the kerchief" was by far the least beautiful.

* * *

Paris, 15 April

Yesterday, lunch at Rouché's with Gabriele d'Annunzio. I had originally refused, caring very little about seeing him again; and I replied to Rouché that I had too good a memory of my meeting with d'Annunzio fifteen years ago to risk spoiling it by seeing again a writer for whose talent I no longer had much esteem. But Rouché would not take no for an answer (I have kept this amusing correspondence), and my reluctance yields to his kindly insistence. There were present: Henri de Régnier, Desvallières, Besnard, Suarès, Saglio, Marcel, Ernest-Charles, and so on. I was placed between Henri de Régnier and Suarès, almost opposite d'Annunzio: I could not have been more pleasingly placed. D'Annunzio, primmer, more constricted, more contracted, and also more sparkling than ever. His eye lacks kindness and affection; his voice is more cajoling than really caressing; his mouth less greedy than cruel; his forehead rather beautiful. Nothing in him in which natural gifts yield to genius. Less will than calculation; little passion or else cold passion. He generally disappoints those who have been taken (that is, mistaken) with his work. "He sums up all of Italy," says Mme Rouché, who is among the latter. "Less Dante," adds Suarès, who eloquently declares to me how little he likes the "Bluffer." The amusing thing is that d'Annunzio has smiles for only two persons: Suarès and me (less for me than for Suarès, whose grandiloquence quite naturally impresses him).

After lunch we gather in the den, Desvallières, Suarès, I, d'Annunzio, and Saglio, who launches into an exaggerated praise of the last pages of the novel (*Forse che si, forse che no*) [3] which *La Grande Revue* has just finished bringing out. It must be said that d'Annunzio has just drenched Suarès and me with the greatest praise a moment before. Saglio's compliments are probably hardly enough for the "Master" (who rather anxiously looks toward Desvallières, toward Suarès, toward me; but he can search us without finding any sugar. He will get only Saglio).

A moment later, nevertheless, d'Annunzio insists on seeing me again. It is agreed that he will write to invite me to lunch (I doubt very much that he will do so). Meanwhile, one by one, the guests leave. There remain only the "Master," Henri de Régnier, Suarès, and I. D'Annunzio starts downstairs first; we follow close behind him.

From the entrance hall we see the rain pouring down. Suarès, on

---

[3] *Perhaps So and Perhaps Not.*

the threshold, somewhat wild-looking, hastily shakes hands and starts to rush out into the rain.

"What!" I exclaim; "are you leaving without a hat?" Suarès collects his wits. "Why, you're right! . . . Oh, I often do this. . . ."

And he rushes to the coatroom and back out again. Outside, I understand why he was upset: d'Annunzio is taking him home in his car.

24 April

Good piano-practice since my return from Cuverville. I dare to tackle Beethoven again — after having got successfully through Chopin's Barcarolle and the Nocturne (in G) in thirds and sixths.

I hardly go out any more at all and get up every morning with the joy of feeling a long succession of hours stretching out before me. I hurl myself into my work (*La Mivoie* [4]), but not with all my heart and not altogether certain that I am writing what I ought to write first. According to my taste, the tone is not sufficiently different from that of *La Porte étroite*; here I am again obliged to shade, to write subtly and softly. I dream of the *Caves*,[5] which I imagine written in a quite lively style, very different.

My most recent adventures have left me an inexpressible disgust.

Went to hear *Coriolanus* at the Odéon. Knowing my lack of patience with the theater, I have ceased allowing myself anything but seats in the gallery. And indeed, yesterday, despite my great satisfaction — or perhaps because of it — I couldn't keep myself at the show after the third act. Copeau and Ghéon scolded me vigorously for not having waited until the scene with Aufidius. The truth is that I went home to read it. (In another connection I wrote for my *Journal sans dates*[6] a praise of the performance.)

On my way home, stopped at the *Cahiers de la Quinzaine*.[7] The little room is full of faces unknown to me except for Sorel and Benda. I leave almost at once.

---

[4] Probably the tale eventually entitled *Isabelle*, published in 1911.

[5] *Les Caves du Vatican* (*Lafcadio's Adventures*), which appeared in 1914.

[6] "Undated Journal," a less intimate chronicle than the *Journals*, written for immediate publication and doubtless intended as a continuation of the "Letters to Angèle" of the *Ermitage*, appeared in the *N.R.F.* from December 1909 to May 1910. It contains many pages taken directly from the *Journals*.

[7] The *Fortnightly*, Charles Péguy's review and bookshop on the Place de la Sorbonne.

Between Christ, Calvin, and the worthy Senator Bérenger confusion is possible only from the terrace of a café.[8] But it may be expedient to dump them all into the same bag, and to put me with them, as M. Eugène Montfort, the author of *Montmartre et les boulevards*, has just amused himself by doing in the latest issue of *Les Marges*.[9] I have apparently written (if you take his word for it) a "passionate defense" of Calvin.[10] I detest that figure; but recently I spoke against M. de Gourmont; and that can be done only in the name of Calvin, it seems. Willy-nilly, I shall be a Calvinist.

I was trying to show in that article how harmful Remy de Gourmont's negative skepticism [11] is to the work of art. M. Montfort suggests to M. de Gourmont to reply "by showing how the Protestant spirit can be equally ruinous and injurious to the work of art." *Equally ruinous*, he says; but I claim that it can be much more so! And I do not believe that one can imagine a form of thought more contrary to the work of art (and to my work in particular) and even more hostile (most often without knowing it) than Calvinism. This is what made me break away from it as soon as I began to write. At M. Montfort's invitation, Remy de Gourmont may well write such an article; but it won't be directed *against me*.

"No more sin! Everything goes! But M. Gide wants to be a sinner, he desires laws to enjoy the pleasure of transgressing them, he calls for forbidden acts (how delightful it is to perform them! . . .). If sin did not exist, it would have to be invented. And there are people who suppress it! . . ."

Despite M. Montfort, this conception of sin as a delicious ice,[12] of sacrilege and Satanism (which was Barbey d'Aurevilly's, for instance, and often Remy de Gourmont's), is as far from Protestantism as it can be. Nor is it any more mine for that reason.

Indeed, it is impossible for me to conceive of ethics as independent

---

[8] In a campaign to purify the streets of Paris and outlaw pornographic publications, Senator Bérenger, a self-appointed censor, had written in *L'Écho de Paris* that he refused to recognize a special privilege for talent. André Gide answered him in a witty and annihilating article in *L'Ermitage* of 15 April 1906.

[9] Issue of May 1910. [A.] *Les Marges* (1903–14) was edited by Eugène Montfort, and the first twelve numbers (1903–8) were entirely written by him.

[10] M. Montfort is doubtless alluding to what I recently wrote on Balzac's *Catherine de Médicis*, inspired by an article by Charles Maurras. [A.]

[11] And not his spirit of inquiry, as M. Montfort tries to make us believe. [A.]

[12] An allusion to the story of the beautiful Italian lady who enjoyed the Florentine ices so much that she exclaimed: "Peccato che non sia una peccata (What a shame it's not a sin)!"

from psychology, as Calvinism tends to do. But conceiving of psychology as a mere matter of mechanism, not taking into account the moral quality of acts or their intimate resonance . . . leads directly to the picaresque.

"No more sin! Everything goes!" The author of *La Maîtresse américaine* and of *La Turque*[13] now wants Phèdre without blushes, Prometheus without his vulture, Andromache without resistance, Orestes without his Erinyes. And he thinks he is freeing literature in this way. I am not surprised that he should cry out: "At times I feel a profound need of lyricism!" I should think so! I believe, however, that the word *profound* is an overstatement.

14 May
     Last night went with M. to Piot's. He is leaving soon for Florence with a new collection of drawings that he wants to show me even more than I want to see them. They are studies for the new frescoes he is getting ready for. The drawings lack the decisive quality, the gravity, even the attractiveness of the first ones. "They are *broader*, don't you think?" Piot keeps repeating by way of eliciting a compliment that I cannot pay him. Easier perhaps, and as people pleasantly say: "happier" — which means achieved with an ever decreasing effort. But I should like to see him tend toward severity. It was becoming for him to remain close to the masters; their intelligence advantageously supplemented his (which is only mediocre). As he stretches out, he clearly exhibits a rather vulgar nature that only the most rigorous art could develop properly.

23 May
     Were I to die today, my entire work would disappear behind *La Porte étroite;* the world would pay attention to it alone.

     Obviously the word *cad,*[14] which Copeau used last night, applies almost exactly to Montfort. His article is not so bad as they claim it to be. In other words, it is precisely what it aims to be: harmful. I write my books so slowly that I often let the epoch catch up with me until I seem to be borne along by it, whereas I was originally reacting against it.

30 May
     I shall probably be obliged to write a preface for my *Aveugle*[15] — which otherwise would only add to the confusion.

[13] Two novels by Eugène Montfort: *The American Mistress* and *The Turkish Woman.*
[14] The slang word *pignouf* is used in the text.
[15] Doubtless an early title for *La Symphonie pastorale* (*The Pastoral Symphony*), first published in 1919.

In it I should say: If being a Christian without being a Catholic amounts to being a Protestant, then I am a Protestant. But I cannot recognize any other orthodoxy than the Roman orthodoxy, and if Protestantism, either Calvinist or Lutheran, attempted to impose its orthodoxy upon me, I should turn toward the Roman, as the only one. "Protestant orthodoxy" — these words have no meaning for me. I do not recognize any *authority;* and if I did recognize one, it would be that of the Church.

But my Christianity springs only from Christ. Between him and me, I consider Calvin or St. Paul as two equally harmful screens. Oh, if only Protestantism had rejected St. Paul at once! But it is to St. Paul, rather than to Christ, that Calvin is related.

Where character can already be seen to take shape:

T. B.'s children play with those of the E. R. and the V.'s. The great game for T. B.'s children is always to "fight"; but this is the way they do it: when he wants to knock down J., smaller than he to begin with, A., the elder, says to his brother: "Hold his feet."

This is indeed the son of the man who, returning from England with M. D. soon after the Zola trial, gave two cents to the newsboys to shout: "Down with Zola! . . ." but didn't dare shout it himself.

"Hold his feet!" — certainly this trait will be found later on in the course of A. B.'s career. It promises well.

Cuverville, 13 June
What is the good of constantly repeating to myself that I am beyond forty: I have never felt younger.

Isn't it for the purpose of rejecting it at times with greater joy that I have made my conscience so exigent and scrupulous?

15 June
Each year, upon returning to my garden again, the same dismay: disappearance of the rare species and varieties; triumph of the common and mediocre ones. "Suppression of the fortunate cases . . . inevitable domination of the average types and even of those which are below the average," said the anti-Darwinian Nietzsche; and again: "It is not the happy sports, the results of selection, that win out, but rather the results of decadence." [16] And farther on: "Nature is cruel to those favored by fortune; it favors, protects, and loves the *humble* . . . the average and inferior types; the latter possess the greatest fecundity and the most

[16] *The Will to Power,* Vol. II, pp. 109, 110. [A.]

marked longevity; with the former, the danger increases, rapid destruction and decrease in numbers."*

When my cat catches a bird it is invariably, rather than a sparrow, a
warbler.

17 June

Mius is gaining skill in hybridizing certain flowers; and I have finally
succeeded in convincing him that, in the beds of seedlings thus obtained, the least robust varieties often gave the most beautiful flowers.
But it is only with great difficulty that I can get him to set aside the
common, vigorous varieties that can get along without his attentions, in
order to favor those that are harder to cultivate and require his care.

If, among her artists, Greece does not count a single Spartan, is this
not because Sparta threw her puny children into pits?

Impossible to get Mius to admit that, in order to assure selection, it
is not enough to prefer the delicate and rare variety, that its difficult
victory over the commoner varieties must be assured by suppressing the
latter in its vicinity.

To avoid argument, he pretends to clear my garden of them; but I
find them a little later, transplanted in some corner, just as rugged as the
rare variety is fragile, and infinitely prolific. In less than two years they
have won back their place; the exquisite has disappeared, stifled by the
commonplace. Because, for flowers too, "the exquisite is as difficult as it
is rare"; and however beautiful the most modest flower of the fields may
be, one's heart weeps to think that the most beautiful always has the
least chance of survival. It is at one and the same time the least gifted
for the struggle and the one that most arouses appetites and jealousies.
Oh, if only man, instead of so often contributing to the spreading of the
vulgar, instead of systematically pursuing with his hatred or his cupid-
ity the natural ornament of the earth, the most colorful butterfly, the
most charming bird, the largest flower; if he brought his ingenuity to
bear on protecting, not on destroying but on favoring — as I like to think
that people do in Japan, for instance, because it is so very far from
France! . . .

Were a miracle to produce in our woods some astounding orchid, a
thousand hands would stretch out to tear it up, to destroy it. If the blue-
bird happens to fly past, every gun is sighted; and then people are
amazed that it is rare!

Winged, plumed, down-covered seeds, wrapped in lusciousness and
attracting the bird! what ingenuity each plant shows in scattering its
progeny as far as possible from itself!

A giant parsley bends its enormous stem terminated by the umbel now without petals; as soon as the seed begins to ripen, the stem curves, seems to bend under the weight of the carpels, and in a solemn gesture, having to let that seed fall without any device to propel it in the air, at least it carries it as far as possible away from its own feet.

O Barrès! How different from yours is the teaching that I read in the book of Nature! I wonder at the way each animal drives its young from it as soon as they are able to take care of themselves. If a soil cannot long continue to produce the same crop, this is not so much because it becomes poorer, but rather, according to a recently discovered phenomenon of exosmosis, because each plant distils through its roots a poison for the plant that resembles it. . . .

And moreover, however you explain it, the important thing to note is that the same soil cannot long continue to produce the same crop.

19 June

Each summer I find again the volumes of Fabre that I regret leaving behind in the autumn. I was a "naturalist" before being a writer, and natural adventures have always taught me more than those related in novels. I even come to like the style of these books, which at first repelled me: what Fabre says in twenty pages could often be put into ten lines, but in this way one shares in the slow tempo of his discoveries; he seems to demand from the reader some of the patience he needed for his researches.

How delighted I am to learn today that the primary larvæ of the oil beetles are those extraordinary and mysterious little lice that I used to watch rising up, clinging by the end of their prehensile tail, on the extreme end of the camomile disks when, as a child, I was hunting beetles! What a consolation to discover finally why I never found any eggs in the balls of dung that I used to take away from the dung beetles!

I am unable to approve Fabre's jokes at the expense of Darwinism; not indeed because I feel myself to be a convinced transformist (and the reading of de Vries, far from persuading me, only increases my reluctance), but daring to say that the Darwinian doctrine rewards laziness is simply monstrous: "With the aid of a vague phraseology that juggles with the secret of the centuries and the unknown elements of existence, it is easy to build up a theory that shields our laziness, for we are repelled by painful studies whose ultimate result is more often doubt than affirmation," Fabre writes. Yes, I subscribe to the last words; but if science risks a great deal by relying on the doctrine of evolution, it is certainly not through laziness that Darwin formulated that doctrine. The evil is not (or at least it was not in his time) the doctrine; it is rather relying on it today.

Here and there reflections of this kind are, as it were, childish thrusts, which fail to destroy the beauty of this fine work; and the arguments he brings to bear against the doctrine of evolution are none the less very sensible.

Yet at times one wonders whom he has it in for. Here, in the very first volume, he launches into a violent attack on "noble theories"; a few lines from the introduction to Lacordaire's entomology serve as a springboard: Darwin, having written a whole book "for the express purpose of proving the identity of principle governing the actions of men and animals," supposedly drew an argument from a story of a sphex that he claims to have discovered devouring a fly, whose wings the sphex had removed in order not to be bothered by the wind. Whereupon Fabre launches out for eight pages, and because, to begin with, sphexes do not eat flies, ridiculing both theory and theorist, Darwinism and Darwin, and piling mockery on mockery.

What! Here we have this scholar whose patience in the observation of nature approaches holiness, who, in this great open book over which he leans piously every day, learns many virtues (among them the danger of self-confidence), who performs the same experiment twenty or thirty times, knowing how pervasive error is and to what fallacious deductions haste invites us — here we have him launching an attack against a sentence reported at second hand and translated! Throughout eight pages he establishes the fact that the supposed *sphex* must have been a *wasp* and is not for a moment concerned to find out whether or not Lacordaire correctly translated the English word! — Well, it so happens that the English text had said "a wasp," and this ends the quarrel. It so happens even that the Darwin quoted by Lacordaire is not Charles Darwin, but his grandfather, Erasmus Darwin! Moreover, Fabre recognizes these things in the second volume with the noblest courtesy and the most natural frankness, while asking to be forgiven for his mistake. If I point it out here, it is not only to draw from it a warning against passionate judgments but also, and especially, a fine example of repentance.

Charles Darwin himself wrote of Erasmus Darwin: "I greatly admired at that time" (when he was a student) "my grandfather's *Zoonomia*, but on rereading it a second time after ten or fifteen years' interval I was disappointed: *the disproportion between hypotheses and facts was too great*" (*Recollections Concerning the Development of My Mind and Character*).[17] Francis Darwin writes, in the biography of his father: "Charles Darwin possessed to the highest degree that lively imagination that he notes in Erasmus as being deeply characteristic and which gave him *that pervasive tendency to build up theories and generalizations.*" "That tendency," adds the son, who is doubtless aware of

[17] And of his father, Robert Waring [Darwin], Charles said: "For every fact that presented itself he had a theory." [A.]

its danger, "was in the case of Charles Darwin carefully checked by his determination to submit all his theories to all the possible tests." Finally Charles Darwin, speaking of himself, wrote: "It follows (and this often cost me dear) that one is always inclined to make up for the knowledge one lacks by unfounded hypotheses." And that is precisely what Fabre reproaches him with; but how far we are from the lazy infatuation of which he accuses him also!

20 June

Probably there are no blackbirds at Cambo.[18]
The blackbird is the most consummate musician, the best poet among our birds; if Rostand had heard him sing, I hope that he would not have written *Chantecler*. But, for his drama, he had to have a victim to serve up to the crowd and on whom to pour out his mockery: he chose the true poet.[19]

21 June

Wonderful intellectual activity; I go into the avenue (yesterday) to read *Les Marges*. (*Flaubert's Notes.*) The accusation of moralizing (I a prude!) is made again. Injustice and deliberate bad faith make me ill. Wrote almost without stopping all afternoon (recollections of Em-Barka, Mohammed of Algiers, and the little fellow in Sousse). But, at night, complete insomnia until four in the morning. At three I light my lamp again and finish reading Darwin's *Journal of a Naturalist;* go to see the sunrise from the window of the other room.

Sleep never comes to me against a black background. Some vision always precedes it, by which I escape from the real; so that I can truthfully say that I never go to sleep without first dreaming.

1 July

The memory of my absurd awkwardness still torments me. It seems to me that the kind of remorse I feel will be somewhat diminished if I note it down here.

It was, I think, two days before my departure — in other words, a month ago; upon the insistent urging of Mme de Noailles and Mme Mühlfeld (I had encountered the latter at the former's house in the afternoon), I had gone to join them in their box at a rehearsal of the Rus-

---

[18] Cambo in the Basque country is where Edmond Rostand had his summer home.

[19] Rostand's last play, *Chanticleer,* the twilight of drama in verse, which suffered from the excessive publicity given it before its production in February 1910, relates with animal characters the fable of the poet in modern society. For Rostand, the poet — that is, himself — is personified by Chanticleer the Cock, whereas the blackbird represents a sort of villain.

sian Ballet at the Opéra. In my whole life I had never felt more numb, more out of place, more mute. Mme de Régnier and her sister-in-law, Henri de Régnier, who was being witty, and Vaudoyer, with a dark and fatal look, were also there. . . .

"M. Gide," exclaimed Mme de Régnier, "come and help us calm Mme de Noailles." (The latter was talking so loud and so animatedly that she was attracting the attention of half the audience on the floor.)

Instead of remaining silent (but some remark was expected of me!) what did I find to say? Just this:

"Oh, Madame de Noailles is much more interesting when she is excited." [20]

I believe these were the only words I pronounced all evening long. I am still blushing for them. I wrote shortly afterward to Mme Mühlfeld to attempt to apologize for my sullenness: "You must have realized how much better it was to know me only from a distance," I said to her, or words to that effect (she was seeing me for the first time — and had long wanted to know me). Not long after, I received an enthusiastic letter from her; and Copeau showed me another in which she spoke of my attractiveness, of my secret charm, etc. . . . If I had said "shit" she would have considered it divine.

12 July

Feeling of the indispensable. I have never had it more strongly, since I wrote *André Walter*, than now that I am writing *Corydon*.[21] The fear that someone else might get ahead of me; it seems to me that the subject is floating in the air; I am amazed that no one reaches out to seize it before me. At the time of *André Walter* I used to hurl myself upon certain books (Rod's *Course à la mort* for instance [22]). . . . If this were to be it! I knew a similar fear at the moment of *Les Nourritures*.

Cavalière, August

From beneath the reed roof sheltering the bench on which I am stretched out and the table on which I am leaning, which (for it is still early morning) throws its shadow to my right on the arena marked by the hens' feet, where sand, ashes, and gravel are mingled with the remains of chicken feed — I see, swimming in the fluid liqueur that seems at once blue and gilded those outlines of colonial exoticism that I can

[20] The word *excité*, used here, is generally reserved for sexual excitement or an artificial stimulation.

[21] Gide's "Four Socratic Dialogues" on the subject of homosexuality did not appear openly and under his name until 1924. But two earlier editions, anonymous and without indication of place or publisher's name, had appeared in 1911 and 1920. The edition of 1911 was entitled simply *C.R.D.N.*

[22] *The Mad Rush toward Death* by Édouard Rod appeared in 1885.

imagine just as well at Dakar or Saint-Louis. I shall describe it all like an earnest schoolboy:

A roof of geranium-colored tiles rests, on the right side, on a square of darkness: the forge. On the left it rests on a lean-to serving doubtless as a wagon-shelter, through whose half-open door can be seen the shining straw in the blackness, can be heard the cock's crowing. In front of the lean-to, two enormous rabbit-cages made of bits of packing-cases on which can still be seen printed addresses and names of senders, just as one finds a pagan inscription among the stones of cathedrals. Above or around the cages, a pile of odd objects, which I can only enumerate: a broken caldron, a ladder, a wicker cage for baby chicks, a grindstone, two flat cages of the kind that are used, I believe, to transport chickens, which are now full of old rags; an ironing board, a warped bench, a huge eucalyptus log, a spiral spring (I am adding this), bits of wire, pieces of wire neeting. A yard away from the lean-to a sort of solitary mast rises into the azure. The sea is there, right near. On the moist sand a maid has built a pile of branches, rubbish, and garbage; now she is setting fire to it; the smoke, the vibration of the hot air, increase the impression of distance between us and the largest of the Iles d'Hyères, make it seem even less real as it floats above the sea. A little farther, almost within reach of the wave, and as if they had been washed up on the beach, two barrels. A green and black boat is approaching with the calm movement of its oars. A whole race of pigeons lights on the tile roof. The guinea-hens slept last night on the top of the big pine. Already the heat is torrid.

A tendency to take into account, in another, only the elements in which he is superior to me.

At Pontigny: [23]

How ridiculous we are! Already I have such trouble in taking myself seriously when I am alone. . . . Each one of us here looks to me as if he were in the tailor's fitting-room, surrounded by mirrors reflecting one another, and seeking in the minds of others his multiplied image. In spite of oneself, one assumes a pose; one throws out one's chest; one would like so much to see oneself from the back!

ÆSTHETICS

It is not enough merely to create the event most likely to reveal character; rather the character itself must necessitate the event. (See Corio-

---

[23] Before the war of 1914–18 Paul Desjardins organized annual meetings of literary men from all over Europe at the abandoned Abbey of Pontigny in Burgundy. Each *décade*, or ten-day period, during the vacation months was devoted to discussion of a specific topic.

lanus, Hamlet.) The succession of events is the development of the character. (Macbeth — who cannot escape his own *realization*.)

Or else, quite to the contrary, the revealing event should already have taken place (Sophocles, Ibsen) and the drama should then furnish the progressive explanation of the event; the prototype of this kind of drama is Œdipus, who advances from happiness in ignorance to unhappy knowledge.

Van de Velde sends me, in a supplement to the *Berliner Tageblatt*, an article on Nietzsche (by Karl-Georg Wendriner) of 22 August 1910, in which I read: "*So trat Nietzsche als ein Verderber der Jugend in die Ewigkeit ein.*" [24]

This is perhaps the most tempting path.

Reprinting of the "Traités"

I beg the reader to note that this first treatise (*Le Narcisse*) dates from 1892; the second, from 1893. I do not have to disavow my youthful works; but I should not wish to have them looked upon with the same eye as the products of a more mature age.

I have not written a single work without having felt a profound need to write it, with the sole exception of *Le Voyage d'Urien*,[25] and yet it seems to me that I put into it a large share of myself and that, for him who knows how to read, it too is revelatory.

Novel

He will say: "The taste for sensual pleasure has always been deplorably keen in me — to the point where it often dominated all others. But often a sort of curiosity preceded and even commanded my desire.

"The fortuitous invitation of pleasure at times made me miss a whole trip."

It is not altogether true that Cardif's early education was, properly speaking, neglected; but the first words he learned were filthy.

For the preface to Charles-Louis Philippe, explain the importance of Claudel's influence. — One is willing to be on the side of the believers; but one prefers not to be on the side of the fools.

---

[24] "Thus Nietzsche entered Eternity as a corrupter of youth."

[25] *Urien's Voyage*, an imaginary voyage full of symbols, published in 1893 with lithographs by Maurice Denis.

ANTHIME ARMAND-DUBOIS[26]

. . . He is always too hot. White duck trousers; alpaca coat; low standing collar, cut out for his wen; a black satin four-in-hand tie; straw hat. Gray eye. Extraordinarily flat, square nails; grayish-yellow hair always flattened down.

Bagnols-de-Grenade

Softness of very early-morning sensations. The limpid air quenches my thirst. Everything seems to me so virgin that I feel today as if I am the first to see it, to want to sing it; but already to name each thing no word seems to me fresh enough.

In the stable, a calf born last night, still only half dry, a delight for the flies. A rope around his neck keeps him within reach of his mother, who is also tied; the cow is chomping some cornstalks. Two dogs have found the placenta, thrown on the manure-pile with the trampled straw, a soiled scrap that they are avidly gobbling. If I had breakfasted, I should perhaps look at this without nausea.

The Garonne has returned to its bed, but the scrubland remains flooded between the river and the cultivated fields; I cannot reach the beach where I used to bathe so voluptuously last year. From a distance I perceive the sparkling sand. It is yonder, in that curve of the river which, although rapid, spreads its warm water shallowly over the pebbles, it is yonder that, looking at the sky, yielding without risk to the current, from the corner of my eyes I watched my flight carry the shore² along swiftly. Oh, sensation even more beautiful than thought! . . .

In an automobile heading toward Marseille

To pleasure is added a sort of heroic foretaste by the inconvenience of the pleasure. Get up before dawn; exhaust the wind and the shower; roast under the noonday sun; deceive one's hunger and one's sleepiness by the uncertainty of hours and places; keep one's life in equilibrium on a narrow ridge and grant oneself salvation only in the rigors of flight. . . .

Before reaching Saint-Pons, where we slept last night, our haste, for more than an hour, crushed the rain against our faces. We didn't even have goggles; the top was not put up. We had been very hot; the first drops were delightful; they penetrated our thirst; then, our fever washed, the downpour became painful.

---

[26] One of the principal characters of *Les Caves du Vatican* (*Lafcadio's Adventures*), the scientist who is converted to Christianity as the result of a miracle.

On my frozen, dripping cheek I might have thought it was hailing.
. . . Why do I speak of this? — For fear of describing a landscape.

There is no art except on a human scale. The instrument that allows
man to go beyond his measure, to exceed his natural agility, escapes the
conditions of the work of art. O light feet of Achilles! you are not
scorned with impunity. Yes, the work of art was easy in a time when
Pegasus of the ideal flight alone outdistanced the speedy son of Peleus.
There can be no question of art as soon as the idea of establishing a record enters in.

Locating the idea of perfection, not in equilibrium and the middle
path, but in the extreme and exaggeration is perhaps what will most set
off our period and distinguish it most annoyingly.

To succeed on this plane, one must agree never to be embarrassed
by anything. The *"quod decet"* of art is the first obstacle to be forgotten.

The young men I have known who were most crazy about automo-
bile-driving were, to begin with, the least interested in traveling. The
pleasure is no longer that of seeing the country or even of quickly reaching a certain place, where nothing really attracts them; but simply that
of going fast. And though one enjoys thereby sensations just as deeply
inartistic or anti-artistic as those of mountain-climbing, it must be admitted that they are intense and indomitable. The period that has
known them will not escape the consequences; it is the period of impressionism, of the rapid and superficial vision; one can guess what gods
and altars it will choose; through lack of respect, consideration, and consistency, it will sacrifice even more on those altars, but in an unconscious
or unavowed manner.

The work of art blossoms forth only with the participation, the con-
nivance of all the virtuous elements of the mind.

Road edged with plane trees from Arles to Raphèle, and every ten
trees an elm. Caper bushes.

Joy. Great soft wind. Flapping canvases. Beauty of the aerial ferry.
X kilometers without running over more than a chicken and a dog.
Two blow-outs: one in the middle of the Camargue, the other in the very
center of the Crau plain.

At Saint-Gilles the rue Émile-Zola, as is fitting, leads to the church.
On the pediment of which, above the sculptured portico, a municipality
with the purest taste has had painted in huge characters:

FRENCH REPUBLIC
LIBERTY   ·   EQUALITY   ·   FRATERNITY

Moreover, however famous this portico may be . . . Romanesque art is never more beautiful than at its purest; a certain ostentation here; profuse ornamentation; a Latin elegance. . . .

That Flaubert should have fought all his life, worn himself out, against that negative thing: human stupidity! . . . Toward the end of his life he had ceased hunting anything but this game.

He became angry or poked fun at expressions such as *"le fond de l'air."* [27] But what could he do about it? The expression wins out over him; it expresses excellently what it sets out to say; and when his mother said to him: "My child, cover yourself; the depths of the air are cold," she meant by this that he should not trust to the temperature of sheltered spots where the sun had somewhat warmed the air, but that in open places where, as soon as the least breath blew, etc. . . . In thirty words I barely succeed in expressing what that banal phrase says so simply.

CHARACTERS

The inconsistent, incoherent creature; you never find him like what he was when you saw him the day before.

Noteworthy that the poisonous animals are those that *do not perspire.*

Edge of the Garonne, 18 August

Feel voluptuously that it is more natural to go to bed naked than in a nightshirt. My window was wide open and the moon shone directly on my bed. I remembered with anguish the beautiful night of the Ramier; but I felt no desire, either in my heart or in my mind any more than in my flesh. With what stiflings would I have heard last year Armand's flute, this evening calling me doubtfully in the darkness. O stammering melody, how I loved you on the edge of the desert! . . . But this was not even a regret; I was calm.

VOYAGE IN ANDORRA

Ax-les-Thermes, Thursday

Arrived at ten p.m. No room in the Hotel Sicre; at this season of the year it amounts to insulting M. Sicre to suppose that he has one. The hotel porter leads us out on the road to Spain until we reach one of the last

---

[27] "The depths of the air."

houses in the village where they take in roomers. The landlady is already in bed; dull wait in a dusty little drawing-room invaded by winged ants, under the stupid gaze of the family portraits.

To reach what is going to serve me as a room I am told to cross through the kitchen, then a sort of dark storeroom; on the way I can clearly make out, by the light of my candle, a heap of newly washed laundry, but not the handles of the wheelbarrow on which it rests. I bump into them, scattering on the floor my night things, my light, and myself stretched out full length. For lack of witnesses, forced to laugh myself, in the dark, while rubbing my bruises.

Friday

Got up too early; my companions are not yet ready and the carriage is not to come for us until six o'clock. Outside; the sky is already overflowing with joy; the air is fresh and acid like a sherbet. How bright it is! On the square a squealing pig is being bled; a horse is splashing in the mountain torrent; the first shops are opening, in which I can buy chocolate, biscuits, and insect powder. At a quarter past six we leave.

Merens, 8 o'clock

A bowl of *café au lait;* Roquefort cheese takes the place of butter, and not at all unpleasantly. Wild joyful light cascades down from the top of the mountains; foam silvers the bottom of the ravines. As I raise my eyes, how I love, on the edge of the sky, the greenish gray of the close-cropped pasturelands! In the depth of the valley, on the higher treetops, a delicate snow remains. Small fields of grain attempt to climb the slopes by surprise, but stop halfway up; a bit higher the rips are not patched and the bare rock appears. The road, rising slowly, follows the trout-colored mountain torrent. Few new plants; a few frail white linaria of which I don't know the name. Shining mulleins whose whole stem is covered with flowers. Some statice on a long stem, which at a distance looks like scabiosa, brothers of the cliff grass edging the paths of my garden. A little higher, delicate pinks, excessively laciniated, almost without color, but having a delicious scent.

A gypsy wagon at the edge of the village has been camping at Merens for the last three days. In the hotel stable I see the performing goat that in the evening, climbing up on a table in the inn, tells fortunes by tapping with its hoof on the tricked card.

10 o'clock

We reach Hospitalet in the stifling heat; seven hours' walk to this stop; we decide to lunch at once. Here is the old guide we have notified;

but it is his youngest son, a lithe handsome youth of sixteen, who will lead us.

Little by little the statice becomes mingled with blue pompons that I think are shepherd's scabious. Higher up, big stemless thistles fixed close to the earth like spits. Over a field of lavender euphrasy is flying a *Parnassian Apollo;* I remember my delight when as a child I first saw this superb butterfly in the Jura; I thought then that it was found only in the Alps. We follow the stream separating Andorra from France; for some time we have been in Andorra.

My burning feet were slipping in my overwide sandals; I was ashamed of feeling so tired. A little before reaching the pass, we sat down a moment beside a trickle of a spring without beauty. It filtered, ice-cold, between the sheets of shale; you think you are merely going to moisten your lips, but you cannot refrain from drinking. Companions! If I had been alone, there I should have stopped, lying beside the spring; I should have drunk more than one glass; then I should have gone down slowly toward Hospitalet. — We set out again.

The hay is being drawn; the peasants are bringing the shocks home on their heads. Herds of cows and bulls as we go through the pass; herds of horses.

Dead snow, before reaching the summit; on the edge of the snow, gentians. The vegetation does not seem to me different from that of the Alps; yet dwarf pines take the place of the annoying larches and spruces.

In short, these mountains have no other advantage over the Alps than that they are a bit less high, a bit more to the south, and, hence, bathed with a little less crude light. Yet the Greeks or the Latins would have experienced here the same terror of the chaotic: "This region that God created to be horrible," Montesquieu would have repeated nevertheless.

On the Spanish side, dark-blue aconites; lower down, the china-blue sword-shaped iris; surprised to find it here in the wild state.

Unable to go any farther than Soldeu (which is pronounced Sol-déou), a paltry village where we can spend the night. For some time now I have been thinking only of a bath. As soon as we have made sure of a lodging in the inn, we go down toward the stream. A waterfall was foaming not far off, which we reached over huge slippery blocks of stone; more aerated, the water seemed less cold; each of us in turn got under the deep shower; it was amidst a thick eddy of foliage into which the sun plunged its last rays.

Rosada: I shall tell of the meal on the covered terrace. The torrent seemed to swell its voice in the evening. At the moment I am writing this, a flickering candle lights the table where we are finishing dinner. The full moon appears over the mountain, exactly at that point in the pass where we came through. Shall I remember the fried eggs, the far too savory ham, the grilled nuts that we nibbled with salt, the vigorous wine whose perfume seemed wrapped in tar; and above all, as we came out of our bath, the glasses of ice water cut with a drop of anisette? . . . With nothing ahead of us but rest, we indulged our thirst; I felt as if made of sand.

The excessive fatigue enfevers my night. Yet the bed is good, and free of fleas and bedbugs. In the same room, Iehl occupies a bed up against the wide-open window, through which the moon shines all night long.

Awakened at four thirty, we shall set out at five; touched by the cordiality of our hosts. Beside a huge fire in the kitchen are huddled the three children, who were chasing each other barefoot last night through the bedrooms.

We have succeeded in renting a horse, which I mount as we start, for I feel far from nimble. In the distance, in the valley beneath our path, can be seen flocks of sheep still in the folds.

At ——, on the upper floor of a little *posada* we are served bread, a flat sausage liberally peppered, some lamb's cheese, and eggs fried in a rather nauseous oil; blackish, harsh wine.

Las Escaldas; watering-place; we were dreaming of pools like those of Alet, hot and cold waters at will. . . . We find only a very ordinary hotel lying in ambush on the road; the bathtubs that are offered us are hardly attractive. . . . As soon as we have ordered our lunch, we set out back along the rapid stream we have just come down, looking for a protected spot.

The hateful inn! While I am writing this a phonograph is barking in the dining-room, where we soon go in to eat. Six priests arrive and are immediately at home. We wanted to lunch at eleven, then set out again so as to be able to sleep at Seo d'Urgel. We are forced to wait for the general meal.

"You are not in a hurry," asserts the innkeeper.

"What do you know about it?"

"Oh, you are not the first travelers I have detained."

What a meal! No matter how robust it is, our appetite broad-jumps over unqualifiable courses; but all through the meal the innkeeper takes care to fan his guests with a sort of enormous feather-duster fly-whisk made of varicolored cloth streamers.

At Andorra la Vieja can be seen: a goose with its wing turned the wrong way so that it comes up to the level of his beak; a duck without a beak; a chicken with its leg patched up; on the way out of the village, a mule that swings its broken leg out on the side like a victim of loco-motor ataxia. That's all.

The heat reverberates from the rock walls. Road edged with box-wood; hellebores. Having reached Saint-Julia de Loria at about four o'clock, our first desire was to push on to Seo, but I feel all done in and, besides, this evening we cannot find a donkey to carry our luggage into Spain. The one we got at Hospitalet, which hasn't the right to cross the frontier, is unloaded. Ropes had held tied to his back the mountain of coats, blankets, and the big brown canvas sack in which clothing and provisions are all rolled topsy-turvy together. After a few days of co-habitation in the sack, the most varied objects enter into intimate rela-tionships with each other; the boxes burst and pour forth their contents; everything becomes gummed and stuck together in a nameless con-glomeration. The most accommodating object is my umbrella — which I certainly don't need, but which I could neither put into a traveling-bag nor check anywhere — and which the donkey-driver hands back to me the first evening bent in an arch, having assumed, molded to the don-key's back, a shockingly suggestive form. I succeeded in straightening out the metal stem, but as soon as I tried to open it, the cotton, worn by the rubbing of the ropes, burst everywhere at once.

End of the day along the stream; children are laying nets, which they will take up the next day at dawn.

Heat on the terrace where we are dining, lighted by acetylene. Heat in the bedrooms; bedbugs. Iehl explains to me his conviction that they come down from St. Joseph. Benevolent saint whose smile is hung over his bed (above mine, St. Ignatius), is it true that your image, half off its backing, is sheltering them? Between the iron of the bed, which forms a decorative medallion, and the chromo, Iehl, standing on the bed, sprays insect powder, which makes him sneeze vigorously without much frightening the bugs. . . .

Sunday

Four o'clock; first sounds on the square; a cat is mewing its hunger in the corridor; I hear the eldest of yesterday's fishermen, the innkeep-er's son, getting ready and going downstairs; already the two other boys are waiting for him on the square; I get up and lean over the balcony; the square is ash-gray. The children recognize me and call to me. They have got back into their soaked clothing of the day before. The top of the mountains is trembling and growing pale, but all the colors are still asleep; an old woman leads some thin horses by. . . . I have hardly closed my eyes all night. The air is full of a winy scent. I go back to bed for a few minutes.

Five o'clock; I start out ahead of the others to spend a minute with the fishermen, who signal to me from the other bank. They complain that their nets have been raised, for they have caught only one fish, just one! Here they are all soaked again, still laughing.

Extraordinary narrowness of this valley. Without noticing it, we are in Spain again; already in Andorra we had met some of these mules fringed with red. The stream is getting deeper; a canal branches off, which we follow, leaving the road, where from a distance we see our horses raising dust.

As soon as we have passed the customs, a *posada* where we are served black sausage and mothy goat's cheese. At the end of the large room, which the outer brightness darkens, a stairway with slate steps; on the last step is seated a little girl, naked. She is watching a lamb being cut open; the innkeeper hangs the intestines from the low ceiling; in a moment, getting up without looking, I bump my forehead into them. Our guide, seated with us, is sprinkling gray salt on a tomato. On the table, having escaped from the cheese, a thin worm is squirming. The old wife of the innkeeper weighs the sausage to know how much of it we have eaten.

Moist fields; luminous rocks. On the happy Cerdagne the valley opens; the light pours down from the top of the mountains like milk.

Back in Spain! Yet I had sworn not to set foot in it so soon again!

Seo de Urgel

The grapevines, locked in the wall up to the second story, spread out over the balcony. Narrow streets, overhanging roofs narrowly channel the sky. Dark cathedral; beautiful Romanesque cloister (see Baedeker), deep arcades in which shops are set up; frugal market.

Between Seo and San Vicente from three o'clock to five; it is very hot; my companions say nothing but inanities; if I were not more silent than they, I should doubtless say just as many as they.

Sunday to Monday: night spent at the baths of San Vicente.

The moon, by some wonderful mystery, has been full for four or five nights now. My room, at the end of the hotel, overhangs the stream at a great height, and through the branches a little upstream I can just make out the sparkling of the water; not another sound but that of the rushing water. How slowly the night flows on! Anything that fell from the balcony would hardly be heard in its fall. Oh, to remain here, drunken and naked under the moon, with no other concern than to sleep off the heat of the day! It is so beautiful that the silence of the night birds is incomprehensible; it is amazing; everything seems to be waiting. . . .

Left at five o'clock; an hour in a rattletrap carriage. At —— the road ends. We pass over a shaky and bent wooden bridge. The mules loaded with our duffel and blankets ford the stream. Immediately afterward the path climbs into the mountains.

At six o'clock we encounter the Jabiru, who, having left Seo de Urgel at three, gets out of another old carriage just as we are arriving. The Jabiru is traveling with his son. While our friend Eugène Rouart is discovering that he and the Jabiru have interesting friends in common, Iehl and I agree to see in him the well-characterized representative of a species — a species that certain psychologist friends of ours have been attempting to define for some time; recently baptized by the charming caricaturist Georges Delaw, it belongs to the family of stilt-birds. The Jabiru most often has a pointed beak; yet the example before us has a spatulate beak, which leads us to seek elsewhere the distinctive signs of the Jabiru. It has been left to our epoch to fix them once and for all, since up to now the species has remained vague and vacillating between two or three settled types from which it is now differentiating itself. I encourage Iehl to write the history of the Jabiru's evolution; already we are defining some of the essential features.

The Jabiru's conversation is rather difficult to report, for each of his sentences bears the mark of impersonality.

The Jabiru never uses anything but the proper word.

The Jabiru loathes the banal, but he flees the tragic.

We note that the obliging qualities of the spatulate variety are limitless; thanks to Rouart's friendships, his kindness even extends to offering us a place in the automobile that is going to meet the Jabiru at Bourg-Madame.

Every boarding-house table that respects itself has its Jabiru; you rarely meet more than one Jabiru per table.

The Jabiru is never aware of the bad impression he makes.

The Jabiru has studied law; is a lawyer, but, because of a weak voice, never exercises his profession in court.

The Jabiru never travels without his Kodak.

The Jabiru prefers to the Basque sandals that I renew in Belver the mountaineer's iron-studded boots.

The little Jabiru is riding a donkey; he stops on the way and takes his time because the oil in the cooking has somewhat loosened his bowels.

Arrival in Belver, where we shall lunch. Iehl and I are letting the caravan go on without us. The Jabiru learns with disapproval of our intention to bathe in the canal at the foot of the hill on which the town stands. Far from the Jabiru's sight, we get undressed in a meadow under the willows, between the stream and a shallow but rather rapid canal, in which each stroke taken with the current sweeps us along as on a flying carpet.

The Belver inn. Soft olives that we suck while waiting for the meal. Huge barn decorated like a palace; corridors with vaults of gilded grain; in a courtyard under the broad sunlight horses turning in a circle trample the wheat. The Jabiru, who never bathes save in a tub and never relieves himself in the fields, is shocked at the state of the "lavatory."

The Jabiru's outfit starts out ahead; our horse is done in. On the heights we make out Puigcerdá too long before reaching it, but Bourg-Madame is right beside it. At Bourg-Madame the auto that has come to meet him with his wife and younger son sweeps away the Jabiru.

Bourg-Madame, the gate of Spain, owes whatever favor it enjoys entirely to the proximity of Puigcerdá. Baedeker tells us that Puigcerdá is frequented by Spanish high society. At the hour when we arrive — that is, at the end of the day — the high society is wildly deserting the town; sumptuous autos are whizzing down the slope we are climbing. Where are they going? We shall find out an hour later when, going back down to Bourg-Madame, we find them all parked along the single short street. Between five and seven o'clock, the autos of Puigcerdá go down to fill up with gasoline, which costs less in France. How rich they are! Some of them, for a horn, sport a dragon of gilded copper which seems to have flown over from Brazil. Nothing to do, nothing to see, nothing to drink at Bourg-Madame. For a distance of twenty yards a row of wooden benches lines the houses; there sit the señoras and señoritas of the high society, of which each Spanish auto unloads eight or ten representatives. Other señoras and most of the men remain standing without saying a word, apparently without thinking of anything. All of them, of both sexes, very ugly, very vulgar, insolently rich, and immensely stupid. What do they do the rest of the day? Now that their autos have drunk, what are they waiting for? . . . On the other side of the street the chauffeurs are taking on airs of Spanish grandees.

At seven we sit down to dinner; all the autos are still there. At a quarter past seven, when I get up to see what has become of them, all the autos have disappeared.

Stagecoach from Bourg-Madame to Montlouis.

At Montlouis we are served a bottle of elegant liqueur wine that would have made Keats renew his experience of seeing the sun's round and songs.

Visit to the barracks; I should have liked to see the library used by the soldiers who are snowbound for such a long time; but, because of repairs, all the books are locked up in cupboards.

Quillan, six a.m.

I have taken my three companions to the station; the sky is purer and silkier than ever. A laughing mystery floats under the avenue of plane trees, a light dust imitating a fog. Alibert will not come for me until eight o'clock. Yesterday he left me his manuscript, which I shall read while waiting for him. His verses fill and sustain my joy. Is our trip already over? How fast I should walk! How high I should climb, this morning!

* * *

"Why yes, of course, I can appreciate delicacy too," Georges protested when I reproached him with being sensitive only to bad smells. "For instance, take Aunt Desmarest; I realize that she often said charming things. One day, for example, the whole family except for her and me had gone on a picnic to Étretat; as they left they had carefully recommended us not to let Mirza out because she was in heat. As soon as the carriage was out of sight, Aunt turned toward me. "Oh!" she said, "we might as well let her out all the same."

"Is that," I asked, "what you call a charming thing? . . ."

"But why did she say it?" Em. asked.

And Georges, almost getting angry:

"How should I know?" And he added: "Out of senility!"

17 October

Certain days my mind, like my body, suffers from every contact. A smile or a remark is enough to hurt me. Everything I do or say seems wrong to me. In Rivière's letter this morning this sentence: "You are not loved at *Paris-Journal*" was enough to poison my whole morning.

I fear I shall soon have to struggle against a false image of me that is being built up, a monster to which my name is given, which occupies my place, and which is terrifyingly ugly and stupid.

The fundamental disloyalty of certain critics.

20 October

Yesterday, opened by chance *L'Appel au soldat* [28] — with great admiration, but with a touch of the feeling that, as a child, I had in contact with certain books that I felt to be written "for grown-ups."

This morning an article by Tancrède de Visan on *"André Gide et le lyrisme contemporain"* that is a tonic.[29]

---

[28] *The Call to Arms*, one of Maurice Barrès's "Novels of National Energy," first published in 1900.

[29] Visan's enthusiastic study of "André Gide and Contemporary Lyricism" was reprinted in 1911 in his book: *L'Attitude du lyrisme contemporain*.

Even now, when, before going to sleep or upon awaking in the middle of the night, I have the misfortune to think of Jammes, all hope of sleep is gone.

Read last night to Em. what I have written of my novel [30] — that is to say, up to the first departure from the Quartfourche. It is too subtle, too broken up into *nuances*. When I write *Les Caves*, beside a flat tone I shall boldly place another flat tone.

"Oh yes, and, besides Henri Ghéon is a deaf man. With him it's easy to carry on a conversation," says Péguy, who has come out to the Villa after me to see if I can influence some of those who will vote for the Goncourt prize or the *Vie Heureuse* prize.[31] What a horrible invention those prizes are! Here is poor Péguy, who for the past fortnight has been doing nothing but climbing stairs and ringing doorbells, etc. . . .

Went to see (for Marguerite Audoux, who is also in the running) Élémir Bourges. The greatest charmer since Mallarmé.

Saw Suarès too; but he pays too much attention to his legend; he wants to be notified the day before you come; according to him, he fears not hearing the bell; the truth is that he doesn't like to be taken by surprise; the lamp has to be placed in the right spot so as to light him very little, from a certain distance and very much from the side. He is rather short, rather swollen; his hands are plump. I should like him to be more emaciated.

VIIIth Court. — Monday, 14 November

He had held up until this moment; I saw him come in fresh and pink, his features only very slightly drawn; but as soon as he had been led to the place of the accused, he looked for his father among the crowd filling the back of the hall, and as soon as he had made out the stooped, unhappy man, who used to crush him under his scoldings and reproaches, then all the muscles in his pale little face seemed suddenly to contract. Those who come in through that door come from the house of

---

[30] *Isabelle,* which appeared in 1911.

[31] According to the will of the Goncourt brothers, finally approved in 1900, there was established a Goncourt Academy of ten writers, each receiving a pension, and a Goncourt prize of 5,000 francs to be voted annually by the Academy to "the best work of imagination in prose." Some of the winners are Claude Farrère (1905), the Tharaud brothers (1906), Henri Barbusse (1916), Georges Duhamel (1918), Marcel Proust (1919), André Malraux (1933). The *Vie Heureuse* prize was founded in 1904 by the magazine of that name and also amounted to 5,000 francs. In 1910 it went to Marguerite Audoux for her sensitive, realistic novel *Marie-Claire*. The literary prizes have always been even more important in France for the publicity they confer on a work than for their cash value.

detention. I was able to observe him well; I was seated on the lawyers' bench, right beside him; without having to get up, just by leaning over the railing, I could even see his thin, bare calves; he was completely covered by a blue-black cape, threadbare and worn to a fringe, caught in a hook at the collar. The old father is called to the stand. I learned from the questioning that the boy is only twelve; three older "comrades" were being judged with him; the lad had let himself be led by them into an easy robbery; by means of a broken window, without even going into a garden house, they had managed to carry off various carpenter's tools.

"There wasn't even fifteen francs' worth," said the eldest.

The old father would like to get his child back; he was satisfied with him until this day, he says. . . . When the judge finally reads: "Transferred to the care of . . . (?) until his majority," the boy, being led off by the policemen, sobs.

Finished my novel the night before last — with too great ease, and this makes me fear that I did not put into the last pages all that I was *charged* to put in.[32]

It is now high time to break with certain habits, certain indulgences in writing. I wish to try at once. And since this notebook happens to be filled, begin another one in which I shall get in training, in which I shall cultivate *new relations*. Keep from living on one's impetus.

Edmond Jaloux came to dinner last night. I suffered to feel so far from him, for I have a very old (though somewhat hardened) affection for him. From contact with society, he is taking on ever more polish; he talks with great tact and sweetness. He had come in evening dress, obliged, upon leaving the Villa, to attend a supper, at which he could get over the boredom I caused him; for I had nothing but gloomy things to say to him; the sight of his tail-coat froze me up, together with the thought that this is his real costume, in which he is more comfortable than in an ordinary coat.

There were not very many to notice that I had never written anything more perfect than *Amyntas*. People looked for descriptions, for the picturesque, for information about the country and its customs. There is hardly anything in the book that I could not just as well have written elsewhere, in France, or anywhere whatever. To whom could the secret value of the book speak? Only to a few rare souls; the others were disappointed.

---

[32] The word *chargé* also means "loaded" both in the sense of a creature or vehicle and in the sense of a firearm.

Paul A. Laurens, who at that time was paying court to Mme Dickemare, spent all his evenings at the Casino of Biskra. I spent all of mine
in a low and ill-lighted little shop that in the daytime did a meager business in henna and where in the evening Bachir, Mohammed, Larbi,
Bachir's brother, and a few other friends of theirs gathered together.
They used to play the three-card trick or checkers. Bachir would prepare the coffee. The pipette of kief would go around from mouth to
mouth. I used to amuse Athman by calling this gloomy spot "the little
casino." Yes, really, I spent every evening there. What did I do? I wonder today. I neither smoked nor played with the others and was not exactly in love with any one of them — no, but rather with that very atmosphere, with that darkness, with that silence, with their company,
which I could not do without. Each one of them was, if not very handsome, at least full of grace and lithe; elsewhere I have spoken of them. I
am well aware that today, more restless, alas, further advanced in debauch, I could not remain the observer that I then was. Not a single evening of the two months that I went there did I fix my desires on one of
them. This is also what allowed me to prolong my pleasure endlessly.
Time passed; never since have I so completely lost the sense of time,
both of age and of the hour. The kief would have added nothing to this.

1 December
Last night went with Ghéon to hear Carissimi's *Jephthah* (Salle
Gaveau). With great art Mme Raunay sings two cantatas by Schutz. The
overture to the *Marriage of Figaro;* the Chevillard Orchestra gives too
great a volume of sound to that airy and passionate music. Of all musicians Mozart is the one from whom our *epoch* has taken us farthest
away: he speaks only in a whisper, and the public has ceased to hear
anything but shouts.

The pleasure I enjoy and the education I get from these evening excursions never make up for my fatigue. I was able to go to sleep afterward only with the help of chloral.

Leaving the dentist's, went into the shop of a little naturalist I didn't
yet know (almost opposite Saint-Germain-des-Prés). Bought (irresistibly) a few wonderful shells.

2 December
Bad night; I wake up with grippe. Delight at the thought of having
to spend a fortnight in the house.

I finish the book by Photiadès (on Meredith). His considerations on
the art of Meredith rather tire my attention; I should have preferred him
to limit himself to speaking of the life and career.

This evening the shells bought yesterday have come. I spend a long time gazing at them and learn to understand them deeply. Certainly I could more easily have made of myself a naturalist, a doctor, or a pianist than I am succeeding in making a writer — but it just happens that I can bring to this career more varied qualities. The other careers would have had to be more exclusive; but it is to this one that I must bring the most will to bear — because I am not as naturally gifted for it as for the others (and the proof is that this is very badly put).

5 December

A vicious grippe has kept me in bed the last two days. However, I was unable to call off the meeting at the Villa of the group of the *N.R.F.* and they have each in turn come into my room for a few minutes' talk. Thanks to Paul Desjardins, I think that the readings with commentaries that I was planning are going to shape up rather well.

Dominique Drouin brings me a little notebook written by his classmates — which interests me greatly.

One of these children of twelve thought up a questionnaire (or more precisely he pinched this questionnaire from a slightly older cousin, and several of them amused themselves by filling it out).

Here are the questions, some of them inept and others rather significant. I am copying faithfully:

1. What is your motto?
2. Who is your best friend?
3. What is the dominant trait of your character?
4. What vocation would you like to have?
5. How would you prefer to die?
6. What is your favorite book?
7. What real-life hero do you prefer?
8. Where do you most like to be?
9. What is your idea of happiness?
10. What is your idea of unhappiness?
11. What is the quality that you prefer?
    Etc. . . .

I notice without surprise that detective novels and the heroes of aviation are at the top.

But this is odder: out of fourteen children questioned, four answer "marriage" to question No. 10: "What is your idea of unhappiness?" Only two attach the idea of marriage to happiness: a foreigner (Russian) and a Jew (J. Sachs).

Among those who link the idea of happiness with that of the single state, one (E. Weiss), a Protestant (considerably older, it seems), replies: *sensitivity* to the question: "What is the dominant trait of your character?" He would like to be a *surgeon;* his favorite book is *Manon;* the quality he prefers is *energy.*

Another (happiness = single life) replies that the dominant trait of his character is *friendship.* The quality he prefers: *love for one's friends.* A. Weiss (a brother, I suppose, of the preceding one) shows himself violently patriotic (motto: *everything is possible to whoever is French*). How would you like to die? — *under the French flag.*

Of two Jews, one (J. Sachs) would like to be: *a shopkeeper;* the other (Lacloche): *a man living on an income.*

Mauclair. He carries his pen a bit too close to his bonnet.

I am going ahead in *Robinson Crusoe,* step by step, with the greatest admiration.

Very beautiful and dignified letter by G. G. in the latest *Cahier de la Quinzaine* (late December 1910), which shows how unjustly Péguy had spoken.

Péguy is a sort of Bernard Palissy who throws his friendships into the fire to keep his oven going.[33]

---

[33] In the second *Cahier* of the twelfth series Péguy had attacked Georges Guy-Grand for acting through professional jealousy to undermine the *Cahiers de la Quinzaine* and get subscribers to withdraw their support. In the fourth *Cahier* of the same series a simple and irrefutable letter from Guy-Grand dated 28 November 1910 vigorously replied to this unjust criticism.

Bernard Palissy (1510–89), man of science, worked sixteen years against incredible difficulties to discover the secret of Italian enamels. To keep his oven at the proper temperature he had to burn all his furniture.

1911

Every evening I read for Dominque Drouin from eight thirty to nine o'clock. Read the first evening Töpffer's *Le Col d'Anterne,* then *"Kanut"* and *"Aymerillot,"* both of which struck me as very bad; then *"Oceano Nox"* and the end of *"Les Malheureux"* and other bits of *Les Contemplations,* which plunged me into the deepest admiration. Yesterday *"Les Djinns";* this evening Turgenyev's short story "The Dog." [1]

Then, withdrawing into the little recess in the hallway, I read an hour of English before going to bed (*Robinson Crusoe* and Macaulay's study on the *Life of Byron*).

Leaving the Palais de Justice, where I had gone so that Fargue could not suspect my zeal. (He had come the evening before, panic-stricken, to beg me to intercede for a friend whose signature had been misused by some scoundrels — and the worst of it is that Fargue himself was not there, at the Palais de Justice. . . . He wanted me to intercede with Judge Flory; fortunately Marcel Drouin, whom I went to consult in the morning about the advisability of such a step, pointed out how contrary it was to all decency — and I was aware of this myself; but nothing is harder for me than an act that seems to be a side-stepping of responsibility; that is why I felt myself obliged to go to the Palais!) In the VIIIth Court I had seen only a few vague robbers appear. I had left Auteuil very early, hoping to stop at the Louvre on the way; but my fear of missing Fargue made me get there a half-hour too early. (I didn't tell him this in my letter this evening, in order not to seem to be complaining; I wrote that I had waited for him from noon until one o'clock; in reality I was there at eleven thirty.)

But, upon leaving, I went to the Louvre and, going up by the staircase of the Assyrians, went through all the galleries of drawings. I felt unresponsive and the light was as dull as possible. Saw the Thony-Thiéry collection without any pleasure; admired at length the Persian and Hispano-Moresque enamels — particularly a white bowl of the twelfth century (?). Had no real emotion except in front of Rembrandt's drawings. Naked body of a young man lying down; lord offering a flower (every line in perspective is suppressed — *absent* suggestion of the shoulder, which is seen from the front — wonderful; foreknowledge or forefeeling of the effect, which makes each suggestion eloquent). After that I

---

[1] "Kanut or the Parricide" and "Aymerillot" are both narrative poems from Hugo's *Légende des siècles;* "Night over the Ocean," "The Unfortunates," and "The Jinns" are also poems by Victor Hugo, as is the collection of *Les Contemplations.*

couldn't look at anything; hurried through the rooms and the big gallery to reach the Chauchard collection. In the big Rubens gallery met Free-grove-Wenzer, of whom I just happened to be thinking. He drags me to his place and shows me his albums and sketches for paintings; but in his library I notice an album by his young friend from Brunswick, illustrations of the most delectable sort of *Les Liaisons dangereuses;* [2] he suggests my taking the album away with me to show it, as I did the drawings by both of them. His friend's studio is in rue des Beaux-Arts; he has the key; he wants to take me there, although the friend is not back yet. We go there, but impossible to open the door. On the way (rue de Seine) the window of a small shop attracts us; a Guérin and a Naudin are exhibited in it. We go in; a little woman in a dark dress, very young and attractive-looking, asks me after a moment if I am not M. Gide and tells me that I must have received, the day before, a letter from her husband. I realize that I am at Vildrac's. From this moment on I begin to have *too good* a time; that is, the curiosity of this new amusement makes me forget every other consideration and I begin to act like a madman. Having discovered that Vildrac is at Rouveyre's, who is to give a portrait or a caricature of me to the *Mercure,* I jump into a carriage with my Englishman and give the coachman Rouveyre's address. At Rouveyre's I find Vildrac and his business associate, whom I mistake for Rouveyre; then, my infirmity getting worse, when Rouveyre himself appears I confuse him so completely with the other that I think I have already shaken hands with him. (Impossible to explain this; on occasion now I *cease* to recognize the person with whom I am talking; and this lasts several minutes — enough, in any case, to fill me with a sort of anguish.)

To all three of them I must have seemed mad; I wanted to appear at ease, so that I talked too much and too loud. Meanwhile Rouveyre kept leaning over on one side as if he had the colic; Vildrac disappeared in his beard; the business associate alone, whom I didn't know, smiled at me with excessive affability; the Englishman effaced himself, or at least remained outside the circle that we formed; he leaned against a mantel and I could no longer understand myself why I had brought him. And no one understood or could give any reason for my sudden visit, flanked by this unknown person. I pretended for a moment to have come to show Rouveyre the drawings for *Les Liaisons dangereuses,* which I was carrying under my arm; and all together we looked at them. Then I took leave of them and departed, leaving them dazed.

When shall I have ahead of me days to be filled only with reading, meditation, and work!

---

[2] *Dangerous Relations,* the famous eighteenth-century novel by Choderlos de Laclos, which Gide has often praised.

Getting home, wrote to Ruyters; good piano-practice. First and third ballades by Chopin, which I am beginning to play *as I wish to;* as I think they are meant to be played.

February

A letter from Jammes even more distant than his silence was and unfortunately more obviously inspired by the pleasure caused him by my praise of his latest poems than by a resurgence of friendship. This letter convinces me that there is more than a mere misunderstanding between us; that is to say, just as I feared, much literature, and offended literature.

27 March

Saw Vielé-Griffin yesterday; charming cordiality. He accuses some writers or other of not knowing French and of writing, for instance, "fallow land" (*friche*) where they should have said "plowed land" (*guéret*); — but he himself writes "*opprobe*" and "*frustre*" (*passim*).[3]

He forgives Régnier nothing; as if he suffered from still liking him, he cannot refrain from talking of him every time I go to see him or meet him.

Lunched with Barrès (at Blanche's). Great anxiety about the figure he cuts; he knows how to maintain silence in order to say nothing but important things. He has changed greatly since almost ten years ago when I last saw him; but he has kept his very active charm, though constantly holding back and knowing how to keep his reserve. What prudence! What economy! He is not a great intelligence, not a "great man," but *clever*, using everything in him until he achieves the appearance of genius. Especially using circumstances, and knowing how to take advantage of what he has, to the point of hiding what he lacks.

8 May

At the studio of R. B., a painter and engraver, perhaps a Jew, certainly a Russian — who wants to do a portrait of me. This is a kind of flattery that will always get me. This portrait (dry-point) is to figure in an album together with a very few others: Rodin, Bartholomé, both sculptors; two painters, Besnard and Renoir; two musicians, Debussy and Bruneau; two philosophers, Bergson and Poincaré, etc. . . . Finally Verhaeren, who introduced him to my *Porte étroite* and has sent him to me.

It is in Montmartre, rue V. You ring at the third-floor apartment but

---

[3] Instead of the correct forms *opprobre* and *fruste*.

have to go down an inside staircase to reach the studio, on the level of the second floor or even between the first and second, for I fancy that the house has two studios for every three floors. A universal man, B. indulges — with the same genius and no shame whatever — in sculpture, engraving, and oil painting. Right now he would like to make stage sets for R. Like many today, he proves to himself that he is a colorist by using only the crudest colors; he has a cruel eye. He intends to achieve mystery by neglecting drawing. You can recognize in a large clay woman, half-naked, the same model as in a big portrait reproducing the harmonies of a wild parrot (buttercup background, aspidistra-green dress, tomato-colored book in her hand): his wife.

Considerable time is spent in seeking the pose I am to take. As soon as I am settled, I like the long silence of this study; I, usually so easily distracted by some muscular impatience, I find that this forced immobility invites my thought to roam; but B. wants to talk. I foresee even worse: twice, smiling at the sheet of metal he is cutting into, he said: "There is someone upstairs who is burning to meet you." Suddenly, starting at a little sound from the upper floor — which must be a signal:

"Véra! Véra! You know that Monsieur Gide is here. We are expecting you!"

The woman of the portrait comes down the steps smiling at my reflection in a large mirror in front of which I am posing.

Mme B. was born on Réunion Island, whence the sparkle of her lips and the languor in her eyes. Without a corset, the points of her well-formed breasts can be seen through the tussah silk of her dress; voluptuous face and body; auburn hair arranged in a turban. A little more familiarity with women would have warned me that the beautiful Véra wrote and that she planned to take advantage of my pose in order to inflict a reading on me. The conversation (for which, moreover, I was as little as possible responsible, for fear of breaking my pose) had no other purpose than to lead up to that reading. But they had to attack the subject from a distance. B. told me his desire to add two women to his album. "Probably Madame Curie . . . and, on the other hand, Madame de Noailles." But this first attempt not having started anything, the conversation was falling off when, at some turning or other, after we had talked of the husband's universal gifts, quite innocently I asked:

"And you, madame, what do you do?"

"I? Oh, nothing," she replied in haste.

A silence during which B., leaning over his sheet of metal, smiles with a knowing air, then, cupping his hand as if to keep his voice from anyone but me:

"She writes."

Whereupon Véra: "Will you be quiet! How absurd he is! Monsieur Gide, don't listen to him. . . . Can it be called 'writing' when all you

do is set down on paper a few poems that you can't keep to yourself?
. . . When I read them to Verhaeren, he wouldn't believe that I was not
accustomed to writing. . . . But why should I write? This is what I ask
myself every day in front of my sheet of paper: Who would be interested in this?" (And repeating her sentence with an accent on each syl-
lable): "Who would be interested in this? — Who could be interested
in it? . . ." (Obviously she is waiting for me to reply: "Why — perhaps
I would," but since I remain silent, she becomes more precise): "Come,
Monsieur Gide, I ask you."

Then B., coming to her aid: "When the emotion is sincere . . ."

And she: "Oh, as for the sincerity! . . . In fact it's very odd: I begin
without knowing what I shall write; when I reread, it's always lines of
poetry; I write in rhythm despite myself; yes, I can't do anything about
it, everything I write is in rhythm. M. Gide, I wish you would tell
me: do you think it's possible to achieve anything by work and
pruning? . . .

Here, somewhat stupidly, I try to establish a distinction between
the two words, suggesting that "*work* does not necessarily imply *pruning.*" But I am not understood and it is better to skip it. The conversation starts off again on a new track.

"Do you know Verhaeren very well? What a charming conversationalist! Have you heard him tell stories? Ah! the other day at Saint-Cloud
we spent the whole day telling each other stories. . . . Indeed, that is
one of the things that have encouraged me to write. 'It would be criminal not to write up these recollections!' he told me. That was after I had
just told him about my grandfather's death. . . . Just imagine, two coffins had been ordered! Yes, two coffins; the maid had made a mistake.
. . . That morning two dealers arrived, each one with his coffin; of
course there followed a heated dialogue; you can guess that, despite the
circumstances, each one could hardly keep from laughing. One was
pointing out the quality of the wood, the other the comfort of his cush-
ions. Finally I remember that my uncle managed to get rid of one of
them, who said to him as he left: 'I'll take the coffin away, but I see that
you will need it soon.' Do you too think that I ought to write this
up? . . . Verhaeren claims that in Brittany he saw this sign in a shop
window: 'Hygienic coffins. . . .' But X." (I don't remember what important name she used), "who was with us, exclaimed: 'With poets you
never know where reality ends. . . .' It's like this other memory he
liked so much. . . . Just imagine that I had got into the habit of buying a bouquet of flowers every morning from a little Paris urchin of
about fourteen who was always in the same spot. According to the season it was violets or mimosa. . . . This lasted two years. Finally one
day I was unable to go out, but a friend of mine who knew the urchin
gave him my address so that he could take the bouquet to me. I see the

urchin arrive and, as soon as the door is open, he throws the bouquet at me across the room, shouting: 'Ah, you think urchins don't feel anything! Yes, every day for the past two years, when you pass you look at me and you don't see that I am also looking at you. . . . Ah! you think that Paris urchins don't feel anything because they haven't the right to say anything? . . .' And, slamming the door, he dashes away. I never saw him again. . . ."

I: "He killed himself."

She, dreamily: "Perhaps. . . . Oh, I have many recollections of that kind!"

I: "And that is what you write?"

She: "No. But it comes to the same thing; what I write is, after all, made up of memories. For instance, I read Verhaeren a poem he liked very much — that is, he thought the form wasn't perfect, but the feeling was there all right."

He: "That's the important thing!"

Etc. . . . etc. . . .

"My hair is coming down," she said, stepping in front of the mirror; "I must go up and fix it."

She disappears, and reappears a moment later.

"Let's see, M. Gide, if you have any Sherlock Holmes in you. Guess what I have in my right hand?" (She is holding her hands behind her back.)

It is her poems, unimaginably dull, and decidedly I have to endure the reading of them.

Then, in the vast silence that immediately follows, she plays her last trump, desperately.

"And suppose I told you that now I am writing a play!"

I: "Ahem!!!" (I take out my watch.) "Why, it's much later than I thought. Will it take you much longer?"

He: "Twenty minutes."

I, resigned: "All right! And what is your play about?"

She: "No, I don't want to talk about it. I haven't yet told it to anyone," etc.

Yet, since I don't ask any questions, she makes up her mind:

She: "Well, here it is! I start out from the observation that in contemporary literature the women characters are always very ordinary, even shameful. I want to show a woman who gradually feels a maternal love taking the place of her conjugal love. Do you understand?"

I: "Not at all."

She: "Yes, she has married someone rather ordinary, and little by little she feels developing for him a sort of maternal love. To begin with, she raises him to her level; she gives him wings and eventually he rises above her. . . . Tell me what you think of it." Etc.

Nine days in Bruges

At Verbeke's printing-house to correct the proofs of *L'Otage,* of *La Mère et l'enfant,* of *Isabelle,* of *Corydon* and of the June issue of the review.[4]

The issue appears with Saint-Léger's *Éloges* bristling with printer's errors.[5] The experience makes me ill and, to divert my mind from it, I imagine what might have happened the first time Debussy was played:

The conductor attached great importance to the music; unfortunately he had against him the theater manager and the organizer of the concerts; at least they did not approve it, so that in the beginning he had to struggle to get the new composition accepted on his program.

He knew, moreover, that he was going to displease his public, but it was a point of honor with him to prefer pleasing the composer and himself; indeed, he felt that he had become a conductor solely for this reason: to make possible the presentation, beside the most classic harmonies, of the newest harmonies.

Debussy himself, who feared an imperfect execution, would have preferred not to be played; to convince him, it took the conductor's insistence and the urging of a few rare friends.

An unfortunate precaution that Debussy had thought it necessary to take made everyone wait some time for the scores, so that this composition, especially difficult because of its originality, could not be rehearsed by the whole orchestra together. The players arrived quite green before their sheets of music the day of the concert and played in defiance of common sense. The conductor had any amount of courage to fight against the ill will of the public, but not to betray a musician he liked, who was hissing with the public and was right to hiss. He himself would have liked to hiss and then to explain. . . . Someone said to him on the way out, when he was attempting an explanation, an excuse: "With music like that what does one note matter in place of another? This simply proves that you are wrong to include it on your program; it deserved such an execution — which, as far as I am concerned, didn't

---

[4] The *N.R.F.,* following the custom of most French literary reviews, had founded a publishing house under the name of Librairie Gallimard — Éditions de la Nouvelle Revue Française. Among the first books issued over this imprint were Claudel's drama *The Hostage,* Charles-Louis Philippe's novel *The Mother and Child,* and Gide's novel *Isabelle. Corydon* appeared in a very limited private edition the same year, anonymous as to author and publisher, as *C.R.D.N.* Verbeke directed the St. Catherine Press, Ltd., of Bruges, which printed the first issues of the *N.R.F.* and is still known for fine work.

[5] The statesman Saint-Léger Léger has always written under the pseudonym of St.-J. Perse. His first published work was formed of the beautiful lyric poems of *Praises.*

seem so bad." It was this that put the finishing touch to the conductor's despair; he fell ill that very evening; the next day he swallowed his baton and died.

Between oneself and the world raise a barrier of simplicity. Nothing so baffles them as naturalness.

I prefer the friendship, esteem, and admiration of one gentleman to that of a hundred journalists. But since each journalist, all alone, makes more noise than a hundred gentlemen, you must not be astonished if my books are surrounded by a little silence, or much unkind noise.

NOVEL

His simple decency — and a certain scruple about the quality of the arms he deigned to use against his adversaries (a scruple he could not get over) gave his adversaries a terrible advance over him. Handicap.

NOVEL

The man who begins to drink. Very harmonious family; eight children.

The wife dies. The father unable to keep an eye on the children. Collapse and complete abandon. The old boarder (with spectacles) rapes one of the daughters whom the father is obliged to leave at home while he goes to work. He suspected him, however, but didn't dare accuse him before. Sudden outbursts of rage. He struggles. He ends up by drinking with the old man. Moral decay.

NOVEL

X. has a generous, even chivalrous character; somewhat utopian. He is vying with Christian feelings (he is a Jew); generosity without morality. He offers his wife to Y., his unfortunate friend who has been eating his heart out for the last five years. Y. and the wife do not consummate the adultery; but in a theater during a rehearsal when they think they are protected by the darkness in their box, the band of actors sees them in each other's arms. The tale is immediately spread abroad and commented on. . . . There begins, for the husband, a struggle with the phantom; he cannot maintain the nobility of his attitude; the viciousness of the environment lowers him to the level of common cuckolds.

Cuverville

The bad weather and my work keep me from observing this year, as I did for three successive years, the finches that live in my garden. Now that they are more numerous it is harder to observe them. In the beginning a single couple nested in the bush near the bench where I was accustomed to sit. Couple? No, it was a triangular arrangement. For a long time I refused to accept the evidence, considering as accepted and indubitable the hatred of rival males; yet I was forced to admit it: the two males that I saw attending to the same female, feeding the same nest, got along perfectly together.

And if it is not the same trio that I saw the following year, then these customs must be current among finches.

What inclines me to believe this is that I encountered them at Arco, in the Italian Tyrol. At the end of the winter season — that is, at nesting-time — from the hotel terrace, almost deserted at that season, during a fortnight we were able to observe some rather tame finches that the hotel-keeper was protecting. There were three of them, a female and two males, very easily distinguishable one from the other but equally solicitous in regard to the female and equally good providers for the nest.

Not claiming to be the only one to have noticed these strange customs among finches or other birds, for a long time I planned to write Henry de Varigny, who was then writing for *Le Temps* an interesting column on rural life, was glad to answer unknown correspondents, and on occasion even would launch a little inquiry. But wouldn't such a subject seem to him to belong to the novel rather than to natural history?

Cuverville, 3 July

X. (I later on) was accustomed to say that age had not forced him to give up a single pleasure of which he did not just happen to be on the point of getting tired.

After *Robinson Crusoe* I read *Tom Jones*, and in the intervals *Olalla* and *The Bottle Imp* by Stevenson, numerous *Essays* by Lamb, then aloud with Mlle Siller *The Mayor of Casterbridge*, and *The End of the Tether* by Conrad; some Milton (*Samson Agonistes*), Thomson (*Evolution of Sex* — the first four or five chapters); Stevenson, *Weir of Hermiston.*[6]

Les Sources, 15 October

A Friday the 13th, I couldn't have missed it.

Traveled beside a bespectacled little tart who kept the whole compartment awake until one thirty a.m. to read *Baiser de femme,*[7] which she began when we were still in the Paris station and devoured at one sitting. Too annoyed with her to be able to go to sleep afterward; and

---

[6] These titles are all given in English in the original. "Olalla" is one of the stories in Stevenson's *The Merry Men.*

[7] *A Woman's Kiss.*

especially annoyed not to have dared say something cutting to her because of the corpulent protector who was snoozing opposite her.

Worked on *Les Caves*. Probably Lafcadio had already met Protos before his adventure in the train.[8]

Rain outside. But on changing trains at Avignon, the exquisite quality of the air refreshed me.

I was no sooner settled in my new compartment than there entered, half supported by his wife, a corpse. She is in deep mourning — you might think it was already in his honor — her face somewhat swollen, somewhat yellow, somewhat shiny; rather insignificant, effacing herself before him. Very tall; one might rather say: very long; a face that must have been rather handsome (he can't be more than forty-five), but which has lost every expression save that of suffering and anguish; not the waxlike color of dead men, but an ashen, leaden hue. . . . His gestures are broad and lacking in co-ordination, and while his wife says to him :"Don't be afraid: the conductor promised me not to do the coupling until you would be settled" (she repeats this several times), he tumbles into the corner seat (we are in first class) and throws one leg up much higher than he needs to in order to cross it over the other. Occasionally he moans weakly. His wife says, as if speaking to someone behind the scenes or by way of sympathy:

"From Nancy to Dijon it was all right, but it was from Dijon on that *I* began to be so tired. And yet we had been promised that we would have to change only once. . . ."

Then he, very quickly, as if fearing to run out of breath, and in an angry voice:

"I told you we hadn't taken the right train. It's that employee in Dijon who made a mistake. . . . Hm! hm!"

At this moment a brakeman goes down the passageway (the train hasn't started yet). The wife asks once more if this is the right train for *Amélie-les-Bains*. What diseases is that little dump supposed to cure? I haven't yet succeeded in discovering what is the matter with *him*.

I look at my time-table. It is barely eight o'clock. The train does not reach Amélie-les-Bains until four o'clock; *he* will never make it!

His nose is constantly running, and as he wipes it once more:

"Take out your other handkerchief," his wife says; "you can see that you already used this one when you had your chocolate."

And indeed the handkerchief is repulsive; but he doesn't give a damn. His cap slips onto one side; his wife straightens it; she spreads a little Scotch plaid over his pointed knees; then helps him slip on a pair

---

[8] Indeed, in the finished novel that fantastic encounter gains piquancy from the fact that Lafcadio and Protos had been classmates and intimate friends in Paris.

of black cotton gloves; very painful; his extraordinarily thin and long hand is out of joint; his middle fingers fall backward like a doll's fingers. What is his disease? Suppose I should catch it! But I cannot take my eyes off him. (The only other traveler, in the corner opposite me, is resolutely hiding behind *Les Pirates de l'Opéra*[9] — and doesn't raise his eyes during the whole trip.) The invalid says:

"It's the jolts that have shaken up my guts like this."

He tries to cough but chokes, while his wife reassures him:

"You know it always does you good to sneeze."

She calls that "sneezing"! On my word, he is beginning the death rattle; he can't catch his breath; she herself becomes a bit worried and in a rather loud voice, as much, I think, for us as for him:

"There's nothing to worry about; everyone knows that it's nervous."

Finally, having caught his breath, he says:

"Ah! I am very low. . . ."

And then she begins to lament not having taken advantage of the stop at Avignon to give him an injection. (She gives him one at Tarascon, shortly afterward.)

"That's right! I hadn't thought of it a moment. Do you want a little piece of sugar? Do you . . . ? How do you feel?"

He says nothing. I see a thread of liquid dripping onto his vest; I think he is crying; but no, it comes from the corner of his mouth.

We are coming to Nîmes. She says to him:

"Nîmes: the Tour Magne!"[10]

Oh, go to hell! . . . But this is where I get off.

21 December

Les Caves. Necessity of drawing the naked form under the clothing in the manner of David, and of knowing about my characters even the things I am not going to use — or at least that are not to appear on the outside.

Mlle Emma Siller is having trouble with her landlord. She writes to Em.: "It is enough to make you sick of life; and this is very sad at my age." (She is sixty.)

Finished *Rhoda Fleming.*[11]

---

[9] *The Pirates of the Opera.*

[10] One of the landmarks of the town is a famous Roman tower on Mount Cavalier.

[11] Meredith's novel.

DETACHED PAGES

I find a great danger in a too ready sympathy. It proposes in rapid succession divers paths, all leading to equally charming landscapes. In rapid succession the soul becomes enamored of that languid lush country which shelters only the soft, the flexible, and the voluptuous and produces it abundantly; then it waxes enthusiastic over the glare of a sandy dune where everything glitters.

✵

FOR MARCEL D.

He taxes me with having badly economized my appeal to the emotions since I exhaust it in the beginning of the book,[12] so that I cease to stir as soon as I try to persuade. This is because I am addressing myself and wish to address myself to the head and not to the heart; this is because I do not seek to win over the reader's sympathy, which would risk becoming indulgence; and it is precisely because, as I am well aware, certain words springing from the heart would touch the reader more deeply than all these more or less specious reasonings — it is precisely for this reason that I have kept from using those words. Compare the device of the lawyer who tries to pass off his client's crime as one dictated by jealousy. I do not want any of that. I intend that this book should be written coldly, deliberately, and that this should be evident. Passion must have preceded it or at most be implied in it; but above all it must not serve as an excuse for the book. I do not want to move to pity with this book; I want to embarrass.

I do not feel any imperious attraction (toward this book). It is undeniable that I am writing it out of season and when I no longer need to write it. This is what I explained yesterday to Marcel, fearing that he might see in it some almost unhealthy obsession, an impossibility of getting my mind off this subject. But, on the other hand, the difficulty comes rather from the fact that I must artificially revive a problem to which I have found (as far as I am concerned) a practical solution, so that, to tell the truth, it no longer bothers me.

✵

It is noteworthy that animal forms, as they become complicated, become less and less numerous. The remarkable success achieved with man is unique.

But immediately there is found *in him*, I mean in the heart of the species itself, all the differences he had left behind.

---

[12] *Corydon.* [A.]

The individual is opposed to the race. Effort toward individualization.

Under another form this amounts to repeating the remark of Darwin and of many others: "The creatures placed on the lower rungs of the ladder are more variable than those which are at the top." (*Origin of Species*, p. 161.)

But once the top is reached, it is in the individual that this variability reappears.

FOR PAUL LAURENS

"Don't you think the word that we were seeking the other day, and which by defining our thought would have given us a better chance of understanding it more fully, is simply *shrewdness* — yes, artistic shrewdness. And what brings this word to mind is a passage of Buffon that I was reading yesterday which seems to contain in germ our conversation at Yport: "Through the *shrewdness* conferred by the constant habit of writing, one *can feel in advance* what will be the result of all these operations of the mind.""

CONCERNING JUDGMENTS

. . . and recalling that of notes of music among themselves: When the E flat entered the drawing-room, the C and the G looked upon her as a third person.

"She's a dominant one," thought the A flat, while the E natural exclaimed:

"I know her: she's my leading note."

PRODIGAL SON

When he returns to the house he blames himself for having left. . . .

And when he sees again this little garden from which he promised himself so much delight, he is amazed not to find the flowers larger, the fruits more tasty, and the affection of his family more joyfully effusive.

Whether he be named St. Paul, Luther, or Calvin, I see him as beclouding the whole truth of God.

It is worthy of consideration that the two most *solemn* dramas that antiquity has bequeathed to us, *Œdipus* and *Prometheus,* offer us, one the notion of good and evil, or rather of the permissible and the forbidden, in its most arbitrary terms, the other the sanction, etc. . . .

❊

She is painstaking;
She is making a collection of happiness;
Her love is all in depth;
She expends a great enthusiasm on very small things. To herself she exaggerates infinitely the value of everything she possesses. (The doll's golden dress; the gardens; the plant from America, which she surrounds with little plants she has gathered on the cliff.) When he doesn't come she takes care of his garden.

A bit too careful.

Unlimited faculty of admiration.

Charming enlargement of the most insignificant bit of reality — by these children.

Their imagination: with three trees they make a forest.

❊

Character of X.

Stubbornness perhaps even more than fidelity. At one and the same time curiosity and need of returning to things. Obstinacy.

Absurdity of always saying: "He will be like the others." The pride of his humility. A certain attention to detail in duty.

He is always rereading the same books, returning to the same places; is aware of how faithful he is and esteems himself for it. Feels no joy at being free. Always throws himself completely into things.

The minor details of gardening: he removes the mistletoe, the suckers, the plant lice.

His fidelity binds him.

Meditative, introverted childhood.

He reads the Gospels on the playground.

"Hold that fast which thou hast."

His classmates make fun of him. Appointment on the Place Vendôme. He waits in the rain. Warmly sheltered, his classmates have a good time watching him.

❊

Advice to the Young Man of Letters

With regard to praise or blame I cannot recommend to you an indifference I have never known myself and, moreover, have been inclined to envy. It is good to be moved to emotion, to vibrate under caresses and even more so under bites. And no doubt there is something to be gained from not protesting immediately against them, but . . .

(Education through one's enemies.)

The important thing is not to let oneself be poisoned. Now, hatred poisons. Etc. . . .

DIMINUTIVE NOVEL

My profoundly creative mind was nourished especially by the still amorphous beauty of things. The work of art, purified (*drained* of ugliness), interested me only by the lasting element one feels in any fixing of a more perfect harmony. Life interested me more; more dramatic and pressing just because of its evanescence. The perfect harmony, always imaginable, appealed to me less than the crusty deformation of that harmony according to a personality. The will of the artist seemed to me to reside not so much in a choice of lines, tones, or sonorities with a view to a harmonious work as in a work in complete harmony to divert (distort) that harmony according to oneself. In any work I invariably looked for the trace of *man*.

Before the expectant beauty of crude nature my liberated brain became more excited than before the work of art. Admiration seemed less compromising, closer to adoration. I was ever more annoyed by the error of those who think it necessary to join art and nature. Certainly art hates nature; if it always seeks after her, it does so as a hunter in ambush or like a rival who embraces her only to strangle her.

Just now I am enjoying a country where no work of art reminds me of man's tiresome anxiety to exalt a passing emotion outside of time. I enjoy provoking God everywhere in persistent nature; I call him forth on all fields; this is to allow myself constantly a complete, a total admiration.

It is only through restraint that man can manage not to suppress himself.

All the causes of ruin are in us; but artificially dominated: culture.

DIMINUTIVE NOVEL

Avignon.

The smell of the pines, the scent of the lavender.

Behind the arches of the bridges, those great swells that the water slowly carries along.

I grieve to think that, later on, my weakened memory will be unable to offer me my sensation of today, however lively, which, losing all sharpness of outline, all accent, will merely seem to me like one of those medals of which the effigy has been effaced, alas, now blurred like any other medal that one can guess to have been precious only by the luster of the worn metal.

Later on, taking this perfumed memory in my hand, pressing it affectionately against my lips, I shall think:

What was it? I no longer see it very clearly. The name of that child? Shall I get it mixed, alas, with so many others? The day was delightfully radiant; the water in the *saqiyas*, I remember, charming. I should like to define the line of the young body and again find it adorable.

❄

I believe that never did the "rules" embarrass any genius, neither that of the *unities* in France nor that of the three actors in Greece, and that Racine and Corneille as well as Æschylus have sufficiently proved this. (That moreover they have no absolute value and that any great genius masters them, whether he finds support in them or negates them — and that to come along and claim that this or that great man was embarrassed by them is just as ridiculous as if a painter said that when painting he is embarrassed by his frame and exclaimed: "Oh, if only I could spread out a little farther!" and that those who protest against them are like Kant's dove, which thought it would fly better in a vacuum.)

In general, insubordination with regard to the rules comes from an unintelligent subordination to realism, from a misunderstanding of the ends of art, from that specious insinuation of empiricism which aims, through a scandalous generalization, to scoff at art by attacking it only where it has become artifice, and to label as factitious all supernatural beauty.

❄

You have found happiness, you say. Take care! For this is the oasis, and Pegasus is not going to carry you any farther.

❄

Contemporary fiction and drama are in the same situation as present-day architecture. The usefulness of the monument is an excuse for its ugliness; and when simple dwelling-places are being built, this is especially evident: that in general one is rather comfortable in them and in particular rather uncomfortable; for they have to be made so that anyone whatever can live in them. As for the newspaper, it is a hotel room.

❄

"You don't seem to understand, sir," the worthy Lyon, my teacher, used often to say to me, "that certain words are made to go with others; between them there exist certain relationships that must not be changed."

"I can't help it, dear teacher, but for words too I am a firm believer in the virtue of bad company."

Let us mistrust "foregrounds"; everything that seems to us big in them changes rapidly.

Sometimes we realize that certain bad characteristics we had found in others are just what we lack to succeed as they do in life. On such days certain qualities we had found in ourselves cease to seem so good. Whereupon we decide to think that they stand in our way and work to our detriment and to the great advantage of others, while the bad characteristics are prejudicial only to others.

But Nietzscheism is like a road that seems to us all the more beautiful because we don't very well know where it leads.

That need of nobility which makes Nietzsche, after twenty-six, still prefer Schiller to Goethe. — Prefer? Perhaps it is a bit risky to say this — but at least he quotes Schiller and not Goethe.

"*Kämpfen wir, und wenn es geht, nicht für Windmühlen. Denken wir an den Kampf und die Askese wahrhaft grosser Männer, an Schopenhauer, Schiller, Wagner!*" (*Correspondence*, Vol. I, p. 150.) [13]

It is just because it is very difficult (if not impossible) to reduce Nietzscheism to a system — that we shall not get over it easily.

Creusa or Lot's wife; [14] one tarries and the other looks back, which is a worse way of tarrying.

It is also Ariadne who, after he has killed the Minotaur, makes Theseus return to the point from which he started.

---

[13] "Let us do battle, and if possible, not for windmills. Let us think of the struggle and the asceticism of the truly great, of Schopenhauer, Schiller, Wagner!"

[14] Creusa, the daughter of Priam and Hecuba and first wife of Æneas, delayed as she left the burning city of Troy and disappeared in the flames; Lot's wife turned to a pillar of salt when she looked back at the destruction of Sodom.

There is no greater cry of passion than this:

And Phædra having braved the Labyrinth with you
Would have been found with you or lost with you.[15]

But passion blinds her; after a few steps, to tell the truth, she would
have sat down, or else would have wanted to go back — or even would
have made him carry her.

In the *Thésée* this must be brought out — the apron-string, to express
it vulgarly. After having conquered the Minotaur, he would like to go
on. — He is held — obliged to return.[16]

TALE

of the island whose inhabitants have invented the idea of not dying.
(This is where Tithonus, the fiancé of Aurora, lives.)

This is on condition that they don't have any children. Eventually
one couple gets bored and prefers to yield life to something new.

The child they raise slowly pushes them out of life — and they will
never know the *novelty* he brings, for which nevertheless they are willing to die.

Not that I never knew how to enjoy metaphors, and even of the most
romantic kind; but, loathing artifice, I forbade myself the right to use
them. Even as early as my *Cahiers d'André Walter* I attempted a style
that aimed toward a more secret and more essential beauty. "Rather poverty-stricken style," said the excellent Heredia, to whom I presented my
first book and who was astonished not to find more images in it. That
style, I wanted it even more poverty-stricken, more stringent, more purified, deeming that the only justification for ornamentation is to hide
some defect and that only insufficiently beautiful thought need fear
utter nudity.

Vannicola; the face of an affectionate punchinello; his habit when
paying of keeping the copper for himself and leaving the silver as a tip.
Twisted like a vine-stock; amorous like a vine-shoot.

---

[15] The famous lines of Racine's *Phèdre* when the heroine contrasts herself with her sister Ariadne, who remained at the entrance of the labyrinth to
guide Theseus' steps by a thread:

> *Et Phèdre au Labyrinthe avec vous descendue*
> *Se serait avec vous retrouvée ou perdue.*

[16] This reference to the project of a *Theseus* in 1911 is interesting since
the work did not appear until 1946.

Marinetti enjoys a lack of talent that permits him to indulge in every form of audacity. After the manner of Scapin, he alone makes the sound of a riot when he has got a few silly readers into the bag: 'Sblood! [17]

(And now it's *Le Roi Bombance!* [18])

He paws the ground and sends up clouds of dust; he curses and swears and massacres; he organizes oppositions, contradictions, and intrigues just for the pleasure of triumphing over them.

Otherwise he is the most charming man in the world with the exception of d'Annunzio; animated in the Italian fashion, which often takes verbosity for eloquence, ostentation for wealth, agitation for movement, feverishness for divine rapture. He came to call on me some ten years ago and displayed such incredibly polite attentions that they forced me to leave for the country at once; if I had seen him again, I should have been done for; I might have decided he had genius.

NOVEL

The Santa Margherita hotel-keeper (a lawyer, it seems), Milanese, short, and with a beard pointing forward, bright and excessively amiable, serves at table himself; and since he is aided only by a single servant-girl (Austrian but Irredentist), whereas there are twenty of us guests, he hustles about, jumps from one end of the dining-room to the other, urges me to have a second helping of a poor dish of which there is too much: "Help yourself again; it's very light!" says to me as he rushes by: "It's not quantity we lack . . ." flies off to give bread to a neighbor, then, on his way by again, finishes the sentence: ". . . it's service." The table wine being almost undrinkable, I order a bottle of Barbera; nothing out of the ordinary, but he serves it *wrapped in a table-napkin*. That is the key to his character (worth examining what this might produce in the serious circumstances of life).

The 15th of August, a holiday, when we were too numerous in the little dining-room, when the lunch didn't begin until one o'clock, and when the "service" lost its head, the main course was a strange stew of *bones*, which he passed me, gallantly leaning over me and whispering very quickly, like a secret: "Knuckle of veal *à la milanaise!* What is called *ossa bucca* in Italian."

[17] The great comic scene in Molière's *Fourberies de Scapin* (*The Deceits of Scapin*) is that in which Scapin persuades his dupe to hide in a huge bag from an imaginary band of pursuers. Then Scapin, alone on the stage with his enemy in the bag, simulates a group of thugs and rains blows on the bag.

[18] *King Carouse*, a satiric tragedy in four acts by Marinetti, produced by the Théâtre de l'Œuvre on 2 April 1909 and inspired by Alfred Jarry's famous farce of *Ubu roi* (1896).

This morning, while I am writing this: "A rather delicate little dish: red mullet with tomato sauce. Do you like it? This is French cooking, nothing to do with Italy." All this said very rapidly and *confidentially*.

A little later:
"It's not for me to offer you sweets . . . but if you like them . . . Do you like this?"
"I don't know; what is it?"
"The most original and at the same time the commonest thing in the world: custard."
And he pours into my plate a sort of inedible paste.

He baptizes as "veal roastbeef" this hideous white meat with red edges.

As proprietor of the hotel-pension L'Hermitage, he claims (in my presence) to be an ardent francophile and talks of committing suicide because I point out to him that it would have been more French to write Ermitage without an *h*.

In the window of the large pastry and candy shop in Santa Margherita, in gold letters protected by a sheet of glass:
"The principle languages spoken here."

❈

DIMINUTIVE NOVEL
The vegetables, I told him, are no more made for man than man is made for them or for anything else.
Perfect adaptation of each thing to itself, in its place, without the slightest care whether it is an advantage or disadvantage to man.
Too slight foliage of the pines. Narrow leaves of the palms.
Eucalyptus with vertical leaves, which barely throw light strips of shadow on the ground when the sun is directly overhead.

❈

MORÉAS
The Greek exoticism (of Moréas) [19] not even apparent to many, because they became accustomed to it in school; habit of the mind that consists in seeing in the externals of life only the plastic side (I was about to say sculptural) and to recognize the most authentic movement of the heart only from gestures.

---

[19] Born in Greece, his real name was Papadiamantopoulos.

For Moréas the *point of view* always remains the same, whatever may be the object he is looking at; he never shifts his position.

He is not stupid, as some have thought whose point of view was different. On the contrary, the least of his judgments reveals an extraordinary clearness of mind; and the relationship he establishes between the object and himself is always right; indeed, all the more right since he himself remains motionless.

As a Greek he hardly admitted that a work of art could be born of any other need than the plastic one; more French, he would have been better able to understand the æsthetic value of thought, in which he was rather poor, besides. He could never believe that I was in love with his poems.

S U A R È S

Doubtless everything is not equal in this little book,[20] although I should not wish to remove anything from it; but the finest pages rise to so surprising a beauty that one forgets the difficulty one often had to get to them. You have to make up your mind with this amazing writer: he excites enthusiasm as naturally as he rebuffs; he makes no effort to enlarge himself or to raise his voice, nor does he to reduce and concentrate himself; the least thought is amplified by all the echoes it awakens in his great cavernous soul, and often, long after it has uttered its cry, Suarès keeps right on speaking. He never runs out.

It is extremely rare that a mountain is precipitous on all sides.

To the famous "three unities" I should be glad to add a fourth: the *unity of the audience*. It would imply the importance for the poetic creation, whether a play or a book, to address itself, from one end to the other of its duration, to the same reader or listener. These reflections rise in me while reading Wells's latest book, which his faithful translator Davray has just brought out in the *Mercure*. Wells has the most ingenious mind; he skillfully interests us by opening up before us the most unforeseen perspectives; but his reputation has no need of further praise. If he is addressing us today, why didn't he always address himself to us? Read by too large a public, which he recruited in all countries and from all social classes, he now addresses himself alternatively to people who are too different from one another. In this book there are

---

[20] *Tolstoi vivant* (*Tolstoy Himself*), by André Suarès (1911).

pages that could only amuse children, or new people; other pages to interest old experienced people like us, but which would repel the former; and finally others in which he seems to be amusing only some alter ego or other; both children and I cease to listen. Occasionally I feel like pulling his sleeve: Mr. Wells! you are forgetting us! And yet it was for us that you began your story; don't make any mistake about it, we were your best public.

※

"Milton's whole genius lies therein: he brought the sparkle of the Renaissance into the seriousness of the Reformation, the magnificences of Spenser among the severities of Calvin." (Taine: *English Literature*, Vol. II, p. 415.)

It is improper, it is almost paradoxical, to claim that we owe to Calvinist puritanism the wonderful English school (I mean the school of novelists), for we cannot easily distinguish in them what belongs to upbringing and what belongs to the race, nor to what a degree the former suits the latter. Furthermore, one must consider that, aside from a few very rare exceptions (Thackeray, for instance), it is by escaping from Calvinism, and only by escaping from it and often by turning against it, that those novelists were able to succeed. So that it could be said that if Calvinism helped them it did so as a sort of restraint that curbs and tightens one's strength and makes Joseph de Maistre utter the remark that has been somewhat misused: "Whatever constricts man strengthens him." This is also because the habit of a certain gloominess, the desire or even the need of finding oneself at fault, and the rejection of the most charming solicitations of life invite them to seek the source of an action and its most secret repercussion rather than what immediately follows it, as do a great many of our novelists.

Thus it is that Calvinism can be an excellent school of psychology, but, let me repeat, on condition that one get away from it, and if . . . (Quote Taine, Vol. II, p. 415.)

※

J. A. had a frozen mustache as if cosmetics had been invented for him; his hair was of just the right length; and a part that you felt he must have kept while sleeping. His hands were utterly inexpressive, and consequently he put them in his pockets as soon as he spoke. He would then throw his head back and talk loud, and talk alone.

The tone of his voice seemed to say: it's useless to interrupt me; I listen only to myself. The wonderful thing is that a circle always formed around him. People didn't exactly admire him, but all the same he astounded them. His voice hissed a little, for he never took out of his teeth a big cigar or the amber tube that held it; this little hissing sound allowed him to be affected without seeming so and to appear witty. He would never stop talking except to draw on his cigar.

"You didn't leave Paris this summer?" M. P. nevertheless risked asking him during a puff of silence.

"I don't like changing beds," J. A. declared sharply as one utters an aphorism. "But when you have your own yacht, perhaps . . ." (J. A. is rolling in money, but he likes letting it be understood that he could endure being even richer.) "But the country! Do *you* find any fun in the country?"

In the jury-box again I look at my colleagues. I imagine these same faces on the opposite bench; badly outfitted, unshaved, unwashed, their hair uncombed, with soiled linen or with none at all, and that fearful hunted look in the eyes that comes from a combination of worry and fatigue. What would they look like? What would I look like myself? Would the judge himself recognize under that frightful disguise the "respectable man"? He would have to be very clever to distinguish the criminal from the member of the jury!

Jules Lemaître's toast to the Duke of Orléans moved me, I confess; in a few sentences he evoked an image of the master that any country whatever might long for, as soon as it longs for a master.

At first I was saddened not to find the same masculine dignity, the same sincere conciseness, in the letter that the Duke of Orléans sends to him. But the reservations I then made do not hold, upon reflection. The important thing is not that a prince should talk well, but rather that he should surround himself with men possessing the qualities that he recognizes he lacks. And moreover, in our epoch, who can say how much the authority of a king would be reduced, just how far the Chambers would limit his initiative? And, indeed, haven't we the right to demand greater personal merit from the representatives of a republic than from the representative of a monarchy? Renan's witticism about Louis-Philippe: "One must forgive kings their mediocrity; they didn't choose themselves," is not necessarily disrespectful.

But, alas, it is just that reassuring limitation of royal power that worries me; everything depends on the value of the areopagus that limits it, and so long as universal suffrage decides the matter, we shall not have changed masters. The king will be a king only when he has freed us from that. Can a king do so, and to free us from it is a king really necessary?

Even Montaigne has been overdone; he is not always racy. I notice that he is never more so than when he gives himself full rein, never less so than when he behaves in a studied fashion. The so famous *Apology* of Raymond de Sebonde is almost devoid of amusing touches.[21] I was not able to finish reading it without a certain obstinacy; in my little six-volume edition it fills almost a whole volume and I, who always read Montaigne with a pencil in my hand ready to note in the margin my astonishment or my joy, I advanced here from page to page without finding a single living word, not one of those nonchalant and quivering sentences that abound among these abandoned pages. The desire to compose that chapter stood in his way.

✻

At times I deeply regret living in an epoch when respect is so rarely shown and so difficult. Not everyone can do without it with impunity. "My mind was naturally inclined toward veneration," Goethe (or at least his translator) says somewhere. If curvatures of the mind were as obvious as those of the spine, I know more than one that would not dare show itself in conversation, etc. . . .

✻

"What do you mean by manners?"
"I mean a general submission and conduct consistent with good or bad laws. If the laws are good, the manners are good," etc. . . . (Diderot: *Supplément au Voyage de Bougainville*, Part IV, p. 205, Centenary Edition.) [22]

"Manners are the hypocrisy of a nation." (Balzac.)

"If, as Buffon says, love lies in the sense of touch, the softness of that skin must have been active and penetrating like the scent of daturas." (Balzac: *Les Paysans.*) [23]

✻

"It is certain that the Mohammedan peoples would have preceded it in that path if, at the very beginning, the Koran had not protected Islam-

---

[21] The "Apology" forms Chapter XII of Book II of the *Essays* and, as the center of the work in its first form, expresses Montaigne's skepticism at its height.

[22] Diderot was inspired to write in 1772 an argument of naturist philosophy (supporting Rousseau's theory that man is naturally good) by the account of Louis-Antoine de Bougainville's voyage to Oceania.

[23] *The Peasants.*

ism by forbidding gaming, and if it had not directed the imagination of Moslems toward the *discovery of hidden treasures.*" (Burckhardt: *The Renaissance,* Vol. II, pp. 193–4.)

Very important to note in fact the absence of games in the *Thousand and One Nights.*

❊

Exemplary sentence of the Goncourt brothers:

"Leaning over the transparency of that water, in which the clayey-ness of the bank, in which the russet of the roots were soon lost in the deep bluish bottom . . ." etc. (*Frères Zemganno,* p. 7.)

"The two brothers led a calm, ordered, sober, almost chaste life. They lived without a mistress and rarely drank anything but reddened water. *Their greatest distraction was to take a little walk on the boulevard every evening, during which they approached every theater-column, one after another, to read their printed names on each of the posters — after which they would go back home to bed.*" (*Frères Zemganno,* p. 243.)

Strange that in as special and documented a book as *Les Frères Zemganno* Goncourt writes *haltère* without an *h* (p. 275).

❊

"Leveling is not God's work and every proper man must have moments in which he is tempted to weep over that work of desolation." (Kierkegaard.)

"That ambitious woman [Cornelia] had early prepared for her sons all *the instruments of tyranny: eloquence,* in which they surpassed all the men of their time; *gallantry:* Tiberius was the first to climb the walls of Carthage; *honesty* itself; for such ambitions could not stop at avarice. *The Stoics who raised the two children,* as they had raised Cleomenes, the reformer of Sparta, *inculcated in them that policy of leveling which serves tyranny so well,* and the classic fables of the equality of wealth under Romulus and under Lycurgus." (Michelet: *Roman History,* Vol. II, p. 162.)

1912

Sunday, 8 January

I had promised myself to return to this journal and to keep it regularly from the first of January on. But I have crawled along so miserably these last few days that, even begrudgingly, I could not have written a thing. To tell the truth, I didn't even try.

14 January

. . . But it is true here as it is for music, where the chord of G sharp does not have the same meaning depending on whether you have reached it by way of the sharps or by way of the flats, and does not sound the same as the chord of A flat to the sensitive ear, though composed of the same notes.

The night before last, excellent conversation with Paul Albert Laurens, who showed me the possibility of writing *Corydon* in an entirely different mode. He would like me to make of it a work as serious as my *Enfant prodigue;* and this causes me to reflect at length.

Late afternoon yesterday at Mme R.'s, where, for an hour, my mind endured the torture of the boot. She is charming nevertheless and shows a disarming kindness and goodwill; but what was I doing there? Speaking of T., I said to her: "He lives on an income, and in literature I like only those who eat up their capital." "As you so well express it," she immediately remarks, "that charming fellow hasn't the means." It is not at all that she is incapable of understanding; but she simply wants to have understood too quickly.

Then Péladan came; strange lack of accent to his face; fat, soft aspect of his whole body. He makes a few remarks in the d'Aurevilly manner: "Coffee and tobacco are the riding-whip and spurs of the mind," etc. . . . He accuses Gautier of "being short on general ideas" and adds: "As for me, I consider it quite natural that M. de X., meeting Y. for the first time" (he is alluding to a real fact, as far as I could understand, and cites the names), "should ask him at once: 'What do you think of the infinite?' And whoever is amazed by that is an imbecile."

It is a great mark of wisdom to dare to appear an imbecile, but it takes a certain courage that I have not always had.

15 January

Yesterday, lunch with the Espinases, the Drouins, and Uncle Charles. Ghéon joins us; then, after lunch, Ruyters arrives. Long debate on politics. At about five Jean Schlumberger comes and we go out with him after having finished up the work for the *N.R.F.* Once outside, he tells us of his worries. Inextricable situation of the *Revue;* impossibility of either keeping it going or getting out of it.

And there is one less day to live. But all work becomes impossible for me as soon as the table on which I am writing does not stand squarely. I repeat to myself Renan's sentence that I used to quote: "In order to think freely, one must feel assured that what one is writing will be of no consequence."

This morning I go to meet Jacques Rivière at the office of the *Revue,* where Jean Schlumberger joins us, whom I lead off to Eugène Rouart's —where I am to meet Copeau.

The three of us lunched together at Vian's; long study of the situation. It seems to us to offer no way out. What an odd thing to think that necessarily time will bring one!

Written in the train (*on the way to Vichy*), *19 January*
I met Copeau at eight o'clock at the little English tavern of the rue d'Amsterdam (the one, I believe, of the trip to London in *A Rebours* [1]), where we dined. Copeau's very good advice: Jean Schlumberger withdrawing from the editorial board of the *N.R.F.,* which would continue with its two other editors, and even if need be with Copeau alone should Ruyters be recalled to Abyssinia.

Hotel Bellevue, Neuchâtel
In this hotel, of which I had such an excellent memory, I get only a miserable little room filled with a devil-may-care taste. I shall not dine, but simply go to a near-by café and get, at nine o'clock, a *café au lait,* which will keep me awake until four o'clock, together with the racket my neighbors make from midnight until two. In the café I had written to Miomandre to congratulate him on an article on Mme de Ségur I had just read in the *Gazette de Lausanne.* Before returning to my pitiful room, I tarry at the cinema; the tot in a light-tan velvet suit with a torn sleeve (he had a white wool *"Mütze"*), so vulgar, so healthy, so full of laughter, who comes and sits beside me, talks with me, tries to keep me there when I want to go, by asserting that I have a right to more of the show. . . .

Have I reached the limit of experience? And shall I be able to catch hold of myself again now? I need to put my remaining energy to some studious use. How easy it would be for me now to throw myself into a confessional! How difficult it is to be at one and the same time, for oneself, he who commands and he who obeys! But what spiritual director

---

[1] In Huysman's novel *Against the Grain* the strange æsthete Des Esseintes, who lives in a dream world, "takes a trip to London" by simply spending an evening in an English tavern in Paris.

would understand with sufficient subtlety this vacillation, this passionate indecision of my whole being, this equal aptitude for contraries? Depersonalization, obtained by an effort of the will and with such difficulty, which could be explained and excused only by the production of works that it authorizes and with an eye to which I have striven to suppress my preferences. Absurdity of the objective method (Flaubert). Cease to be oneself in order to be all. Danger of aiming toward a limitless empire. To conquer Russia, Napoleon had to risk France. Necessity of linking the frontier with the center. It is time to return home.

(This will be the subject of *Alexandre aux Indes.*[2])

Constant *vagabundance*[3] of desire — one of the chief causes of the deteriorating of the personality.

Urgent necessity to recover possession of oneself.

But can one still make resolutions when one is over forty? I live according to twenty-year-old habits. Did I know what I was doing at twenty? When I made the resolution to look at everything, never to prefer myself to anything and always to give preference to what differed most from me. . . .

Even my insomnia struck me last night as a form of perplexity, a kind of difficulty in making up my mind to sleep.

Never go out without a definite aim; hold to this.

Walk along without looking in every direction.

In a train choose any compartment whatever; and enter the subway train by the first door you see, without looking for something better. Do not scorn little victories; as soon as it is a matter of the will, the *much* is only the patient addition of the *little.*

Forbid oneself every kind of vacillation.

Zurich, Tuesday evening

Everything I wrote this evening will strike me as silly in a short while. Already I feel better; this brisk air has put me back on my feet; I am again becoming aware of my strength. This state is the very one I wanted; but as soon as I weaken, I cease to be anyone because of having wanted to be all (state of the perfect novelist), for fear of being only *someone.*

It is as a conqueror, not as a traveler, that Alexander advances in new lands; he is seeking the *limits* of the world, etc. . . .

---

[2] No work by André Gide entitled "Alexander in India" has been published.

[3] The French text has the same made-up word from *vagabondage* and *abondance.*

Zurich, Wednesday

I should like never to have known Claudel. His friendship weighs on my thought, and obligates it, and embarrasses it. . . . I can still not get myself to hurt him, but as my thought affirms itself it gives offense to his. How can I explain myself to him? I should willingly leave the whole field to him, I should give up everything. . . . But I cannot say something different from what I have to say, which cannot be said by anyone else.

How much more sensuality invites to art than does sentimentality — this is what I repeat to myself as I walk in Zurich. To tell the truth, I don't understand anything here; I feel more foreign to these people, and they to me, than I should be among Zulus or Caribs.

Thursday

When I hear myself in a conversation, I feel like becoming a Trappist. And all the disgust and exasperation I feel does not correct anything in me. The indulgence others must have to have, at times, to put up with me! . . . There are certain shortcomings of my mind that I know and loathe but that I cannot overcome. If at least I could not be aware of them!

Heavy fog over the town and over my thoughts. Lunch with that M. Simon whom Bernard Spicket introduced to me two years ago at the Opéra and who, in turn, had introduced to me his friend Dehmel.

After lunch Simon shows me the books of his library with a very evident anxiety not to let me touch them. The assurance of that mind, which clings firmly to what it has and is never distracted.

He talks to me at length (while we go together to the Federal Museum) of the state of nameless barbarism into which Germany is sinking. "The ideal of their sensuality," he says, "is the bottle of champagne. The Emperor still holds them in check; but when Wilhelm dies, they will begin to elbow their way. Their strength and health increase with their stupidity. I assure you that I am not exaggerating anything; I have the opportunity to observe them very closely: you cannot imagine the stupidity of those people. But what an advantage it is to be interested in nothing but one's work! People talk a great deal of the wonderful German method; that method has nothing particularly wonderful about it; it is childishly simple; the wonderful thing is not the method but the fact of following it. . . . A German who gets dead drunk Sunday evening (and this is the supreme debauch for him) is behind his desk again on Monday morning, stupefied, but not much more so than usual, just as exact and diligent as if he had drunk nothing but water the day before. Their great virtue is patience; their great force lies in never letting themselves be distracted by anything."

Howbeit, the conversation with Simon tires me out rather quickly, as with all those who are anxious about their limits and fear going beyond them. I speak to him of Chopin; he replies that he sticks to Beethoven; of Dostoyevsky and he confesses to being too great an admirer of Goethe to follow him, any more than he does Ibsen.

Visit to the Federal Museum. Wonderful rooms; a porcelain stove that is prolonged on both sides into an armchair; understanding of comfort and intimacy, more skillfully arranged than I have seen anywhere else (I am speaking particularly of a sumptuous Renaissance hall and of the next one, so simple, with wainscoting of inlaid-work that would have delighted Théo).

Andermatt, 27 January

Here I am again in this land "that God created to be horrible" (Montesquieu). The admiration of mountains is an invention of Protestantism. Strange confusion on the part of brains incapable of art, between the lofty and the beautiful. Switzerland: a wonderful reservoir of energy; one has to go down how far? to find abandon and grace, laziness and voluptuousness again, without which neither art nor wine is possible. If of the tree the mountains make a fir, you can imagine what they can do with man. Æsthetics and ethics of conifers.

The fir and the palm tree: those two extremes.

29 January

E. P. has come to join us, together with a school friend . . . an Alsatian with glasses and a pointed nose. His intellectual poverty and lack of curiosity, which he hides under an air of disdain; mediocrity of his reactions; yet great kindness and decency; but as soon as you talk to him of anything but practical matters, particularly money matters, he has no more resonance than a wooden bell. As soon as his smile leaves him, his face looks glum and expresses nothing but boredom.

I spent two days of fog and snow up there, more becoming to the landscape than the blue sky we had hoped to find after several weeks of rain. And, paradoxically, now we have a cloudless azure since Olten. I am writing this in the train taking me back to Paris and to Em., who is ill and whom I am eager to see. Wonderful descent from Andermatt to Göschenen this morning; I was plunging into one of the circles of Dante's hell. The fog, frozen by the wind, covered with hoar-frost my cloak, my gloves, the coachman's blond lashes, and the tail of the horse, which looked like an enormous ostrich feather, as in one of Goya's *Proverbs*. The little one could glimpse of the mountains and their wonderful romantic hideousness faded away immediately in a fantastic unreality. Sensual pleasure in the strange, just as intense as in the desert when, on the way back from Tolga (?) (with P. A. Laurens, Mother, and Marie) the carriage-wheel raised a mane of sand; and the crunching of the sleigh in the snow made me think of it.

The clearer air this morning lets us see the distant peaks cutting off the valley in the direction of the Furka, pink and violet, without any of the usual suggestion of cruelty or hideousness.

Tuesday

Got home last night at midnight. This morning I write a few letters (answers to invitations), which I send to my Aunt Charles Gide so that she can mail them from Andermatt. Short piano-practice. This evening, I finish my rereading of *The Possessed.*[4] Crushing admiration. I penetrate, this time, still deeper into the secret reason of this work, lighting it still better by my recollection of the others. I retain the detail and the mass, but am amazed by the manner in which the dialogue and the action come to meet the idea, so surely yet in a manner apparently so empirical.

Unable to write anything all day long, through a total *absence of slope.*

After dinner, after reading the last pages of *The Possessed,* I go to smoke a cigarette at Ruyters's.

At that age (twelve or thirteen) I was a great taker-apart of clocks and, when I used to arrive at Uzès at my grandmother's, would not rest until I had cleaned all the works and set in motion all the pendulums in the house.

Wednesday

In order to be more economical of it, I shall note in minute detail the manner in which I spend my time.

Seven thirty: bath, reading of Souday's article on A. S.

Eight thirty to nine: breakfast.

Nine o'clock: piano (first Bach-Liszt Prelude for organ). Practice interrupted by the arrival of Dr. D. to dress Em.'s arm.

Ten to eleven: letters to Rilke and Eugène Rouart.

Eleven o'clock to twelve: walk, then cleaning up my notes on *The Possessed.*

Lunch.

One o'clock to two: practice at the piano.

Two to three: reading of *Clayhanger;*[5] then intense fatigue and frightful let-down. I am going to sleep from three to four.

---

[4] Dostoyevsky's novel, the title of which, as is usual with Russian works, Gide cites in French.

[5] By Arnold Bennett (1910).

Through a desire and a need to attach myself to something solid, I am tying myself to the translation of Hebbel's letters (those dated from France). I find both hard work and great interest in it, so that I continue this work until dinner-time.

With all my heart and all my soul I listen to this call of virtue.

Thursday

Managed somehow to catch a cold, which further complicates my restlessness; but already yesterday's short period of work has strengthened me. No one is yet informed of my return. I should like to regulate my day and decide as to the allotment of my hours as I used to do, rue de Commailles; I had a "daily routine" pinned to the wall and made it a matter of pride not to get away from it in any way. What strength I should have had if I had not soon given myself leave! . . .

Nothing but Marcel Drouin's visit (very cordial conversation) distracted me from the translation of Hebbel.

Friday

A slightly better day which I spend altogether in the little room beside the library, between a fire of wood-blocks and the little electric radiator. Translated Hebbel all morning and part of the afternoon; I finally stop, not discouraged, but more and more convinced that these letters will hardly interest ten readers and that the *N.R.F.* cannot be willing to publish them.

I write a few lines of the *Traité des Dioscures,*[6] which I have been carrying in my head for so many years; but it doesn't go very well either. Right now I think that it is better to keep these ideas on Greek mythology for the novel I shall write after *Les Caves.* I shall have them developed by some character, with all the slowness and complexity that is necessary. So that this work too is dropped.

Read the first chapter of *Clayhanger,* which I leave to go back to *Captain Singleton.*[7]

Saturday

Uncertain and painful thought. Nothing to note here, despite my application in keeping account even of the insignificant. Alone my practice of the piano and reading (*Clayhanger* and *Singleton*) save this day from oblivion.

─────────────

[6] The "Treatise of the Dioscuri" does not seem ever to have been published.

[7] *The Life, Adventures, and Piracies of the Famous Captain Singleton,* by Daniel Defoe (1720).

Sunday

My old cat has again given birth, the night before last. Four milk-white little ones with tails shaped like cornets. Upon Em.'s insistence, I make up my mind to do away with two of them. Old Moune took almost no interest in the two others, which we find this morning, one dead of cold on the dining-room mat, the other still in its basket, but hardly breathing and frigid. I warm and revive it somewhat; but when I try to make it suck a scrap of sponge, it becomes obstructed; little bubbles form at the nostrils; the sides rise four or five more times with great effort; then I have nothing but a rag of flesh in my hands. Moune looks on all this without any emotion; her milk has not risen and this is the secret of her indifference. When the milk rises, maternal love begins.

Nothing yet. I am living in expectation of myself. The Drouins came to lunch, as usual.[8] Went back up to my room immediately after the meal. I am letting my beard grow; that is to say that I have not shaved for the last five days; through a need to feel ugly. Ruyters came in the late afternoon; I hardly enjoyed his visit at all; yet he reveals himself a rather good doctor.

I am continuing *Clayhanger* with a growing interest. Wrote my teacher to return; all my hours that I can invest. . . .

The benefit and encouragement I derive from reading the story of the Pope's condemnation of Mgr. Duchesne's *Histoire de l'église*[9] enlighten me somewhat on the secret cause of my unhappiness. Variations on the fear of the *Index*.

Monday

That state of equilibrium is attractive only when one is on a tight-rope; seated on the ground, there is nothing wonderful about it.

This, however, checks my restlessness a bit: the memory of having already gone through such periods of *lack of interest*. Probably it is connected with a physiological state; but I cannot succeed in establishing a relationship. . . . To be always oneself, in mediocrity or genius! . . . From me to me what a distance! This is why I never dare plan or promise anything and never achieve anything without using evasions and deceiving myself, through what shilly-shallying! . . .

---

[8] The last two words appear in English in the text.
[9] The monumental *Histoire ancienne de l'Église* (*Early History of the Church*), in three volumes, by Monsignor Louis Duchesne, began to appear in 1907 and by 1911 had reached a fifth edition.

Tuesday

Last night read *Clayhanger* until midnight. I am greatly disappointed by this book and do not yet grasp its value. It is not a very long stream, but a slow-moving creek. It is not hard to fill eight hundred pages this way. Bennett stops off everywhere with no other apparent reason than to prolong his journey. I am still looking for the reason that made him write this book. Yet I go on.

Begun my English lessons again.

This morning went out for a half-hour. I feel myself a little less negated by myself. And I have even had occasion to think of *Les Caves* again without disgust or revulsion. Piano-practice and reading of *Clayhanger*.

Em. went to see Uncle Charles; didn't find him in, but spent some time talking with the old maidservant, who tells her that in the beginning she could hardly put up with being constantly upbraided by my aunt; that she then became accustomed to it, having discovered that "at bottom Madame is very good"; then she adds: "If I can only stick it out two years more, then I won't even want to change."

Wednesday, 7 February

If I were to disappear right now, no one could suspect, on the basis of what I have written, the better things I still have to write. What temerity, what assumption of a long life, has allowed me always to keep the most important for the end?! Or, on the contrary, what shyness, what respect for my subject and fear of not yet being worthy of it! . . . Thus I put off *La Porte étroite* from year to year. Whom could I persuade that that book is the twin of *L'Immoraliste* and that the two subjects grew up concurrently in my mind, the excess of one finding a secret permission in the excess of the other and together establishing a balance.

Thursday

I have dropped *Clayhanger* (at the hundred and twenty-fifth page), the book becoming less and less good as one gets into it. Resumed *Captain Singleton*, which I am now reading with ease.

Ghéon came to lunch yesterday; his conversation revivified me. After an English lesson we went out together.

Read some *Singleton*, and tried to launch again Julius's visit to Lafcadio.[10] This evening I again feel so tired that I have trouble in writing these few lines and do so only through a sense of duty.

New attacks against me in *L'Indépendance;* new attacks in *Les Marges* (in three places). What perseverance in hatred!

---

[10] An important scene in *Les Caves du Vatican* (*Lafcadio's Adventures*).

At Eugène Rouart's request, I had gone to rue de Lisbonne to get news of Y. and of S. Frightened by the sound of voices and warned by the concierge of the presence of the E.'s and of some foreign bodies, I didn't go up.

Finished the day at Paul Desjardins's, where my fatigue suddenly increased greatly. Where does that insurmountable embarrassment come from that I invariably experience in his presence? And why does he always appear so embarrassed in my presence? He is a self-dominated figure who (for he never lets himself go) always succeeds in being, in any circumstance, just the way he thinks he ought to be; I always feel petty and personal compared with him.

Nothing can express the weariness of my mind.

Friday

To my low physical condition is now added a constant headache and a great intellectual fatigue. I feel desperately far from myself. I had trouble going to sleep and, as the night was drawing to a close, Montfort's hatred and misrepresentation of my thought began to make me suffer so much that I got up to write a preface for *La Porte étroite*. It was not yet five o'clock. I struggled for some time (but how make those understand who will not understand?); then, exhausted, went to bed again fully dressed and sank into sleep.

Yet I went to see Jacques Rivière this morning. How I like and admire the resourcefulness of his intelligence and the grace of his sympathy! Then Alain-Fournier came in and I tried not to cut too poor a figure in his eyes.

This afternoon, after my English lesson, I go to take Paule Gobillard the address of the druggist that Paul Desjardins gave me yesterday, where she can get pitchblende muds. Through weariness I note these little details without attempting to comment.

The friend who came with E. P. to Andermatt had a pointed nose like Alain-Fournier's. Pointed noses: only moderately sensual people.

Saturday, midnight

I start out too late, this first day when I happen to have something else to write but whimperings.

Catholicism is inadmissible. Protestantism is intolerable. And I feel profoundly Christian.

Our Grandfather Rondeaux, of a very Catholic family, but himself an Encyclopedist and admirer of Voltaire, had exacted of Mlle Pouchet, his wife, a very ardent Protestant, that their male children should be

declared Catholic. Later, as a result of some action that he considered
an abuse on the part of the Church . . .

Sunday

The weather is again rainy; my headache this morning probably has
no other cause. Yesterday morning, after weeks of rain, it was fine; immediately I felt better. I went to Jean Schlumberger's to tell him how
desirable I thought it was for the *N.R.F.* to include the Tharaud brothers among its writers. I was thoroughly convinced and talked to him
very enthusiastically about this. Jean, as usual, let me express myself to
the end; and, as it almost always happens, I let myself be convinced by
the contrary argument. Was I really convinced by Jean? No, but properly *resigned*. So that when the afternoon mail brought a letter from
Copeau entirely of my opinion, I ran back to Jean's to urge him to clinch
the matter if there was still time. Fortunately Jean had not found the
Tharauds in, either in the morning or in the afternoon, and had missed
the visit that they, in turn, had come to pay him at about seven o'clock.
Nothing was lost, then. So much the better!

Also went to see Gallimard in the morning.

Already I was beginning to blush for the dismay I had let myself
sink into the last few days and for having, with so little pride, "given
voice to my lamentation." But in the late afternoon, after an English
lesson, with a pretense of exercise and also for want of something better
to do (restlessness also), I went out again; I trailed through the Bois de
Boulogne at great length and some distance, lamentably. The sky was
again quite covered. Copeau's letter restored me (and also one of the
best conversations I have ever had with Em. But of everything concerning Em. I forbid myself to speak here.).

Yesterday evening, opening by chance the little volume of Saint-
Évremond from the Heredia sale, I fall on this sentence: "It is a characteristic of great men never to precipitate anything and never to get impatient over anything. . . . It takes a certain period of time to bring
great plans to maturity. Those who know how to wait are usually paid
with interest for their patience; for, in many things, delaying achieves
more than strength . . ." etc.

"Haste spoils the best-planned undertakings. Whereas patience rip-
ens the most difficult plans and makes their execution easy." (Vol. IV,
pp. 156 and 157.)

Having gone out for a moment yesterday, I let myself be carried
away by curiosity, following the crowd to the stadium of the Parc des
Princes, which I had never entered. For almost an hour I watched a
football game, in which I understood almost nothing. Æsthetics of the

grouping, of the mass, tending to take the place of the æsthetics of the individual. Hideous crowd of spectators.

On getting home I find Ruyters and Pierre de Lanux; Ghéon soon came to join us. He has just come, full of enthusiasm, from a presentation of *Electra* "danced" by Isadora Duncan.

In the evening I read to Em. Iehl's story that I want to put into shape for the *N.R.F.*

Wednesday

Copeau came yesterday; we spent the whole day together from lunch on; he slept at the Villa and only left this morning at eleven o'clock. What good I get from the feeling of his worth! He read me his review of Louis Bertrand; in the evening we went to see Mme Théo, who had just got back from Brussels after spending a week in London. After dinner at the Gaîté Montparnasse we listen to two acts of *La Tour de Nesle*.[11]

The hope of soon going to meet André Benjamin-Constant in Algiers electrifies my every thought.

Saturday, 17 February

I can only note in haste the rather whirlwind life of the last few days. I am writing seated on a bench in the Bois; the weather was radiant this morning; this is the secret of my happiness. But already the sky is clouding over again; I need Apollo; I must set out.

How hard it is for me to remember what I have done since Wednesday!

Let's try: Wednesday afternoon I went to see the Valéry ladies; I had not had the heart to write them the bad news I had received from Switzerland about the Bataglia muds on which Paule G. was counting: those muds are not exported. Then went to pick up Eugène Rouart, who has just got back to Paris. Together we made an excursion to the exhibit of Italian futurists; then went to discover at the M. Bank that Ruyters, whom we hoped to see there, had not been in all day. Right after dinner I rush to ask after him; too late; the whole household is down with grippe.

Thursday morning at Valentine Gilbert's with Em. to liquidate the affairs of Édouard.

After lunch, visit of Verhaeren, then of Élisabeth R. accompanied by her two daughters and a young nationalist poet, who "wanted to meet me." Impossible to recall how I spent the rest of the day. . . .

Oh yes, I can: I had promised to be present at the little lecture that

---

[11] A romantic melodrama by Alexandre Dumas *père*.

Jacques Rivière gives every week at the Gallimards' on French literature. He was to speak that evening on Rabelais and had asked me to
read some passages for him. To tell the truth, I wanted to give the reading and had arranged it so that Jacques would ask it of me; petty pretense that I don't believe took anybody in; everything went off very
well, however; but I had the embarrassment of thinking that Rivière
would have read better than I; of feeling that the others thought so too
and considered my intrusion into their group rather indiscreet, as it in-
dubitably was. I became clearly aware of this as soon as I entered the
drawing-room, and the feeling of my indiscretion deprived me of all
assurance: I read miserably, almost dolefully, modestly, with an air of
excusing myself, a text that on the contrary called for cynicism and
bravura. Well, it's my fault!

Such little mortifications and blows to my vanity are very good
lessons.

Took Ghéon to dinner. He drags me off to spend the evening at the
Théâtre des Arts, where the first performance of *Mrs. Warren's Profession* [12] is being given. I arrived bristling, predisposed against it by the
author's unbearable immodesty. And the first scenes were worse than I
expected; you cannot imagine anything harsher, drier, or more abstract.
But during the second act I let myself be captivated without thinking
of resisting (it is only fair to say that the actress who played Mrs. Warren was excellent). I recovered myself toward the end of the third act.
It is annoying that the fourth should be so bad. What a grimacing art
and what creaking thoughts!

Unable to go to sleep before dawn.

Friday morning I felt obliged to hurry to Jean Schlumberger's to give
him a manuscript by Alibert, hoping that I could satisfy the latter's request still to get into the next number. Not having found Jean, I hastened after Copeau, for whom I had waited in vain at the Occident last
Tuesday. Then, not having found Copeau, I went and rang at Paul
Laurens's studio; he had a model posing and could receive me for only
a moment. Returned to Auteuil having lost the whole morning.

In the evening I took Em. to the first recital of Jean d'Udine's pupils.
It would have been very good if it had not been so mortally long. Being
the first to arrive, we were placed at the very back of the stage; cut off
by twelve rows of audience and kept in place until the end; fearing constantly that Em. was going to feel ill; how I blamed myself for having
taken her there!

(Very ingenious method of solfeggio, making every scale start
with C.)

---

[12] The comedy by George Bernard Shaw.

This morning, article by Sauvebois (?) in *La Critique indépendante* (on Ghéon's book [13]), to which I reply at some length, explaining to him the attitude of the *N.R.F.*

Sunday

The weather is beautiful. If only I could catch hold of myself! Restlessness and not work still fills my days.

Yesterday morning Iehl came to talk to me about his doubtful situation. . . .

"I came to Paris to make up my mind," he says.

Through fear of making someone suffer, and through lack of will, what cruelties one can commit!

Took tea with Em. and worked until evening noting the addresses of our subscribers.

I was expecting Rivière after dinner. We were to go together to Wonderland. Not seeing him come, I was unable to keep myself in the house; I was afraid of my restlessness; I was unable to calm or to satisfy it by going out.

Went to kill an hour at the new cinema near the Pont Mirabeau; then walked for some time; then got on the top deck of a trolley and did not come home until I had gone around the Trocadéro. Absurd. And, back home, I felt even less calm than before.

Monday

We have had Valéry, Ruyters, and Ghéon to lunch; I was so tired that I left them after lunch to go and rest. Valéry and Ruyters were tired themselves. Ghéon too noisy; the conversation produced nothing. What patience my friends must have to put up with me on certain days! The days on which I am most colorless my outbursts are most sudden and most violent; especially with Valéry, as soon as he launches into a question of literature or art, my only desire is to cut it short at once.

At about three o'clock the Piots came, then Paul Dukas, with whom conversation was easier than usual, the first friends having left.

At five o'clock I went to join A. B. at rue de T. He strives to form opinion among those close to him. He succeeds in convincing himself, and his opportunism involves a sort of sincerity. When he gets ready to drop someone, he is likely to say: "The poor fellow. . . . After all, I can console myself by thinking that I did everything I could for him!" and "At least I can tell myself that . . ." Yesterday his political declarations (by this I mean that showy kind of declamation behind which hide intrigue and spite), his noble and empty sentences, so completely

---

[13] *Nos Directions (Our Directions),* a collection of literary essays voicing the æsthetics of the *N.R.F.* group, published in 1911.

clothed his real feelings that I couldn't make out anything sincere or fundamental in his words. For each of his decisions he insists on furnishing a noble motive; he succeeds in persuading himself that that noble thought, which he goes out of his way to exhibit, was the original cause of his deed — even if it were to bring in a fifty-per-cent interest.

"He is the first one taken in by what he says," Em. says to me, and I add:

"I don't want to be the second one."

And it is through his weaknesses, inconsistencies, and shortcomings that he gets himself liked in spite of everything; his best friends are just those who take him least seriously.

He accompanies me to the boulevard Saint-Germain, where we take a cab to go to the rue d'Assas, to Jean Schlumberger's, where the meeting of the *N.R.F.* is being held. Griffin had just left. I find still there Ruyters, Ghéon, Lanux, Gallimard, Bertaux, Alain-Fournier, Duhamel, Vildrac, Pilon, Fargue, etc. Conversation broken up in little groups.

After dinner I busy myself copying into a notebook the list of subscribers to the *N.R.F.*

Morning spent at the office of the *Revue* with Rivière and Ghéon. Afternoon spent almost entirely in insignificant correspondence. This evening I go to pick up Copeau at the P.L.M. station (back from Annecy-Talloires, where he had gone to give an expert opinion on the canvases that Besnard has brought back from India).

Thursday

Copeau's assurance and calm exaltation were a tonic to me.

He left me Tuesday morning to pick up Miomandre, who was to introduce him to Suarès. I went to lunch at the Théos' with Verhaeren and Marianne Delacre, who after lunch sang various melodies of Bach, Beethoven, Schumann, Mozart, which I accompanied. Good conversation about Dickens. At three o'clock Copeau comes to get me; we have to make a rapid decision about Suarès. We agree to do everything to make him join us; and this everything still seems very little to us. Copeau goes back to see Suarès the evening of the same day to make him the *N.R.F.*'s offer — which our *condottiere* accepts with very moving joy and gratitude, Copeau tells me.[14]

Copeau, who has dined at his mother's, comes back in the evening and we stay up late correcting the proofs of his review and reading the

---

[14] The first part of Suarès's *Voyage du Condottière* began to appear in 1911, recounting the travels in Italy of the imaginary modern *condottiere* Jan-Félix Caërdal, who is obviously the author himself.

fragments of *Ajax* and of *Proserpine* that I was planning to give to *Vers et Prose.*[15]

Wednesday morning Copeau goes back to Le Limon; the cab that takes him to his mother's, then to the station, drops me at the house of A. B.

An A. B. in best form, supple and unstarched, for whom my friendship blossoms out again; he talks again of a trip and invites me to join him in Morocco in June. . . .

Very calm afternoon, during which, without exactly working, I get a bit nearer to work.

Valentine dines with us and we go together (with Jeanne, whom we pick up on the way) to the Théâtre des Arts. I stupidly ask for a box; the boxes of the Théâtre des Arts are so ridiculously arranged that one can see only a third of the stage. The nerve of a neighbor who stretches out and leans against the railing of the next box makes me furious. Em.'s whole horizon is formed of his shoulders, and naturally she withdraws, resigns herself; however little one leaves her, it is always enough for her. The worst of it is that she was much better placed before, when she was in the back and could get up; I am the one who made her sit in the front for the second act; if only she would lean forward a little! . . . but in order not to get in the way of her two sisters, she draws back, on the contrary, restricting herself deliberately. . . . I touch the elbow of the man who is in the way; he turns around, and when I signal to him to sit back a little more:

"Why I declare! No, I won't!" he said, thinking moreover that I am protesting only on my own account (like that swaggerer who in the train from Switzerland was amazed to see me smoking and said: "I thought smoking bothered you," the imbecile, because an hour earlier I had begged him not to smoke his nauseating cigar in the compartment where Em. and Jeanne were sitting, but to go to the next compartment, reserved for smokers, where I myself had gone to light my cigarette).

Em. begins to get worried; I am aware that I can no longer control myself; I want to strike out, to shout, to weep; I leave the box trembling all over and go back alone to Auteuil.

Friday

Yesterday morning received Einstein, a little round German who wants to found a new review to struggle for modern tendencies, which he reproaches for something or other. Likable, but still in the pasty state; like all Germans.

[15] These two dramas by Gide were never finished; *Proserpine,* "fragment of a drama," did appear in the issue of *Vers et Prose* for January–March 1912. Years later he returned to this theme and wrote *Perséphone* for Ida Rubinstein.

Iehl comes and I keep him for lunch. I read him the *Récit de Michel* [16] and am helped by his remarks.

After lunch useless wait for Chapon. Tea at the Lerolles'; appalling insignificance of the conversation.

I barely grieve over these various wastes of time; I don't feel good for anything and shall not resume life until some distance from this spot.

(My will has become so weak that the least breath bends it or stands in its way; this morning a charming letter from Papini depicting Vannicola as poor and ill, and already I was setting sail for Florence.)

Saturday, 24 February

Yesterday after dinner I went to Drouin's; then to Ruyters's, without finding him (stayed talking to Mme Ruyters for a quarter of an hour); then to Elie Allégret's. Long conversation on the Chinese revolution, which Elie Allégret considers as "a great step forward on the part of humanity."

He informs me that François de Witt-Guizot took me as whipping-boy in his lecture at *Foi et Vie*.[17] Coming from that direction, any attack strengthens me.

Cuverville, Wednesday

Beautiful weather at last. I let myself be won over by the serenity of this beautiful light, and rest in the certainty of my forthcoming departure.

Copernicus: The wonderful revolution effected by Christianity consists in having said: the kingdom of God is within you. Happy paganism saw no enemy that was not outside man.

The Augean stables, the hydras, the swamps to be cleaned up are *within us*. It is within us that Hercules must labor. Christianity = the inner operation.

Radiant morning of the world; man's powers undivided.

It is altogether that Ajax, suddenly, turns against himself; he no longer finds anything whatever in him to defend itself.

Theseus adventuring, risking himself *amidst* the labyrinth, assured by the secret thread of an inner fidelity . . . etc.

Written in the train, Thursday

My whole day yesterday was spent in copying the subscriptions and the complimentary lists of the *N.R.F.*, of which I had taken the collection of cards with me.

---

[16] *Michel's Tale.* No work by André Gide with such a title has been published.

[17] *Faith and Life* was a highly serious Protestant group of liberal tendency, which also published a periodical of the same name.

At this date we have five hundred and twenty-eight subscribers and we distribute two hundred and forty-four complimentary copies. I note a rather large number of errors in our list.

Driving rain this morning; reinvasion of gray ideas.

The notary comes at ten o'clock and with him Em. and I go to see Mme Freger, who is to sign some deed or other by which she yields the succession of her farm-rent to her son Louis.

Wonderful dignity of the old woman (she has just recovered from pleurisy and wanted to put her affairs in order, though she still has a year and a half of her lease). Near the door, a little apart from the others, her son Louis; he is now twenty-eight. The brothers and brothers-in-law are to get together soon and sign a deed bearing witness to the fact that they consent to the mother's yielding to Louis four thousand francs' worth of furnishings, equivalent to the sum that Eugène, the elder son, received at the time of his marriage, in addition to two thousand francs coming to each of them from the father's estate.

The notary has prepared a letter; but instead of asking Mme Freger simply to sign, he invites her to write above her name: "good for security." The poor old woman, somewhat bewildered, calls her son to her aid; but Louis cannot write for her. The notary offers her a model. Em. has the better idea of writing the letters in lightly in pencil, so that she will only have to cover them in ink. Her hand casts a shadow; she doesn't see very well and twice has to clean her glasses. We urge her to change her place and to sit facing the window; then the notary dictates the letters to her one by one; or says to her: "*o*, a circle; *n*, two downstrokes; two more downstrokes. . . ." And while she is writing, I look at the old wooden table on which the notary has laid the deed, in which successive scourings have hollowed little valleys (where the wood is soft between the harder lines of the grain). So many memories *inscribed* in this table; the story of each one of those spots, of those scratches. . . . What the story of the Freger family must be! Character of the father: the harsh upbringing of his sons, sending them out to gather dung on the roads despite the gibes of passers-by; making a point of honor of always having the best-kept fields in the district; beauty, *nobility*, of that form of avarice; the children taught always to give us the least attractive ·ggs, saving the heaviest ones for the market, etc. . . . Ferocious sense of property: the time he shot at our dog after he had strangled one of their ducks (although Em. had immediately gone to pay them for it) and not trying to hide it; the barbs of the wire fence cut off at the spot where the cows could take advantage of the grass in the avenue by sticking their heads through the fence. Recall the father's childhood, a mere farm-hand in the beginning and *raising* himself by dint of severity. The beauty of his children — the daughter in particular, who now (as always happens) reaches marriage already quite out of shape. The night work in the fine season; the harvesting; the full bucket of cider that Louis, the second of the sons, used to drink daily at that time, whence diarrhea; his shame to admit his illness. The marriages of the elder son, Eugène, planned and missing fire one after another, as Mme Freger related to my brother-in-law: "I don't know how for us to go about it. M'sieur Georges, wouldn't you perhaps ask for her hand in place of us?"

Saturday, 2 March
I leave this evening for Marseille — and Monday sail for Tunis.

* * *

7 May
    Got back ten days ago (the Sunday before last in the evening); I should have gone back to this journal immediately. The very day after my return I went back to work; that is to say, I began to polish the pages of *Les Caves* that I had not gone over. Impatient to show them to Copeau. He came last Friday to spend three days at the Villa. Excellent reading, but it gives me a glimpse of how far I still am from what I owe to myself. My characters, whom I saw in the beginning only as puppets, are gradually filling with real blood and I am not doing my duty by them as easily as I had hoped. They demand more and more, force me to take them more and more seriously, and my original fable reveals itself to be less sufficient. Necessity for tremendous work.

    Visit of Jean-Marc Bernard the morning before yesterday; likable, but more passionate than intelligent; amazingly lacking in culture, like all those nationalists who, under pretense of cultivating only their earth and their dead, are ignorant of almost all the rest of the world. Confesses, moreover, and very nicely, his ignorance and the monstrous lacunæ of his party.

    How he makes me regret again that Lasserre did not write the article on Claudel that he was planning to do. I hope that it will be known later on that he let himself be intimidated by the letters of young men who, terrified by the "howler" he was about to commit, warned him and begged him not to let himself be carried away in the direction he hinted at in closing a preceding article — in which he announced that in his next column he would tell off the author of *L'Arbre*.[18]

    He informs me that Henri Clouard no longer edits *La Revue critique* (I should have known this from the cover), but rather Pierre Gilbert, who annoys them because he has no other criterion than the opinion of Maurras, etc. . . .

---

    [18] In *The Tree,* published in 1901, Paul Claudel gathered together his first five dramas.

Rather embarrassed by the quotation Péguy makes of a sentence from *Isabelle* in his *Mystère des Saints Innocents.*[19] He takes the sentence and sets it in italics, but nothing indicates that it is a quotation. He counts none the less on my gratitude. But I don't know what to say to him; and, in my uncertainty, say nothing.

Anything that turns (or even *can turn*) into a device becomes hateful to me. As soon as the emotion decreases, the pen should stop; when it continues to run on just the same (and it only runs on the more easily), writing becomes detestable. Whole pages of this most recent Péguy, and groups of pages, he could have had written by a secretary; they cease to be *really animated;* they imitate the good ones, those in which the emotion *demanded* this intellectual stuttering.

The craft I wish, may it be so discreetly original, so mysterious, so hidden, that it can never be seized in itself! I should like no one to be aware of me save by the perfection of my sentence and, because of that alone, no one able to imitate it.

I intend to prevent its ever being said of anyone that he is imitating me or that he resembles me (or else that it should be for a very fundamental reason), as it can be currently said today of this or that one: he is indulging in a little Francis Jammes or a little Henri de Régnier, and as it will be said tomorrow: a little Péguy. I don't want to have any *manner* — but that which my subject demands. (What is needed here is the English *but*). Amen.

Written on 8 May

I did not go to Tunis. Met Mme Mayrisch at Marseille. Let the Monday boat leave without me; slept in Toulon; then to Cannes, where I found Valery Larbaud and Arnold Bennett (the latter, installed at the Californie, earns around a thousand francs a day; he is paid at the rate of a shilling a word; he writes without stopping every day from six a.m. to nine a.m., then gets into his bath and doesn't think of his work again until the next morning). Through fear of bad weather and through impatience, I drop Tunisia and head for Florence, where, the very day of my arrival, I manage to get settled at 20 Lungarno Acciaioli in a very pleasant bedroom and sitting-room (*primo piano* on the quay) at three lire a day. I was still so tired and reduced to so little that Vannicola and Papini, whom I saw in the very first days, wondered what I had been suffering from (they have told me this since). I was able to get back to work and to myself only after a week of constant efforts. Nevertheless, little by little, work won me back and I was able to bring my book to the point I had hoped to reach in Italy. Neither churches nor museums (ex-

---

[19] *The Mystery of the Holy Innocents,* by Charles Péguy, a long poem of religious inspiration, appeared in 1912.

cept for Santa Croce and the Etruscan Museum), but I felt that everything was there within reach, ready to consult. Almost daily letter to Em.; voluminous correspondence with Claudel; all my time spent at my table and at my piano, hardly going out except for meals and, in the evening, a bit of a spree. What a city Florence is!! Poor Vannicola's decline. Larbaud comes to join me and considerably upsets my work; but so nice! And how interesting his conversation!

Finally, the 16th, putting all my papers in the drawer, I go to meet Ghéon at Pisa, bring him back to Florence that same evening (a bed is set up for him in my sitting-room), and for six days we lead an amazing, unrelatable life, of inestimable value — interrupted, just as we were going to set out for Siena and Assisi, etc., by the bad news of Ghéon's little niece, which calls him suddenly back to Orsay. I haven't the heart to prolong my trip without him and return at the end of April.

4 June

From 13 May to the 25th, session at the Rouen Assizes.

The value I get from it, to which I had greatly looked forward, goes beyond all hope. I have noted this elsewhere.[20]

During the following week in Paris I unfortunately lost the impetus I had brought back with me. At Cuverville for the last four days, my mind flabby and my style utterly flat.

Cuverville, 7 June

"Fine heads of cabbage, waving their hairy leaves, which look like the ears of great oxen."

This is what I read in *Trois Villes saintes,*[21] which I received yesterday.

The *"hairy* leaves" of cabbage!! Ah! dear M. Baumann, the Virgin must not have had much trouble in appearing to you.

GOSPELS

I consider detestable all moral teachings that are not dictated by the love of humanity — but I tell you that these counsels are dictated by the love of humanity and that, through the apparent and resolute severity of that voice, I feel stirring a great suffering love, that only the dryness of your hearts, O skeptics and rationalists, prevents you from recognizing.

---

[20] See *Souvenirs de la Cour d'Assises* (*Recollections of the Assize Court*). [A.] This volume was published in 1914.

[21] *Three Holy Cities,* by Émile Baumann, a Catholic novelist.

30 June

Beethoven's ample phrase. Absurd habit I had got into of letting the breath drop in the middle. It should swell with a single *inspiration* from one end to the other. It is just a fortnight ago that I became convinced of this (I should even say: that I became aware of it) and I am striving to correct myself to give nuances to the content of the phrase. Important progress.

29 July

I stop two thirds of the way through *Marius the Epicurean;* the advantage I get from it is not what I am looking for in English. Yesterday evening I read one after the other a chapter of *Vanity Fair* and one of *Oliver Twist;* this morning I finish the chapter I had begun of *Captain Singleton.* I am doubtless going to decide in favor of *Vanity Fair.*[22]

Cuverville, 9 October

I had left Cuverville with the intention not to return until November — or not to return at all and to go back directly to Paris. Ruyters, whom I wanted to take along with me to the south, brought me back here, where we dragged out twelve days under the rain and Marcel's bad mood. His hostility toward me, or at least the irritation I cause him, becomes more and more evident; and I believe he is in no way sensitive to the grief I feel about it. Each day I said to myself: I should have done better not to come back; in the future I shall yield the place to him at once.

The end of the month at Pontigny; rather hybrid ten-day period.

Immediately afterward I leave for Italy.

A week in Florence.

A week on the Adriatic (with a cold), at Grottamare, where I finished *Oliver Twist,* and at San-Benedetto.

A fortnight (wonderful) at Acquasanta (where I read *Paradise Lost* and Gosse's *Critical Kit-Kats*).

Return by way of Florence.

10 November

Got back yesterday morning from a visit to Les Sources while Em. is finishing closing Cuverville, which I left the last day of October.

I feel in an excellent mood for work; but disposed rather to read than to write, extraordinarily avid and as on my best days. Found by a miracle, at the scrap-iron fair in Toulouse, a little volume of Spenser in an

---

[22] All these titles are cited in English. *Marius the Epicurean* is by Walter Pater; *Vanity Fair,* by Thackeray; *Oliver Twist,* by Dickens; *Captain Singleton,* by Defoe.

excellent edition with abundant notes and a glossary, in new condition. They ask four sous for it. Rouart insists on giving me the book, which he knows will give me great pleasure. I plunged into it at once; it was exactly the book among all others that I wanted to read just now; but I was impatient to get back to Paris and to my big etymological dictionary by Skeat, which now makes that reading even more attractive. At the same time I am continuing to read *The Mirror of the Sea*.[23]

The Faerie Queene gives me a great desire to tackle Ariosto. Unfortunately, today I was unable to find an hour's rest. This morning I had to go and see old Espinas about the offers that Eugène Rouart is making to his son; lunched very pleasantly at the Ruyters'. What a good afternoon I could have spent with my books! But Ghéon and Drouin were waiting for me at the Villa, then Maurice Desmarest and his wife came. Howbeit, I acted very cordial; but I promised myself to lock myself in my room next Sunday and let my friends get along without me.

Went out with Drouin and Ghéon, to whom I wanted to relate my night at Narbonne with Alibert and the two C. brothers. Wonderful night which put me back on my feet physically and intellectually. The extraordinary overexertion of that night left me in a state of radiant equilibrium.

I was wondering at the ease with which I achieve happiness, and how natural bliss is to me — as I read some article or other in which X. and Y. confessed to having known only two or three moments of perfect happiness in life. The other night, with L. C., this morning with Spenser, first my body, then my mind were as happy as both can be. And what does it matter to me if they were not happy at the same time, since one achieves bliss only while the other sleeps.

11 November

From day to day I put off and carry a little farther into the future my prayer: may the time come when my soul, at last liberated, will be concerned only with God!

This morning at work at six o'clock. Spenser and Skeat, then Conrad. I write to my teacher to resume my lessons.

12 November

Stupid use of my morning (yesterday). I took an auto to save time; went to reserve the little dining-room of the Vian restaurant, where Em. and I can lunch comfortably with the young Iehl couple; then to the *Mercure*, where I did not find Vallette (I was taking back the volume of

---

[23] A collection of essays and reminiscences by Joseph Conrad (1906).

Prétextes [24] corrected for a new printing); then to the *N.R.F.*, where I did not find Rivière; then to rue d'Assas, where I did not find Schlumberger; back at the *N.R.F.*, I learned from Tronche that Rivière no longer came in the morning, but in the afternoon. I went after him at his place on the rue Froidevaux; he was working on the sequel to his article on Faith, of which we talked at some length. I repeated to him the word of Christ that is opposed to his article, and as I was reading it, I kept hearing within me: "No man cometh unto the *Father* but by *me*." And I want to take these words literally, which Rivière does not appreciate.

I thought also of going to find Bourdelle, who wanted to show me his new work; but I didn't have time.

Charming lunch with the Iehls. I come home and close myself in to work until evening in a state so close to bliss that I wish for nothing better here below.

I have read much of Jusserand's *Histoire de la littérature anglaise* [25] and made synoptic tables. Worked wildly on Skeat. Read before going to bed Keats's notes on *Paradise Lost* and the quotations he makes from it.

Today I have not left the house; distracted from work only by my correspondence and various tidyings-up.

Begun my English lessons again. But the worthy W. W., my teacher of last year, now seems to me sinisterly insufficient. He could not believe that I had read the whole of *Paradise Lost*.

13 November

I discover *Hero and Leander* [26] and, dazed with intoxication, penetrate that ardent and magnificent poetry.

Keats, to whom I want to return next (*Endymion*), seems to me in comparison, I am ashamed to write it, almost cold and colorless, and especially so subtle in his rhythm that he often eludes one through his delicacy.

Went to the baths this morning. Worked the rest of the day.

Thursday, 14

Very bad, dissipated day. Receive a letter from Copeau, who urges me to come right away to Le Limon.

---

[24] Originally published in 1903, *Pretexts* contains the two lectures on influence and on the limits of art, the series of three articles on Barrès and "uprooting," and some articles and book reviews on contemporary subjects. Most of the contents had appeared in *L'Ermitage*.

[25] *History of English Literature.*

[26] By Christopher Marlowe (1598).

Friday

I spend the whole day at Le Limon with Jacques Copeau — who reads me the first act of *La Maison natale*.²⁷ I come back somewhat braced up.

Monday, 18

This evening great effort to get back to work on *Les Caves*, but too many preoccupations have disorganized my thought. No matter; I keep at it, knowing well that the fruit of one's effort is not harvested at the moment.

My day is already completely mortgaged: at ten a.m. I am to meet Eugène Rouart, and until four o'clock we talk business (organization of the corporation to exploit the Seintein mines; formation of the Electrolysis Corporation, etc. . . .). I come home done in.

What interest can there be in noting all this? Yet I force myself to do so, hoping to find in the very boredom that I feel in going over these dull days some weapon against myself. Meanwhile, I have nevertheless somewhat progressed in my work; but to get ahead properly with *Les Caves*, the study of English must be neglected. I have, however, finished the amazing *Hero and Leander* — and continued *The Faerie Queene*.

19 November

Went to see Paul Claudel yesterday at his sister's. He receives me with great cordiality. I enter right away the little room he is occupying, which is dominated by a crucifix above the bed.

Paul Claudel is more massive, wider than ever; he looks as if he were seen in a distorting mirror; no neck, no forehead; he looks like a power-hammer. The conversation immediately starts on the subject of Rimbaud, whose complete works in one volume prefaced by Claudel, which the *Mercure* has just published, are on the table. He has recently had an opportunity to talk with some employee or business representative who, for some period of time, had frequented Rimbaud at Dakar or Aden; ²⁸ who depicted him as an absolutely insignificant creature, spending all his days in smoking, sitting on his haunches in the Oriental man-

---

²⁷ *The Family Homestead,* a three-act drama of bitter misunderstanding within a family, on which Copeau worked for fifteen years; it was finally presented at his own Théâtre du Vieux-Colombier in December 1923.

²⁸ After renouncing literature in 1873 at the age of nineteen, Arthur Rimbaud lived as an adventurer until he settled in Harar, Abyssinia, in 1880 as representative of a French firm of Aden. By Dakar André Gide doubtless means Harar.

ner, telling silly gossip stories when he had a visitor, and occasionally putting his hand in front of his mouth as he laughed the sort of private laugh of an idiot. At Aden he used to go out bareheaded under the hot sun at hours when the sun on one's head is like a blow from a club. At Dakar he lived with a native woman, by whom he had had a child, or at least a miscarriage, "which is enough to upset" (says Claudel) "the imputations of homosexuality still occasionally attached to his name; for if he had had such tastes (and, it seems, nothing is more difficult to cure), it goes without saying that he would have kept them in that country where they are accepted and facilitated to such an extent that all the officers, without exception, live openly with their boy."

As I chide him for having, in his study, glossed over the ferocious side of Rimbaud's character, he says he wanted to depict only the Rimbaud of the *Saison en enfer*, in whom the author of *Les Illuminations* was to *result*.[29] Led, for a moment, to speak of his relations with Verlaine, Claudel, with an absent look, touches a rosary in a bowl on the mantel.

He talks of painting with excess and stupidity. His speech is an unceasing flow that no objection, no interrogation even, stops. Any other opinion than his own has no justification and almost no excuse in his eyes.

The conversation, by a natural slope, reaches matters of religion; he rises up violently against the group of Catholic politicians of the Action Française,[30] then against Sorel and Péguy, whose "motives he begins to understand better."

In too great a hurry to get back to my book, I cannot note here all the turns of our conversation.

22 November

A few letters this morning painfully remind me that today I am entering my forty-fifth year.

Yesterday, in the late afternoon, after a rather good period of work, I went to Paul Desjardins'; Thierry was there and soon Pierre Hamp arrived. Thierry said nothing during the whole time. Paul Desjardins read us Milton's wonderful sonnet on his blindness. Pierre Hamp began to attack the "tendencies" of the *N.R.F.*, which I defended rather bitterly and at much too great length, losing my footing (or my head) several times, especially after Pierre Hamp alluded to a new attack by Variot in

---

[29] Rimbaud's two great works are the poems in verse and prose of *The Illuminations* and the prose *Season in Hell*.

[30] The Royalist group of L'Action Française, with its newspaper of the same name, remained militantly Catholic even after its leader, Charles Maurras, was censured by the Vatican.

L'Indépendance apropos of Ghéon's article on Francis Jammes. I knew nothing of that attack and for several minutes was unable to pay attention to Pierre Hamp. All this leading me on, I prolonged my visit beyond the limits of decency, not having grasped at once that Hamp and Thierry were staying to dinner. Finally Paul Desjardins got up and discreetly left me with the two others (perhaps to ask that a place be set for me, or to notify me indirectly, or merely to go and wash his hands). Immediately I looked at my watch and hastened toward the hallway, where Paul Desjardins joined me, smothering me with thanks according to his custom.

On getting home I find a note from Vannicola, who announces his arrival. What is that unfortunate fellow coming to Paris for? I write him at once that I shall go and lunch with him tomorrow; very sorry, however, to cut into a day that I hoped to be able to devote entirely to work. After the business letters that I had to write in the evening, I wonder if I shall manage to get to sleep.

23 November

Slept well; thanks perhaps to a generous libation of orange-flower water. Work all morning. At one o'clock Iehl arrives, who is returning to Fronton two days from now. I go out with him to pick up Vannicola at his hotel, lunch with him, then, as soon as possible, get back to Auteuil to work. I write the greater part of the conversation between Julius and Lafcadio after the crime, without too much nervous irritation, but incapable of judging right away the quality of what I have written. Perhaps when I reread it tomorrow, I shall find it abominable; nevertheless, I think at least that the general outline of the scene is good.

Em. went to see Allain at the house of education where he is still being kept. She gets back at about tea-time with a number of *L'Opinion*, which she bought to read on the way, expecting to find in it Pierre de Lanux's article on Serbia. Instead she falls upon Pierrefeu's article against Iehl and against me, which infuriates her; but the article is written in such a way that on the contrary it greatly encourages me. Such disparagements, instead of crushing me, exalt me, and even more completely than praises.[31] After dinner, I go back to work after having finished the second canto of *The Faerie Queene*, of which I read a few stanzas to Em.

---

[31] I write to Pierrefeu: "Sir, a single thing displeases me in your article: the reproach you make me of seeking to hide what I owe to Dostoyevsky. I have the greatest gratitude toward Dostoyevsky and yet cannot proclaim it any louder than I have done, not having, as you have said, a strong voice. I beg, etc. . . ." (And I enclosed with my letter my booklet on Dostoyevsky.) [A.]

Stupidly, after a good session of work, not making up my mind to go to bed yet, I go back to reading Conrad, then Spenser again — and this considerably upsets my night. Great trouble going to sleep afterward, and for a sleep all shot full of holes.

. . . .

Rather good work all these last days; I interrupt this journal, which is reduced to the dull notation of facts. Good solely as a way of getting into the habit of writing.

1913

Yesterday evening reread fifty pages of *La Porte étroite;* each time I pick up that book again, I do so with an indescribable emotion; but if the dialogues, the letters, and Alissa's journal strike me as excellent — as well turned out as possible — on the other hand the intervening passages are not devoid of preciosity. Could it be said that the subject demanded this? Then I should have taken another subject. I no longer want to choose a subject that does not permit, that does not require, the frankest, the easiest, and the most beautiful style.

Monday, 19 May

Back from Italy since last Wednesday.

Everything I am writing this morning should have been noted earlier, but I didn't have time. This work of simplification, of arrangement, in which my mind engages in spite of myself in regard to everything it takes up — excellent exercise if it leads to the work of art — is deplorable here where the particular is more important than the essential.

Interrupted again in the very first lines (went with Em. to see the David exhibit and the Bonnard exhibit). This evening my ink is muddy and my pen blunted. Before writing the first word of my sentence I wait until the whole sentence has taken shape in my head; deplorable; rather the incorrect expression. Need of rereading some Stendhal. Dare to write without order.

21 May

First finish my book.[1] Spurn everything that distracts me from it.

Cuverville, 24 June

Finished *Les Caves* yesterday. Doubtless there will still be much to change after I have given it to Copeau to read and in the proofs. Odd book; but I am beginning to be fed up with it. I cannot yet realize that it is finished and can't stop thinking of it. More than one passage in the first and second books seem to me weak or forced . . . but I think the hardest parts are also the best-turned-out.

Of late I have been able to work only in a very broken-up fashion, constantly leaving my pen for an English book or for my piano.

I have gone back to Chopin's Barcarolle and Bach's *Two-Part Inventions.*

Since *The Way of All Flesh,* I have read much Keats, resumed *Mar-*

---

[1] *Les Caves du Vatican* (*Lafcadio's Adventures*).

ius the Epicurean at the point where I had dropped it last year. Aloud we have just finished George Eliot's very ordinary *Amos Barton*. Now we are reading *The Merry Men* with delight.[2]

26 June

It seems to me at times that I have never yet written anything serious; that I have always presented my thought in an ironic manner, and that, were I to disappear today, I should leave an image of myself from which even my guardian angel could not recognize me.

(The belief in angels is so disagreeable to me that I hasten to add that this is only a manner of speaking — but one that expresses my thought rather well.)

Perhaps, after all, my belief in the work of art and the cult that I make of it prevent that perfect sincerity which I henceforth demand of myself. What interest have I in any limpidity that is not a quality of style?

29 June

Every day I read a chapter of *Marius the Epicurean* (with the greatest delight); aloud, for an hour, *The Merry Men;* I spend from three to five hours (and more often five than three) in piano-practice (exclusively Bach and Chopin). When one adds Ransome's book on Wilde, some Milton, some Keats, some Byron, etc., plus the correspondence, which every day takes one or two hours more, there is hardly any time left for personal work. I am putting it off until I travel again, when I shall have neither the piano nor any reading to finish.

Ransome's book strikes me as good — and even very good in spots. Perhaps he admires a bit too much the trappings with which Wilde liked to cover his thought and which still seem to me rather artificial — and on the other hand he fails to show to what a degree the plays *An Ideal Husband* and *A Woman of No Importance* are revelatory — and I was about to say confidential — despite their apparent objectivity.

Certainly in my little book on Wilde I was not altogether just to his work and turned up my nose at it too readily — I mean before having known it sufficiently. As I think it over I wonder at the good grace with which Wilde listened to me when, in Algiers, I criticized his plays (very impertinently it seems to me today). No impatience in the tone of his reply, and not even a protest; it was then that he was led to say to me, almost as an excuse, that extraordinary sentence which I quoted and which has since been quoted everywhere: "I put all my genius into my life; I put only my talent into my works." I should be interested to know if he ever said that sentence to anyone else but me.

---

[2] *The Way of All Flesh* is by Samuel Butler; *Marius the Epicurean*, by Walter Pater; and *The Merry Men*, by R. L. Stevenson.

Later on I hope to return to the subject and relate everything that I didn't dare tell at first. I should like, too, to *explain* Wilde's work in my own way, and especially his drama – of which the greatest interest lies between the lines.

2 July

I have been busy these last few days writing a fair copy of my *Souvenirs de la Cour d'Assises*. It is, I think, a very good exercise and I am taking the greatest interest in it. My imminent departure makes me positively ill; at moments I hope that the situation in the Balkans will become worse so that it will be impossible for me to go.

I tried to return to *Trois Hommes* by Suarès, but his grandiloquence gets on my nerves.[3] I know too well and feel too clearly that he has known Dostoyevsky for only a short time, that he discovered him only after a conversation we had together, in which I complained that he seemed to pay attention only to Tolstoy. All the pathos of the beginning of his portrait is there only as a cover; he doesn't want it to be apparent that he has not always admired Dostoyevsky. Perhaps when he gets to him it will be the same with Goethe.

He says some extraordinarily perspicacious things about Dostoyevsky, such as only he can say today; but it is monstrous to remove Dostoyevsky as far as possible from Nietzsche only to bring him closer to – Wagner!

3 July

Yesterday evening, after dinner, my eyes tired, I was seated on the bench in front of the house watching the cats play, when Mius's voice rang out:

"Ah, what a game! Ah, what fun we are going to have!"

However gloomy and old-appearing, Mius, at moments, recovers all his youth; quivering with joy, he lays his rat-trap on the steps. A big female and seven little ones are caught in it. You can imagine what that family walk must have been, at twilight, with this catastrophe as its conclusion. The little ones are charming and don't seem very frightened, but the mother, who knows something about life, is furious; she jumps heavily against the wires, hurting her snout; she leaps, not to get away, but aggressively to throw herself on us. At each leap she utters an odd little war-cry. Em., whose heart is wrung at the thought of the carnage about to ensue, runs away as is her wont. The dogs are wildly excited; they are making such a rumpus that eventually they have to be locked

---

[3] The subjects of *Three Men* (1913) are Pascal, Ibsen, and Dostoyevsky.

up. Jeanne and the two maids have come running; Mius, they, and I gather around the cage, like the gods leaning over human misery.

"Well, how are we going to kill them?" Mius finally asks.

Marthe suggests pouring boiling water on them.

"No," says Mius, "I'm going to get my knife."

"You must try to keep them from suffering too much," says P., ordinarily so foolish, but who seems enlightened in this circumstance.

"Too bad for them! It serves them right," exclaims Juliette, the gardener's wife, two of whose rabbits the rats have eaten; "all they had to do was not to harm us."

"But they don't know that what they do is harmful," says P.

I hold myself in check to keep from upsetting the trap as if by accident; and choosing the least evil, I suggest dropping the cage into a bucket of water.

The little ones did not resist for long. But the mother's suffering went on longer than I should have thought. She leapt about frightfully; occasionally you could see a new air bubble rise to the surface. Finally her lungs were filled; all together it lasted three minutes.

10 July

I had to interrupt my work and leave Cuverville to go and get little D. These four days in Paris have done me in. I cannot collect my ideas, nor especially my self-confidence. The article that I just about promised Rivière I do not feel capable of writing; I should like, I *ought*, to travel. I spend my best hours clearing up the passages in *Les Caves* with which Copeau was not entirely satisfied; I have great trouble doing so and succeed only after terrible nervous irritation. Rivière's article on the "novel of adventure," which I read this afternoon, adds to my confusion; he says in it almost what I should have liked to say in my article and much better than I could have done.[4] In two days the arrival of the young people A. and D. will finish upsetting me.

* * *

Trip to Italy. Sojourn at Tivoli, at Vallombrosa, at Santa Margherita.

I reproach myself bitterly for not having gone to see poor old Papa La Pérouse as I went through Paris on my return journey. Probably he has no one to hold out a hand to him and is wallowing about in the darkness.

---

[4] Rivière's long article on the psychological novel of adventure, which appeared in the *N.R.F.* for June and July 1913, may have been inspired by the recent novel of his friend Alain-Fournier, *Le Grand Meaulnes* (*Big Meaulnes*), but it was prophetic as regards the literature of the twenties.

2 September
At that time he used to repeat to himself, not without anguish, that the last act would perhaps not be a comedy ending and that life would fail him, not even all at once in screams and tears, which still involve a sort of glory and solemnity, but slowly in silence.

He felt all his faculties weakening and wildly regretted all the joys and all the beauty of life that he had not hugged to his flesh and to his heart.

4 September
The most extraordinary visions — he will have them when he is no longer in a state to describe them. . . .

Milton's blindness is frightful; but how much more horrible is Baudelaire's loss of speech!

8 September
I long ago became reconciled to not having anything glorious in my manner. If only the work is born, even at the price of a tremendous effort! . . .

25 September
Excellent visit of Paul A. Laurens and his wife (they spend four days with us); I talk with him as of old. I read him *Les Caves*. He recalls that I already talked to him about it at Biskra; that is farther back than I remembered.

It seems to me that everything I have written up to now has been nothing but barking and outside show before the *real* show begins and that it is only now that the public is going to enter the booth.

3 October
Much pretense in all this. My satisfaction on seeing them is great; but I play it up and my laugh is artificial.

Paris, 2 November
Ten days of otitis and partial deafness. Excellent condition for work. Tomorrow my secretary begins work and a new regime starts.

This morning visit to poor Papa La Pérouse. I am noting the conversation elsewhere.

17 November
Since 3 November a secretary has been coming every morning. I work with her from nine to eleven thirty and she types from two to five what she took down from dictation in the morning. (*Souvenirs de la*

Cour d'Assises and translation of the *Gitanjali*.[5]) I cannot find a minute for the piano, alas! Go almost every day to swim for an hour at rue de Chazelles — which makes me feel very good. Reading of English is almost abandoned for a while; I have great trouble finishing *The Master of Ballantrae*.[6] Odd book in which everything is excellent, but heterogeneous to such a degree that it seems the sample card of everything in which Stevenson excels.

If Montfort's animosity toward me deserves to interest scholars some day, I should like us not to be judged without a knowledge of the full text of Charles-Louis Philippe's letters to Van de Putte. Then it will be seen whether the passages I suppressed are likely to embarrass Montfort or me.

DETACHED PAGES

I mean to speak of the rules.

If it is true that genius escapes the rules, this puts me at ease.

I was just seeking in what way that genius escapes which I so often see anxious to force into the strictest forms the impulse least likely to submit to authority; and I shall try to find out why.

Art is just as far from turmoil as from apathy.

Neuchâtel

How much I love this calm lake ringed by low shores and peopled by gulls, where neither my eyes nor my mind encounters anything accidental or foreign!

How does it happen that I, generally so susceptible to cold, felt nothing but comfort this morning seated on the bench when it was barely five degrees above freezing, and with nothing in front of me but water and fog? I should be glad to live here.

That abominable effort to take one's sin with one to paradise.

Beware of artistic protestations; the real artist does not sport a red waistcoat and is not eager to talk of his art. Among those who shout so loud, you can be sure that there are not many who, to the immediate success of Pradon, preferred the attentive perfection of the other *Phèdre*.[7]

---

[5] Gide translated from the English the *Gitanjali* (1912) of the Bengali poet Sir Rabindranath Tagore.

[6] A romance by R. L. Stevenson (1889).

[7] A cabal organized by the Duchesse de Bouillon and her brother the Duc de Nevers produced Pradon's inferior play, *Phèdre et Hippolyte*, simultaneously with Racine's *Phèdre* (1677), and assured its success by buying out the house at both theaters for the first six performances.

Indeed, he cannot doubt of our affection; but perhaps he is not yet aware how much pride, ambition, and exigence it involves.

The scent of the hay near Pavia.
The oleanders near Genoa.

The truth is that, as soon as the need to provide for it ceases to force us, we don't know what to do with our life and we waste it wantonly.

NOVEL

Almost at the start of the book, dining together in a restaurant, they examine the wrinkles they *will have*.

Hasn't there been any bankruptcy in their life, any surrender — any renunciation?

He who protests will later on make of the ability to renounce the wisdom of his whole life.

(That too can be a rule of conduct based on complacency.)

The fox with his tail cut off: he who pretends to have wanted and to prefer everything that happens to him; from this alone he wins a reputation for wisdom.

The friend to whom he had confided his youthful dreams is well aware that this is a form of bankruptcy.

Establish the bankruptcy of Christianity — those who wanted to practice it had to withdraw from the world; Christianity was unable to form a world in the image of Christ as Buddha or Mohammed did — show that this is the *superiority* of Christ. But Catholicism set out to form a society and succeeds in doing so only by getting rid of Christ.

(All this wants to be said very mildly; horror of the tone of voice that belongs to the dispenser of justice or to the revolutionary.)

That the first duty of the Christian is to be happy; and so long as he has not achieved happiness he has not put into practice the teaching of Christ. — Christ's wonderful words: "Why weepest thou?" (To be commented on.)

Richard Feverel, *waking up* after the accident (it is essential that the accident should be caused by love), has completely forgotten that he had reached happiness (the odd feeling he has however: apprehension).

Subject: the two lovers who wake up after having drunk of Lethe (but one after the other).

They will not begin their love all over again — quite the contrary.
. . . If they disliked each other. (She, sure of the past love, of which he is ignorant, seems *bold* to him.)

CAVES

Funeral of Fleurissoire.

I must put:

In the first carriage: Blaphafas and the widow. (Conversation.)

In the second carriage: Mme Armand-Dubois and the Countess de Baraglioul.

In the third: Anthime Armand-Dubois, Baraglioul.

CHOPIN

For Beethoven surely the *quantity* of sound is important; for Chopin only the *quality* (pianissimo in the Barcarolle).

No more limpid diamond.

No pearl of finer water.

(To say after the Algiers night in the *Mémoires*.[8])

How often the joy of love, particularly the most charming, left me in such an exasperated, atrocious delirium of all the senses that, for a long time afterward, I could not relax and overexerted my frenzy, not consenting to be released, to take leave of the instant, but insatiably avid and as if pursuing through pleasure something beyond pleasure.

---

[8] Gide commonly refers to his *Si le grain ne meurt* (*If It Die* . . .) as his *Memoirs*. This volume was openly published in 1926; a private printing, without name of publisher, had been made in 1920–1.

Glossary of Persons

MENTIONED IN THE JOURNALS

N.B. Not all the names listed in the Index are to be found in this
Glossary. Servants, tradesmen, chance acquaintances, and others sufficiently identified in the text — together with the most famous in all domains — have been omitted here. Other names have simply resisted
research.

Originally intended to identify the specifically French names that
are presumably known to the author's compatriots, the Glossary has
grown in the making to include all the persons about whom English-
speaking readers might have questions.

André Gide and his friends have been most helpful in supplying
information.

J. O'B.

ADAM, PAUL (1862–1920), French novelist of manners and history
(*La Force, Le Lion d'Arras*) and dramatist.

ALAIN-FOURNIER (1886–1914), French poetic novelist of charming
fancy, killed at the front soon after his first work, *Le Grand Meaulnes,* had established his genius.

ALBERT, HENRI (1869–1921), French writer of the symbolist movement, editor of the quarterly review *Le Centaure* (1894–6), which
published Gide, Valéry, Régnier, etc.; translator of Nietzsche.

ALBINONI, TOMMASO (1674–1745), Italian composer of nearly fifty
operas and many instrumental works.

ALIBERT, FRANÇOIS-PAUL (1873–   ), French poet of Virgilian
temper, strongly influenced by Mallarmé.

ALLÉGRET, ANDRÉ, second son of Élie Allégret, with whom André
Gide traveled in Corsica (1923).

ALLÉGRET, ÉLIE, Protestant minister, tutor of André Gide and best
man at his wedding. Founded the French mission at Talagouga in
the Gaboon and later became director of the Center of French Protestant Missions. Of his five children, André Gide adopted the third,
Marc.

ALLÉGRET, JEAN, eldest son of Élie Allégret; died of tuberculosis at
Arcachon.

ALLÉGRET, MARC, third son of Élie Allégret; adopted by André
Gide, whom he accompanied on trip to the Congo (1925–6). Excellent scenario-writer, author of *Lac aux dames.*

AMYOT, JACQUES (1513–93), French humanist, tutor to the sons of
Henri II, and translator of Plutarch.

ANDLER, CHARLES (1866–1933), French professor of history and
political economy, who specialized in the subject of modern Germany.

ANDRÉÆ, DR., Swiss doctor whom André Gide first consulted in Geneva in 1894 and whom he considers responsible for having cured him of a lung infection.

ANDRIAN, LEOPOLD (1875–   ), Austrian diplomat and poet of Catholic and philosophical nature, appreciated for his prose treatise *Der Garten der Erkenntnis* (1895).

APOLLINAIRE, GUILLAUME (1880–1918), French poet, story-teller, and art critic of great talent and originality, who wrote on cubism, discovered many modern painters, and created the word *surréalisme*.

ARVERS, FÉLIX (1806–50), French poet known for only one sonnet, which is in most anthologies, "The Secret."

ATHMAN (*ca.* 1897–   ), Arab youth whom André Gide met at Biskra in 1893 and again in 1895, and whom he brought to Paris in 1899.

AUDOUX, MARGUERITE (1865–1937), French realistic novelist who related her working-class life most vividly in *Marie-Claire* (1910). She belongs to the new tradition of Lucien Jean, C.-L. Philippe, and Émile Guillaumin.

BAHR, HERMANN (1863–1934), Austrian critic, novelist, and dramatist who founded in 1891 the *Jungwein* group, became the spokesman of the new expressionism, and wrote such successful plays as *The Concert.* He directed the Deutsches Theater of Berlin.

BANVILLE, THÉODORE DE (1823–91), French poet of *Odes funambulesques* and dramatist of *Gringoire*. Disciple of Théophile Gautier and exponent of art for art's sake.

BARBEY D'AUREVILLY, JULES (1808–89), French poet, novelist, and critic of originality and colorful personality.

BARRÈS, MAURICE (1862–1923), French novelist who early won a place of distinction through his youthful "cult of the ego" and then evolved into a traditionalist and advocated "the cult of the earth and the dead"; his novels of Alsace-Lorraine preached a return to regionalism and expressed his ardent nationalism.

BARTET (pseud. of Jeanne-Julia Régnault, 1854–1941), French actress, chiefly of tragic roles, at the Comédie-Française from 1879 until her retirement in 1919.

BARTHOLOMÉ, PAUL-ALBERT (1848–1928), French sculptor, most famous for his Monument to the Dead in the Père-Lachaise cemetery, Paris.

BAUER, HENRY (1852–?), French dramatist and author of essays on Nietzsche.

BAUMANN, ÉMILE (1868–1941), French Catholic novelist of sin and redemption.

BAYARD, PIERRE DU TERRAIL, SEIGNEUR DE (1476–1524), the French knight "without fear and without reproach."

BEAUNIER, ANDRÉ (1869–1925), French novelist and critic, who for many years wrote most of the literary criticism in the *Revue des deux mondes.*

BELLINI, VINCENZO (1802–35), Italian composer of operas.

BENDA, JULIEN (1867–), French philosopher and essayist, who has consistently defended intellectualism against Bergson and Sorel. His most famous work is *La Trahison des clercs* (1927).

BENJAMIN-CONSTANT, ANDRÉ, French bookseller in Algiers; son of the once famous painter, Jean-Joseph Benjamin-Constant and close friend of Jacques Copeau.

BÉRENGER, RENÉ (1830–1915), French jurist and political figure, Senator from 1875 until his death, who consistently raised his voice against pornography, white slavery, and immorality.

BERGSON, HENRI (1859–1941), French philosopher of "creative evolution," who exalted the faculty of intuition over the pure intellect.

BERNARD, JEAN-MARC (1881–1915), French poet and critic of the neo-classical movement, who was one of the founders and editors of the little review *Les Guêpes* (1909–12). He was killed at the front.

BERNARD, TRISTAN (1866–), French comic dramatist, famous especially for *L'Anglais tel qu'on le parle, Le Petit Café, Triple-patte.*

BERNARDIN DE SAINT-PIERRE (1737–1814), French disciple of Rousseau and pre-romantic writer, whose sentimental novel *Paul et Virginie* (1787) sounded a new note in literature.

BERNHARDT, SARAH (1844–1923), French actress.

BERNSTEIN, HENRY (1876–), French dramatist of great force and wide popularity (*Le Secret, La Jalousie, Judith*).

BERTAUX, ÉMILE (1869–1917), French historian of art, appreciated for his studies of Rome, Donatello, Hugo as an artist, etc.

BERTHELOT, PHILIPPE (1866–1934), French diplomat who after numerous successful missions became director of political affairs (1919) and general secretary (1920) of the Ministry of Foreign Affairs.

BERTRAND, LOUIS (1866–1941), French novelist of the Mediterranean area and exponent of Latin imperialism; elected to the French Academy in 1926.

BESNARD, PAUL ALBERT (1849–1934), French painter of the impressionist school and engraver.

BLANCHE, JACQUES-ÉMILE (1861–1942), French painter, known especially for his portraits, who also wrote his interesting recollections.

BLEI, FRANZ (1871–), Austrian writer who, besides other translations from English and French, translated Gide's *Bethsabé*, *Prométhée*, and *Roi Candaule* into German; founder of the review *Hyperion*.

BLOY, LÉON (1846–1917), French Catholic novelist and essayist of passionate, iconoclastic vigor, most famous for the eight volumes of his journal (1898–1920).

BLUM, LÉON (1872–), critic, essayist, and political figure. Member of the Council of State (1895), president of the Socialist Party; director of the newspaper *Le Populaire* (1921–40); Prime Minister (1936–7, 1938 and 1946).

BONHEUR, RAYMOND, French composer, great friend of Carrière, Samain, Jammes, etc. André Gide wrote the first act of a light opera scenario for him, but the project was dropped before completion.

BONNARD, PIERRE (1867–1947), French painter and illustrator of the impressionist school.

BONNEFON, JEAN DE (1866–1928), French popular historian and journalist.

BOUGAINVILLE, LOUIS-ANTOINE DE (1729–1814), French mathematician, diplomat, and military man, fought under Montcalm at Québec, explored the South Pacific, fought in the American Revolutionary War, and became a Senator under Napoleon. The relation of his *Voyage around the World* was made famous by Diderot's philosophic "Supplement" to it.

BOUHOURS, FATHER (1628–1702), French literary critic and arbiter of style at the height of the classic period.

BOUILHET, LOUIS (1822–69), French poet of mixed romantic and realistic tendencies, popularizer of Oriental exoticism, and friend of Flaubert.

BOURDELLE, ÉMILE-ANTOINE (1861–1929), French sculptor of monumental stylized allegories, who also painted and wrote.

BOURGES, ÉLÉMIR (1852–1925), French critic and idealistic novelist of lyric symbolistic works, such as *Le Crépuscule des dieux* (1884).

BOURGET, PAUL (1852–1935), French novelist, dramatist, and essayist, who with Anatole France and Maurice Barrès dominated the literary scene before the first World War. His most characteristic novels are the psychological study *Le Disciple* (1889) and the sociological thesis *L'Étape* (1902).

BOUTS, DIERIK (1410?–75), Dutch painter.

BOYLESVE, RENÉ (1867–1926), one of the masters of the French psychological novel (*La Becquée*, *L'Enfant à la balustrade*).

BRANDON, MME, friend of André Gide's mother, whose literary and artistic *salon* was the first he frequented.

BRASSEUR, ALBERT-JULES (1862–1932), popular French comic actor of the Théâtre des Variétés.

BRAÜNIG, teacher in charge of the lower classes at the École Alsacienne, which Gide attended as a boy.

BRÉAL, AUGUSTE, son of the eminent philologist Michel Bréal; French painter who studied under Gustave Moreau, and author of a penetrating study of Velázquez.

BRÉVAL, LUCIENNE (1869–1935), Swiss-born French soprano of the Paris Opéra and Opéra-Comique.

BRIAND, ARISTIDE (1862–1932), French statesman, who repeatedly occupied the most important ministries and was twelve times Premier, working consistently from the Armistice until his death for international peace (Locarno, Thoiry, and the League of Nations).

BRION, MARQUISE DE, sister of the German diplomat and æsthete Count Harry von Kessler; intellectual and social center of the German colony in Paris before 1914.

BRISSON, ADOLPHE (1860–1925), French literary and drama critic.

BROGLIE, PRINCESSE DE, famous in the nineties and early years of this century for her great beauty and unusual, rich costumes.

BRUNEAU, ALFRED (1857–1934), French composer and music critic of *Le Matin,* famous for his lyrical dramas such as *Le Rêve* and others based on Émile Zola's novels.

BRUNETIÈRE, FERDINAND (1849–1906), scholarly French critic and historian of literature, who applied theories of evolutionism to literary genres such as the novel, poetry, criticism, the theater.

BRUNOT, FERDINAND (1860–1938), French linguistic historian and honorary dean of the Paris Faculty of Letters, whose monumental *History of the French Language* in 15 volumes appeared from 1905 to 1935.

BRUNSCHWICG, LÉON (1869–1944), French philosopher known for his studies of Spinoza and Pascal as well as for his analyses of the philosophy of the sciences.

BUFFON, GEORGES LOUIS LECLERC, COMTE DE (1707–88), French naturalist.

BURCKHARDT, JACOB (1818–97), German historian, author of *The Civilization of the Renaissance in Italy.*

BURNAND, ROBERT (1882–   ), French journalist and author of books on London, Reims, *Paris Restaurants,* etc. Great friend of Paul Gide.

BURNE-JONES, SIR EDWARD (1833–98), English painter of the romantic school, a friend of Rossetti and William Morris.

CABANIS, GEORGES (1758–1808), French doctor and materialistic philosopher.

CAPUS, ALFRED (1858–1922), popular Parisian dramatist of witty light comedies.

CARPEAUX, JEAN-BAPTISTE (1827–75), French sculptor.

CARRIER-BELLEUSE, ALBERT-ERNEST (1824–87), French sculptor, famous for a bust of Renan and, with his son Pierre Gérard (1851–1933), for decorative statuettes found on every middle-class mantelpiece during the period 1880–1910.

CARRIÈRE, EUGÈNE (1849–1906), French painter, known for portraits, religious pictures, and his interest in the theme of motherhood.

CASTELLANE, BONI, MARQUIS DE (1867–1932), French society figure and writer of informal memoirs.

CÉZANNE, PAUL (1839–1906), French painter, who broke with impressionism to create a solid new style.

CHAMISSO, ADELBERT VON (1781–1838), German zoologist and poet, remembered chiefly for his *Peter Schlemihl*.

CHANVIN, CHARLES, French poet who gave up literature for the magistrature; friend of C.-L. Philippe.

CHAPON, ALBERT, French man of letters and managing editor of the neo-classical review *L'Occident* (1901–14).

CHARMOY, JOSÉ DE, French sculptor known for his busts, statues, and tombs — especially of Renan, Zola, Baudelaire, etc.

CHAUMEIX, ANDRÉ (1874–), French literary critic, who wrote regularly in the *Revue hebdomadaire*, the *Revue de Paris*, and the *Revue des deux mondes*. He was long editor-in-chief of the *Revue des deux mondes* and a member of the Academy.

CHÉNIER, ANDRÉ (1762–94), French poet, whose work, published after his early execution by the revolutionary tribunal, seemed to the romantics a powerful romantic outburst, but was in reality soberly classical.

CLARETIE, JULES (1840–1913), French essayist and journalist of the 20-volume *La Vie à Paris* and incidentally novelist and dramatist.

CLAUDEL, PAUL (1868–), French poet and diplomat (Ambassador to Tokyo and to Washington) whose odes and verse dramas (*L'Annonce faite à Marie* and *Le Soulier de satin*) struck a new note of genius. Elected to the Academy in 1946.

CLIFFORD–BARNEY, NATALIE, American who lived her mature life in Paris, where she gave famous receptions for her illustrious literary friends and inspired Remy de Gourmont.

CLODION (pseud. of Claude Michel, 1738–1814), French sculptor.

CLOUARD, HENRI (1885–), French critic and essayist of the neoclassic revival, editor of the reactionary *Revue critique des idées et des livres* from 1908 to 1913.

COLLIGNON, MAXIME (1849–1917), French archæologist and historian of Greek and Roman art.

COMTE, AUGUSTE (1798–1857), French philosopher, chief exponent of positivism.

CONSTANT, BENJAMIN (1767–1830), French statesman and author of a powerful novel of psychological analysis, *Adolphe*.

COOLUS, ROMAIN (1868–?), French writer of light comedies, such as *Cœur à cœur* and *Pardon, madame*, and journalist.

COPEAU, JACQUES (1879–), French critic and theatrical producer, who, after founding the *Nouvelle Revue Française* with Gide and others in 1909, revolutionized the French theater in 1913 by creating the Théâtre du Vieux-Colombier with its new style of simplicity and sincerity.

COPPEE, FRANÇOIS (1842–1908), French poet and dramatist of the simple life, whose work is often prosaic.

COTTET, CHARLES (1863–1925), French painter, pupil of Puvis de Chavannes. He especially painted scenes of Brittany.

COUTARD, great friend of Paul Gide.

CRANE, WALTER (1845–1915), English painter, decorator, and illustrator of the Pre-Raphaelite group.

CROSS, HENRI-EDMOND (1856–1910), French impressionist painter, who used the divisionist technique of Signac.

CROUX, French nurseryman at Val d'Aulnay, from whose catalogue Gide quoted irrefutable arguments in favor of transplanting during his memorable polemic with Maurice Barrès.

CUREL, FRANÇOIS DE (1854–1928), dramatist of social and philosophical preoccupations (*Le Repas du lion, La Nouvelle Idole*, etc.).

CUVIER, GEORGES (1769–1832), French naturalist.

D'ANNUNZIO, GABRIELE (1863–1938), Italy's greatest literary artist since the mid-nineteenth century, who in his poems (*Laudi*, etc.), his novels (*Il Fuoco, Il Piacere*) and plays (*La Città Morta, La Gioconda*) broke with classicism and introduced the new inspiration of foreign writers such as Hugo, Baudelaire, Whitman, Bourget, Dostoyevsky, Nietzsche, etc. Eventually, abandoning æstheticism, sensualism, and his international reputation, he became the national prophet of Italian imperialism.

DARWIN, ERASMUS (1734–1802), English man of science and poet, whose *Zoonomia* anticipated the views of Lamarck and whose long poem *The Botanic Garden* (1791) contains a real scientific enthusiasm and little poetry; grandfather of Charles Darwin.

DAUCHEZ, ANDRÉ (1870–), French painter, pupil of Gustave Moreau.

DAUDET, ALPHONSE (1840–97), realistic novelist and conteur of *Le Petit Chose, Lettres de mon moulin, Tartarin de Tarascon*, who, like Dickens, combined a deep sympathy for human suffering with a delicate sense of humor.

DAVRAY, HENRY-D. (pseud. of Henry Durand, 1873–1944), French critic, journalist, and translator of Wells, Kipling, Wilde.

DEARLY, MAX (1874–), French comic actor of stage and screen, who achieved great success in the farces of Flers and Caillavet.

DEBUSSY, CLAUDE ACHILLE (1862–1918), French composer, whose new harmonies and literary associations (as a faithful member of Mallarmé's group he composed lyric poems inspired by Verlaine, Mallarmé, Louÿs, Rossetti, etc.) led to the apotheosis of symbolism in music in his opera *Pelléas et Mélisande* (1902).

DEGAS, EDGAR (1834–1917), French painter, important member of the impressionist school.

DE GROUX, HENRI (1867–1930), Belgian painter of dramatic subjects.

DEHMEL, RICHARD (1863–1920), German poet, the most distinguished representative of the transition from extreme naturalism to classic restraint.

DELAW, GEORGES (1877–), French caricaturist and journalist, who wrote and drew for *Le Matin, Le Journal*, and other dailies and also issued his own albums.

DELVOLVÉ, son-in-law of the painter Eugène Carrière.

DENIS, MAURICE (1870–1943), French painter of the neo-impressionist school and illustrator, many of whose works are of religious inspiration.

DESBORDES-VALMORE, MARCELINE (1786–1859), French poet of the romantic movement, famous for her elegies.

DESCAVES, LUCIEN (1861–), French naturalistic novelist of *Sous-Offs* and defender of justice, who entered the Goncourt Academy in 1900 and was long literary critic and editor-in-chief of *Le Journal*.

DESCHAMPS, GASTON (1861–1931), literary critic of *Le Temps*, conservative Paris daily.

DESJARDINS, PAUL (1859–1940), French moralist whose *Devoir présent* (1892) proclaimed the necessity for a moral awakening, which he worked to achieve in founding the same year L'Union pour l'Action Morale, later L'Union pour la Vérité, and finally the Entretiens de Pontigny, which embraced in a spirit of inquiry all the great literary, social, æsthetic, political, and religious problems of the age.

DESMAREST, ALBERT, French painter and first cousin of André Gide.

DESMAREST, AUNT, née Claire Rondeaux, older sister of André Gide's mother.

DESMAREST, MAURICE (1844–?), cousin of André Gide (son of his mother's sister Claire).

DESPRÉS, SUZANNE (1875–   ), French actress who achieved fame in the Théâtre de l'Œuvre, directed by her husband, Lugné-Poë, and later acted at the Gymnase, the Antoine, and other Paris theaters, including the Comédie-Française, where she became a member of the company in 1901.

DESVALLIÈRES, MAURICE (1857–1926), French dramatist of popular light comedies, whose greatest successes (*L'Hôtel du Libre-Échange*, 1894) were written in collaboration with Georges Feydeau.

DICKEMARE, MME, wife of a French doctor whom Paul Laurent frequented at Biskra in 1893–4.

DIDEROT, DENIS (1713–84), French philosopher, critic, dramatist, etc., who edited the great *Encyclopédie*; a fecund writer and one of the great forces of the age of Enlightenment.

DONNAY, MAURICE (1859–1945), French dramatist of love and psychological analysis, whose masterpiece, *Amants*, was played in 1895.

DOUMIC, RENÉ (1860–1937), French literary historian and critic, who wrote regularly in the conservative *Revue des deux mondes*; elected to the Academy in 1923.

DROUIN, DOMINIQUE, son of Marcel Drouin; he spent much time in Ethiopia.

DROUIN, JEANNE, née Rondeaux, sister of Mme André Gide and wife of Marcel Drouin.

DROUIN, MARCEL (1870–1946), French professor of philosophy in Alençon, Bordeaux, and Paris and, under the pseudonym of Michel Arnauld, essayist and critic. As a classmate of André Gide and Pierre Louÿs, he founded with them *Potache-Revue* and *La Conque* (1891); in 1908, after a brilliant record at the École Normale Supérieure and sojourns in Germany, was instrumental in founding *La Nouvelle Revue Française* with his brother-in-law, André Gide.

DRUET, E., French photographer, who established an art gallery dealing in such modern painters as Bonnard, Rouault, Vuillard.

DUCHESNE, LOUIS-MARIE-OLIVIER (1843–1922), French prelate and archæologist, professor at the Institut Catholique de Paris, director of the French School in Rome, famous for his studies in ecclesiastical history; elected to the French Academy in 1910.

DUCLAUX, ÉMILE (1840–1904), French scientist and long director of the Pasteur Institute.

DUCOTÉ, ÉDOUARD (1870–1929), French poet, who became editor of *L'Ermitage* (1897–1906), grouping around him Gourmont, Ghéon, Claudel, Gide, Jammes, Copeau, etc.

DUHAMEL, GEORGES (1884–), French novelist (incidentally poet, essayist, dramatist), who won fame for his depiction of suffering humanity as seen by a military surgeon and proceeded to paint a picture of modern society (*Pasquier Chronicles*). After being a most effective editor of the *Mercure de France*, he was named perpetual secretary of the French Academy.

DUJARDIN, ÉDOUARD (1861–), French founder (1885) of the *Revue wagnérienne*, editor (1886) of the *Revue indépendante*, one of the great disseminators of symbolist ideas, poet, dramatist, and student of early Christianity.

DUKAS, PAUL (1865–1935), French composer of *The Sorcerer's Apprentice*, etc.

DUMAS, ALEXANDRE, *fils* (1824–95), realistic and social dramatist of *La Dame aux camélias, La Question d'argent*, etc.

DUMONT-WILDEN, LOUIS (1875–), Belgian poet and art critic, known as well for his books on Belgium.

DUPOUEY, PIERRE DOMINIQUE (1877–1915), French naval officer, a close friend of André Gide from 1903 until his death at the front. He became converted to Catholicism, and his example was the dominant factor in Henri Ghéon's conversion. Gide and Ghéon published his fervent letters in 1916.

EM., *see* Gide, Mme André.

ÉPINAY, MME DE LA LIVE D' (1726–83), rich intellectual of the age of Enlightenment, who befriended Rousseau, Grimm, and Diderot and left interesting memoirs.

ERNEST-CHARLES, J. (1875–1925), French literary critic and sociologist, who wrote regularly in *La Revue politique et littéraire*.

ESPINAS, PIERRE, mining engineer, son-in-law of Charles Gide.

FABRE, ÉMILE (1869–), French dramatist of such plays of social satire as *L'Argent, La Rabouilleuse, Ventres dorés;* administrator of the Comédie-Française.

FABRE, FERDINAND (1827–98), French novelist.

FABRE, JEAN-HENRI (1823–1915), French arithmetician, physicist, chemist, and naturalist, who because of his famous studies of entomology has been called "the insects' Homer."

FALCONET, ÉTIENNE MAURICE (1716–91), French sculptor.

FARGUE, LÉON-PAUL (1878–   ), French poet in verse and prose of the delicate world of imagination and hallucination.

FAURE, ÉLIE (1873–1937), French essayist and art critic, better known for his ambitious and provocative *History of Art* (1909) and his art monographs than for his practice of medicine.

FAURÉ, GABRIEL-URBAIN (1845–1924), French composer, who wrote for the piano, chorus, chamber orchestra, and full orchestra as well as for the church and the stage. With Debussy he contributed to the rebirth of French music, and he renewed the classic tradition of Couperin and Rameau.

FAZY, EDMOND, French author of a study of *Ludwig II and Wagner* and of a book on modern Turkey.

FÉNÉON, FÉLIX (1861–1944), French art critic, who in various symbolist reviews revealed the new impressionist school of painting. Great influence on literature.

FERRERO, GUGLIELMO (1871–1942), Italian historian and essayist, who championed democracy in such works as *The Greatness and Decline of Rome* (1902–7) and became professor of modern history in Geneva when he left Italy in opposition to Fascism (1930).

FEYDEAU, ERNEST (1821–73), popular French dramatist and novelist, author of *Fanny* (1858).

FLINCK, GOVAERT (1615–60), Dutch painter of the school of Rembrandt.

FLORY, GEORGES (1858–?), French jurist, who was *juge d'instruction* or state prosecutor in Paris from 1898 to 1908, later vice-president and councilor of the Appellate Court.

FONTAINAS, ANDRÉ (1865–   ), Belgian-born symbolist poet and disciple of Mallarmé, interpreter of English poets such as Shelley and Poe, and sensitive art critic.

FONTAINE, ARTHUR (1860–1931), French sociologist and economist.

FORD, JOHN (1586–*ca.* 1640), English dramatist.

FÖRSTER-NIETZSCHE, ELISABETH, sister of Friedrich Nietzsche, who took care of the philosopher during his illness.

FORT, PAUL (1872–   ), French poet of the *Ballades françaises*, founder of the first symbolist theater, and editor of the review *Vers et Prose* (1905–14).

FOUILLÉE, ALFRED (1838–1912), French philosopher and sociologist, author of numerous studies on the evolution, the psychology, and the ethics of *"idées-forces."*

FRANCE, ANATOLE (1844–1924), French novelist and story-teller (who began his career as poet and literary critic), famous for his limpid style, delicate irony, and skepticism (*Penguin Island, The Revolt of the Angels,* etc.).

358   GLOSSARY OF PERSONS

FRANC-NOHAIN, MAURICE (pseud. of Maurice Le Grand, 1873–
1934), French poet and writer of light comedies and adapter of
Andersen, Gulliver, etc., for juvenile reading.
FRANCK, CÉSAR (1822–90), Belgian composer.
FRIZEAU, GABRIEL, French book-collector and art-lover of Bordeaux, who was one of the first admirers of Claudel and the introducer of Jacques Rivière to the literary world of Paris.
FROMENTIN, EUGÈNE (1820–76), French painter and perspicacious art critic, who wrote one classic novel of psychological analysis, *Dominique* (1863).
FUSTEL DE COULANGES, NUMA-DENIS (1830–89), historian of
the Merovingian and Carolingian epochs, who drew everything
from the rigorous study of ancient texts.

GALLIMARD, GASTON (1881–   ), French publisher, who became
administrator of the *Nouvelle Revue Française* when founded in
1908–9 and later of the publishing house; also acted as business
manager of Copeau's Théâtre du Vieux-Colombier.
GANZ, HUGO (1862–?), German dramatist and journalist, best known
abroad for a book on Russia, *The Land of Riddles*.
GARNIER, GEORGES–LOUIS (1880–   ), French poet, dramatist,
and director of the Salon des Tuileries.
GATTESCHI, ROBERTO PIO (1872–   ), Italian poet and painter of
Florence, whose first poems appeared in 1893.
GAUGUIN, PAUL (1848–1903), French painter who began as an impressionist and developed a highly personal style in his Tahitian
works.
GAUTIER, THÉOPHILE (1811–72), French poet and novelist, who,
heading the school of art for art's sake, acts as a pivot between romanticism and naturalism.
GÉMIER, FIRMIN (1865–1933), French actor and stage producer,
who, after many revolutionary experiments, became director of
the Odéon theater.
GEORGE, STEFAN (1868–1933), German poet strongly influenced
by French symbolism, who renewed German poetic style; besides
Shakespeare and Dante, he translated Baudelaire and several
more recent French poets.
GÉRARD, see Gide, Paul.
GHÉON, HENRI (1875–1944), French novelist, dramatist, and critic,
who began writing tragedies of the people (*Le Pain*, *L'Eau de
vie*) and, after his conversion to Catholicism in 1917, revived the
miracle play (*Le Pauvre sous l'escalier*). Closely associated with
the early *Nouvelle Revue Française* and with the Théâtre du
Vieux-Colombier.

GIDE, MME ANDRÉ (1867–1938), née Madeleine Rondeaux.

GIDE, CHARLES (1847–1932), younger brother of André Gide's father; famous professor of economics in Paris, who wrote more than a score of studies on political economy.

GIDE, GÉRARD, pseudonym for Paul Gide.

GIDE, PAUL, son of the economist Charles Gide and cousin of André Gide. (He figures in the *Journals* under the pseudonym Gérard.)

GIDE, MME PAUL (1833–95), née Juliette Rondeaux, André Gide's mother.

GILBERT, PIERRE (1884–1914), French critic, who in the last year of his life succeeded H. Clouard as editor of *La Revue critique.*

GILBERT, VALENTINE, née Rondeaux, sister of Mme André Gide and wife of Marcel Gilbert.

GILBERT DE VOISINS, AUGUSTE (1877–1939), French novelist of exoticism, poet, and translator of Browning.

GOBILLARD, PAULE (?–1946), French painter who studied with her aunt Berthe Morisot and with Renoir; elder sister of Mme Paul Valéry and close friend of Mallarmé, Redon, Degas, etc.

GONCOURT, EDMOND DE (1822–96), with his brother Jules (1830–70) was a leader of French naturalism in both the documentary novel and the theater. He also ranks as an art critic through his studies of Hokusai, Utamaro, and eighteenth-century art. The 9 volumes of *Journals* depict the society of their time. By his will he founded the Goncourt Academy.

GOSSE, SIR EDMUND (1849–1928), English critic, biographer, and poet, best known for his scholarly studies of Scandinavian and English literature. He was librarian of the House of Lords, 1904–14.

GOURMONT, REMY DE (1858–1915), fecund French literary critic and novelist, one of the founders of the *Mercure de France* (1890), for which he wrote assiduously for the next twenty-five years, apologist and spokesman of the symbolist movement.

GREGH, FERNAND (1873–), French poet and critic of poetry.

GRÈVE, FÉLIX-PAUL (1879–), German translator of *The Arabian Nights* and of several works by André Gide (*Paludes, Saül, La Porte étroite*).

GRIMAREST, JEAN LÉONOR LE GALLOIS DE (1659–1713), French author of a biography of Molière, which first appeared in 1705.

GRIMM, MELCHIOR (1723–1807), German chronicler of Parisian intellectual life, whose correspondence records the achievements of the *philosophes.*

GROLLEAU, CHARLES (1867–?), French dramatist and translator of works by Oscar Wilde, G. K. Chesterton, etc.

GUÉRIN, CHARLES (1873–1907), French poet of melancholy temper and classic form, who was an intimate friend of Francis Jammes.

GUÉRIN, CHARLES (1875–), French painter, pupil of Gustave Moreau.

GUILLAUMIN, ÉMILE (1873–), French novelist of the Bourbonnais region, appreciated for his sympathetic *Life of a Simple Man.*

GUY-GRAND, GEORGES (1879–), French sociologist, author of *Syndicalist Philosophy* (1911) and *The Future of Democracy* (1928), and director of "L'Union pour la Vérité" – a very active discussion group.

HAASE, ALBERT, German grammarian, author of a syntax of seventeenth-century French.

HAGUENIN, ÉMILE (1872–1924), French professor of modern literature, a close friend of Marcel Drouin at the École Normale. From 1901 to 1914 he taught at the University of Berlin and after the war was head of the information service of the Reparations Commission in Berlin.

HAMP, PIERRE (1876–), French novelist of the working man (*Le Travail, Le Rail, La Peine des hommes*) and the hardships of the various trades.

HAMSUN, KNUT (1859–), Norwegian novelist of peasant background, whose *Hunger* (1890), *Growth of the Soil* (1917), etc., won for him the Nobel prize for literature in 1920.

HANOTAUX, GABRIEL (1853–1944), French historian of the seventeenth century and of the contemporary period.

HAN-RYNER (1861–?), French poet and short-story writer of Norwegian descent.

HEBBEL, FRIEDRICH (1813–63), German poet and dramatist.

HEREDIA, JOSÉ-MARIA DE (1842–1905), French poet of the Parnassian movement, whose single volume of sonnets, *Les Trophées* (1893), won him election to the French Academy.

HERELLE, GEORGES (1848–1935), French historian, journalist, and translator of numerous Italian writers, chiefly d'Annunzio.

HÉROLD, ANDRÉ-FERDINAND (1865–?), French poet and lyric dramatist of classic and Parnassian inspiration with a penchant for the Middle Ages and for Oriental literature; drama critic for the *Mercure de France.*

HOFMANNSTHAL, HUGO VON (1874–1929), Austrian poet, dramatist, novelist, and essayist of symbolist tendency, much of whose work was performed in co-operation with the composer Richard Strauss or the producer Max Reinhardt.

HOUDETOT, ELISABETH, COMTESSE D' (1730–1813), French in-

tellectual of the Enlightenment, sister-in-law of Mme d'Épinay
and friend of Rousseau.

HUYSMANS, J.-K. (1849–1907), Belgian-born French novelist, who in
1884 broke with naturalism and was one of the first to herald the
symbolist movement (*A rebours*); his later conversion to Catholicism and the novels it inspired (*La Cathédrale*) kept him in the
forefront of French letters.

IBELS, ANDRÉ-ALBERT (1872–1932), French poet, novelist, and
chiefly dramatist of light comedies.

IEHL, JULES, Alsatian novelist and great friend of Charles-Louis
Philippe; in 1909 his first book, *Cauët*, was highly praised by discerning critics. When Gide met him he was a clerk in an express
office, but Eugène Rouart helped him to become justice of the
peace first at Albi and then at Poitiers, where he later held more
important judicial offices. In 1910 André Gide made his trip in the
Pyrenees and in Andorra with Iehl and Eugène Rouart. Sometime
between 1909 and 1912 he took the pseudonym of Michel Yell.

JACOBY, PAUL (1842–?), Russian alienist, author of *Studies of Natural Selection in Mankind* (1881), which analyzes two neuroses:
that of power in royal families and that of talent in families of artists, writers, and men of science.

JALOUX, EDMOND (1878–   ), French novelist of subdued atmosphere and literary critic of sound judgment, who entered the
French Academy in 1936.

JAMMES, FRANCIS (1868–1938), French intimist poet, who sang of
his native Pyrenees with a childlike sensuality and an increasingly
orthodox Catholic faith.

JANVIER, FATHER MARIE-ALBERT (1861–1939), French Dominican priest of great eloquence, who for twenty-two years preached
an annual lenten mission in Notre-Dame de Paris.

JANZÉ, COMTESSE DE, French member of society, who maintained
one of the most important Parisian *salons* of the late nineteenth
century.

JEAN, LUCIEN, French writer of realistic character studies of the lit-
tle people of Paris, among whom he lived. His contributions to
L'Ermitage between 1902 and 1906 were collected in the volume
Parmi les hommes (*Life among Men*).

JEANNE, see Drouin, Jeanne.

JEANNIE, see Valéry, Jeannie.

JOUBERT, JOSEPH (1754–1824), French philosopher, author of maxims.

JOURDAIN, FRANCIS (1876–   ), French painter and decorator, famous for the modern simple style of decoration he inaugurated in 1913.

JUSSERAND, JULES (1855–1932), French literary historian and diplomat.

KAHN, GUSTAVE (1859–1936), French poet, novelist, and critic, theoretician of symbolism and of the vers libre, founder of the review *La Vogue*, and editor of *Le Symboliste* and *La Revue indépendante*.

KASSNER, RUDOLF (1873–   ), Austrian essayist, whose writings on music, philosophy, mysticism, and English poetry fill 12 volumes; translator of Gogol, Pushkin, Tolstoy, and Gide (*Philoctète*).

KESSLER, HARRY VON (1868–1937), German diplomat and essayist, author of *Recollections of a European, Germany and Europe, Hugo von Hofmannsthal*, etc.

KIERKEGAARD, SOEREN (1813–55), Danish philosopher.

LABICHE, EUGÈNE (1815–88), French writer of light comedies, such as *La Cagnotte, La Poudre aux yeux*, etc.

LACLOS, CHODERLOS DE (1741–1803), French officer and author of *Les Liaisons dangereuses*.

LACORDAIRE, HENRI-DOMINIQUE (1802–61), French Dominican preacher of great eloquence and liberal ideas, who became a deputy in 1848 and entered the Academy in 1860.

LA FAYETTE, MME DE (1634–93), French writer of the classical period, famous for her *Princesse de Clèves*.

LAFORGUE, JULES (1860–87), French poet of the early symbolist movement, famous for the ironic vers libres of his *Complaintes*.

LA MOTTE-FOUQUÉ, FRIEDRICH, BARON DE (1777–1843), German poet, dramatist, and story-teller, best known for the romance *Undine*.

LANSON, GUSTAVE (1857–1934), French literary historian, who imposed scientific methods in literary history on the French University and is remembered for his *History of French Literature* and his bibliographical manual.

LANUX, PIERRE DE (1887–   ), French essayist and journalist, at one time secretary to André Gide and, briefly, to the editorial board of the *N.R.F.*; in charge of the Paris office of the League of Nations (1924–34).

LA PÉROUSE, pseudonym for Marc de la Nux, André Gide's piano teacher, whom he always venerated. (The same pseudonym figures in *Si le grain ne meurt* and in *Les Faux-Monnayeurs*.)

LARBAUD, VALERY (1881–   ), French poet, novelist, and essayist especially appreciated for his penetrating *Journal d'A. O. Barna-booth* (1913), which introduced into literature a new cosmopolitanism, and for his sensitive translations of Samuel Butler, W. S. Landor, Walt Whitman, etc.

LA SALLE, GEORGES DE, French author of a book of travels in Manchuria (1905).

LASSERRE, PIERRE (1867–1930), French literary critic of conservative tendency, who studied French romanticism and also contemporary writers.

LAURENS, CLAUDE, son of Paul-Albert Laurens.

LAURENS, JEAN-PAUL (1838–1921), French painter of the Life of Saint Genevieve in the Panthéon, of the Théâtre de l'Odéon ceiling, etc.; member of the Institute; father of Pierre and Paul-Albert Laurens.

LAURENS, PAUL-ALBERT (1870–?), son of Jean-Paul Laurens; painter and professor at the École des Beaux-Arts; intimate friend of André Gide, whom he accompanied on first trip to Africa (1893). His portrait of Gide is in the Luxembourg Museum.

LAURENS, PIERRE, son of Jean-Paul Laurens, and a painter himself; professor at the École des Beaux-Arts; great friend of Charles Péguy, whose portrait he painted.

LAUTRÉAMONT, COMTE DE (pseud. of Isidore Ducasse, 1846–70), French poet of the revolutionary *Chants de Maldoror*.

LAVALLIÈRE, ÈVE (pseud. of Eugénie Fenoglio, 1866–1929), French actress, who became the chief star of the Théâtre des Variétés, creating roles in light comedies.

LAVATER, JOHANN KASPAR (1741–1801), Swiss poet and divine, known as the inventor of phrenology.

LÉAUTAUD, PAUL (1872–), French self-taught novelist and critic, long associated with the *Mercure de France* and appreciated for his outspoken drama criticism and caustic wit.

LEBEY, ANDRÉ (1877–1938), French poet, then sociologist and historian; abandoned symbolism in favor of studies of Freemasonry and of the Bonapartes.

LEBLANC, GEORGETTE (1875–1941), French singer and actress, who met the poet Maeterlinck when she was eighteen and for twenty years acted in his plays, maintained a brilliant *salon* for him in Paris, and exercised a great influence over his career.

LECONTE DE LISLE, CHARLES (1818–94), French poet of the Parnassian school, whose work is steeped in classical culture.

LE DANTEC, FÉLIX (1869–1917), French biologist and philosopher.

LEMAÎTRE, JULES (1853–1914), French literary critic and exponent of the impressionist method.

LEROLLE, French painter, and brother-in-law of the composer Ernest Chausson.

LITTRÉ, ÉMILE (1801–81), French positivist philosopher, whose dictionary of French is still a standard work.

LORDE, ANDRÉ DE (1871–   ), French dramatist, who created the style of the Grand Guignol terror plays.

LOUIS, GEORGES (1847–1917), eminent French diplomat, Director of Political and Commercial Affairs in the Ministry of Foreign Affairs; Minister Plenipotentiary, Conseiller d'État; half-brother of Pierre Louÿs.

LOUIS-PHILIPPE (1773–1850), King of the French, 1830–48.

LOUÿS, PIERRE (1870–1925), French poet and novelist of *Chansons de Bilitis* (1894), *Aphrodite* (1896), and *Les Aventures du roi Pausole* (1900).

LUGNÉ-POË, AURÉLIEN-FRANÇOIS (1869–1940), French actor and theatrical producer, who founded the Théâtre de l'Œuvre (1893–1929), which revealed to France such idealistic dramatists as Ibsen, Maeterlinck, Claudel, etc.

MAETERLINCK, MAURICE (1862–   ), Belgian poet and lyric dramatist of *Pelléas et Mélisande,* who evolved in the direction of a mystic rationalism and moral optimism.

MAILLOL, ARISTIDE (1861–1944), French sculptor of vigorous classical tendency, whose solid nymphs are famous.

MAINDRON, MAURICE (1857–1919), French writer of historical novels.

MAISTRE, JOSEPH DE (1754–1821), French philosopher and essayist, who, as Ambassador of the King of Sardinia to the Russian court, wrote his *Considerations on France* and *St. Petersburg Evenings* to contradict the philosophy of Voltaire, Montesquieu, and Rousseau in favor of absolute monarchy and papal infallibility.

MALHERBE, FRANÇOIS DE (1555–1628), French poet, more important for his influence as codifier and purifier of language at the beginning of the classical period than for his poems.

MALLARMÉ, STÉPHANE (1842–98), French poet, whose intellectual purity and hermetic style influenced a whole generation of writers despite the limitation of his first *Complete Poems* to forty copies. His weekly receptions in his Paris apartment (1886–98) gathered the artistic élite of the Continent in fascinating conversation.

MARDRUS, DR. J. C. (1868–   ), French Orientalist, and translator of *The Thousand and One Nights* in 16 volumes.

MARINETTI, FILIPPO TOMMASO (1876–1944), Italian poet, novelist, dramatist, and critic of aggressive temperament, who, writing in French and Italian, started the futurist movement, which foreshadowed Dadaism and surrealism, and founded in Milan the review *Poesia*.

MARIVAUX, PIERRE CARLET DE CHAMBLAIN DE (1688–1763), French dramatist and novelist of great sensibility and psychological penetration, whose name (*marivaudage*) stands for witty banter about love. His journals were inspired by Addison, and his novels in turn influenced Richardson.

MARX, ROGER (1859–1913), French art critic, who wrote numerous monographs on French artists and studies of medals.

MATISSE, HENRI (1869–), French painter of the expressionist school, leader of the *"Fauves"* in early years of the century, and now one of the classics of modern painting.

MAUCLAIR, CAMILLE (1872–), French poet, novelist, and critic, who revealed and defended most of the best in modern French art and literature.

MAUREL, ANDRÉ (1863–), French critic and novelist, best known for his numerous books on the beauties of Italy.

MAURRAS, CHARLES (1868–), French poet, essayist, pamphleteer, and political leader of the Action Française movement; exponent of decentralization and a return to monarchy, who was tried in 1945 as the ideologist of the Vichy government and sentenced to life imprisonment.

MAUS, OCTAVE (1856–1919), Belgian writer and lawyer, who was one of the founders of the advance-guard literary review *L'Art moderne* (1881) and later of La Libre Esthétique, the society before which André Gide lectured in Brussels.

MAX, ÉDOUARD ALEXANDRE DE (1869–1924), Rumanian-born French actor, who frequently played opposite Sarah Bernhardt and enjoyed a great reputation in lyric tragedy.

MAYRISCH, MME ÉMILE (?–1947), wife of the Director of the great Luxemburg metallurgical syndicate named Arbet. A woman of great culture in French, English and German, she received poets, philosophers, painters and sculptors in her château of Colpach in Luxemburg, which became a meeting-place of French and German cultures. She traveled in the Orient with the late Director of the Musée Guimet and in the Near-East with André Gide.

MÉGARD, JOSEPH (1850–?), Swiss landscape painter and etcher.

MEMLING, HANS (*ca.* 1430–94), Dutch painter.

MENDÈS, CATULLE (1843–1909), prolific French poet and dramatist.

MÉRIMÉE, PROSPER (1803–70), French novelist, dramatist, and, chiefly, writer of short stories, such as *Carmen* and *Colomba*, famous for their objectivity and artistry.

METZYS, QUENTIN (1466?–1530), Dutch painter.

MICHELET, JULES (1798–1874), French historian, who joined poetic intuition to scientific research and in his voluminous work consistently defended the lower classes.

MILLARD, CHRISTOPHER SCLATER (1872–   ), English writer under the pseudonym of Stuart Mason who translated André Gide's essay on Wilde from *Prétextes* and wrote studies of Wilde.

MIOMANDRE, FRANCIS DE (1880–   ), French novelist of subtle fancy and translator of Spanish masterpieces.

MIRBEAU, OCTAVE (1850–1917), French novelist, dramatist, and critic, famous for his social satire and outspoken manner.

MITHOUARD, ADRIEN (1864–1929), French poet and editor of *L'Occident* (1901–14), a neo-classical literary review of Christian inspiration.

MOCKEL, ALBERT (1866–1945), Belgian poet and critic and founder of the Liége review *La Wallonie,* which played a foremost part in the symbolist movement.

MONET, CLAUDE (1840–1926), French painter of the impressionist school, famous for his water-lilies and cathedrals and seascapes.

MONTFORT, EUGÈNE (1877–1936), French novelist, editor of *Les Marges* (which he wrote entirely himself from 1903 to 1908), and author of a tableau of modern French literature.

MONTICELLI, ADOLPHE JOSEPH (1824–86), French painter of landscapes and groups, much appreciated for his finesse.

MORÉAS, JEAN (pseud. of Jean Papadiamantopoulos, 1856–1910), Athens-born French poet, who founded within the symbolist movement (which he had been the first to name and defend) the "Romanesque school" and achieved a vigorous return to classicism.

MOREAU, GUSTAVE (1826–98), French painter, who, like Redon, painted visions and ideas rather than visual experiences; a great draftsman, he taught Matisse, Rouault, and many others.

MORICE, CHARLES (1861–1919), French poet and literary and art critic, whose *Littérature de tout à l'heure* (1889) summed up the tendencies of the day and had a great influence, but who failed to become the great critic of symbolism.

MORISOT, BERTHE (1841–95), Belgian painter of the French impressionist school.

MOUNET, PAUL (1847–1922), French tragic actor of the Odéon and the Comédie-Française; younger brother of Mounet-Sully.

MOUREY, GABRIEL (1865–1945), French poet, historian of art, and translator of Poe and Swinburne into French verse.

MÜHLFELD, MME, widow of the literary critic Lucien Mühlfeld, maintained an important politico-literary *salon* in Paris that was frequented by Régnier and Valéry.

NADELMAN, ÉLIE (1885–1946), Polish-born sculptor, who has worked in Paris and in America.

NATANSON, ALEXANDRE, Polish-born editor, who with his brothers founded *La Revue blanche* in 1891 and also the weekly *Cri de Paris*.

NATANSON, THADÉE, brother of Alexandre Natanson, with whom he founded the symbolist *Revue blanche;* also collaborated with Octave Mirbeau on the play *Le Foyer* and with G. Frazer on a book about Léon Blum.

NAUDIN, BERNARD (1876–), French painter and engraver, pupil of Bonnat.

NAZZI, LOUIS, French editor of a little review entitled *Sincérité* and founder of a poetic school or group called *"sincérisme."*

NOAILLES, COMTESSE ANNA DE (1876–1933), French poet and novelist of delicate talent and vibrant sensitivity.

NODIER, CHARLES (1783–1844), French novelist and poet, around whom was formed in 1823 the first coterie of romanticism.

NYROP, KRISTOFFER (1858–1931), Danish philologian, author of an exhaustive historical grammar of the French language.

ORLÉANS, DUC D' (1869–1926), the last of the name, and pretender, after his father's death in 1894, to the throne of France; banished by a law of 1886, he made England his home.

ORVIETO, ANGIOLO (1869–), Italian poet and editor, who was chief founder and editor of the Florentine literary review *Il Marzocco* (1896–1932), of æsthetic, d'Annunzian tendencies.

OTWAY, THOMAS (1652–85), English dramatist.

PALISSY, BERNARD (1510–89), French chemist and naturalist, who, among other discoveries, invented after twenty years of experiments a new process of enamel-work.

PANIZZI, ANTONIO (1797–1879), Italian man of letters and patriot, who lived most of his life in exile in England, where he became librarian of the British Museum. He kept up a lively correspondence with Mérimée, Ugo Foscolo, etc.

PAPINI, GIOVANNI (1881–), Italian poet, novelist, and essayist, significant for founding the reviews *Leonardo* (1903–7), and *Lacerba* (1913–15), for his popularization of pragmatism, and for his conversion to Catholicism (*Life of Christ*, 1921).

PASCAL, BLAISE (1623–62), French Catholic polemicist and philosopher, famous for the vigor, conciseness, and beauty of his *Pensées*, composed as an apology of Christianity.

PÉGUY, CHARLES (1873–1914), French poet and essayist, who exerted a very great influence through such works as his *Jeanne d'Arc, Notre Patrie,* and *L'Argent,* as well as through the review he founded and edited, *Les Cahiers de la Quinzaine* (1902–14).

PÉLADAN, JOSÉPHIN (1859–1918), French disciple of Barbey d'Aurevilly, who, aiming to renew art through mysticism, founded the Rosicrucian Order and organized Rosicrucian art exhibits in 1892 and after.

PELLERIN, AUGUSTE, wealthy French industrialist and collector of modern paintings, chiefly by Manet, Cézanne, and Derain.

PERSE, ST. J. (pseud. of Alexis Saint-Léger Léger, 1887–   ), French poet of vigorous, imagistic strophes of *Éloges* (1910) and *Anabase* (1924) and general secretary of the Ministry of Foreign Affairs (1933–40).

PETIT, GEORGES, owner and director of an important art gallery, where Jacques Copeau was the chief employee.

PEZARD, MAURICE (?–1923), French archæologist and Orientalist.

PHILIPPE, CHARLES-LOUIS (1874–1909), French realistic novelist of the simple life, who left several masterpieces.

PHILLIPS, STEPHEN (1868–1915), English poet and dramatist.

PHOTIADÈS, CONSTANTIN, French literary historian and critic, author of a study of George Meredith.

PIERREFEU, JEAN DE (1883–   ), French journalist, known for his reportages on the war of 1914–18.

PILON, EDMOND (1874–   ), French poet in vers libre, and art and literary critic whose regular fortnightly column in *La Plume* was remarkable for its impartiality.

PIOT, RENÉ (1869–1934), French painter, illustrator, and designer for the theater, who renewed the art of the fresco in the early years of the century.

POINCARÉ, HENRI (1854–1912), French physicist and philosopher of eminence.

POLYCLITUS, Greek sculptor who flourished 450–420 B.C.

POUCHET, JULIE, wife of Édouard Rondeaux, André Gide's maternal grandfather.

POZZI, SAMUEL-JEAN (1846–1918), famous French surgeon and book-collector. His wife wrote a remarkable little volume of poems.

PRADON, PIERRE (1632–98), French dramatist, who rivaled Racine in his time.

PRINCE (pseud. of Charles Petit-Demange, 1872–1933), French comedian of the Variétés theater and of over six hundred silent films, known internationally as Rigadin.

PUTTE, HENRI VAN DE (1877–   ), Belgian poet, who with A. Ruyters edited *L'Art jeune* in Brussels as a review of "naturist" tendency. In his poems he was inspired by Jules Laforgue.

QUINTON, RENÉ (1866–1925), French biologist, noted for his study of *Sea Water as an Organic Milieu*, and pioneer in aviation.

RACHILDE, MME (pseud. of Mme Alfred Vallette, 1860–1935), French novelist, dramatist, critic, and personality in Paris literary life, who helped her husband to found *Le Mercure de France*, in which she reviewed fiction for many years.

RANSOME, ARTHUR (1884–   ), English literary historian, who wrote a study of E. A. Poe, a book on Oscar Wilde (1912), etc.

RAUNAY, MME JEANNE, French singer at the Opéra-Comique.

RAY, MARCEL, French writer on art and translator from the German.

REBELL, HUGUES (1868–1905), French novelist, critic, and poet, who was secretary of *L'Ermitage*. His poems in verse and prose, inspired by Whitman and Nietzsche, and his very successful novel *La Nichina* won him fame in the nineties.

REDON, ODILON (1840–1916), French painter and engraver of the post-impressionist group, who painted his visions in a new color-scheme and created a highly personal art, instinct with thought and literature.

RÉGNIER, HENRI DE (1864–1936), French poet and novelist of great delicacy and fluidity, one of the leaders of the symbolist movement, elected to the French Academy in 1912.

RÉGNIER, MARIE DE (1875–   ), daughter of the poet J.-M. de Heredia and wife of the poet Henri de Régnier, wrote poems and novels under the pseudonym of Gérard d'Houville.

RENAN, ERNEST (1823–92), French philologist, historian of religions, and philosopher, most famous for his unorthodox *Life of Jesus*.

RENARD, JULES (1864–1910), French satirist in both novel and drama, author of *L'Ecornifleur, Poil de Carotte*, etc.

RENOIR, AUGUSTE (1841–1919), French painter of the impressionist school, famous for the rich coloring and palpable volume of his portraits, nudes, and animated scenes.

RESHETNIKOV, FEODOR M. (1841–71), Russian self-taught writer, who painted a realistic picture of the ignorance, savagery, and suffering of the masses in his novelette *Those of Podlipovka*.

RETINGER, JOSEPH H. (1888–   ), Polish author of a book on Conrad, a history of modern French literature, a study of the Mexican labor movement, *All about Poland*, etc.

RETTÉ, ADOLPHE (1863–1930), French poet and vigorous literary critic, who turned against his original fervent symbolism and social anarchy to become a militant Catholic.

RETZ, PAUL DE GONDI, CARDINAL DE (1613–79), French historian of society, whose racy *Memoirs* depict the courts of Louis XIII and Louis XIV.

RICHTER, JOHANN PAUL (1763–1825), German romantic novelist, who wrote under the name Jean-Paul.

RILKE, RAINER MARIA (1875–1926), German poet, born in Prague, who lived long in Paris in close association with the sculptor Rodin. His elegies and other poems are works of philosophy and of great artistry.

RIMBAUD, ARTHUR (1854–91), French poet of great originality, whose two works revolutionized modern poetry. Abandoning literature entirely at the age of nineteen, he ended his life as an adventurer and business representative in Abyssinia.

RIVAROL, ANTOINE (1753–1801), French essayist and pamphleteer, best known for his *Discourse on the Universality of the French Language*.

RIVIÈRE, JACQUES (1886–1925), French critic, and editor of *La Nouvelle Revue Française* from 1919 to 1925 after having been identified with the review from 1909. His vivid correspondence with Alain-Fournier and with Claudel is famous.

ROBERTY, MATHILDE, daughter of the Rouen minister who officiated at André Gide's marriage at Étretat and friend of Mme Gide. Later she presided over a horticultural school near Neuchâtel in Switzerland.

ROBIDET, gamekeeper at André Gide's estate of La Roque in Normandy.

ROD, ÉDOUARD (1857–1910), novelist of French Switzerland, who wrote psychological novels with moral intentions, as in his essays.

RODIN, AUGUSTE (1840–1917), French sculptor, famous for *The Thinker, The Bronze Age, The Kiss,* and for statues of Balzac, Hugo, etc.

ROGGERS, HENRIETTE, French actress, who created the role of Nyssia in André Gide's *Roi Candaule* opposite de Max as Gyges and Lugné-Poë as Candaules; married the novelist Claude Farrère.

ROLMER, LUCIEN (1880–1916), French poet and novelist.

RONDEAUX, GEORGES, brother of Mme André Gide and long mayor of Cuverville.

RONSARD, PIERRE DE (1524–85), French poet of the Renaissance, who with Joachim du Bellay and others founded the group known as the Pléiade and revolutionized French poetry as much by his theories as by his beautiful odes and sonnets.

ROSENBERG, FÉDOR, Russian from Livonia, whom André Gide met in Florence during his wedding trip (1895).

ROSSETTI, DANTE GABRIEL (1828–82), English painter and poet of the Pre-Raphaelite school.

ROSTAND, EDMOND (1868–1918), French poetic dramatist, whose *Cyrano de Bergerac* renewed the romantic drama brilliantly at the end of the century.

ROTHMALER, AUGUSTINE DE, professor of French literature in Belgium, who had taught Mme Théo Van Rysselberghe.

ROUART, EUGÈNE, son of a famous industrialist and collector of modern French paintings; he married one of the daughters of the painter Henri Lerolle. As a graduate of the School of Agriculture at Grignon, he directed various large agricultural enterprises, and, entering politics, was elected Senator from the Haute-Garonne. Great friend of writers and painters, he contributed to the early interest in Francis Jammes. He and Jammes joined André Gide at Biskra in 1895 and Gide dedicated his *Paludes* to him. He himself wrote a novel, *La Villa sans maître*, which did not enjoy much success despite the interesting psychological problem it sets forth.

ROUART, LOUIS, younger brother of Eugène Rouart; wrote articles for *L'Occident*.

ROUCHÉ, JACQUES (1862–), director of the Paris Opéra since 1913, after having founded *La Grande Revue* and directed the Théâtre des Arts (1910–13). He has consistently shown a predilection for new works.

ROUSSEL, K.-XAVIER (1867–), French painter, who admired Cézanne, Degas, and Renoir and painted mythological subjects.

ROUVEYRE, ANDRÉ (1879–), French caricaturist, who contributed to *Le Rire*, etc., and collected his drawings in several volumes.

ROYÈRE, JEAN (1871–), French poet and critic, strongly influenced by Mallarmé; editor of *La Phalange* (1906–16) and champion of "pure poetry."

RUDE, FRANÇOIS (1784–1855), French sculptor, most famous for his relief of the *Marseillaise* on the Arc de Triomphe.

RUYSDAEL, SALOMON VAN (*ca.* 1600–70), Dutch painter.

RUYTERS, ANDRÉ (1876–), Belgian writer and banker, who was one of the founders of the *Nouvelle Revue Française*. He went to Addis Ababa as a bank director, then managed the Far Eastern branches of the Banque d'Indochine. He has long lived in China.

SAGLIO, ANDRÉ (1869–), French art critic, who wrote a well-known book on French furniture.

SAINTE-BEUVE, AUGUSTIN (1804–69), French critic belonging to the Romantic school whose "Monday Chats" and "Literary Portraits" have outlived his poems and single novel.

SAINT-ÉVREMOND, CHARLES DE SAINT-DENYS DE (1610–1703), French essayist, known for his voluminous, witty correspondence written during his forty-year exile in England.

SAINT-LAMBERT, JEAN-FRANÇOIS (1716–1803), French poet of the Enlightenment, whose *Seasons* shows the inspiration of Thomson and Young.

SAINT-PAUL, ALBERT (1864–?), French poet, who contributed to Mockel's review *La Wallonie*, experimented with the fifteen-syllable line, and won the praise of Mallarmé.

SAINT-SIMON, LOUIS DE ROUVROY, DUC DE (1675–1755), French historian of society, whose *Memoirs* are the memorial of court society in his age as well as a masterpiece of literature.

SARDOU, VICTORIEN (1831–1908), French dramatist of manners, much appreciated in his time for his consummate but mechanical technique.

SARRAUT, ALBERT (1872–?), French statesman of the Radical-Socialist Party, who occupied ministries in several cabinets, was twice Governor General of Indo-China, and specialized in colonial questions.

SAUVEBOIS, GASTON, French literary critic, who contributed to *La Vie* and *La Revue mondiale*.

SCHLUMBERGER, JEAN (1877–   ), French novelist of psychological insight and one of the founders of the *N.R.F.*

SCHUTZ, HEINRICH (1585–1672), German composer of religious music and of the first German opera.

SCHWOB, MARCEL (1867–1905), French prose poet of the symbolist period, whose great erudition, visual imagination, and ironic, flexible style gave him a significant place in modern letters.

SEBONDE, RAYMOND DE (?–1432), Spanish theologian, who professed in Toulouse and wrote a *Natural Theology*, translated and commented on by Montaigne.

SÉGUR, SOPHIE, COMTESSE DE (1799–1874), French novelist, whose fictions, printed in a collection called "The Pink Library," are widely read by children.

SERT, JOSÉ-MARIA (1876–1945), Spanish painter, best known for his vast murals in France and America. He drew an illustration for Gide's *Bethsabé*.

SHACKLETON, ANNA (*ca.* 1830–84), talented Scottish girl who entered the Rondeaux family in 1850 as tutor to the seventeen-year-old Juliette (André Gide's mother) and remained her great friend until death. Her angelic disposition, her great interest in botany, and her intimate knowledge of English and German deeply influenced André Gide's childhood.

SHCHEDRIN, N. (pseud. of M. E. Saltykov, 1826–89), Russian realistic and satiric novelist, whose *Golovlyov Family* and *Bygone Days in Poshekhonie* expose the venality of the ruling class and empty traditions of manorial society in czarist Russia.

SICKERT, WALTER (1860–1942), English painter and illustrator, who frequented Aubrey Beardsley, Oscar Wilde, Charles Condor, etc.

SIGNORET, EMMANUEL (1872–1900), French poet of Wagnerian and Parnassian inspiration, whose poems André Gide collected in one volume in 1908.

SILLER, FRÄULEIN EMMA, for many years the tutor of the Rondeaux girls, of whom the eldest became Mme André Gide; often visited Cuverville and helped André Gide in his study of German; eventually returned to her native Regensburg (Bavaria), where she died recently at a very advanced age.

SIMON, LUCIEN (1861–1945), French painter, pupil of Gustave Moreau, and specialist in genre scenes.

SINCLAIR, UPTON (1878–   ), American novelist of iconoclastic nature.

SISLEY, ALFRED (1839–99), French painter of English descent, who ranks with Monet and Pissarro as a leader of the impressionist school.

SKEAT, WALTER WILLIAM (1835–1912), English philologist.

SOREL, GEORGES (1847–1922), French social philosopher of revolutionary syndicalism, famous for his influential *Reflections on Violence* (1906) and *Illusions of Progress*.

SOUDAY, PAUL (1869–1929), French critic, who from 1912 until his death wrote the regular literary criticism in *Le Temps*.

SOURY, JULES (1842–1915), French materialistic philosopher and psychologist, disciple of Renan, who took an active part in the Dreyfus Affair as a member of Action Française.

SOUZA, ROBERT DE (1865–?), French poet and critic, learned æsthetician of poetic prosody, who worked to prolong the symbolist movement.

SPICKET, BERNARD, childhood friend of Jacques Copeau.

STEIN, LEO, American expatriate, brother of the writer Gertrude Stein, who settled in Paris in the first years of the century and collected paintings by Picasso, Matisse, Braque, etc. He is referred to in his sister's *Autobiography of Alice B. Toklas* and in the Memoirs of Fernande Ollivier.

SUARÈS, ANDRÉ (1866–   ), French poet and essayist of flamboyant nature and broad views, whose studies of Wagner, Dostoyevsky, and Pascal are penetrating and original.

SULLY, MAXIMILIEN DE BÉTHUNE, DUC DE (1559–1641), famous French statesman, who served Henri IV as Finance Minister, rebuilding the royal treasury, encouraging agriculture and industry, rebuilding roads, and establishing frontier fortifications. He was much loved by the King.

SULLY-PRUDHOMME (1839–1907), French poet of the Parnassian school, who introduced philosophy and science into his impersonal poems and also composed popular poems in the elegiac mood. He received the Nobel prize in 1901.

TAGORE, SIR RABINDRANATH (1861–1941), Bengali poet of the *Gitanjali*, who translated his verses into English prose.

TAINE, HIPPOLYTE (1828–93), French historian, critic, and philosopher, most widely known for his *History of English Literature*.

THARAUD, JÉRÔME (1874–), and JEAN (1877–), French novelists, who have always written in collaboration and handled a wide variety of fiction. Their most famous works are *Dingley, l'illustre écrivain*, and *La Maîtresse servante*.

THIERRY, ALBERT (1881–1915), French schoolteacher and author of sensitive stories of childhood, who was killed at the front.

THOMSON, SIR JOHN ARTHUR (1861–1933), English biologist.

THOMY-THIÉRY, French owner of a large plantation on the Ile Maurice, who in 1895 willed to the Louvre his collection of paintings representative of the Barbizon school and 144 sculptures by Barye; the collection in the Louvre bears his name.

TÖPFFER, RODOLPHE (1799–1846), Swiss painter, novelist, and writer of short stories.

TOULOUSE-LAUTREC, HENRI DE (1864–1901), French painter and lithographer, famous for his posters and ironic canvases of circus and night-club life.

TRONCHE, Frenchman employed by the *Nouvelle Revue Française* in the early years.

VALENTIN (Jean Boulogne, 1591–1634, called), French painter born at Coulommiers.

VALENTINE, *see* Gilbert, Valentine.

VALÉRY, JEANNIE, Mme Paul Valéry, née Gobillard.

VALÉRY, PAUL (1871–1945), French poet and essayist, who began his career when as a law student he met Pierre Louÿs and André Gide, then Mallarmé, whose chief disciple he became. After a brilliant start he abandoned literature for twenty years and was persuaded to return in 1917 by André Gide. His mature career was crowned by his election to the French Academy in 1925.

VALLETTE, ALFRED (1858–1935), French writer, who was one of the founders and, from 1890 until his death, the editor of the *Mercure de France*. He was instrumental in the growth of that important review from a 32-page brochure of symbolist literature to a powerful force in modern letters, with its own publishing house.

VALLOTTON, FÉLIX-ÉDOUARD (1865–1925), Swiss painter of portraits, flowers, and landscapes.

VANDEPUTTE, see Putte, Henri van de.

VAN GOGH, VINCENT (1853–90), Dutch painter of great importance in the French post-impressionist group, known for his crude colors and obvious brush-strokes in portraits and landscapes.

VANNICOLA, GIUSEPPE (1877–1915), Italian poet and essayist of great spirit but little achievement, who suffered for many years from illness and poverty.

VAN RYSSELBERGHE, THÉO (1862–1926), Belgian painter of landscapes and portraits.

VARIGNY, HENRY DE (1855–?), French physiologist and biologist, scientific editor for *Le Journal des débats, Le Temps,* and *La Revue scientifique.*

VARIOT, JEAN (1881–   ), French Catholic writer of dramas and romantic legends of Alsace.

VAUDOYER, JEAN-LOUIS (1883–   ), French novelist, essayist, and critic of great subtlety, curator of the Carnavalet Museum, and administrator of the Comédie-Française.

VAUGELAS, CLAUDE FAVRE, SIEUR DE (1585–1650), French lexicographer and arbiter of style, whose *Remarks on the French Language* and work on the *Dictionary* of the Academy continued Malherbe's purification of the classical language.

VAUXCELLES, LOUIS (1870–   ), French art critic for *L'Excelsior* and author of a *History of French Art from the Revolution to the Present Day.*

VELDE, HENRY VAN DE (1863–   ), Belgian architect and exponent of the *"style nouveau."*

VERHAEREN, ÉMILE (1855–1916), Belgian poet of the cult of humanity and the tumultuous forces of modern life.

VERLAINE, PAUL (1844–96), French symbolist poet, distinguished for the musical quality of his verse and his rather disreputable life.

VERRIER, CHARLES, French writer and managing editor of *L'Ermitage* (1897–1906) while Édouard Ducoté was editor-in-chief.

VIELÉ-GRIFFIN, FRANCIS (1864–1937), American-born French poet of nature, who, inspired by the Greek classics, the Scandinavians, and Walt Whitman, contributed a new breath to the symbolist movement.

VILDRAC, CHARLES (1882–   ), French poet and dramatist, best known for his play *The Good Ship Tenacity.*

VISAN, TANCRÈDE DE (1878–   ), French literary critic, who contributed regularly to the *Mercure de France,* etc.

VOGÜÉ, EUGÈNE-MELCHOIR DE (1848–1910), French novelist and introducer of Russian literature.

VOLLMŒLLER, DR. KARL GUSTAV (1848–1922), German poet and dramatist, who adapted Æschylus, Gozzi, and Molière to the German stage.

VRIES, HUGO DE (1848–1935), Dutch botanist, author of a new theory on the growth of plants.

VUILLARD, ÉDOUARD (1867–1940), French painter of intimist tendency, specializing in interiors and portraits of women.

WALCKENAËR, ANDRÉ (1869–), sickly, ill-favored friend of Gide, who for three years "posed" three hours every Wednesday before Gide, who was then planning to make him the hero of the unwritten *Éducation sentimentale;* graduate of the École des Chartes for paleographers, he became assistant librarian of the Mazarine Library in Paris.

WARENS, MME DE (*ca.* 1699–1762), lady of Annecy in Savoie, who befriended Rousseau, converted him to Catholicism, and lived with him for a time in a country house near Chambéry called Les Charmettes.

WENDRINER, KARL GEORG (1885–), German critic, who has written studies on Goethe, Nietzsche, etc.

WERTH, LÉON (1879–), French novelist.

WIDMER, GEORGES, cousin of André Gide.

WITT-GUIZOT, FRANÇOIS DE (1870–), French officer of Foch's staff, banker, and social benefactor, author of articles in *Revue des deux mondes.*

WOJTKIEWICZ, WITOLD (1879–), Polish painter whose first exhibit was held in Paris at the Galerie Druet in May and June 1907; André Gide wrote the preface for the catalogue.

WYZEWA, TÉODORE DE (1862–1917), Russian-born French poet and critic of music, literature, and painting; translator of Tolstoy, Stevenson, Charles Lamb, R. H. Benson, Vasari, etc.

THE WORKS OF ANDRÉ GIDE

POETRY IN VERSE AND IN PROSE

Les Cahiers d'André Walter (Librairie de l'Art Indépendant, 1891)	The Notebooks of André Walter
Les Poésies d'André Walter (ibid., 1892)	The Poems of André Walter
Le Traité du Narcisse (ibid., 1891)	The Treatise of the Narcissus
La Tentative amoureuse (ibid., 1893)	The Attempt at Love
Le Voyage d'Urien (ibid., 1893)	Urien's Travels
Les Nourritures terrestres (Mercure de France, 1897)	*Fruits of the Earth* (London: Martin Secker & Warburg, 1949; New York: Alfred A. Knopf, 1949, in *The Fruits of the Earth*)
El Hadj (ibid., 1899)	El Hadj
Amyntas (ibid., 1906)	Amyntas
Le Retour de l'enfant prodigue (Vers et Prose, 1907)	The Prodigal's Return
Les Nouvelles Nourritures (Gallimard, 1935)	*New Fruits of the Earth* (see *Fruits of the Earth* above)

TALES

L'Immoraliste (Mercure de France, 1902)	*The Immoralist* (New York: Alfred A. Knopf, 1930; London: Cassell & Co.)
La Porte étroite (ibid., 1909)	*Strait Is the Gate* (New York: ibid., 1924; London: Martin Secker & Warburg)

N.B. Since 1935 the author and his French publisher have ceased classifying Gide's works in categories. The translator therefore assumes full responsibility for this pigeonholing.

* The titles preceded by an asterisk have been published in English translation. Unless otherwise indicated, all translations are by Dorothy Bussy.

*Isabelle
(Gallimard, 1911)

*Isabelle
(New York: ibid., 1931; London: Cassell & Co.; in *Two Symphonies*)

*La Symphonie pastorale
(ibid., 1919)

*The Pastoral Symphony
(ibid.)

*L'École des femmes
(ibid., 1929)

*The School for Wives
(New York: ibid., 1929, also 1950, in *The School for Wives, Robert, and Geneviève;* London: Cassell & Co.)

Robert
(ibid., 1929)

Robert
(New York: ibid., 1950, in *The School for Wives, Robert, and Geneviève*)

Geneviève
(ibid., 1939)

Geneviève
(ibid.)

*Thésée
(ibid., 1946; New York: Pantheon Books, 1946)

*Theseus
(London: Horizon Publications, 1948; New York: New Directions)

SATIRICAL FARCES

Paludes   Morasses
(Librairie de l'Art Indépendant, 1895)

*Le Prométhée mal enchaîné
(Mercure de France, 1899)

*Prometheus Ill-Bound
(London: Chatto & Windus, 1919; trans. by Lilian Rothermere)

*Les Caves du Vatican
(Gallimard, 1914)

*The Vatican Swindle
(New York: Alfred A. Knopf, 1925) or *Lafcadio's Adventures* (ibid., 1927; London: Cassell & Co.)

NOVEL

*Les Faux-Monnayeurs
(Gallimard, 1926)

*The Counterfeiters
(New York: Alfred A. Knopf, 1927) or *The Coiners* (London: Cassell & Co.)

CRITICISM

Prétextes
(Mercure de France, 1903)

Pretexts

Nouveaux Prétextes
(ibid., 1911)

Further Pretexts

*Dostoïevsky
(Plon-Nourrit, 1923)

*Dostoevsky
(London: J. M. Dent, 1925;
Martin Secker & Warburg,
1949; New York: Alfred A.
Knopf, 1926; New Direc-
tions, 1949; trans. anon.)

Incidences
(Gallimard, 1924)

Angles of Incidence

Journal des Faux-Monnayeurs
(ibid, 1926)

The Counterfeiters' Day-Book or
Journal of The Coiners

*Essai sur Montaigne
(Éditions de la Pléiade, 1929)

*Montaigne
(New York: Horace Liveright,
1929; London: Blackmore
Press; trans. by S. H. Guest
and T. E. Blewitt)
*The Living Thoughts of Mon-
taigne
(New York: Longmans, Green
& Co., 1939; London: Cas-
sell & Co.)

Divers
(Gallimard, 1931)

Miscellany

*Interviews imaginaires
(New York: Pantheon Books,
1943)

*Imaginary Interviews
(New York: Alfred A. Knopf,
1944; trans. by Malcolm
Cowley)

Attendu que . . .
(Alger: Charlot, 1943)

Considering That . . .

*L'Enseignement de Poussin
(Le Divan, 1945)

*Poussin
(London: The Arts, No. 2,
1947)

Poétique
(Neuchâtel: Ides et Calendes,
1947)

A Definition of Poetry

Préfaces
(ibid., 1948)

Prefaces

Rencontres (ibid., 1948)	Encounters
Éloges (ibid., 1948)	Praises

DRAMA

Philoctète (Mercure de France, 1899)	Philoctetes
Le Roi Candaule (La Revue Blanche, 1901)	King Candaules
Saül (Mercure de France, 1903)	Saul
Bethsabé (Bibliothèque de l'Occident, 1912)	Bathsheba
Œdipe (Gallimard, 1931)	Œdipus
Perséphone (ibid., 1934)	Persephone
Le Treizième Arbre (*Mesures*, No. 2, 1935)	The Thirteenth Tree
Robert ou l'intérêt général (Alger: *L'Arche*, 1944–5)	Robert or The Common Weal
Le Retour (Neuchâtel: Ides et Calendes, 1946)	The Return

MISCELLANEOUS

*Souvenirs de la Cour d'Assises (Gallimard, 1914)	**Recollections of the Assize Court* (London: Hutchinson & Co., 1941; trans. anon.)
Morceaux choisis (ibid., 1921)	Selections
Corydon (ibid., 1924)	Corydon
*Si le grain ne meurt . . . (ibid., 1926)	**If It Die . . .* (New York: Random House, 1935)

Numquid et tu . . . ?
(Éditions de la Pléiade, 1926)

Numquid et tu . . . ?

Un Esprit non prévenu
(Éditions Kra, 1929)

An Unprejudiced Mind

L'Affaire Redureau
(Gallimard, 1930)

The Redureau Case

La Sequestrée de Poitiers
(ibid., 1930)

The Poitiers Incarceration Case

Jeunesse
(Neuchâtel: Ides et Calendes,
1945)

Youth

TRAVELS

Voyage au Congo
(Gallimard, 1927)

Travels in the Congo
(New York: Alfred A. Knopf,
1929; London: ibid., 1930)

Dindiki
(Liége: Éditions de la Lampe d'Aladdin, 1927)

Dindiki

Le Retour du Tchad
(Gallimard, 1928)

*in *Travels in the Congo*
(New York: Alfred A. Knopf,
1929; London: ibid., 1930)

Retour de l'U.R.S.S.
(ibid., 1936)

Return from the U.S.S.R.
(New York: ibid., 1937; London: Martin Secker & War-
burg, 1937)

*Retouches à mon Retour de
l'U.R.S.S.* (ibid., 1937)

Afterthoughts on the U.S.S.R.
(New York: Dial Press, 1938;
London: Martin Secker &
Warburg, 1938)

JOURNALS

**Journal, 1889–1939*
(Gallimard, 1939)

The Journals of André Gide,
1889–1939
(New York: Alfred A. Knopf,
1947–9; London: Martin
Secker & Warburg, 1947–9;
3 vols., trans. by Justin
O'Brien)

Pages de Journal, 1939–1942   Extracts from the Journals, 1939–
(New York: Pantheon Books,   1942
1944; Paris: Gallimard, 1946)

Deux Interviews imaginaires suivies   Dialogues on God
de Feuillets
(Charlot, 1946)

COLLECTED EDITIONS

Œuvres complètes   Complete Works
(Gallimard, 15 vols., 1932–9)

Théâtre   Drama
(Gallimard, 1942)

Théâtre complet   Complete Drama
(Neuchâtel: Ides et Calendes, 8
vols., 1947–   )

INDEX

THE WORKS OF ANDRÉ GIDE

Referred to in *The Journals*

A NOTE ON THE TYPE IN WHICH THIS BOOK IS SET

The text of this book is set in Caledonia, a Linotype face designed by William Addison Dwiggins, which belongs to the family of printing types called "modern face" by printers—a term used to mark the change in style of type-letters that occurred about 1800. Caledonia borders on the general design of Scotch Modern, but is more freely drawn than that letter.

The text typography is by W. A. Dwiggins.

University of Illinois Press
1325 South Oak Street
Champaign, Illinois 61820-6903
WWW.UILLINOIS.EDU